The Age of
Constantine and Julian

THE AGE OF CONSTANTINE AND JULIAN

Diana Bowder

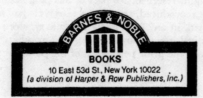

BARNES & NOBLE
BOOKS
10 East 53d St., New York 10022
(a division of Harper & Row Publishers, Inc.)

FAMILIAE MEAE CARISSIMAE

Published in the U.S.A. 1978 by
HARPER & ROW PUBLISHERS, INC.
BARNES & NOBLE IMPORT DIVISION

ISBN 0–06–490601–9

First published in Great Britain 1978 by
Paul Elek Ltd, London

Printed in Great Britain by
Latimer Trend & Company Ltd Plymouth

Contents

List of Illustrations   vii

Acknowledgements   ix

Introduction   xi

Map   xiv–xv

I   The Beginning of the Late Empire: Diocletian and the
Tetrarchy   I
The Great Persecution 10

II   The Constantinian Period: Imperial History and the
Official Monuments   15
*How Constantine Came to Power 15, From Emperor of the West
to Sole Emperor (312–24) 28, Constantine Sole Emperor (324–
37), and the Foundation of Constantinople (324–30) 32, The Reforms of Constantine 39, The Succession Crisis of 337. The Reign of
the Sons of Constantine (337–61) up to 353 42, Constantius II Sole
Emperor (353–61). Gallus Caesar (351–4) and Julian Caesar
(355–61) 47, The Reign of Julian (361–3) 53*

III   The Churches of Constantine and Helena   55
*The Churches in Rome 55, Trier Cathedral 60, The Churches of
the Eastern Capitals 61, The Churches of the Holy Land 62*

IV   The Emperors, the Church and the Pagan Establishment   65
*Privileges for the Church 65, Constantine and the Donatists of
Africa 67, Constantine, Arius and the Council of Nicaea 70, The
Arian Controversy Continues under the Sons of Constantine 75,
Were the Pagans Persecuted? 79, Christian Emperors and Pagan
Men of Letters 85, The Coinage 89, The Religion of Court,
Government and Army 93*

V   The Pagan Revival of Julian the Apostate   97
Julian's Conversion to Paganism 97, The Pagan 'Church' 99,

Contents

Theology 102, *The Paganization of the Government* 103, *Julian and the Cities* 103, *Education* 106, *Julian and the Church* 108, *Religious Minorities* 111, *Julian's Supporters* 112, *The Coinage* 116, *The 'Beard-Hater'* 118, *The Monuments: (i) The Inscriptions* 122, *The Monuments: (ii) Temples in Rome and Arabia* 123, *The Monuments: (iii) The Corbridge Lanx* 124, *The Celtic Pagan Revival* 125

VI   Christian and Pagan Life and Art   129
Temples and Churches 131, *Christian and Pagan Saints* 145, *Pagan and Christian Festivals* 149, *Mosaic Pavements* 157, *Tableware Exalted and Humble* 170, *Tomb Furniture* 179

Bibliography and Notes   194

Appendix I: The House of Constantine   213

Appendix II: Chronological Table   214

Index   218

List of Illustrations

NOTE: Plate references appear in the text as bold numbers in brackets, e.g. (**49**)

pp. xiv–xv Map of the Roman Empire, A.D. 306–A.D. 363

1 Arch of Constantine, Rome
2 Colossal head of Constantine
3 Head of Diocletian
4 Colossal head of Constantius II
5 Santa Constanza, Rome: (a) exterior; (b) interior
6 Coin portraits: (a) Constantine; (b) Helena; (c) Fausta; (d) Constantius II; (e) Constans; (f) Magnentius; (g) Vetranio
7 Reverses of FEL. TEMP. REPARATIO series: (a) Virtus spearing falling horseman; (b) Phoenix on globe; (c) emperor in galley
8 Chi-rho reverse of Magnentius
9 HOC SIGNO VICTOR ERIS reverse of Vetranio
10 Bull coin of Julian: (a) obverse; (b) reverse
11 Contorniate reverses: (a) Sol in chariot; (b) Circus Maximus
12 Isis coin: (a) reverse; (b) obverse
13 Fresco showing interior of St. John at the Lateran, Rome
14 Street of tombs beneath St. Peter's, Rome
15 Christus-Helios mosaic in Tomb of the Julii
16 Part of Megalopsychia mosaic with Golden Church of Antioch
17 Apse mosaic of Santa Pudenziana, Rome
18 Medallions of Constantine: (a) obverse with busts of Sol and Constantine; (b) obverse with chi-rho badge on emperor's helmet
19 Statue of Julian the Apostate
20 The Corbridge *Lanx*
21 Mosaic pavement of Basilica of Theodorus: (a) Jonah and the Whale; (b) Eucharistic Victory; (c) Good Shepherd
22 Temple of Syrian gods on Janiculum, Rome
23 Basilica of Santi Giovanni e Paolo: the Clivus Scauri
24 Lydney: reconstruction drawing of sanctuary
25 Pesch: reconstruction model of sanctuary
26 Church of Qirqbize, south façade

27   House of the Horses, Carthage: mosaic of horse with she-wolf and Romulus and Remus

28   *Calendar of 354*: (a) Constantius II; (b) November; (c) Trier

29   Europa mosaic, Lullingstone

30   Hinton St. Mary mosaic pavement

31   Cock-headed man mosaic, Brading

32   Detail of Small Hunt pavement, Piazza Armerina

33   Winged Seasons mosaic, Carthage: Summer

34   House of the Horses, Carthage: mosaic of sorcerer making sacrifice

35   Coronation of Venus pavement, Ellès

36   Constantinian Villa, Antioch: (a) main pavement; (b) Autumn, and part of hunting panel; (c) Bust of Dionysus

37   Mosaic of Gê and the Karpoi, Antioch: (a) Gê and Aigyptos; (b) Aroura and *putto* and the Karpoi

38   Mildenhall Treasure: (a) pair of Bacchic platters; (b) Great Dish

39   Kaiseraugst Treasure: (a) Achilles Dish; (b) Ariadne Tray

40   Water Newton Treasure: bowl dedicated by Publianus

41   Cologne glassware: (a) Wint Hill hunting bowl; (b) bowl with Sacrifice of Isaac; (c) Hercules and Antaeus bowl

42   African light *sigillata* C plate with Mithraic scenes

43   Gold glass medallion with Raising of Lazarus

44   Jet pendants and bronze medals from graves at Cologne

45   Via Latina Catacombs: (a) Jesus and the Samaritan woman; (b) Hercules slaying an enemy; (c) Vision of Abraham at Mamre; (d) Earth-Goddess (?); (e) View of a funerary chamber

46   Hypogeum of Trebius Justus: (a) building scene; (b) main wall

47   Frescoes from public catacombs, Rome: (a) Allegory of Susanna and the Elders; (b) Orante; (c) Adam and Eve; (d) Virgin and Child

48   Constantinian frieze sarcophagus

49   Two Brothers Sarcophagus

50   Sarcophagus of Junius Bassus: (a) front, general view; (b) detail, Christ and St. Peter; (c) side, vintaging Cupids

51   Dumbarton Oaks Season Sarcophagus

Acknowledgements

I have received help from a great many sources while I have been engaged in research for this book, and for the thesis on the religious history of the period with which it is linked. I should especially like to thank Professor Peter Brown, my first supervisor at Oxford University, and Professor Jocelyn Toynbee, for their interest and encouragement and for the fascinating discussions of late Roman life and art which we have had. Professor Toynbee and also Dr. Roger Tomlin kindly read through this book in manuscript, and made some detailed suggestions. Dr. J. F. Matthews, my second supervisor, has also seen it in manuscript and made valuable suggestions. A number of people gave me information when I was preparing for travels abroad. I have very happy memories of a long stay at the British School at Rome, where I was given assistance by the director at that time, Professor Ward Perkins, and, of a practical nature, by the indefatigable Signorina Anna Fazzari, to whom I owe visits to a number of monuments difficult of access. While there, I also profited by the advice of Dr. Brandenburg and Dr. Christern of the German Archaeological Institute, of Dr. Salomonson of the Dutch Institute, Professor Testini of the Pontifical Institute of Archaeology, and Professor L'Orange of the Norwegian Institute. Dr. K. Dunbabin gave me information on the mosaics of North Africa, and when I went there I met, among others, Dr. Yacoub at the Bardo Museum in Tunis, Père Ferron at Carthage, and Dr. Salama at Algiers. A week at the British Institute of Archaeology in Ankara prepared the way for extensive travels in the Middle East; at Istanbul I met Dr. Jale Inan and others, at Beirut I met Père Tallon and others. An earlier visit to the Rhineland introduced me to Dr. Doppelfeld at Cologne, and Professor von Petrikovits and Dr. Rüger at Bonn, and Dr. Gose at Trier. For these travels I benefited from generous grants from the Craven Fund at Oxford University and from the British School at Rome. While working on the coinage I received much assistance from Dr. Kent at the British Museum (including access to unpublished work), and also from Mr. Carson at the same establishment, and from Dr. Sutherland at the Ashmolean Museum in Oxford.

I owe a debt of a different kind to my husband and family, without whose active support this book could not have been written; and to Mrs. Dorothy Hill, whose outstanding generosity with her time and help

Acknowledgements

made it possible for me to reconcile the demands of small babies with the needs of research. Her daughter, Mrs. Jenny Aley, beautifully typed the manuscript of this book, and minimized the difficulties occasioned by preparing it for publication while living in Brussels. Many other friends have helped with their encouragement and practical assistance of various kinds. Miss Moira Johnston of Elek has been most patient and helpful.

The Author and Publishers would like to thank the following for their help in supplying photographs and/or granting permission for their reproduction: Edwin Smith, 1, 5b; Musei e Monumenti Communali, Rome (photographs Studio Aldo Reale), 2, 4; Archaeological Museum, Istanbul (photograph Hirmer Fotoarchiv, Munich), 3; Deutschen Archaeologischen Instituts, Rome, 5a; Heberden Coin Room, Ashmolean Museum, Oxford, 6, 7, 8, 9, 10, 11, 12; Pontificia Commissione di Archaeologia Sacra, Rome (photographs Benedettine di Priscilla), 13, 14, 15, 23, 45, 46, 47a–c; Department of Art and Archaeology, Princeton University, 16, 37; Fratelli Alinari, Florence (Collection Anderson), 17, 47d; Cabinet des Médailles, Bibliothèque National, Paris, 18a; Staatliche Münzsammlung, Munich, 18b; Musée du Louvre, Paris, 19, 36a, b; His Grace the Duke of Northumberland, 20; Museo Archeologico, Aquileia, 21; Society of Antiquaries of London, 24; Rheinisches Landesmuseum, Bonn, 25; Archeologisch Institut, Rijksuniversiteit, Utrecht, 27; Biblioteca Apostolica Vaticana, 28, 43; National Monuments Record, London, 29, 30; Mrs. M. E. V. Oglander, Brading (photograph Dixons of Newport), 31; Colorvald s.n.c., Valdagno, 32; Musée du Bardo, Tunis, 33, 35; Musée de Carthage, 34; Museum of Art, Rhode Island School of Design, 36c; British Museum, London, 38, 40; Römermuseum, Augst (photograph Elisabeth Schulz, Basle), 39; Department of Antiquities, Ashmolean Museum, Oxford, 41a; Rheinische Landesmuseum, Trier, 41b, c; Museo Nazionale Romano, Rome, 42; Römisch-germanisches Museum, Cologne, 44; Vatican Museums, 48, 49; Reverenda Fabbrica di San Pietro in Vaticano, 50; Dumbarton Oaks Collection, Washington D.C., 51.

Introduction

The tides of historical fashion, which have for so long relegated the Later Roman Empire to obscurity, unattractively labelled 'an age of decline', have since the Second World War been turning in its favour. For it has been newly recognized as an age of transition such as the one through which we are ourselves passing. In the West, the transition was between the rule of Rome and eventual barbarization, heralding the beginning of early mediaeval times. In the East, it was between the Eastern Roman Empire and the rule of Byzantium. The full process lasted some three hundred years, from the end of the third century to about A.D. 600. Within this large span there were many cross-currents and reversals and renewals: the process of transition was far from being a smooth and even stream. In particular, the fourth century stands out as a period of revival and renewal after the invasions and internal chaos of the middle fifty years of the third century, which threatened to engulf the whole Empire and put a premature end to it. It was the relentless pressure building up on the Rhine and Danube frontiers, which made itself felt as early as the reign of Marcus Aurelius (161–80), as wave after wave of barbarian tribes moved westwards, driven by others from the steppes of Russia—Alamans, Franks, Burgundians, Sarmatians, Goths, Huns, Vandals—that was responsible for the collapse of the Western Empire in the fifth century; responsible, too, for the iron regime of the fourth century and the ever-present need for military campaigns on the frontiers. These were the basic conditions of life under the emperors of the fourth century.

Yet within the hard, militarized structure, largely the creation of the Emperor Diocletian, there was room for a new flourishing of civilian life, which took place under Constantine and his successors. The early and mid fourth century was an age of confidence, in which only a rather strident insistence on the eternity of the Empire and of its embodiment, the emperor, reveals that the fears bred by the insecurity of the third century were not entirely banished. New buildings, public and private, rose apace, and in their train followed the minor architectural arts, such as mosaic and fresco, some of whose fruits we can still admire today. Luxurious furnishings and tableware helped to make life pleasant for the rich, and although the 'iron regime' bore harshly on the poor, many of whom were now reduced from free peasants to the status of serfs, bound to the land they tilled, there were still many people of modest means who could afford to buy decorated pottery or even glass or, at a humbler level, to lay coins and cooking-pots in the graves of their dead. But as compared with the early Empire there was certainly a polarization of wealth and poverty, especially in the West, with over-powerful lords amassing vast estates and the riches from them, which leads historians to talk of a pre-feudal society. The leading senators of Rome were poised midway between their Republican predecessors and the barons of the mediaeval period.

Above all, the fourth century was a time of religious change. A century that opened with the last Great Persecution of the Christians, and ended with the effective proscription of paganism, could not be otherwise. Fed by the insecurity of the third century and the new spirit of the times, with its emphasis on things spiritual rather than things temporal, Christianity had already grown strong. But nothing made its final victory inevitable. It was Constantine, utterly sincere in his conviction that he had been granted a personal sign by God, and given a mission to fulfil within the Empire, who was the architect of the Church's triumph. The belief in the close contact between men and gods, through visions, dreams, portents, and even physical appearances, was deeply rooted in the ancient world, and superstition of all kinds was particularly rife in the fourth century. It was no cynical calculation that made Constantine a Christian, and at the date of his conversion Christianity was far too unimportant, especially in the West, to justify an appeal to its adherents. It is clear from our sources that Constantine was a deeply religious man, quite incapable of any self-interested pretence in this sphere. Although it was some years before he realized the exclusiveness of Christianity, and the solar monotheism that was one of the leading features of late paganism blurred for him the distinction between the two, to the end of his life he acted out his conviction that he had been chosen by the God of the Christians to inaugurate a Christian Roman Empire. The sons who were his successors on the throne, especially Constantius II, consolidated their father's work, both religious and secular, and helped to make the Christian Empire a reality.

Yet the majority of the inhabitants of that Empire were still pagan. Many were humble people of town and country, still loyal to their local, native cults, who in many cases had scarcely heard the name of Christ; while others were people of rank and education for whom Graeco-Roman civilization was embodied in the worship of the gods, new and old, of Greece and Rome. It was to their support that Julian the Apostate appealed when, successful in his bid for the throne, he found himself sole emperor and declared full liberty of worship, going on to enact the full programme of his celebrated revival of paganism. This fascinating figure sometimes seems to speak directly to our modern age—in his

identification of loneliness as one of the greatest of human ills, for example—though in his obsession with ritual he was as much a product of
the superstitious age he lived in, and as alien to us, as was Constantius II
in his preoccupation with theological niceties. Constantine, too, found
that these were a major subject for his attention, but his motive was
different: divisions in the Church were unpleasing to its heavenly Lord,
and therefore likely to bring down his wrath upon the Empire in secular
disasters. Julian's paganism was as sincere as Constantine's Christianity,
and like him he was endowed with the zeal common to converts. His
campaign for the restoration of paganism was pursued with feverish
energy during his short reign, and cast its net wide, leaving few resources untapped. It was channelled mainly through the cities, the
sacred hearths of the original Greek civilization that was his chief
inspiration and love. Much of his work was directed towards reviving
the declining institutions of the cities, and there are signs of an enthu-
siastic response in some quarters. Christian writers of the period and
after were clearly dismayed by the degree of success achieved by Julian,
and still afraid, even in the fifth century, of another pagan reign. But
Julian was the last pagan Roman emperor, and by the mid to late fourth
century the balance was already tipping decisively in Christianity's
favour. By the end of the fourth century the Emperor Theodosius and
his sons could not only issue but enforce, throughout most of the Empire,
laws forbidding the practice of the pagan cults, and a new and con-
fidently Christian world begins to come into being, peopled by such
men as Paulinus of Nola, Jerome and Augustine. It is on the earlier
period of greater fluidity, under the House of Constantine and Julian,
when the balance was much more even, and the final triumph of
Christianity and extinction of paganism still far from certain or obvious,
that this book is focused; and a large portion of it is devoted to the
depiction of religious life under those emperors, both public and private,
with the help of the great volume of archaeological and artistic material
—such things as churches and temples, mosaics, coins, frescoes, silverware and engraved glass—that has survived from this exciting and
fascinating period, for our greater illumination.

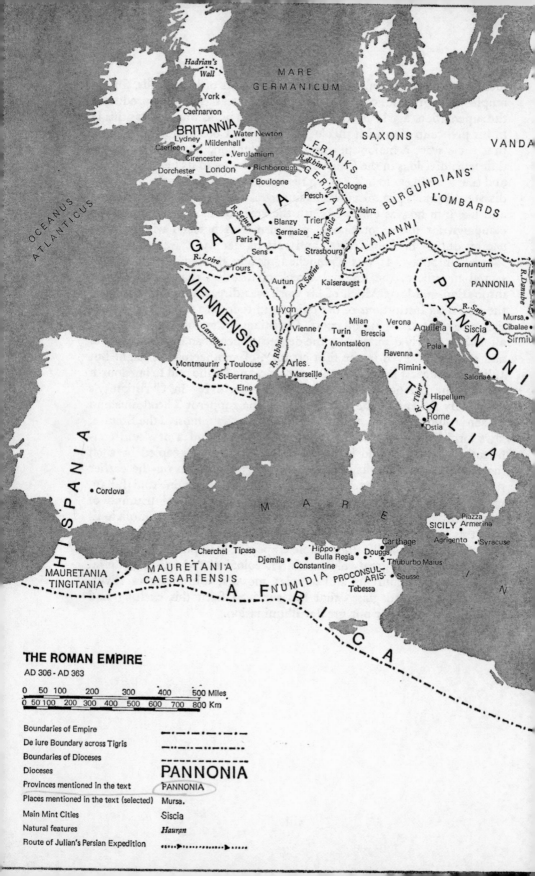

THE ROMAN EMPIRE

AD 306 - AD 363

0 50 100   200   300   400   500 Miles
0 50 100   200 300 400 500 600 700 800 Km

Boundaries of Empire	▬ ▬ ▬ ▬
De iure Boundary across Tigris	▬ · ▬ · ▬ ·
Boundaries of Dioceses	─ ─ ─ ─
Dioceses	**PANNONIA**
Provinces mentioned in the text	PANNONIA
Places mentioned in the text (selected)	Mursa.
Main Mint Cities	Siscia
Natural features	*Hauran*
Route of Julian's Persian Expedition	●···▶···●···▶··●

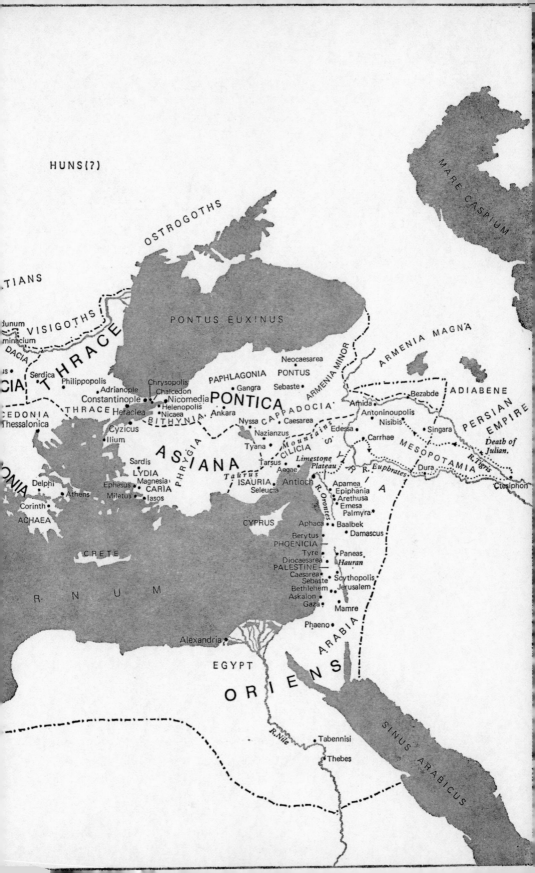

Chapter I

The Beginning of the Late Empire: Diocletian and the Tetrarchy

By the fourth century A.D., the high tide of the *pax romana*, the peace and security which Rome guaranteed to the peoples of her Empire, was long past. As a result, the fourth century has been seen all too often as a period of decline, of religious squabbles on the brink of the abyss. In reality, it was a renaissance cut short.

One of the principal architects of this renaissance was a man named Valerius Diocles, who seized power in A.D. 284 and became the Emperor Diocletian. The previous fifty years, from the assassination of the boy emperor Alexander Severus in 235, and the end of the Severan dynasty, must have looked to agonized contemporaries very much like the end of the Roman Empire. Usurper succeeded usurper on the throne, and the average length of reign was less than two years. Moreover, restless and land-hungry tribes of barbarians on the frontiers, many of them driven westwards into the area between Rhine and Danube by mass migrations of nomadic peoples from the Russian steppes (notably the Huns, against whom the Great Wall of China had been built in the third century B.C., the Goths and the Vandals), took advantage of the internal weakness to raid and invade far into the interior of the Empire, pouring across the Rhine and Danube into Gaul and the Balkan provinces; while nomads of the Sahara caused trouble in Africa, and in the East the new and expansionist dynasty of the Sassanids replaced the Parthian Arsacids on the throne of Persia in A.D. 226, and made it once more a thorn in the side of Rome. It was only with great difficulty that the invasions were beaten back, and in both East and West it was only accomplished at the expense of a temporary loss of control of some of the affected regions by the central Roman authority, principally when Zenobia, Queen of Palmyra, created her own empire in and around Roman Syria from 261 (when her husband Odaenath was entrusted with the defence of the East by the Emepror Gallienus) until its recapture by the Emperor Aurelian in 272-3, and when a series of independent emperors ruled in Gaul from 260 to 274.

Nor was this all. The twin evils of indiscipline in the army and the barbarian invasions brought further ills in their train. The social and economic structure of the Empire was seriously weakened. From the Severan dynasty onwards, each emperor or usurper, struggling to maintain his authority against all comers, raised the pay of the troops

I

under his command. As the system of taxation was very complicated, and could not be quickly reformed, it was easier to debase the currency in order to satisfy the soldiers than to find fresh supplies of money. In consequence, inflation, so familiar to a modern age of printed paper money, was rampant during the third century. The standard silver coin, the *denarius*, had become by the end of the third century a badly struck bronze piece thinly washed with silver; and from being rated at 1,250 to a pound of gold had sunk to a rate of 50,000. Its decline was attended by the virtual collapse of the monetary economy, and a return was made to trading in kind whenever possible, a step that was comparatively easy in a largely agricultural economy. Taxes and rents were exacted in kind, and the State used the foodstuffs that came in in this way to grant rations to the soldiers and civil servants, to supplement the dwindling real value of their pay. It also began to supply them with uniforms, from the taxation of weavers or from State clothworking concerns. Even so, this was not enough, and the soldiers often resorted to looting and the minor officials to charging fees to the public for everything they did, to augment their incomes—further sources of misery for the common people.

The financial chaos itself, although it is unlikely to have brought ruin to many, was a potent addition to the uncertainties of the times, after centuries of stability. Moreover, numerous peasants were overwhelmed by the combination of barbarian invasions, pillage by Roman soldiers, ordinary taxation, and special requisitions of their produce, and abandoned their little farms to try and scrape a living in the towns or to live as brigands. Much of Gaul became a prey to large bands of such rebels, known as the Bagaudae, who even put up usurpers. The decrease in the area of cultivated land brought famine whenever there was a bad year of drought or unseasonable weather, and the consequent malnutrition led to epidemics. Many third-century coinages were a mute appeal to Salus, the goddess who personified safety and salvation from danger, or to Apollo Salutaris, god of healing and protection from disease.

The psychological consequences of all these disasters and the prevailing insecurity on the population of the Empire can well be imagined: on the worldly plane, a desperate craving for order and stability and strong government and a respite from their various afflictions, and a readiness to accord great devotion and almost divine honours, in a reality of imperial cult far removed from the formal 'worship' of earlier emperors, to any leader who could provide them; and on the spiritual plane, a growing need for a religion that could offer the maximum consolation and strength in adversity, and an unshakeable sense of inner security, and could impart significance to their manifold woes. Detachment from 'the world' and a heightened sense of spiritual values were inevitable in such an age, and it was during the third century that Christianity, with its doctrine of a loving Saviour who had really lived and shared the sufferings of mankind, began to make large inroads into the mass of pagan faithful. It is one of the paradoxes of history that Diocletian, the emperor who restored strong and stable government, was also the author of the last Great Persecution of the Christians.

Although Diocletian, while a private citizen, had risen from the ranks by his talent to become commander of the imperial bodyguard, he was no great soldier-emperor: it was as an administrator that he was pre-eminent. Some of the military action that was necessary to restore the Empire to its former territorial integrity had been carried out by his more recent predecessors, notably Aurelian (A.D. 270–5), who re-conquered the separatist Gallic and Palmyrene empires. The campaigns fought during Diocletian's own reign (A.D. 284–305) were usually delegated to his lieutenants. But he inaugurated a system of defences of the Empire that was further refined by Constantine, and the two emperors' reforms laid the military foundations that made possible the fourth-century renaissance. Diocletian sought to ensure the security of the frontiers themselves by establishing chains of forts, sometimes on the old alignment, sometimes on a new one, for example in Syria, where the frontier had been moved southwards and eastwards following the conquest of the kingdom of Palmyra and the acquisition of upper Mesopotamia during Diocletian's reign. These forts were manned by 'frontiers-men' (*limitanei*), made up of the old auxiliary units of the Roman army together, perhaps, with some of the legions. Some of the forts were built to house just the actual garrison, while others had an outer enclosure that could serve as a refuge for the surrounding population in time of need. Behind the frontier, stationed in strong camps located at the main strategic points for its control, were the legions and cavalry units of the main army. In certain areas of the frontier, the troops were put under the command of newly created military leaders, the *duces*, leaving the provincial governors concerned with civil functions only. Unlike the *limitanei*, these detachments of the main army could be transferred from one province to another, even from one part of the Empire to another, at the emperor's bidding, to deal with a crisis. The strong defences and the division into mobile and non-mobile troops made for some flexibility without jeopardizing the permanent protection of each frontier. But Diocletian found it necessary to increase the total strength of the army, creating many new units, and this was a permanent strain on the resources of the Empire. Still more money was needed for pay; and voluntary enlistment was no longer a sufficient source of recruits, so he was obliged to make service in the army compulsory for the sons of veterans, and institute conscription. State armour and clothes factories were set up to supply weapons and uniforms.

It was in response to various military emergencies that Diocletian evolved his remarkable system of government, the Tetrarchy or Rule of

Four. In 285, the year after he came to the throne, he nominated as Caesar, or junior emperor, an army officer called Maximian, a man of Illyrian peasant stock as he probably was himself. Diocletian remained in the East and sent Maximian to the West, principally to deal with the peasant revolt of the Bagaudae in Gaul. Then, the following year, when a rebel naval commander, Carausius, declared himself Augustus (i.e. emperor, *tout court*) in Britain, Diocletian promoted Maximian, too, to the rank of Augustus. Diocletian remained senior Augustus, however, and was the only one entitled to legislate. He was 'Jovius', agent of Jupiter, ruling on earth under the special protection of the king of the gods, while Maximian was 'Herculius', under the patronage of Jupiter's son Hercules. It was in 293, after a serious rebellion in Egypt in 292, that the pair of legitimate rulers became a foursome on the appointment of two Caesars, one to serve under each Augustus. Diocletian's own Caesar was Galerius Maximianus, of Dacian birth from the lower Danube, and he was married to Diocletian's daughter Valeria. Maximian chose as his Caesar—doubtless with Diocletian's approval—Flavius Constantius, father of Constantine, later nicknamed Chlorus (the Pale). He also came from the Balkans, like the two Augusti, and was of low birth, despite Constantine's later claim that he was descended from the Emperor Claudius Gothicus (268–70). Constantius Chlorus married Maximian's stepdaughter, Theodora, on the pattern of his fellow-Caesar Galerius. In order to do this he had to divorce Helena, mother of Constantine, who at this juncture, while still a child, was sent to the court of Diocletian, a useful hostage to deter his father from any thoughts of rebellion.

The tetrarchic system was thus complete, and was to operate smoothly for the rest of Diocletian's reign. The three subordinate emperors carried out their largely military and administrative duties, while the senior Augustus poured forth a flood of legislation, and engaged in occasional frontier campaigns on his own account. In the West, Carausius, the emperor of Britain, was for a time recognized by the tetrarchs as legitimate ruler of that diocese, and he took the opportunity to begin the build-up of its defences against the new threat of marauding Saxon pirates. But in 293 he was assassinated by one of his ministers, Allectus, a far less talented man, and this change of leadership enabled Constantius Chlorus to reconquer Britain for the tetrarchs three years later, defeating and killing Allectus. He proceeded to set the seal on Carausius' system of maritime defences, strengthening it and extending it to become the famous line of Saxon Shore forts, running round south-east England from Norfolk to the Isle of Wight. These were garrisoned by a mixture of soldiers and sailors, to combat sea-borne raids, and were under the command of the newly-created Count of the Saxon Shore. Both Britain and Gaul (including the southern diocese,

Viennensis) were now under Constantius Chlorus, who established his capital at Trier on the Moselle. In Gaul he conducted campaigns against the Germans who threatened the Rhine frontier, and on both sides of the Channel he set in hand the restoration of war-damaged cities. One of these was York, where a magnificent new fortress was built, probably as the seat of the military governor (*dux*) of Britain. Another was Autun, which had been the principal university town of Gaul: in 298 the orator Eumenius, who had been one of the Caesar's State secretaries and had just been appointed professor at Autun with the mission of restoring the university, delivered a speech of thanks to his imperial patron, in which he describes how Constantius gave money from the treasury, allowed the use of troops as labourers, and even brought over skilled builders from less ravaged Britain, for the restoration of the temples and other public buildings and private houses of Autun. Further south, Maximian, his defeat of the Bagaudae and his German campaigns over, was now in charge of Italy, Spain and Africa. His capital was probably Milan.

In the eastern half of the Empire, the Caesar Galerius was nominally ruling the Danube lands, while Diocletian himself took charge of the dioceses round the east Mediterranean. But this geographical division of spheres of influence was more fluid than in the West. Diocletian led a number of campaigns on the Danube, and when, after the quelling of the revolt of Domitius Domitianus in Egypt in 297/8, the Persians invaded Syria, he sent Galerius against them. After an initial defeat, Galerius won a great battle at the city of Nisibis in Mesopotamia, and achieved the most advantageous peace that the Romans ever made with Persia. Armenia, on the borders of the two empires, had for centuries been a shuttlecock between Roman and Persian hegemony; it now became once more a Roman client-kingdom, with the restoration of its pro-Roman ruler Tiridates, whom the Persians had expelled. Moreover, the Roman hold on Mesopotamia was consolidated, and even some land beyond the Tigris acquired.

In celebration of his oriental victories, Galerius erected a triumphal arch at Thessalonica, his capital city, carved with friezes depicting his campaigns. One relief shows Diocletian and Galerius making sacrifice for the successful outcome of the war. The surviving parts of the arch form the largest and most beautiful creation of the official art of the Tetrarchy that has come down to us. The age was not one favourable to art, for the emperors were too heavily preoccupied with the work of restoration and reconstruction, military, administrative and physical, to spare much thought for its patronage. Only when they required a portrait or a more ambitious monument to mark some special occasion, like Galerius' arch or the monument raised in the Forum at Rome in A.D. 303, the year of the twentieth anniversary (counted inclusively) of

Diocletian's coming to power (and of Maximian's too by a courtesy arrangement in the interests of symmetry) and the Caesars' tenth anniversary, was the stimulus of imperial patronage forthcoming. The sole survivor of the Forum monument is the so-called *Decennalia* Base, with inscription and flat reliefs of a procession and sacrifice celebrating the Caesars' jubilee. Of the portraits, the double group of the four emperors shown embracing fraternally, carved in Egyptian porphyry, that is built into the corner of St. Mark's in Venice, is perhaps the most typical. They wear military uniform and the cylindrical leather caps that became fashionable at this time. The hard and unyielding purple porphyry, a material much favoured in this period for imperial statues (and throughout the fourth century for imperial sarcophagi), was well adapted to the rather squat and ugly figure-style, expressive of strength at the expense of grace, that characterizes most tetrarchic art. Much of the industry engaged in producing beautiful objects for the adornment of private houses and public buildings—mosaics, statues, reliefs, frescoes and the like—had been severely disrupted by the invasions and civil wars of the third century, or had simply gone out of business as a result of these and the increasing poverty of the population. There were still workshops in the imperial capitals, such as those in Rome that turned out pagan and Christian sarcophagi and catacomb frescoes (see Chapter VI) in addition to works of public art like the jubilee monument in the Forum, and there were some also in certain dioceses that had come off more lightly—mosaicists in Britain and Africa, for example; but the total volume produced cannot have been very great. The military and political foundations of the state of relative security enjoyed by the Empire during the fourth century were only just being laid, and the siege mentality induced by the recent disasters had yet to give way to a more relaxed atmosphere in which art could again flourish.

Building was another matter. It had always been a favourite activity of emperors, conscious as they were that edifices bearing their name might well constitute their most lasting monuments, as well as giving present employment, use and aesthetic pleasure to their subjects. Under Diocletian, the physical restoration of ruined cities and the building of fortifications was an urgent necessity, and the creation of entirely new buildings was an obvious means of instilling confidence. We have already come across the work of Constantius Chlorus at York and Autun. The other Caesar, Galerius, built a palace and a mausoleum for himself at Thessalonica. Little is known of the building activities of Maximian, though one historian reveals that he had what was probably a sumptuous villa in the countryside near Rome, where he went to live on his retirement in 305. Diocletian himself was responsible for a large number of new buildings, restorations, and road reconstructions and developments, and not only in the East, witness the Senate-house and the

Baths of Diocletian at Rome. His own chosen residence was Nicomedia in Asia Minor, an enormously significant break with the centuries of tradition that had sanctified Rome as the capital of the civilized world, in favour of the richer and more populous East that was to prove itself militarily the more viable half of the Empire; a move that was to be confirmed by the creation of Constantinople. The hostile Lactantius, a Christian rhetorician from Africa who was summoned to the court at Nicomedia and witnessed the Great Persecution there, and later became tutor to Constantine's eldest son, has left us a vivid description of Diocletian's efforts to endow this former mere provincial capital with monuments suited to its new status: 'A large part of a city is suddenly demolished. Everyone moved away with their wives and children as though the city had been captured by the enemy. And when it was all complete, having ruined the provinces in the process, he would say, "It is not right, it must be done differently." Again it had to be pulled down and changed, and perhaps yet again. Such was his mad behaviour in his eagerness to make Nicomedia the equal of Rome.' The same passage speaks in general of his 'boundless greed for new buildings', and how he drained the provinces of workers and craftsmen and waggons and building supplies, constructing 'here a law-court, there a race-course, here a mint, there an arms factory, here a mansion for his wife, there one for his daughter.' Lactantius' prejudice appears most clearly here, for the erection of new buildings was one of the stock items on which praise was lavished in panegyrics of living emperors, and after the almost total cessation of it during much of the third century the need was especially great. (3)

Diocletian's great work of reconstructing the Empire was not limited to its physical manifestations and the vital task of providing for its defence against external enemies. Many of the misfortunes of the preceding fifty years had stemmed from internal divisions and civil wars and the ease with which usurpers could arise. One way of combating this was to increase artificially the degree of awe in which the monarchy was held, by building up the emperor from being a mere leader and prince of men into a great king ruling by divine right and enjoying a special relationship with the gods. We have seen how Diocletian took the surname Jovius and gave Maximian that of Herculius; and these two gods were given great prominence on the coinage. To some extent this was a development of earlier tendencies: the Emperor Aurelian had regarded himself as being under the patronage of Sol Invictus, the Unconquered Sun, and had built that god a great temple in Rome, as well as honouring him on the coinage, and an occasional earlier emperor had done likewise with his favourite god (see also Chapter IV). Diocletian followed these precedents more systematically, seeking theological sanction for the Tetrarchy itself. His main innovation was the elaboration of court ritual, borrowing some of the ceremonial from the court of the Great King of Persia, with the intention of setting the emperor on a higher plane than the rest of his subjects. Public appearances by the emperor were restricted so that each one became a solemn occasion, and access to him was now more difficult, jealously guarded by a band of eunuch chamberlains whose main use lay in keeping ambitious nobles at bay. At imperial audiences, those present prostrated themselves as if before the revelation of a god. All this was not, however, a wholly artificial creation, for it seems to have answered to an increased need for imperial pomp and circumstance, perhaps partly as a public reassurance of the stability of government and Empire.

This, however, was not enough to deter would-be pretenders, as Diocletian well knew. The separation of civil and military powers in the provinces, and the creation of the *duces*, would be more effective. The subdivision of most of the existing provinces into a large number of much smaller units might seem to have been an additional weapon, but was probably done in the interests of governmental efficiency. Lactantius laments the consequent multiplication of officials: 'So that the whole world should be terrorized, the provinces were chopped into tiny pieces: numerous governors and officials oppressed individual areas and almost individual cities, together with dozens of accountants and chief officers and deputies of prefects . . .' There is certainly some truth in his disparaging remarks, though the new arrangements did decrease the area of authority of each governor and, while incidentally reducing his power, made it easier for him to cope with a growing burden of administration. However, some kind of counterpoise to the increasing divisions was needed, and this took the form of grouping a number of provinces together in a 'diocese' under a 'vicar' or deputy of the praetorian prefect who, from being the commander of the imperial bodyguard in the early Empire, had developed over the centuries into the emperor's chief minister. The twelve dioceses (Moesiae was subsequently split into Dacia and Macedonia) were organic groupings that foreshadow the post-Roman nation states, especially in the West: Britain was one, northern and central France (extending to the Rhine) was another, with the climatically distinct South of France as a separate diocese; Spain and Portugal (with Morocco) formed a fourth. The new diocesan organization provided a convenient half-way stage between the provincial and central government.

In the financial sphere Diocletian did something to bring order out of chaos, although even he was not able to accomplish as much as he wished. The monetary system had collapsed, inflation was rampant, and taxation, even in kind, had run into difficulties because of the large areas of abandoned land, for which the local town councils or *curiae* were still obliged to collect taxes but were frequently unable to do so, with unfortunate if not disastrous consequences both for the councils and for the imperial exchequer. Diocletian reformed the currency, returning to a genuine three-metal system, with gold coins struck at the rate of 60 to the pound, real silver at 96 to the pound, and large bronze coins. But the issues of gold and silver were too small, and too much of the cheap bronze was put into circulation to compensate, which upset the fixed relationship between the metals, and inflation continued. So in 301 Diocletian promulgated his celebrated Price Edict, the first recorded attempt to impose a wage and price freeze. It laid down in minute detail the maximum wages to be given for various services and the maximum prices to be charged for a very wide range of goods. The edict, preserved in several inscriptions, is a valuable source of information on the commoner commodities of the time. We learn, for instance, that Britain's finest products included a hooded, waterproof, woollen cloak, a woollen rug, and beer. But as a measure to stabilize prices the edict was a failure: despite the heavy penalties—including capital punishment—prescribed and in some cases carried out for over-charging or withholding goods from sale, some goods quickly disappeared from the market, and enforcement became impossible.

Diocletian was more successful in his reorganization of the system of taxation. He established a single common unit (*iugum*), equivalent in assessment to the poll-tax for a single person (*caput*), and all land was divided up into these units, not on acreage alone but according to the use to which the land was put. Thus olive-groves and vineyards, being more valuable, were assessed in smaller units than arable land, and in some provinces this, too, was graded according to productivity. Animal stock was assessed as fractions of a *caput*. This basic system was used not only for ordinary taxation in money and in produce, but for levying cloth for uniforms (to supplement the output of the State factories), horses for the public post that carried officials and State-owned goods (mostly rations for the army and for officials' salaries) along the main roads, and, most important of all, recruits for the army. Where necessary, small holdings were grouped together into larger units for furnishing recruits. The new system was fairer than the inequitable special requisitions that had become the rule during the third century to make up the shortfall from ordinary taxation, and was easy to administer—in fact it was rather too easy to increase the taxes. Although there were numerous minor variations from one part of the Empire to another, it exemplifies to a high degree, by its reduction for fiscal purposes of people and land to equivalent units, the tendency of the late Empire towards standardization and symmetry. Indeed this tendency was writ large in the tetrarchic system itself, and in all Diocletian's reforms. It took a mind of military precision and tidiness to re-lay the foundations of an Empire under siege.

The Great Persecution

Diocletian linked the Tetrarchy, as we have seen, with a revival of the traditional Roman religion, putting it under the special protection of two of the oldest Roman gods, Jupiter and Hercules. It was this that brought it into conflict with the growing Christian Church, whose main crime in Roman eyes was its adamant withdrawal of worship from the pagan gods, thus breaking the *pax deorum*, the unwritten contract whereby the gods watched over the Empire with benevolent care in return for honour and worship by all its inhabitants; together with their refusal to participate in the imperial cult, which laid them open to the charge of sedition. The Jews, who also refused to worship the gods, did at least have their own ancestral God, and had long reached a *modus vivendi* with the Romans. But the Christians proclaimed an upstart deity, who had died a brigand's death, as the only true God, and were a breakaway sect, rejecting and rejected by traditional Judaism. We can trace the growth and hardening of anti-Christian sentiment in the Empire, from the early days when Christianity was just a new and unpopular sect, whose leaders caused riots by preaching disloyal sermons in the market-place, and about whom there were ugly rumours of child-eating and incest; useful scapegoats, in fact, as Nero found. Some decades then elapsed before the question was first raised in a general form as to whether Christians, as such, were acting in breach of the law. It was under Trajan that this occurred, in the early years of the second century, during the governorship of Pliny the Younger in Bithynia in north-west Asia Minor, and we have Pliny's letter to his emperor in which he expresses his doubts and honest bewilderment over the proper procedure when confronted with the denunciation of some Christians by informers. Yet despite his question as to whether 'the name itself' or only the crimes that accompany it are to be punished, Pliny assumes the first, for he had already executed a group of Christians for no other 'crime' than their obstinate refusal to renounce their allegiance to Christ. Trajan's reply shows that he, too, regards the guilt of obdurate Christians as proven. He and Pliny are unanimous, however, that those who apostatize are to be pardoned and released. Pliny's procedure in this matter was the same as that of governors in succeeding persecutions: 'I ordered statues of the gods and of the emperor to be brought in, and those who said that they were not and had never been Christians, and repeated after me prayers to the gods and offered incense and wine to the emperor's image, and also cursed Christ—it is said that nothing can compel real Christians to do this—I saw fit to release.' Trajan's further instructions on the subject accord well with his reputation as a just and merciful ruler: although obstinate Christians who are denounced to the authorities must be punished, there is to be no witch-hunt, and the governor is not to take action, as Pliny had done in one instance, on lists of names posted up by anonymous informers—'a very bad precedent and unworthy of our reign.'

At the end of his letter, Pliny reveals the anxieties that underlie the course of action he took. Above all, it is the numbers involved and the deplorable effect which the new cult is having on religious—and corporate—life that worries him, while the benefits of persecution are already manifest, making him lend the weight of his authority to repression, as St. Augustine was to do three hundred years later in the struggle against the Donatist schismatics, for much the same reasons. 'Many of every age,' says Pliny, 'of every rank and of both sexes are or will be involved in the prosecution. Nor is it only cities to which the infection of that superstition has spread, but villages and the countryside too; it can and must be stopped and put right. Already rites have begun to be celebrated at temples that were lately abandoned, and sacred festivals long discontinued are being held again, and everywhere meat from sacrificial victims, for which there had been very few purchasers hitherto, is being bought.'

If this was the situation—even allowing for some exaggeration—in Bithynia c. A.D. 100, how much worse, from the point of view of a rootedly pagan emperor, will it have been two hundred years later, in the time of Diocletian. His was not, however, the first general persecution. For 150 years after Trajan, violent repression of Christianity was still limited to sporadic local outbreaks, for instance in Asia Minor and in Gaul (at Lyon in A.D. 177) under Marcus Aurelius, and in Africa in 180 and under Septimius Severus, around A.D. 200. It was the grant of Roman citizenship to all or most of the inhabitants of the Empire by Severus' son Caracalla in 212 that made Empire-wide persecution possible, by putting the religious obligations of a Roman citizen on masses of humble provincials as well as on their leading dignitaries, who alone had possessed the citizenship previously. By 250, amid invasions on several fronts and a serious epidemic, the time was ripe for such action: the short-lived emperor Decius (whose troubled features are recorded in one of the major triumphs of Roman portraiture) sought, like Diocletian, to renew the great Roman traditions, including religion; he staged an attempt to revive the cult of the deified emperors and, after a preliminary attack on the Church's main leaders, ordered everyone in the Empire to make sacrifice to the gods for its safety and as a sign of loyalty. Those few who had the courage to refuse were executed, but enormous numbers of Christians lapsed—a sure indication of how Christianity was spreading to more worldly and less dedicated people—and set a great problem for the Church authorities when the persecution was over (Decius was killed in battle with the Goths in 251).

Decius' protégé Valerian became emperor in 253, and persecution continued, in a lower key, to the end of the decade. The Church then enjoyed about forty years of peace and quiet, and made great progress in evangelization in the fearful and highly charged atmosphere of the later third century.

The peace was broken in about 298, and we have Lactantius' partly eyewitness account of how it happened. Diocletian and Galerius were sacrificing to obtain omens for a military operation, but these were persistently elusive (according to Lactantius, a Christian servant had caused the upset by crossing himself). Tages, the chief soothsayer, said that 'profane persons' were present. Diocletian, greatly angered, ordered everyone in the palace to sacrifice; those who refused were flogged, and soldiers dismissed from the army. But he was unwilling to go any further, and it was only at the instigation of the highly superstitious Galerius, who came a few years later to winter at Nicomedia after a campaign, that the local persecution was turned into a general one. Galerius, son of a barbarian priestess, was driven by the popular superstition that the 'atheist' Christians brought down the wrath of the gods on the Empire in the form of natural disasters and other misfortunes, rather than by the fear of potential revolutionaries that had principally animated the Roman authorities earlier. Galerius spent all winter working on Diocletian, whose advisers also gave their opinion in favour of persecution, some of them apparently influenced by the treatise *Against the Christians* written by the Neoplatonist philosopher Porphyry, pupil of Plotinus. Still undecided, Diocletian sent a soothsayer to consult the oracle of Apollo at Miletus, which 'gave the answer of an enemy of the Christian religion'; whereupon the emperor gave in, but insisted that no blood must be shed. The day of the ancient Roman festival of the *terminalia*, 23 February, was chosen for 'setting a term' to Christianity in 303. 'At first light . . . the prefect came to the church with *duces* and tribunes and finance officials; and bursting open the doors, they hunted for an image of God, found and burned the Scriptures, and looted and plundered the church, causing great panic and confusion.' As the church was an imposing building—evidently a sizeable house-church—in a high part of Nicomedia, the emperors watched the proceedings from the palace, discussing how to destroy the building. Diocletian rejected the use of fire because of the many large houses near by, so the praetorian guard was sent in with drawn swords and crowbars and demolished it in a few hours. These dramatic events reported by Lactantius were part of the action taken under a general edict issued that day, ordering the burning of all copies of the Scriptures and the demolition of all churches, and prohibiting the assembly of Christians for worship. 'The next day another edict was posted up, stripping Christians of their rank and making those of all classes liable to torture' (it was normally reserved for people of low degree) and depriving them of all civil and legal rights. A rash but heroic Christian who tore it down was roasted alive.

The next episode was a damaging fire at the palace. Lactantius alleges that Galerius was at the bottom of it. Be that as it may, the Christians were natural objects of suspicion. The bishop of Nicomedia was executed, and Christians of the imperial household were interrogated under torture; Eusebius, in his *Church History*, records the martyrdom of three of them, once-powerful eunuchs. A little later there was another fire, less serious than the first, but it coincided with the news of rebellions in two eastern provinces, allegedly incited by Christians. In consequence, another edict ordered the arrest of all Christian clergy, and this was followed by a command that they should be compelled to sacrifice to the gods. The authorities (normally the local magistrates) used whatever means they could to enforce compliance, including torture and forcible propulsion through the motions of sacrifice, especially as the *vicennalia* festival, with its accompanying amnesty for criminals, was imminent. Some clergy died under torture, while others, also obdurate to the end, were executed for their contumacy.

Even this was not enough: in 304 yet another edict was promulgated, ordering everyone to sacrifice, as under Decius. This was the culmination of the Great Persecution. In the areas where Christianity was strongest, notably, therefore, in the East of the Empire, large numbers of courageous men and women, who preferred the crown of martyrdom to the horror of disavowing their Lord and Saviour, were burnt alive or otherwise executed. In Upper Egypt, ten, twenty, thirty, sixty or a hundred men, women and children were put to death on a single day, according to Eusebius; while some other Egyptian martyrs were sent to Tyre in Phoenicia, to be killed by wild beasts in the amphitheatre there. A little town in Asia Minor, where all the inhabitants were Christian, was surrounded by soldiers and burnt to the ground, its entire population perishing in the flames. Away from the palace, the majority of the martyrs were humble town and counrty folk, although we hear of a noble lady from Antioch who drowned herself, together with her two daughters, while under arrest, and of two young sisters from the same city.

This fourth edict was applied everywhere in the East, but unevenly in the West. 'Maximian, who was scarcely characterized by mildness, gladly enforced it throughout Italy' (Lactantius), though apparently not in Africa. Moreover, in Gaul and Britain, if we are to believe our sources written under Constantine and painting rosy pictures of that emperor's father, Constantius Chlorus 'allowed churches, i.e. mere walls that could be rebuilt, to be destroyed, but he preserved intact the true temple of God that is in men.' So says Lactantius, while Eusebius even denies that he had churches demolished. However, the very small number of known martyrs in Britain (where only three are recorded: Aaron and Julius at the legionary base of Caerleon in South Wales and St. Alban at Verulamium) and Gaul does lend credence to the possibility that they were all victims of earlier persecutions, and that no more were added during the Great Persecution.

After about two years, the situation was saved, temporarily in the East but permanently in the West, by the failing health of Diocletian. He had been taken ill in Italy after the celebration of his twenty-year jubilee, the *vicennalia*, in Rome in 303, and his illness grew increasingly serious after his return to Nicomedia. In 305 he abdicated and retired into private life, to his great fortress-like palace, complete with temple of Jupiter and mausoleum for the Jupiter-emperor, which he had prepared for himself at Split (or Spalato, near the ancient Salonae) in Yugoslavia. The mediaeval and early modern town was built inside its largely intact walls. He compelled Maximian to retire at the same time so that the two Caesars could be promoted to the rank of Augustus simultaneously. Galerius became the senior Augustus, ruling in the East like Diocletian, while Constantius Chlorus became the main emperor in the West. Two new Caesars were appointed: Maximin Daia, an ill-educated nephew of Galerius who had become a tribune of the imperial bodyguard, in the East, and Severus, another soldier-friend of Galerius, in the West. Galerius, like Diocletian, would be the only legislator, and the other three emperors seemed likely to form a harmonious team for him.

Imperial preoccupation with these changes of government gave some respite to the unhappy Christians. The edicts against them, from henceforth a dead letter in the West, remained in force throughout the East, and the new team of emperors, the superstitious Galerius and his lieutenant Maximin, continued to persecute. But the situation had changed dramatically since the persecution of Decius, when the pagan majority was still hostile to the Christians. These had not only increased in number in the intervening period, to the point where a hagiographer in Edessa (modern Urfa, in Mesopotamia) could say, in a famous phrase, that 'the persecuted outnumbered the persecutors', but had come out far more into the open and become on better terms with their pagan neighbours, who were now less willing to acquiesce in their murder by the authorities. No governors refused to enforce the anti-Christian measures, but they could not count on any co-operation from the population at large. The active and passive resistance of the Christians and their sympathizers, together with the march of events, was to wear down all the persecutors within a few years. The worst of the Great Persecution would soon be over.

Chapter II

The Constantinian Period:
Imperial History and the Official Monuments

How Constantine Came to Power

Although Diocletian's reorganized administrative system was a permanent legacy to the Roman Empire, lasting substantially unchanged for three centuries in the East, his hopes that the Tetrarchy itself would be a durable form of government were doomed to disappointment. The forces for disruption were already present in 305, in the form of two over-mighty citizens, Maxentius, the son of the retired emperor Maximian, and Constantine, the eldest son of the reigning junior Augustus Constantius Chlorus; and in the armies whose loyalty to the dynastic principle was to effect the shipwreck of the new, Second Tetrarchy. It seems odd that Diocletian had passed over these two young men, whose upbringing had been so close to the highest sources of power in the State—Constantine, after all, had spent his youth at Diocletian's own court—and who must have appeared such obvious choices for the position of Caesar. But the great emperor, when he acted otherwise, was trying to create for Galerius a team similar to the one he had himself led; and Galerius was no Diocletian, able to dominate other strong characters by his own forceful personality, so the new senior Augustus needed a rather more compliant team. It is Constantine, exceptionally able, energetic and independent-minded, whose claims seem most clearly to have been disregarded for this reason. Maxentius, even allowing for our sources' hostility towards him, seems to have been of a less high calibre. Whatever the reasons, the stage was now set for a renewal of internal conflict, after more than twenty years of relative peace.

In 306, only one year after the inauguration of the Second Tetrarchy, Constantius Chlorus, never the healthiest of men, died at York. Constantine, who had made a dramatic escape from the eastern court on hearing of his father's illness, was at his side, and was immediately proclaimed Augustus in his father's stead by the troops. He was probably just over twenty years old at this time. He sent messengers to Galerius asking him to sanction the granting of this rank, but as it would have been unfair to Severus to promote Constantine over his head, and upset the balance of the Tetrarchy to have two Augusti in the West, Constantine had to be content with the rank of Caesar, while Severus was promoted to junior Augustus. (6 a)

Constantine's success in breaking into the foursome of rulers emboldened Maxentius to encourage the troops to hail him, too, as Augustus. But whereas Constantine's proclamation after his father's death did not upset the numbers, there was no one at present whom Maxentius could replace, and Galerius, understandably unwilling to depart from Diocletian's blueprint, refused to recognize Maxentius even as Caesar, and ordered Severus to eliminate him. But it was Severus himself who was eliminated, in 307, for Maxentius turned for help to his father Maximian, now in rather grudging retirement, and proclaimed him Augustus for the second time. The name and presence of the old emperor worked like magic with his former troops, who deserted Severus and rallied to Maxentius. It had been just the same with the armies of the dioceses which Constantius Chlorus had ruled as Caesar, Britain, Gaul and Viennensis, where Constantine was immediately recognized after his usurpation in 306; and recognition as emperor depended on the army. So the unfortunate Severus was besieged in Ravenna, surrendered to Maximian, and was ordered to commit suicide.

This brought Galerius himself down upon the illegitimate Maxentius-Maximian partnership. The imminence of attack from this quarter sent Maximian off post-haste to Gaul, to concert an alliance with Constantine. Constantine must have had a difficult choice between loyalty to Galerius and Maximian's tempting offers. These were recognition as Augustus and the hand of Maximian's daughter Fausta in marriage. Constantine accepted, divorced Minervina, mother of his eldest son Crispus, and married Fausta. But he made no move against Galerius when the latter gathered his armies and marched upon Rome. In the event his help was not needed, for Maximian had seen to it that Rome was well supplied with provisions to stand a siege, and Galerius was foiled by the great fortification-walls built by the Emperor Aurelian, the strongest city walls in the Empire, much of them still standing today. Galerius' soldiers threatened to desert him, just as Severus' troops had done so short a time before, and he retreated to his own dominions.

The next year (308) Maximian, irked by being treated as a subordinate by his own son, who was taking full advantage of the fact that it was by his invitation that his father had resumed power, fell out with Maxentius, and tried to divest him of his authority by the symbolic gesture of stripping off his son's purple mantle while he was addressing the troops. They, however, supported Maxentius against his father, and old Maximian fled to Gaul, to his new son-in-law Constantine. Again Constantine was faced with a dilemma, and again he decided in favour of Maximian, giving him his moral support and every honour, though careful to exclude him from any share in his own power; and he made no move against Maxentius. Again events soon proved him right, for Maxentius lost control of Africa, Rome's vital granary, from which he had been attempting to extort huge quantities of corn and money. The troops stationed there, supported by the leading men of the diocese, rebelled and declared the aged deputy-prefect, Domitius Alexander, Augustus. This tied Maxentius' hands for the time being and, whether he wished to or not, he was unable to attack Constantine.

The chaotic state into which the Second Tetrarchy had fallen forced Diocletian to come temporarily out of retirement, late in 308, to arrange matters. A conference was held at Carnuntum on the Danube in Pannonia, attended by Diocletian, Maximian and Galerius. Diocletian prevailed upon Maximian to go back into retirement, as he would himself. As for the vacant position of junior Augustus left by the death of Severus, rather than promote Constantine, who remained Caesar of Gaul and Britain, Galerius chose another old comrade-in-arms, Licinius, assigning to him the middle-Danube diocese of Pannonia until he should recover his rightful domains—Italy, Spain and Africa, at present held by Maxentius and Domitius Alexander. These were regarded as usurpers, and omitted from the arrangements. Maximin Daia was to remain Caesar in the East.

It may have been these decisions that prompted the diocese of Spain to detach itself from loyalty to Maxentius and go over to Constantine, by whose father it had been ruled during the brief space of his reign as Augustus. Constantine himself, despite the decision at Carnuntum, was now a legitimate Augustus, for Maximin objected to continuing as a mere Caesar while Licinius, coming newly into the Tetrarchy, was created Augustus straight away, so Galerius, to mollify him, recognized his claim to the title, and Constantine's likewise. So, year by year, crisis by crisis, Constantine was consolidating his position, and was now lawful ruler of the whole of the north-west portion of the Empire.

The new arrangements failed to satisfy old Maximian. In fact he was in a more precarious position than ever, for Constantine no longer needed him to legitimise his title of Augustus. He returned to Gaul, however, and carried on as a mere counsellor to his son-in-law for over a year. But in 310 he seized an opportunity when Constantine was absent fighting the Franks across the Rhine, and tried to usurp power for the last time, taking possession of the treasury at Arles and using it to load with presents the soldiers who were left behind, hoping to secure their allegiance. But the news was quickly relayed to Constantine, who by forced marches at amazing speed was upon Maximian long before he looked for danger from that quarter. Maximian's rebellion collapsed forthwith, and he fled to Marseille with a few troops. There, even while he was parleying with Constantine, who had followed him, his soldiers betrayed him and opened the city gates. He was taken and either strangled or ordered to hang himself, a sorry end for a once-powerful emperor, as Lactantius does not fail to note. The loyalty of the whole Gallic army to Constantine was absolute.

The orator who congratulated him on the crushing of the revolt introduced a strange new detail: Constantine was descended from one of the Illyrian soldier-emperors who preceded Diocletian, Claudius Gothicus (268–70). This certainly spurious attribution of ancestry indicates that Constantine was by now preparing for the assumption of wider power, for, by giving him a title of legitimation superior to that of the Tetrarchy, it dissociated him from his fellow-tetrarchs. It was not enough merely to slough off the Maximian connection: he must have something better even than his recognition by Galerius. Things began to look increasingly ominous for Maxentius, who now had not only the threat of Licinius trying to reclaim his rightful dominions, but also the lurking possibility of attack by Constantine, to contend with. Maxentius succeeded, however, in reconquering Africa from Domitius Alexander in 311, following it up with a brutal and bloody repression. The great city of Carthage was sacked and burnt to the ground.

The same year, 311, saw the death of Galerius. It marked the effective end of the Great Persecution, for he attributed his gruesome end from a horrible disease to the wrath of the God of the Christians. The forcible repression of Christianity had been continuing during these years both in his domains and in those of Maximin Daia. More is known about the latter's proceedings, thanks to the account of Eusebius, who lived at Caesarea in Palestine, of which he was soon to become bishop (in 314). Maximin has the rather dubious distinction of being the most intelligent of the various persecutors of Christianity. In 306, after a year spent settling down, he published an edict of his own ordering a general sacrifice to be carried out with the aid of census lists. But enforcement proved difficult, so the following year he changed his tactics and, instead of the death penalty, the threat of mutilation was used to try to persuade Christians to apostatize. Predictably, this was no more successful, and soon those who, like Eusebius, lived near the south-east corner of the Mediterranean were given the spectacle of gangs of men, with their right eyes gouged out and their left feet lamed with branding-irons, being led from Egypt, where the mines and quarries were now too full of convicts, to work in the copper-mines at Phaeno in southern Palestine, or even further afield. There they kept up their courage, and supervision at Phaeno was so lax that a new governor, inspecting the mines in 310, found that the convicts had even contrived to build churches; he executed some and dispersed the rest to other places. Execution was still the penalty for outstanding acts of contumacy, such as seizing a governor's right hand to prevent him sacrificing, as a few bold spirits did, and the year 309 had seen a return to sterner measures. These were aimed at enforcing an edict laying down that all the food in the markets should be sprinkled with libations and blood from sacrifices, and that everyone should be compelled to taste the sacrifices.

Maximin's measures, however, were not only negative. It was principally in this that he differed from his predecessors. As well as attacking the Christians directly, he mounted a serious and carefully thought out campaign to revive paganism, and was in some ways the precursor of Julian the Apostate, half a century later. He ordered the restoration of all temples and sanctuaries that were falling into ruin, and appointed priests where there were none (in itself a testimony of the extent to which the growth of Christianity was eroding the basis of paganism, as regards both finance and manpower). Furthermore, in an attempt to imitate the hierarchic system of organization that had brought such benefits to the Church, he created a high priest of each province, chosen from among the leading members of the city councils, and to increase their dignity he gave each high priest a bodyguard. All the pagan priests in each province were to be under the control of the high priest, like Christian presbyters under their bishop. Lastly, from Eusebius' sneer about Maximin awarding governorships and other privileges to 'jugglers, as if they were pious and beloved of the gods', it would seem that he was not above showing favouritism to pagans, and elevating unsuitable individuals to high office because of their devotion to the pagan cause. Such partiality in giving patronage again foreshadows one of Julian's chosen weapons against Christianity.

Amid this persecution, with an atmosphere heavy with menace still lowering over the Christians, and with executions still quite commonplace—and the same or worse in Galerius' own dominions (Asia Minor and the Balkans)—the famous Palinode of Galerius burst like a bombshell: 'Among other dispositions which we are constantly making for the advantage and good of the State, we had formerly wished to set all things right according to the ancient laws and public discipline of the Romans [*disciplina* was a favourite tetrarchic word, sometimes personified and treated as a minor deity], and to provide that the Christians, too, who had abandoned the mode of life of their own fathers, should return to sound reason; for the said Christians had somehow become possessed by such self-will and folly that they did not follow those institutions of the ancients which their own ancestors had perhaps first established, but at their own whim and pleasure they were making laws for themselves to observe and were gathering assemblies of different peoples in various places. When, however, our command had gone forth that they should return to the institutions of the ancients, many were subdued by the danger that threatened, many too were thrown into a panic. And when very many persisted in their purpose and we saw that they neither paid cult and due reverence to the gods nor worshipped the god of the Christians, considering our most gentle clemency and our immemorial custom of granting pardon to all men, we have thought it right in their case too to extend the readiest indulgence, so that they may once more be Christians and form their conventicles, provided that they do nothing contrary to public order [*disciplina* again] ... Wherefore in accordance with this our indulgence it will be their duty to pray to their god for our safety and for that of the State and for their own, so that on every side the State may be preserved unharmed and that they themselves may live in their own homes free from care.' A few days later Galerius was dead, freed at last from his appalling sufferings (May 311).

The death of Galerius left a vacuum in his dominions, for his son was too young for power, and as he lay dying he entrusted him, together with his wife, to Licinius. He evidently intended Licinius to succeed him, at least for the time being. But Maximin was too quick for him: he made a dash through Asia Minor and had occupied the whole of it before Licinius, occupying the Balkans in his turn, reached the Bosphorus. War was nearly declared, but the two emperors thought better of it, and met in the middle of the straits to swear friendship.

Maximin, now in control of most of the East of the Empire, had found that the recantation edict of his senior Augustus had already been promulgated in Asia Minor, and although he was unwilling to publish the document itself in the rest of his territory, he had issued instructions to the governors to the same effect. Eusebius and Lactantius describe the dramatic turnabout in the fortunes of the Christians. Throughout the East and the Balkans the prisons were opened, and the 'confessors', who had suffered for Christ but not died in the process, were restored to the companionship of their fellow-Christians, who had escaped more lightly or hidden themselves—or lapsed, laying up a major problem for the Church. One of those released was Lactantius' friend Donatus, to whom he dedicated *On the Deaths of the Persecutors*, who had languished in prison for six years and been tortured nine times; perhaps a typical case among these brave men and women. The mutilated convicts from Phaeno and the other mines and quarries were allowed to return home, and made a truly triumphal progress through the towns on their route, greeted by throngs of joyful, hymn-singing Christians. People crowded into the newly opened churches (some, it would seem, had escaped demolition) to attend the restored services after their long interruption.

In the East, however, all this was only a temporary respite from persecution. Not six months had elapsed before Maximin had found new ways of bringing pressure to bear on the hated Christians. He solicited embassies from the leading cities, whose councils would still have been almost entirely pagan at this early date, requesting from their emperor the privilege of the expulsion of all the impious Christians from their territory; a privilege that was, needless to say, granted with alacrity by the grateful Maximin. Eusebius copied down his rescript to the city of Tyre in Phoenicia (Nicomedia in Asia Minor and Antioch in Syria, Maximin's new and old capitals, were other cities led by dutiful pagans anxious to please the gods and the emperor). In it he sets forth very clearly the belief that the fertility of the earth and the absence of hurricanes, earthquakes and war were directly dependent on the worship given to the gods to secure their favour, and on the corresponding absence of Christian 'impiety'. Look, he says, upon the plains waving with ripe corn, and the meadows bright with flowers after the rain, and see how mild the weather is. Alas for his boasting! The rains failed that very winter and brought famine, with a plague following hard upon its heels: God's judgement upon his wickedness in persecuting the Christians, says Eusebius. Indeed his measures against them were not, even now, limited to exile, their 'removal' from the pious cities being sometimes interpreted in a more sinister sense. In the autumn of 312, several bishops and other Christians were summarily executed. Moreover, anti-Christian propaganda began to be circulated, in the form of forged *Acts of Pilate*, highly derogatory to Christ, that were even ordered to be taught to children in schools; and 'confessions' wrung by threats of torture from some prostitutes at Damascus, alleging all sorts of immorality in Christian churches, were likewise posted up everywhere. It may also have been now, rather than earlier, that Maximin set about his restoration and reorganization of paganism. The last attack on the Christians that formed part of the Great Persecution was one of the most comprehensive.

It was, however, destined to be short-lived, as political events further west caught up with Maximin. There existed at this point a *de facto* tetrarchy and, had the three legitimate emperors—Maximin, Constantine and Licinius—agreed to recognize Maxentius, the situation could probably have been stabilized fairly indefinitely. Any such possibility was, however, excluded by the ambitions of Constantine. Maxentius, while still a 'usurper' or unrecognized ruler, was fair game for anyone strong enough to unseat him. In 312 an alliance was formally concerted between Constantine and Licinius, who was given the hand of Constantine's half-sister Constantia in marriage. The apparently intended victims of the alliance, Maximin and Maxentius, were not slow to react to the implied threat, and came to a secret understanding. The stage was set for the crucial confrontation between Constantine and Maxentius.

Lactantius alleges that Maxentius moved first, ordering the destruction of Constantine's images throughout his domains, thus declaring war. Eusebius has the more probable version: Constantine decided to 'rescue' Italy from the tyrant and, acting with his usual energy and speed, crossed the Alps into Italy. Maxentius sent armies against him in northern Italy, but Constantine defeated them at battles near Turin, Brescia and Verona. The way to Rome lay open, and Constantine took it, marching down the Via Flaminia to fight his main battle against Maxentius, at a place called Red Rocks, some nine miles north of the city. His forces were outnumbered by perhaps more than two to one (though of superior quality), for he had exhibited a commendable sense of responsibility in making his preparations, leaving comparatively large forces behind him to guard the frontiers instead of stripping them of their defenders and laying them open to barbarian attack, as had been done by many a usurper and contender for imperial power before him, with disastrous results for the Empire. Instead, he had enlarged the small nucleus of his field-army, made up of experienced men from the frontiers, by recruiting and training suitable men from among the Germanic prisoners of war captured in his campaigns to protect Gaul. Maxentius, with his larger army, and corn arriving once again from Africa, could have remained safe within the mighty walls of Rome for a considerable length of time, but he was unsure of the loyalty of the populace. At one of the celebrations for the fifth anniversary of his rule (*quinquennalia*), the crowd in the Circus Maximus shouted out that Constantine could not be vanquished. Lactantius goes so far as to speak of sedition, with the common people cursing Maxentius as a traitor to public safety; *they* had no mind to stand a long and painful siege. In the circumstances, Maxentius allowed an ambiguous oracle from the Sibylline books, saying that an 'enemy of the Roman people' would be destroyed on 28 October, his own anniversary of accession, to lure him forth from the city on that day. The Milvian Bridge, by which the Via Flaminia crossed the Tiber, was demolished, and a bridge of boats was carefully constructed in two halves linked by iron bolts that could be withdrawn if the enemy should try to cross.

When battle was joined at the Red Rocks, Maxentius' troops must have been struck by the strangeness and novelty of the device painted on the shields of the men in Constantine's army. It was the celebrated chi-rho monogram, and Lactantius tells how it came to be there. Dreams were widely if not universally regarded, from at least the time of Homer, as possible vehicles for the conveyance of warnings and other messages from the gods, and it was in a dream that Constantine, who had a strong visionary side to his nature and had been granted, according to a panegyrist speaking in 310, an actual vision of Apollo in an important sanctuary of that god in Gaul, had been instructed to place 'the celestial sign of God' on the shields of his army, 'and so join battle'. There is no mention of the famous vision of the Cross in the sky ringed about with the words 'In this sign you shall be victorious' (*Hoc signo victor eris*), which makes its first appearance (in Greek) in Eusebius' *Life of Constantine* written after the emperor's death, a work of rhetorical panegyric rather than of sober historical fact; and it seems likely that it was an embroidery by Eusebius, by Constantine himself (very probably), or by Christian court tradition, on the theme of the dream. Whatever the precise truth of the matter, Constantine was sufficiently impressed by his dream-vision to be willing to commit himself and his army to the protection of the unfamiliar deity of those wretched Christians who had been causing so much trouble to their misguided persecutors in the East of the Empire; to Christ, whose only credential of any weight, apart from the impressive loyalty, even to martyrdom, of a minority of his followers, was that he had struck down the arch-persecutor Galerius the year before. Opportunism can have played no part whatever in his decision, for the Christians were in far too small a minority, especially in the West, for their support to be worth winning, and had, moreover, been deliberately purged from army and administration. The superstition that was a leading characteristic of the age was in Constantine metamorphosed into a grandiose sense of a specially close relationship with the gods. He was their chosen one, led on by his high destiny, and the commands which he was thus privileged to receive were to be obeyed unquestioningly.

Constantine's decision was to have momentous consequences for the whole history of Christendom. For the victory promised to Constantine by his new patron deity in the battle of the Milvian Bridge was soon his, while Maxentius fled back to Rome in the rout and was caught in his own trap, as the temporary bridge collapsed and precipitated him and his entourage into the Tiber, where they were swept away and drowned. Eusebius not unnaturally likens the scene to the crossing of the Red Sea by Pharaoh's army, a subject that was to become popular on Christian sarcophagi, but not until the late fourth century. The victory proved that the God of the Christians was a god who could win battles, and who favoured Constantine and his fortunes, and was worthy of having the Empire entrusted to His protection. Constantine was not slow to draw the inevitable conclusions. The *signum Christi* was added permanently to his personal insignia, in the form of a badge on his helmet, and to those of his army, as the sacred standard known as the *labarum*, on which portraits of the emperor and his family were surmounted by the chi-rho. The monogram of Christ was thus invested from its very origin (its pre-Constantinian antecedents are highly obscure) with a powerful charge of imperial victory-mystique, and the sign of the Redeemer, the spiritual Saviour, came to have connotations of salvation on a more terrestrial plane, of the Empire, of the emperor with whom the safety of the Empire was held to be intimately bound up, and of the soldiers who fought under its protection. A kind of magical power was widely attributed to the Christogram, for in ancient times a symbol was thought to possess some part of the (talismanic) efficacy of that which it symbolized. The victory-mystique of the chi-rho was important for its subsequent history: two usurpers were to make use of it in the early 350s in their struggle for legitimation, as we shall see (Chapter IV).

The battle won, Constantine entered Rome in triumph and was acclaimed with joy by Senate and people. Like many another Roman ruler, Maxentius had run into financial difficulties, and had not been over-scrupulous of the legality of the means which he employed to raise money. Our sources speak among other things of executions of wealthy men and the confiscation of their property. Some of the money had gone on buildings, including a new temple of Venus and Roma, a temple in the Forum (still standing) in honour of his son Romulus who died in 309, and a grandiose basilica (law-court) adjoining the Forum. This was not quite finished when Constantine conquered Rome, so the honour of completing the gigantic edifice, whose three huge vaults with coffered ceilings still dominate the Forum today, fell to him. The brick of which it is built was rendered to look like stone, while luxurious marble revetments once covered the brickwork inside. The interior was divided, as were the later, Christian, basilicas, by two rows of columns, and had an apse at the west end to which Constantine added another on the north. In the west apse was placed, as the focus of the whole basilica, a colossal statue of Constantine, no less than seven times life-size. It was evidently rather makeshift at first, with some of the sculptured parts (the torso would have been hollow beneath bronze armour) purloined from earlier colossi. The enormous marble head that dominates the courtyard of the museum of the Conservatori on the Capitol appears to have been carved in the 320s. There are two right hands, which again suggests a replacement, and opens up an interesting possibility: was the cross-holding statue described by Eusebius, duly inscribed, 'By this saving sign, the true proof of courage, I have saved and freed your city from the yoke of the tyrant; and furthermore I have set free both the Senate and the People of Rome, and restored them to their ancient renown and splendour', perhaps a later substitution, on the orders of a more truly Christian Constantine, for a secular, sceptre-holding image put in the basilica soon after the battle of the Milvian Bridge? There is a world of difference between the placing of a chi-rho on the emperor's helmet or shield, as a kind of talismanic sign for his protection, and the setting of the Cross of Christ in his right hand as a symbol of power, making him an Emperor by the Grace of God; and there was clearly need for a lapse of some years before the one could become the other. Even the statue of Constantine carried round in 330, at the inauguration ceremonies of Constantinople, held a little figure of Victory in its right hand, not a cross or other Christian sign. (2)

In return for the 'liberation' of their city, the senators of Rome voted Constantine a triumphal arch, which likewise still stands, near the

Colosseum. The inscription is fascinating, for it reveals how Constantine's miraculous 'vision' and its consequences appeared to contemporary upper-class pagans in a form that could be expressed on a public monument. 'To the Emperor Flavius Constantinus,' it runs, 'greatest, Augustus, pious and favoured by fortune [*pius felix*—conventional titles, these, part of every fourth-century emperor's official nomenclature], the Senate and People of Rome dedicated this arch to mark his triumphs, because at the instigation of the Divinity [*instinctu divinitatis*], in his greatness of heart, he came with his army and exacted instant vengeance on behalf of the commonwealth from the tyrant and all his minions in righteous warfare.' Subsidiary inscriptions hail 'the liberator of the city, the founder of peace', and refer to the celebration of Constantine's *decennalia*, which means that the Arch was complete by 25 July 315, the date of his 'tenth' (by the Romans' inclusive counting—it was really only the ninth) anniversary of power. It cannot have been started earlier than 29 October 312, the morrow of the Milvian Bridge, and may have been built in a shorter time than this suggests. This, together with the evident shortage of highly qualified artists, helps to explain the fact that the Arch is decorated almost entirely with reused material, and came to be known as 'Aesop's jay' on account of its borrowed plumes. But there was another reason, too: by ransacking the monuments of earlier 'good' emperors—Trajan, Hadrian and Marcus Aurelius—Constantine was associating himself symbolically (in the full ancient sense of the term, which includes a degree of contagious magic—some of the power of the person transferred to the associated object) with them, and inaugurating a reign that was intended to be as crowned with blessings as theirs. And it is no accident that the river-gods and flying Victories holding trophies that occupy the spandrels of the three arches are direct copies of those on the Arch of Septimius Severus, another 'good' emperor. (1)

The most obvious case of reuse is the series of eight Hadrianic sculptured medallions, or *tondi*, that are set in pairs above the two side-arches. They depict the emperor in various scenes of hunting and sacrificing, and the imperial heads were all recut into portraits of Constantine and Licinius (or Constantius Chlorus?). The four on the south face are damaged; one shows Constantine, with veiled head, making sacrifice to Diana after a boar hunt, while the others have Constantine or Licinius (the heads are broken) departing for the hunt, hunting a bear, and sacrificing to Silvanus after the success of the bear hunt. Those on the north face (the front) of the Arch represent (again from left to right) Constantine hunting a boar, Licinius sacrificing to Apollo (in its original form one of the finest works of the Hadrianic period), Constantine and hunters with the lion they have killed, and Licinius, with veiled head, bringing an offering to Hercules after the success of the lion hunt. Thus for the very last time a Roman emperor is depicted, on an official monument, in the act of making a pagan sacrifice. If it seems ironical that the monument in question should be the memorial of the battle of the Milvian Bridge, which initiated the triumph of Christianity and sounded the first faint knell for paganism, the same reliefs also show how far Constantine was from realizing the exclusiveness of Christianity, and from his later concept of himself as the Christian God's vicegerent on earth, his main task being to advance the interests of the Church and turn the heathen from their 'wicked errors'. He had simply extended his special patronage to one cult among the others—a notorious cult that had recently been in trouble with the authorities, it is true—in much the same way as Aurelian, for example, had promoted the cult of the Unconquered Sun (probably for the same reason—a miracle during his eastern wars). This had hitherto been Constantine's own patron deity, witness the long series of SOLI INVICTO COMITI coins ('To the Unconquered Sun, [the emperor's] Companion'), with which he broke with the traditional tetrarchic coin types in 310 and which continued to be issued as a main coinage until 320, and by one mint down to 323. Thus Christ had to share Constantine's special allegiance with a number of pagan gods—not only Sol but Mars, Jupiter and Hercules (all still found on major coinages between 312 and 320). Significantly, two of these gods, Apollo-Sol and Hercules (patron of the lesser tetrarchic dynasty to which Constantine's father belonged), appear in receipt of sacrifice on the front of the Arch. It would be years before Constantine realized the full implications of his choice of the Christian God as his protector.

Two newly created *tondi* were added to the Hadrianic set, one at each end of the Arch. They depict, respectively, the Sun-God in his four-horse chariot (*quadriga*) and the Moon-Goddess in her two-horse chariot (*biga*). The style is classicizing, to blend in with the other *tondi*, and they are passably well executed. The cycle of medallions is heavily symbolic. The primeval activity of hunting had by the fourth century become overlaid with layers of possible meaning. As a theme on sarcophagi of the second, third and early fourth centuries, it betokened the courage of the deceased that had earned him immortality, or was an allegory of the defeat of evil and the hope of overcoming death (powerfully symbolized on a common type of sarcophagus as a lion devouring its prey). It was in this sense of the conquest of evil that the hunting scenes were placed on the Arch of Constantine, for a coin depicting him, and in the parallel version Licinius, as the slayer of a lion is inscribed 'Liberator of the World'. The sacrifice scenes exhibit the two emperors' piety towards the gods of the Roman State, courage and piety being the classic virtues of a Roman emperor. The setting of Constantine and Licinius in each of the closely related pairs of medallions (on the north side it is Constantine who hunts and Licinius who conducts the sacrifice after the hunt's successful conclusion, and apparently the other way round on the south side) is a sign of their *concordia* (actual or wished for).

The inclusion of the Sun (Sol Invictus, with raised right hand) and Moon in the set of medallions indicates that the emperors belong to the same cosmic order as the two luminaries: their powers are not merely temporal, but share in the divine authority ruling the universe (on one coin, Constantine holds the zodiac, and symbols of cosmic power (globes, stars and the like) accompany his representation on other coins). They are Sun-emperors, mystically identified with the Sun-God, who also makes frequent appearances elsewhere on the Arch. Beneath one of the side-arches, his bust faces that of Constantine himself. And he and the goddess Victory are present on two of the reliefs set round the base and on the narrative friezes as the deities protecting Constantine's army in the struggle against Maxentius. It appears from this, and from the total absence of the chi-rho shield-device or any other reference to the 'vision' as Christian, that the *divinitas* of the dedicatory inscription was conceived by the Senate as the Unconquered Sun, with whom Constantine, too, readily identified his new God. Yet the careful ambiguity of the inscription reveals an awareness of a Christian element that would make the actual mention of Sol or other gods unwelcome to the emperor.

There are six 'historical' frieze panels, running anti-clockwise round the Arch at the level of the top of the side-arches, just below the *tondi*. Starting from the west end, they depict: the departure of the troops on the campaign against Maxentius, the siege of Verona, the battle of the Milvian Bridge with Maxentius' army sinking beneath the waves, Constantine's entry into Rome, the emperor making a speech to the people, and the emperor distributing largesse. Various architectural features in the background of the last three help to localize their settings as the Campus Martius, the Forum Romanum and the Forum of Julius Caesar. The style of these reliefs is in total contrast to the classical style of the rest of the contemporary sculptures of the Arch; so completely un-Roman in its rigidity and formality, its repetitions of the same figure to form groups, and its preference for frontality, that the possibility of their having been executed by a group of provincial sculptors, summoned to Rome after working on Diocletian's palace at Split, must be reckoned with. The figures are squat, in the tetrarchic manner, yet, in the static scenes of Constantine making a speech and handing out largesse, the repetition of figures and the hieratic frontality of the enlarged figure of the emperor produce an effect that might be described as proto-Byzantine, heavily impregnated with the tendencies that were to dominate Byzantine art. The Arch of Constantine, with its sculptures of a wide variety of ages and styles, looks both forwards and backwards in the history of Roman art. It is a fitting monument of an age of transition.

From Emperor of the West to Sole Emperor (312–24)

Constantine was now the legitimate ruler of most of the Western Empire—Britain, Gaul, Spain, Italy and North Africa. On his arrival in Rome, the Senate had voted him the title of Senior Augustus (carrying with it the vital right to legislate), which Maximin claimed—with reason—for himself. He spent the winter settling affairs in Rome, which included the definitive disbandment of the praetorian guard, which had been the means of Maxentius' coming to power in 306 when Severus was threatening to suppress it, and had been the instrument of some of Maxentius' more repugnant actions, notably a massacre of some of the populace for reasons unknown. Then in February 313 he set off for Milan, where he met Licinius for the celebration of the latter's marriage to Constantia.

From the conference of the brother-emperors there emerged a document of signal importance for the history of the Church, known as the Edict of Milan. Lactantius recorded the details of the copy that was posted up in Nicomedia not long after by Licinius, addressed to the governor of Bithynia: 'I, Constantine Augustus, and I, Licinius Augustus, met happily at Milan, and in the course of our discussions on all matters relating to public well-being and security, we thought it right that our very first ordinances, which would benefit the majority of our people, should concern the respect due to the divinity, that is to say, that the Christians should be given full liberty to follow the religion of their choice, so that all that is divine in the celestial seat may be appeased and propitious towards us and towards those under our authority. This is why we thought that, with a wholesome and just purpose, we should embark upon this policy of not refusing to anyone the opportunity of devoting himself either to the cult of the Christians or to whatever religion he feels is most suited to him, so that the highest divinity, whom we freely worship, may in all things bestow upon us his customary favour and goodwill. Therefore your Excellency must know that we have decided that all conditions laid down concerning the sect of the Christians in previous writings addressed to your office should be utterly abolished, and that regulations that seemed unfortunate and altogether alien to our clemency should be cancelled; henceforward let every one of those whose pleasure is likewise to observe the religion of the Christians do so freely and completely, without any let or hindrance. We thought it right to communicate these decisions very fully to your Solicitude, that you should know that we have given complete and total freedom to the Christians to practise their religion. While you see that we have granted them this grace, your Dedication will understand that to promote the peace of our reign, open and free liberty has likewise been extended to others, too, that they should be utterly free to follow whatever cult they choose. We have done this lest we should appear to diminish any worship or any religion.' Several clauses follow laying down that all confiscated churches are to be freely and immediately returned to the Christian communities, with the payment of compensation from the public purse to purchasers and even to those who had received the buildings as a gift. 'Thus it will come about that, as we have set forth above, the divine favour towards us, which we have experienced in great ventures, shall continue for all time to assure the success of our enterprises and public prosperity.' The edict ends with provisions for its wide publication.

The elaborate titles, the pompous and circumvoluted prose style, like that of the Palinode of Galerius, seem already Byzantine; but the content is clear. This edict inaugurated the definitive Peace of the Church. Never again were the Christians subjected to systematic and general persecution by the authorities of the Roman Empire. The passages about the Divinity seem to provide further evidence that Constantine was still groping towards a monotheism altogether vague as yet in character; but the extremely guarded language may reflect compromise with the pagan Licinius.

At the time of its formulation the Edict of Milan could only be applied in the West, the Balkans and Greece, where active persecution had already ceased, and the main implementation concerned the handing back of church buildings. But only a few months were to elapse before it brought relief to the unhappy Christians of Maximin's domains. For Maximin, no doubt dismayed by the swift collapse of his ally Maxentius, and knowing that the existence of his alliance with that illegitimate ruler would be discovered by Constantine—as it was—from statues and documents in Rome, and provide Constantine and Licinius with the excuse they wanted to attack him, decided that his one chance of survival lay in striking first. The conference at Milan gave him the opportunity he needed: while Licinius' back was turned, beyond the other side of his dominions, Maximin made forced marches from Syria and crossed the Bosphorus. But the element of surprise in his attack evaporated while he was delayed eleven days by the resistance of Byzantium, and was held up further while he besieged two more cities. Meanwhile the news had reached Licinius, who gathered a small army and marched to Adrianople in Thrace hoping, with his 30,000 men, to stay the advance of Maximin's 70,000 until reinforcements came. Both sides prepared to fight. Maximin prayed to Jupiter, vowing that he would wipe the name of the Christians off the face of the earth if he were victorious. As for Licinius, an angel came to him in a dream and dictated a form of prayer to be used by his troops; that, at least, was the official version, duly recorded by Lactantius. The prayer was as follows: 'Highest God, we beseech you, Holy God, we beseech you: we commend all just causes to you, we commend our safety to you, we commend our Empire to you. Through you we live, through you we are victorious and blessed by fortune. Highest, Holy God, hear our prayers: we stretch out our arms to you: hear us, Holy, Highest God.' The content of the prayer and the recurrence of a dream-vision suggest a less miraculous source: Constantine. It was probably he himself who worked out, with or without Licinius' assistance, a form of words—almost a magical formula—most likely to draw to them again, in succeeding conflicts, the powerful help of the God of the Milvian Bridge.

The prayer and the tidings of its allegedly miraculous origin gave a great access of confidence to Licinius' soldiers, and the sound of their heavenward murmurings dismayed their adversaries. Battle was joined, and the desertion of some of Maximin's troops helped to turn it into a rout. Maximin, in despair, disguised himself as a slave and fled across the Bosphorus. Abandoning his capital, he made for Cappadocia, where he was able to regroup his remaining forces. A few days after the battle, Licinius crossed the straits in his turn and entered Nicomedia in triumph. There he gave public thanksgiving to God for his victory, and posted up the Edict of Milan, adding verbal instructions that the churches were to be handed back in their original condition. Then he continued his pursuit of Maximin, who retreated to the passes of the Taurus mountains and tried to block them with hasty fortifications. When these were stormed, he fell back on Tarsus where, blockaded by land and sea, he took poison. Licinius made a clean sweep of all surviving relatives of the tetrarchs, executing even Diocletian's poor wife and daughter as well as Maximin's own family and Severus' son, in an effort to rule out possible usurpations.

Lactantius' chronological account finishes at this point, on a note of rendering thanks to God for his destruction of all the persecutors; and for the next forty years, until the surviving work of the great fourth-century historian, Ammianus Marcellinus, begins in 353, we are without a detailed narrative of secular events, and have to piece together their course from a variety of sources, principally the fifth-century pagan historian Zosimus, who drew on the lost *History* written by a late-fourth-century admirer of Julian, Eunapius of Sardis. Licinius proceeded to consolidate his hold on the Eastern Empire, smashing Maximin's statues and executing his leading supporters. Even before the defeat of Maximin, that emperor had begun to doubt the wisdom of his renewed persecution of the Christians, and had sent orders to the governors, first to cease molesting them, and then, just before his death, to grant them full rights of assembly and to return their churches, in imitation of the

Edict of Milan. He evidently feared the possibility of a Christian 'fifth column' during his war with Licinius. But his recantation, like that of Galerius, availed him nothing.

It was not long, however, before the victorious allies, Constantine and Licinius, who now controlled the whole of the Empire between them, fell out with each other. Zosimus accuses Constantine of causing the quarrel by trying to appropriate some of Licinius' provinces. There was some justification for this, in that accidents of history had assigned to Licinius parts of the Balkans that had belonged to the Western Empire under the First Tetrarchy. Licinius refused to concede the point, and a battle was fought at Cibalae in Pannonia in 314. Licinius was worsted, and after a second, indecisive, battle in Thrace, had to give up all his European dominions with the exception of Thrace. In return, however, he was permitted by Constantine to legislate, which as junior Augustus under the tetrarchic system he had hitherto been unable to do. The Empire was now truly split in two, with Constantine ruling the larger part instead of the smaller, as far east as Greece and Macedonia.

Three years later, in 317, the two emperors agreed to associate their sons with them in power as Caesars. Constantine's eldest son Crispus, borne to him by his first wife Minervina, was now about twelve years old, and his second son Constantine II had been born during that winter at Arles. Licinius' single Caesar was his small son by Constantia, Licinianus, born in 315. Although this joint decision might be taken as indicating that all was well between Constantine and Licinius, relations between them deteriorated again over the next few years, some of which (322 and 323) were spent by Constantine in major campaigns on the lower Danube, with notable success. Licinius had also been governing well, despite the blood-bath with which he inaugurated his reign, and a deep-rooted antipathy towards culture and its representatives. He kept a tight rein on finances, which enabled him to favour the more hard-pressed sections of society, such as the peasants and the municipal institutions. Long after, in a speech composed in 386, Libanius of Antioch was able to refer to Licinius, without mentioning his name, as 'the man who made the cities flourish'. But Licinius found that the newly liberated Christians were a force to be reckoned with, far stronger numerically in the East than in the West, where they were very much in the minority. He may have feared, like Maximin, a 'fifth column' operating in Constantine's favour, or simply have wished to exert the authority of the State over the Christians as far as he could. Whatever the reason, he began gradually to infringe the rights granted to them by the Edict of Milan. Bishops were forbidden to meet in synods to settle matters of doctrine or discipline—a clever move towards isolating individual churches. Christians were dismissed from the imperial household, the administration and the army, as at the beginning of the Great

Persecution. The visiting of prisoners (who would be awaiting trial—prison sentences as punishments were unknown to Roman law) was forbidden, perhaps on the pretext of possible interference with the course of justice; it had been a standard Christian charitable activity from New Testament times. And restrictions were placed on Christian worship: it was to take place in the open air outside the city walls, and women were not to attend the same services as men. The governor of Pontus, in north-east Asia Minor, apparently exceeded his brief, demolishing churches and executing some bishops.

All this played neatly into the hands of Constantine, who was thus enabled to mount a high-minded crusade against his rival on behalf of the oppressed Christians in his domains. A prolonged state of mutual hostility had allowed time for both sides to assemble impressive armaments, with Licinius having a certain numerical superiority (150,000 infantry to 120,000, and cavalry and fleet in proportion). Constantine invaded Thrace and won a first victory at Adrianople in July 324. Then he summoned his fleet from the Piraeus and from the new harbour he had built at Thessalonica, and, by cleverly deploying only part of it, won a naval battle in the narrows of the Hellespont (Dardanelles) in a carbon-copy of the battle of Salamis of 480 B.C., when the comparatively few Greek ships threw the large Persian fleet into confusion in another circumscribed stretch of water. Constantine was now free to cross over to Asia Minor, where on 18 September he inflicted a decisive defeat on Licinius near Chrysopolis, a city on the Bosphorus. The losses in all three battles were tragically high. Licinius surrendered a few weeks later at Nicomedia, and was sent into retirement at Thessalonica, but was executed after a conspiracy in 325.

Constantine Sole Emperor (324–37), and the Foundation of Constantinople (324–30)

Constantine was now master of the whole of the Roman Empire, which had not been united under one sovereign for thirty-nine years, since Diocletian appointed Maximian as his colleague in 285. He lost no time in arranging matters to suit the new age of expansion and prosperity which he felt himself to be inaugurating. His first two actions, both made on 8 November 324, were the consolidation of the Constantinian dynasty by the elevation of Constantius II, probably the second of his sons by Fausta, born in August 317, to the rank of Caesar; and the tracing with a ploughshare, after the ancient Roman custom, of the circuit of walls of a completely new capital at Byzantium on the Bosphorus, to be renamed Constantinople. The choice of this site was dictated by strategic considerations. Constantine's campaigns on the middle and lower Danube in 322 and 323 had shown him the most beleaguered stretch of the frontier. Byzantium was nearer to this than was Diocletian's chosen Nicomedia, and more central to the whole Empire, on the road linking most of its capitals, and Constantine's brief siege of Byzantium during the recent war against Licinius had given him an opportunity to take note of the city's signal strategic advantages. A mint was established there, probably at the beginning of 326, and was rapidly built up from only two workshops to eleven four years later. Building proceeded apace: the great church of Sancta Sophia (Holy Wisdom) was begun in 326, and the palace and hippodrome were already under way when the new Forum was created in 328.

Meanwhile, tragedy in the form of a double execution had overtaken the imperial family. Constantine, having celebrated his *vicennalia* in 325 during the Council of Nicaea (see Chapter IV), decided to mark what for us was his real twentieth anniversary by festivities at Rome in 326. He was accompanied on the journey to Rome by the Empress Fausta and his eldest son Crispus, who had distinguished himself as admiral in the war against Licinius. But, while they were still at Aquileia in north-eastern Italy, Crispus was suddenly put to death at Pola, and Fausta shortly afterwards at Rome. Naturally enough, nothing concrete is known about the reasons behind the two executions. Rumour was rife, and popular opinion linked the two events into a kind of replay of the famous tragedy of Hippolytus and his step-mother Phaedra, who tried to seduce him and, failing, accused him of an attempt against her, to their mutual destruction. According to Zosimus, Crispus was suspected of having a liaison with Fausta, and Fausta was then put to death in an overheated bath at the instigation of her mother-in-law Helena. Another source accuses Fausta of adultery with a palace official; Crispus' offence is buried in silence. Ironically, Constantine had been issuing laws on moral matters, such as adultery, earlier in the year, and this may have had something to do with the savagery of his reaction, in his fierce anger, when he discovered moral delinquencies—if such they were—in his own family. The involvement of Helena in the tragedy, as asserted by Zosimus, gains credibility from her pilgrimage to the Holy Land, undertaken immediately after, which looks suspiciously like an expiation. As for the main perpetrator of these horrible deeds, the hostile pagan sources—among them Zosimus and the Emperor Julian himself—allege them as the reason for his conversion to Christianity: the pagan priests, when approached by Constantine, replied that there was no means of expiating such crimes, whereas 'an Egyptian come from Spain' (Bishop Hosius (or Ossius) of Cordova, Constantine's confessor, who had been at his court from about 312) offered him the free forgiveness of Christ. In reality, Constantine had been making lavish donations to the Church for years, had recently acted as a kind of chairman of the Council of Nicaea, and in edicts and letters had already spoken quite clearly as a Christian. But it is very likely that the Church, in the person of Hosius and perhaps of others (Bishop Sylvester of Rome?), used Constantine's guilty conscience as a means of tightening its hold upon him. (6 b, c)

One instance of this may have occurred during this very visit to Rome. Zosimus records that when 'the traditional festival came round, at which the army had to mount up to the Capitol and carry out the customary rites', Constantine joined in some of the festival out of respect for the army, but ceded to pressure from Hosius and kept aloof from the sacred rites. This drew down upon him the anger of the Senate and people. If this incident really took place in 326, and not in 313 or 315, an additional reason for the public anger at Constantine's withdrawal may have been that the festival in question was the annual procession of the knights, specially held over from 15 July for a few days so that the emperor could participate in person. Whatever the precise nature and chronology of this particular event, Constantine's visit to Rome for the *vicennalia* was not a happy one, and he was doubtless glad to shake off his feet the dust of a city where he had put his own wife to death, and return to continue the building of his great new capital, to be called by his name.

Military necessities, however, prevented his supervising the works in person. Restiveness among the tribes of the middle and lower Danube, the Sarmatians and the Goths, kept him campaigning there and based at the Balkan capital of Sirmium from late in 326 to 329, underlining the strategic suitability of Constantinople as the principal imperial residence. As for the West of the Empire, after the demise of Crispus, who had been stationed at Trier, the next eldest Caesar, Constantine II, still only eleven years old, was sent to that city in 328 in the charge of a praetorian prefect. Military operations on the Rhine gave the border area a new stability, with trade between Roman and free Germany reestablished, and Roman coins circulating once again beyond the Rhine.

By 330, the great new city on the Bosphorus stood ready for its dedication ceremony. An enormous circuit of walls, rebuilt in the fifth century and still standing today, girded it about, cutting right across the isthmus from the Sea of Marmara to the Golden Horn. The old forum of Byzantium had become the so-called Augustaeum, with a statue of Helena on a porphyry column in its centre, and a grand new Senate-house replacing the old town council-chamber. At each end of one of the four porticoes enclosing the old forum Constantine had a temple built, one dedicated to the Fortune of Rome, the other housing the statue of Cybele from mount Dindymus in Phrygia, duly purged of her wilder and more immoral associations by the removal of her lions and the rearrangement of her hands in the Orante attitude, 'looking over the city and surrounding it with her care'—a talismanic protector for the city, in fact, its new Fortune, parallel to that of Rome. There was another temple in the vast, newly fitted hippodrome, for it was enlarged to enclose the sanctuary of the Dioscuri (Castor and Pollux), who were often regarded as patrons of horsemanship and the circus games. (So much for Eusebius' assertion, in his *Life of Constantine*, that Constantinople was a wholly Christian city, without a single pagan temple!) The imperial palace was built next to the hippodrome, with which it was connected so that the emperor could appear in the imperial box before the people with the *éclat* of the sudden descent of a god. The palace, says Zosimus, was scarcely less magnificent than that of Rome. The new Forum was established on the site of the gate of the old Byzantium. It was circular, and surrounded by porticoes in two stories, with two long, marble-vaulted passages leading from it to 'the porticoes of Severus'. In the centre of the new Forum was a porphyry column (the one piece of Constantinian Constantinople that is still *in situ*, known as 'the Burnt Column' in consequence of the vicissitudes it has experienced), matching the one in the Augustaeum, surmounted by a colossal gilded-bronze statue of Constantine himself with the attributes of the Sun-God, notably the radiate crown. It was an adaptation of a statue of Sol Invictus purloined from Ilium (Troy). Local chroniclers of the city record that a curious pagano-Christian cult came to be devoted to this statue: a priest would pray, and the people would chant the Kyrie Eleison a hundred times; and legend had it that the rays of the crown were made from nails from the True Cross, and that the column enclosed the Palladium, the statue of Pallas Athene brought from Troy to the foundation of Rome, together with many other 'wonders' (Noah's axe and the rock from which Moses struck water, according to one source). The statue was dislodged by a gale in the twelfth century, and was replaced by a cross. It was probably this statue that Julian is alleged to have thrown down and buried, objecting to a cross that adorned it, or perhaps to the insult to his own special divine patron, the Sun, from having the first Christian emperor usurping his attributes.

There was apparently another statue of Constantine tricked out as the Sun-God, replacing the god in a chariot drawn by four gilded horses that had been set up on two columns in the old Byzantium. This statue held in its hand a statuette of the Fortune of the City, and joined the procession of gods at the inaugural ceremonies of the new capital, on 11 May 330. These dedication ceremonies were distinctly pagan in tone—there was as yet no other way. They were probably presided over by the Neoplatonist sage Sopater from Apamea in Syria, a surprising figure to find at Constantine's side, but one who had become a close friend and adviser (see also Chapter IV). Bloodless sacrifices were offered to the Fortune of the City, and the statue of Constantine was escorted round the hippodrome by soldiers carrying candles. The festivities lasted for forty days, ending with magnificent chariot-races in the hippodrome and lavish largesse to the people. One pagan feature does, however, seem to have been omitted: there were no hecatombs of slaughtered animals to win the favour of the gods of Constantinople; and this accords with the anodyne and vestigial nature of the officially permitted paganism.

Such things as bloody sacrifices, as Constantine well knew, were not in place in a city that was to have a markedly Christian character. Some of its most imposing buildings were churches, not relegated to the outskirts as at Rome, but in the very heart of the city. The original church of Holy Wisdom (S. Sophia), replaced after a fire by Justinian's marvellous edifice, was an oblong structure erected on the site of a pagan temple, a significant supersession of the old order by the new. It is possible that the bronze doors survive, reused under Justinian. Even less is known of its sister churches, Holy Peace (S. Irene) and Holy Power (S. Dynamis), all three dedications being strongly redolent of philosophy, that love of Wisdom to which many men of intellectual aspirations devoted themselves in the fourth century, a wisdom that had come increasingly to have the character of a divine revelation rather than of human knowledge and enquiry. In this case it was the Christian 'Wisdom' that was later to fire the young Augustine, for Christ himself was the true Holy Wisdom, the dedicatee of Constantine's great church. There were lesser churches, too: the chroniclers attribute to Constantine the foundation of St. Agathonicus and St. Acacius, and two pagan temples were converted into the churches of St. Mocius and St. Menas. These obscure saints were probably local martyrs. In a letter to Eusebius Constantine asked him to have fifty copies of the Scriptures prepared and sent to Constantinople for the use of the new churches that were to be built to accommodate the increasing numbers of Christians in the city. Towards the end of his life—he died only seven years after the dedication of Constantinople—he embarked upon the construction of another great church, that of the Holy Apostles, which was to serve as his own mausoleum. When it was completed after his death by his son Constantius II, the church was composed of a gilded-roofed and marble-revetted basilica leading to the circular *martyrium*-mausoleum with its gilded dome, all enclosed in a porticoed court flanked by dependencies. Inside the mausoleum, the emperor's tomb in the centre was surrounded by cenotaphs of the Twelve Apostles, making Constantine an honorary thirteenth apostle: a resting-place of fitting magnificence and sacredness for the first Christian emperor, a kind of Christian apotheosis.

For the decoration of his city, Constantine plundered the art treasures of the East (as Nero had done for Rome), taking them without scruple from all over Greece and Asia Minor, especially from the famous pagan sanctuaries that over the centuries had come to resemble museums of beautiful statuary. The celebrated gold tripod on its base of bronze snakes, that was dedicated to Apollo at Delphi by the victorious Greeks in 478 B.C. after the Persian wars, was set up in the hippodrome, where part of the damaged base still remains. Some idea of the scale of the operation can be judged from the fact that no fewer than 427 statues, most of them pagan and apparently only a few added after the reign of Constantine (statues of later emperors), stood in S. Sophia alone. Thus, at minimal expense, the whole city was turned into an art gallery of the ancient masters, a monument to the artistic glories of the Hellenic past, on the threshold of the Byzantine era. The pagan statues were regarded by the Christian populace as infested with demons and pregnant with magic, while the more educated, pagan and Christian alike, could take pride in their cultural heritage. The losers were the unfortunate provinces and temples that had been robbed of their chief treasures.

Who were the citizens of the enlarged city, in addition to its comparatively small existing population? The arrival of the court inevitably brought numerous officials, staff and hangers-on. The existing town council, the *curia*, was elevated to the dignity of a Senate like that of Rome, although the new senators were only given the title of *clari* (distinguished) instead of *clarissimi* (very distinguished). Some genuine Roman senators were transferred to Constantinople, attracted by the offer of a free mansion as well as by the proximity of the emperor. The privileged persons who rented imperial lands in Asia Minor were ordered to build a house in the new capital. Members of the common people who came there knew that they would get a corn dole like the citizens of Rome—the grain from Egypt was diverted for the purpose from Rome, which continued to be supplied by North Africa—in addition to having a large market for the goods or services they had to offer. The city was no longer governed by its erstwhile chief magistrates, nor yet by a prefect like Rome, but by a proconsul, the equal of a provincial governor. It was the existence of the proconsul, the Senate and the corn dole, more than the fine new buildings and the presence of the emperor, that marked out Constantinople actually and potentially as a rival of Rome itself in status, which Nicomedia, for example, had not been. The point was driven home by the commemorative coins issued for the occasion, and struck at every mint in the Empire from 330 to 335 (and, with a different reverse, to the death of Constantine). One of the pair of types has a bust of Dea Roma on the obverse, and the she-wolf with Romulus and Remus on the reverse. The other features the new personification of Constantinople, her bust on the obverse labelled CONSTANTINOPOLIS, and a full-length portrait of her on the reverse, holding a spear and shield and with her foot on the prow of a ship.

Such, then, were the beginnings of the city that was destined to be the great fortress of Christianity throughout the Byzantine period. The cost of the works was a serious drain on the imperial treasury, made worse by Constantine's notorious generosity to his favourites. In seven years the well-filled exchequer of Licinius was empty. Measures taken in 331 to remedy the situation included the confiscation of the treasures, and probably the lands, of the temples (see Chapter IV). New taxes, too, were instituted, notably a special tax (*collatio glebalis*) on the land of senators, whose resources could certainly stand the strain, and the *collatio lustralis* or *chrysargyron*, payable in gold and silver—hence its popular name—levied on craftsmen and traders in the towns. This was a heavy burden, for most of the wealth produced in the Empire was agricultural, and the tax was subsequently abolished.

In 332–4 there was further trouble on the Danube frontier. The Vandals, driven westwards by the Goths, were in their turn putting pressure on the Sarmatians of the middle Danube, who appealed to Constantine for help. The result was a spectacular defeat of the Goths of the lower Danube: 100,000 who had crossed the river into Roman territory in the winter of 331–2 were blockaded by an army under the command of the Caesar Constantine II, and perished. Their fellow-tribesmen sued for peace, and were accorded the status of allies: they agreed to protect the frontier and furnish a contingent for military service in return for supplies of grain. The success against the Goths, however, did not by itself solve the Sarmatians' troubles. They had armed their subject people, the Limigantes, against the Goths, and were now driven out by them. Constantine settled 300,000 Sarmatians in Thrace, Macedonia, Italy and Gaul (where names like Sermaize testify to their presence), and they appear to have integrated more or less successfully with the local population.

There was trouble, too, in the East: plague in Cilicia, famine in Syria and consequent food riots at Antioch in 333, and a usurper in Cyprus—soon put down—in 334. Then, at the very end of Constantine's reign, the Persian menace reawoke. There had been long years of peace during the minority of Shapur (or Sapor) II, who had acceded in 310, but now relations were deteriorating. In the name of the State religion of Zoroastrianism, Shapur was persecuting the Christians in his enormous empire, whom he may well have regarded as secret agents of the Romans. A tactless letter from Constantine did nothing to assist matters. Fuel was allegedly thrown on the fire by the philosopher Metrodorus who, like Apollonius of Tyana (on whom see Chapter VI) in the first century, had gone to India to live among the Brahmins, and on his return presented Constantine with some pearls and pretended that some jewels had been stolen in transit by the Persian king. The Roman defences on the eastern frontier were strengthened: the Caesar

Constantius had been installed at Antioch in 333, and he proceeded to fortify Amida and Antoninoupolis in northern Mesopotamia. In 335 Constantine's nephew Hannibalianus was given the overlordship of the diocese of Pontica in Asia Minor, with the Armenian title of King of Kings, and he made Caesarea in Cappadocia his capital. The Persians apparently declared war in 337, but Constantine, on his way to take the field against them, died at Helenopolis in Bithynia, where he was baptized on his deathbed: baptism was frequently delayed in this period to allow it its maximum effect in washing away sin.

The Reforms of Constantine

Like Diocletian, Constantine was a great reformer and innovator. Some of his reforms neutralized the work of his great predecessor, while others built on it and carried it further. The army of the late Empire was substantially that of Constantine, for he created the central, highly mobile reserve that was its leading feature, while Diocletian had concentrated, like earlier emperors, on strengthening the frontiers. The new field army, composed of the crack troops of the emperor's escort, the *comitatenses*, came into being from the circumstances of Constantine's advent to power. When he marched against Maxentius, he took with him a comparatively small but hand-picked force consisting of men drawn from the armies of Britain and the Rhine together with newly created units. This remained with him after his victory, bound to him by a closer link after the disbandment of the praetorian guard, and was used against Licinius in 314. Between 314 and 324 the new mobile army was enlarged in preparation for the final struggle with Licinius, and given its definitive form and status. It had more privileged conditions of service and more stringent entry requirements than the rest of the army. Zosimus accuses Constantine of fatally weakening the forces manning the frontiers (the *limitanei* or *ripenses*), while the *comitatenses* grew soft with luxurious living in the towns of the interior in which they were stationed. Certainly the thinning-out of the legions and their virtual immobilization was bound to have a demoralizing effect; they could repel minor incursions of the barbarians but not a major invasion, and could not themselves invade barbarian territory—this was now the prerogative of the *comitatenses*. Yet it was principally the lack of a central reserve of highly mobile troops that had led to the near-collapse of the defences of the Empire in the third century, and this was being effectively remedied by Constantine.

Two new posts of command were created to take charge of the *comitatenses*, the *magister peditum* or Master of the Infantry and the *magister equitum* or Master of the Cavalry, responsible immediately to the emperor. These were the highest-ranking officers in the whole Empire, with authority over the *duces* commanding the frontier army, and this hierarchic arrangement tightened the emperor's control over all the troops of the Empire. The separation of military from civil power was now complete, for the praetorian prefect henceforth had only the commissariat and the conscription of recruits under his control. The office of the praetorian prefects, too, was altered, for the *de facto* geographical division of their sphere of influence under the Tetrarchy, when each emperor had his own prefect, was continued when the Empire was reunited. This was a wise move in the Diocletianic tradition, for the permanent reduction in the power of the mightiest official in the Empire would lessen the likelihood of usurpations (a number of third-century emperors had been overthrown by their praetorian prefect). Constantine's system was fluid, with a given area sometimes under one prefect, sometimes under another, and some decades were to elapse before the definitive division of the provinces into four prefectures was evolved. The most powerful of these, emerging already under Constantine, was that of the prefect of the East, generally the emperor's right-hand man, with jurisdiction over Thrace, Asia Minor, Syria and Egypt. The other three developing prefectures were those of the Gauls (with Britain and Spain), Italy and Africa, and Illyricum. These larger groupings to some extent neutralized the Diocletianic system of dioceses under 'vicars' or deputy-prefects.

Another office—honorary rather than real—reformed by Constantine was the consulship, which became again the pinnacle of a man's career instead of a necessary step on the way to provincial government, held by considerably more than two men each year. Julian was to accuse Constantine of being the first to appoint a German, a barbarian, to the consulship—but then he himself selected the German Nevitta as one of his consuls for 362. More seriously, Constantine greatly increased the number of barbarians in the army, and even formed his bodyguard entirely from Germans, as well as settling huge numbers of barbarians within the Empire; and the collapse of the Western Empire a century later revealed—too late—the limit to the numbers which it could safely absorb.

Constantine's other major reform concerned the currency. Diocletian's monetary system had broken down because he was unable to coin enough gold to stabilize the exchange rate between the metals. Constantine, with the treasures of Licinius and of the temples at his disposal, was in a far better position, and he took full advantage of it. He had already (in 309) reduced the weight of the gold coin from 60 to 72 to the pound, and the so-called *solidus*, later known as the bezant, became the foundation of the great wealth of the Byzantine Empire. He also struck, from 324, a silver coin of the same weight (72 to the pound instead of 96), valued at 1,000 to the pound of gold, hence its name *miliarense*. This put an end to some of the ravages of inflation, and the fourth century saw a gradual return to a basically monetary economy, which was a considerable achievement. But gold and silver were for the rich: the bronze was the only currency the poor could hope to use, and here Constantine's record was less good. He debased the bronze (issued in large quantities for army pay) by continually decreasing its size, while that of the gold and silver was pegged (and little of the bronze was withdrawn from circulation through taxation, for the poll-tax as well as the land-tax was now paid in kind). Thus in this sphere he showed a cavalier disregard for the needs of his poorest subjects that was unworthy of the first Christian emperor. The large bronzes of the Diocletianic reform were not struck again until the reign of Julian (361-3).

Constantine's social policies were, however, in general more benevolent towards the poor and defenceless. One law protects widows and orphans from harassment in litigation. Others provide for immediate grants of food and clothing to parents so poor that they would otherwise be forced to sell their children as slaves or expose them to die. When imperial estates were being divided up, slave families were to be kept together; but this enactment seems to have been dictated by Constantine's concern for the sanctity of the family rather than by any compassion for slaves, which in other laws about their rights is conspicuously lacking. Thus, a master was only guilty of homicide if he deliberately killed his slave, not if the slave died after flogging or lying in chains; a woman who formed a liaison with her slave was to be executed and the slave burnt alive; and even freedmen could be re-enslaved for ingratitude or insolence towards their former masters. The divorce rules were tightened up: only men could now divorce for adultery, as well as for poisoning and procuring, while women could only divorce their husbands for murder, poisoning or tomb robbery. Illegitimate children were deprived of all rights of inheritance from their fathers.

Constantine in general extended and reinforced the principle of compulsory heredity of calling applied by Diocletian to at least one of the most vital industries, namely agriculture. Constantine extended it to soldiers, to the shippers who transported the corn supplies, to the bakers, and to the officials in the civil service, and strengthened the principle with regard to the *curiales*, the members of the town councils (for more about them and their plight, see Chapter V). For the civil wars, epidemics and insecurity of the third century—by no means unknown in the fourth century, either—had led to a shortage of manpower, and men shunned the more burdensome professions and industries, forcing the government to act to maintain the services necessary for the organization of the State. Thus the peasant became tied to his holding in a kind of serfdom (the system spread gradually over the Empire), the *curialis* could not leave his town council, nor the shipper or baker his corporation, and soldiers' and civil servants' sons had to follow in their father's footsteps; while unwarlike sons of veterans were made members of their local *curia*, to serve the public in another capacity.

Constantine waged a constant and praiseworthy, if probably fruitless, war against judicial corruption. One celebrated law, issued in 331, seems to have been dictated, or at least partially so, by the furious emperor (Roman emperors appear in general to have played an active part in drafting important legislation and correspondence), outraged by some particularly disgraceful case that had come to his ears: 'Let the rapacious hands of the court officials refrain, let them refrain, I say; for if after this warning they do not refrain, they shall be cut off by the sword.' He goes on to castigate various categories of court officials, who extorted bribes from litigants along every step of the way, from escorting them into the court and bringing them before the judge (usually the governor of the province) to the delivery of the record of the verdict. 'The ears of the judge shall be open equally to the poorest as well as to the rich.' Savage penalties were laid down for this and other offences, but even Eusebius reproaches Constantine with laxity in enforcing the death penalty, which, in the absence of satisfactory alternative penalties, deprived many laws of their teeth. The enforcement of laws against corruption was in any case fraught with difficulty in a society that, like modern Italy, was geared to patronage and the performance of favours, if not to actual corruption. Constantine was neither the first nor the last emperor to encounter this problem, endemic in the Roman Empire: the enforcement of any law depended on the emperor's vigilance and on the consent of the governors and lesser officials whose task it was to put it into practice. This was strikingly so with the laws relating to paganism (Chapter IV). Certain Christian-inspired reforms were made to the penal code: crucifixion was abolished, the branding of convicts on the face was forbidden, and it was laid down that prisoners were to be led forth into the light each day. Lastly, Constantine made a praiseworthy attempt to abolish gladiatorial combats. These, in fact, died out in the course of the fourth century in favour of the cheaper beast-fights.

The Succession Crisis of 337
The Reign of the Sons of Constantine (337–61) up to 353

The political history of the next few years, for lack of full sources, reads like a catalogue of civil and external wars. Constantine had a large family of half-brothers and sisters and nephews and nieces, descendants of his father's wife Theodora, Maximian's stepdaughter. He had already found one half-sister, Constantia, useful as a living pledge to give to Licinius. The rest of the family, especially the brothers, had suffered from Helena's jealous displeasure during her lifetime, and had

lived in a retirement akin to exile, some of them at Toulouse in Gaul.
But Constantine himself was disposed to be more generous to them, and
he brought them out of retirement and promoted them to positions of
honour and authority. His half-brother Dalmatius was made consul
and censor (both largely honorific) in 333, and held a military command in the East in 334–5 (it was he who suppressed the usurper Calo-
caerus in Cyprus). It was also in 333 that Constantine invested his
youngest son, Constans (full brother of Constantine II and Constantius II, born in 320), with the rank of Caesar—on 25 December, the
birthday of the Unconquered Sun, that was becoming identified with
the birthday of Christ (see Chapter VI). Then in 335 he made his plans
for the succession, evidently aware that his time was running out. Constantine II was to rule Britain, Gaul and Spain, Constantius II would
have Asia Minor, Syria and Egypt (i.e. the wealthy East, the most
desirable part), while Italy, Africa, and the Danube diocese of Pannonia
would fall to Constans. Two of his nephews, both sons of Dalmatius,
would also have a small share: Dalmatius the Younger was to rule the
dioceses of Thrace, Dacia and Macedonia, and Hannibalianus eastern
Asia Minor (Cappadocia and Pontus). Constantine's half-brothers were
omitted from the settlement, which was confined to the next generation,
but the eldest one, Julius Constantius (father of Gallus and of Julian),
had been appointed consul of the year and given the rank of patrician
(Constantine revived this ancient appellation as a title of honour).
Julius Constantius' daughter was married to the Caesar Constantius,
and Constantine's own daughter Constantina to Hannibalianus. Thus
fair shares for all and inter-dynastic marriage alliances were the order of
the day. It was an honourable settlement of a thorny problem, there
being so many males of the dynasty of an age for and capable of governing, and Constantine may have died in the happy expectation that all
would run smoothly after his death.

Sed dis aliter visum. Constantine's own experience of the break-up of
the Second and Third Tetrarchies, hitherto held together by ties of
adoption and marriage if not by any actual ties of blood, after the
disappearance from power of the dominating figure of Diocletian,
should have taught him the dangers likely to beset an arrangement such
as he had made. In fact his scheme for the rule of the Empire never got
off the ground. For several months after Constantine's death in May
337, the government was paralysed by mutual fear and suspicion
between his sons and nephews, and was only carried on in the name of
the dead emperor. Then in September the three sons held a conference
at Viminacium in the Balkans: they awarded themselves the title of
Augustus and then had it confirmed by the Senate of Rome. Antici-
pating a revolt by Constantine's half-brothers and nephews, they
instigated an uprising of the soldiery at Constantinople. It was pro-

bably Constantius II, as Julian later alleged, who was behind the massacre of the entire rival faction: no fewer than two of his uncles, including Julian's own father Julius Constantius, and seven cousins, one of them the elder brother of Gallus and Julian, were killed by the troops. Julian and his half-brother Gallus were spared only because Gallus was sick and Julian was still an infant (born in 332, he was five years old at the time of the slaughter); they were kept under close surveillance first in Constantinople and then, under conditions amounting to house arrest, in a remote part of Asia Minor. (**6** d, e)

As the events of the next twenty-four years were to show, Constantius was quite capable of decisive, and sometimes of brutal, action. He was, indeed, the most capable ruler of the three brothers, a fact perhaps recognized by Constantine when he assigned him the important Eastern portion of the Empire, enabling him to become senior Augustus. He would establish himself as the strong man of the new regime. His youth on his accession, when he was not quite twenty, may have been a factor in the later charges levelled against him that he was under the thumb of his leading advisers; but those who made them generally had an axe to grind—St. Athanasius, for example—and the accusations may be regarded as without foundation. From the beginning he showed his determination to choose his own advisers: Constantine had put him under the tutelage of Ablabius, the Christian parvenu from Crete who became a favourite of Constantine and an immensely powerful praetorian prefect, but Constantius soon got rid of him and had him executed on suspicion of treason. The eunuchs who filled the posts of Lord High Chamberlain and of all his underlings were powerful in his reign, but equally powerful under all the emperors, strong or weak, of the late Empire. They fulfilled a vital function in linking the isolated god-emperor to the rest of the court and government, without being themselves part of the network of aristocratic clans and factions; dependent on the emperor alone, they could be sacrificed at need. No, far from being a weak emperor, Constantius II displayed consistent energy, firmness and statesmanship throughout his long reign (337–61). He had no great gifts of intellect or imagination, and was no innovator, yet it was his competent government, more than anything else, that made the Constantinian system work.

The joint reign of all three surviving sons of Constantine only lasted for three years. Constans, only seventeen in 337, was not allowed by his brothers to legislate, but he attempted to assert his rights, and in 340 Constantine II invaded Italy. He met with unexpected resistance from Constans, who sent an army against him, and was killed at Aquileia, leaving Constans in possession of the whole of the Western Empire.

The new arrangement, with the two Augusti Constantius and Constans, was rather more enduring, but was destined to be abruptly terminated by a usurpation after ten years (340–50). During this time and earlier, Constantius was resident at Antioch and preoccupied with the Persian war that had broken out just before his father's death. In 338 Shapur laid siege to the important Mesopotamian city of Nisibis, which was energetically and successfully defended by its bishop, Jacobus. Persian raids and Roman counter-raids succeeded each other during every campaigning season. In 343 Constantius invaded the Persian province of Adiabene and took the title Adiabenicus. Shapur besieged Nisibis a second time in 346, again failed to take it, and signed a treaty with the Romans. Hostilities began again, however, in 348, and the Romans were defeated at Singara to the south-east of Nisibis, because of the indiscipline of the troops. Nisibis withstood yet another siege in 350: Julian, in a later panegyric of Constantius, describes how Shapur had the local river diverted to flow in great dykes round the walls and undermine them, and mounted siege-engines on boats and on high mounds to attack it, but all in vain. Troubles at the other end of the Persian empire then kept Shapur occupied for a few years— fortunately for the Romans, who were in the throes of a civil war. The defence of upper Mesopotamia, finally incorporated in the Empire under Diocletian, was a very worthwhile cause, for this settled and fertile land of ancient cities was sufficiently akin to the neighbouring province of Syria, long in Roman hands, to be a valid part of the Empire, not a meaningless and alien annexe.

Constans, meanwhile, had been active on the Rhine and upper Danube frontier and in Britain, where he apparently established a system of military espionage to operate beyond Hadrian's Wall. He did much to improve discipline in the army, which had been very lax under Constantine, who owed so much to his troops. In 348 the eleventh centenary of the foundation of Rome was celebrated, doubtless with a great festival of which nothing is recorded. This year was chosen for the inauguration of a reformed bronze currency, with two pieces (one thinly plated with silver) heavier than those of Constantine. There was a wide range of types, all bearing the legend FEL(icium) TEMP(orum) REPARATIO (the restoration of a happy and prosperous age). Most of the types are military, with personified Courage (Virtus) or the emperor himself with barbarian captives, or Virtus spearing a fallen horseman, all in several varieties. But some are connected with the theme of renewal, especially the types with the legendary bird, the phoenix, with the radiate halo that symbolized its connection with the Sun, standing either on a globe or on the pyre in which it was consumed and rose from its own ashes—a potent symbol of resurrection and re- newal. One of the types with the emperor depicts him standing in a galley steered by Victory, holding the *labarum*-standard and a phoenix on a globe. Such themes were especially palatable, and necessary, because of an ancient prophecy that the twelve vultures that appeared at the foundation of Rome foretold a life of twelve centuries for the city and its empire—remarkably accurate, as far as the Empire of the West was concerned. But the revaluation was fraught with difficulties in the poorer West, Constans' domain: a black market in the heavier coins was quickly established and some of the silver-plated ones were being melted down for their silver. Trade in and melting down of the new coins was forbidden on pain of death or exile, and customs checks were tightened. (7)

Such measures, and the misery to which they point, were disastrous for Constans' popularity, already low with the army because of his firm control. In 350 one of his highest officials, Marcellinus the Count of the Sacred Largesses, on whom some of the responsibility for the new monetary arrangements would have fallen, put up a semi-barbarian officer, Magnentius, in a bid for the throne. Taking advantage of Constans' absence hunting, Marcellinus gave a banquet at Autun for a large number of important army officers, ostensibly to celebrate his son's birthday, at which Magnentius suddenly appeared dressed in purple. The ploy succeeded: the drunken guests hailed him as emperor, and he was accepted as such by the citizens of Autun, followed by the crucial element, the army. Constans fled in the direction of Spain, but was overtaken and assassinated at Elne near the Pyrenees. Italy and Africa soon recognized the usurper, and Magnentius was now *de facto* emperor of the West. His success shows that there were limits to the dynastic loyalty of the army. His territory did not, however, extend as far east as that of Constans: in Illyricum the aged Master of the Infantry, Vetranio, seized power himself, with the assistance of Constantina, the widow of Hannibalianus and sister of Constantius and Constans, and with the connivance of Constantius himself. Subsequent events were to prove that this 'usurpation' was really a manoeuvre by Constantius to block Magnentius' progress eastwards. There was yet a third usurpation in this same year (350): in Rome Nepotianus, son of Constantine's half-sister Eutropia (he was presumably too young to be included in the massacre of 337), attempted to seize power, but was put down by Magnentius, through the agency of his king-maker Marcellinus, after less than a month. (6 f, g)

Constantius now took advantage of the respite on the Persian front to move against Magnentius. First Vetranio had to be dealt with. Magnentius had tried to win him over to an alliance with himself, but Vetranio sensibly stayed loyal to his understanding with Constantius, and gave the preference to the ambassadors from the legitimate emperor. Magnentius also tried to treat with Constantius, asking for recognition as emperor of the West and for the hand of the princess Constantina, but Constantius would have nothing to do with his brother's murderer. From Constantinople he marched into Illyricum with a small army and met Vetranio for a set-piece abdication scene at Naissus (modern Nish in Serbia). Both rulers were to harangue the assembled troops, setting forth their claims. Constantius spoke first, reminding them of their loyalty to Constantine and his family, and of that emperor's liberality towards them. They were easily won over—it was like Orpheus charming the beasts, according to the orator Themistius—and Vetranio took off his purple robe and handed it to Constantius. He then retired to Bithynia on a good State pension—hardly the usual fate of deposed usurpers, especially at the hands of the suspicious-minded Constantius.

The way was now clear for the campaign against Magnentius, with Constantius in possession of the large Illyrian army. After some indecisive manoeuvring in Illyricum, the usurper was heavily defeated at the bloody battle of Mursa in 351. Magnentius must have been a good general, whose soldiers followed him with devotion, for, though much outnumbered, they fought with frenzy, and even darkness and attempts by Constantius to get a truce failed to stop the fighting, and the savage slaughter continued far into the night. 'Thus perished large forces,' wrote the historian Eutropius, 'that could have conquered any enemy and assured the security of the Empire.' The battle of Mursa was a Pyrrhic victory in a tragic civil war, seriously weakening the armies of the Rhine and Danube.

Magnentius fell back first on Italy, and then, encircled by the fleet and army of Constantius and deserted by most of the senators of Rome, who took ship for Illyricum and the court of the legitimate (and victorious) emperor, he retreated to Gaul, in 352. In 353 Constantius invaded Gaul, where the capital city of Trier had already declared for him and shut its gates against Magnentius' Caesar, his brother Decentius. Magnentius suffered a final defeat at Mons Seleucus (Montsaléon) in the Alps, and took his own life and that of his relatives at Lyon. Decentius, summoned too late to help him, committed suicide at Sens.

Constantius II Sole Emperor (353–61)
Gallus Caesar (351–4) and Julian Caesar (355–61)

After the fall of the usurpers, two of whom—Magnentius and Vetranio —are chiefly memorable for having been the first to issue unequivocally Christian coinages (see Chapter IV), the Empire was once again completely united under the rule of one man, the Emperor Constantius II. He was now in his maturity, an experienced ruler and seasoned campaigner in his late thirties. His leading traits were an unswerving devotion to duty and determination, not to say obstinacy, in pursuing his objectives, and he had proved to be a very capable and efficient, if unimaginative, ruler. But the death of his own brother at the hands of a usurper had, understandably, made him exaggeratedly suspicious; and this meant that the faintest whiff of treasonable conduct made him very harsh and cruel, and laid him open to abuse by malicious informers and persons with a grudge against a private enemy. Constantine had established the corps of the *agentes in rebus* (literally 'doers in affairs'), State couriers who could also act as spies. Constantius multiplied them many times over, and they became virtually secret police, and were probably the worst and most hated feature of his reign.

A number of tragedies occurred over the next few years in consequence, direct or indirect, of the emperor's suspicious mind. There was an unnecessarily harsh and widespread purge of the followers of Magnentius, extended to Britain as well through the medium of a particularly infamous notary (or State secretary), known as 'Paul the Chain' on account of the legal traps and toils in which he involved people, who caused the ruin of many innocent men. Meanwhile Constantius, nothing loth, was celebrating his *vicennalia* with magnificent games at Arles.

Constantius' most important victim was the man whom he had created Caesar in 351 to take charge of the eastern provinces while he marched westwards against Magnentius; perhaps looking also to the future succession, for he himself was still childless. The man whom he selected for the honour was Constantius Gallus, Julian's elder half-brother, son of Julius Constantius who was murdered in 337, and Constantius' own cousin. Suddenly elevated after a youth spent in closely guarded retirement, he was married to Constantina, sister of Constantius and widow of the unfortunate Hannibalianus, and installed at Antioch to keep an eye on the Persians. They, however, were the least of his troubles, which included a Jewish rising at Diocaesarea in Palestine, which was brutally put down, serious raids by Isaurian brigands from the Taurus mountains, minor raids by the Saracens, and a serious corn shortage at Antioch itself. It is at this point, with the events leading up to Gallus' downfall and the purge of Magnentius' supporters, that begins the first of the surviving books (Book 14) of Ammianus Marcellinus' *History* in thirty-one books, from where Tacitus left off at the end of the first century. The lost books must have been far less detailed than the splendidly full account that illuminates the events of the next quarter of a century. Written at the end of the fourth century in a rather laborious Latin by a Greek-speaking ex-army officer from Antioch, the *History* is a monument to the quality of thought and objectivity achieved by the finest products of the late renaissance of classical letters. But Ammianus had his rare moments of bias, especially where his erstwhile, greatly revered, commander—Ursicinus the Master of the Cavalry—is concerned, and his treatment of Gallus is one of them; for just at this time he was serving under Ursicinus, who was playing a not entirely honourable role beside the young prince in the East. His years of exile had brutalized Gallus, but he was not the monster of cruelty, guilty of fearful crimes, which Ammianus portrays.

Things went from bad to worse for Gallus. At the height of the food riots in Antioch he sacrificed the governor of Syria, Theophilus, who was lynched by the mob. Meanwhile Gallus' praetorian prefect, a man named Thalassius who was married to a cousin of the sophist Libanius, was sending unfavourable reports on Gallus to Constantius, accusing him, without any foundation, of having designs beyond his station. Thalassius soon died, but in Constantius' suspicious mind the Caesar's fate was already sealed. First he detached most of the troops from Gallus' command, then he sent out a new praetorian prefect, Domitianus, with orders to urge Gallus to go to Italy. Domitianus, however, behaved with such insolence towards the Caesar that Gallus ordered his arrest, and the palace guard lynched both him and the disloyal quaestor, one of Gallus' own officials. This was followed by the discovery of a conspiracy against Gallus (Ursicinus, the Master of the Cavalry, presided over the investigations). Then his wife Constantina died while on her way to visit her brother to put in a good word for her husband. Isolated, but loyal to Constantius to the last, Gallus obeyed his emperor's instructions to leave Syria and go to him in the West. He never reached Constantius' presence, but was arrested while on his journey, stripped of the purple, summarily tried by a tribunal formed of his personal enemies, and executed at Pola, where Crispus had been put to death twenty-eight years before. Thus died Gallus in 354, victim of a palace plot and of Constantius' fearfulness for the safety of his throne. He had not ruled well, but deserved a better fate.

The dead princess Constantina was buried at Rome in a beautiful mausoleum that is still standing, long since converted into the church of 'S. Costanza'. Purposely set in a piously close relationship with the catacombs and basilica of St. Agnes (the latter built by Constantina herself), it is a circular structure with a high central drum resting upon columns and arches, surrounded by an ambulatory with a solid outer wall, and originally by an external portico as well. Its great glory are the mosaics that adorn the interior, many of which have survived. They represent a curious mixture of Christianity and completely anodyne paganism: Christ enthroned upon the globe of the heavens and giving the keys to St. Peter, and Christ giving the Law to SS. Peter and Paul, respectively, in two tiny apses off the ambulatory; while the ambulatory ceiling is decorated with varied panels, two with a portrait of Constantina surrounded by Bacchic *putti* gathering, carting and treading the vintage, two with birds, fruit, libation vases and other symbolic motifs, and others with medallions enclosing a great variety of motifs—tiny figures such as Victory or Cupid, ornamental heads, a lamb with the *thyrsus* (the ivy-entwined Bacchic staff), other animals, birds, stylized flowers, and the like. Many of the 'pagan' themes, especially the Bacchic ones, are mildly symbolic of the bliss of Paradise. The lost mosaics set below the windows of the drum may have depicted the Evangelists and the Apostles, while the dome was taken up with Old Testament scenes framed by caryatids with Bacchic panthers at their feet. The porphyry sarcophagus that held the body of Constantina is adorned with *putti* among vine scrolls. Thus the imperial funerary ideal, far from being rigidly and narrowly Christian, sought to unite elements of a purified paganism with the themes and doctrines of the new religion on which the salvation of individuals and of the Empire depended. (5)

Constantius' first attempt to appoint a helpmeet had ended in disaster—for the Caesar. There was now only one possible male relative left: Gallus' younger half-brother, Julian. Late in 355, then, Julian was suddenly snatched from his studies at Athens—where he had been allowed to go through the influence of the Empress Eusebia, after a time of great difficulty and insecurity following Gallus' death—was summoned to Milan, invested as Caesar, married to Constantius' sister Helena, and despatched forthwith to Gaul with an escort of 360 soldiers who 'knew only how to pray'. The situation in Gaul was a daunting one: waves of Alamannic and Frankish invasions had devastated much of the eastern side of the province, including the capital cities of Cologne and Mainz, and bands of barbarian raiders wandered there at will, with the Rhine army, weakened by the defeat of Magnentius, its forts overrun, unable to check them. Julian was only nominally in charge, an arrangement justified by his total lack of experience of military affairs, yet he set to work with determination to learn the part of a soldier, and was so successful that he soon gained the right to command the Gallic armies, and in 357 won a resounding victory near Strasbourg (Roman Argentorate) with only 13,000 troops against 30,000 Alamanni. This feat of brilliant generalship was accompanied by a programme of strengthening or repairing the fortifications of key Rhine forts, and was followed up by campaigns against the Franks of the lower Rhine. So many prisoners of war, carried off from Gaul by the barbarians, were released as a result of these campaigns and those of the following two years, that food supplies ran short. Proud Germanic chieftains came hard on each other's heels to Julian suing humbly for peace; and their tribes were compelled to help in the rebuilding, and even in the provisioning, of the forts and cities which they had themselves devastated—an amazing spectacle to those who had recently been terrorized by those bold barbarians.

It was in the year of the battle of Strasbourg that the Emperor Constantius made a triumphal visit to Rome, the almost legendary centre of the Empire, where he had not set foot before, and was not to do so again. Ammianus describes the procession of unparalleled magnificence that dazzled the eyes of the citizens of Rome, ablaze with golden and jewelled standards, with the infantry clad in shining mail, and the heavy-armed horsemen encased in armour like mediaeval knights. Constantius himself, 'as if he were about to terrify the Euphrates or Rhine with a show of arms ... sat alone upon a golden chariot, amid the glittering brilliance of mingled precious stones ...', immovable as a statue. The Byzantine taste for pageantry was already present in full measure. The awe and wonder were not only on one side: when Constantius reached the Forum, he stood amazed at the great and historic monuments of the Roman people, secular edifices and pagan temples alike, all surrounded by an aura of sanctity that made the city appear to him as 'the sanctuary of the whole world'. Although he had but recently been bent on putting an end to the practice of paganism (see Chapter IV), the greatness of the pagan past rose up before him at Rome in such majesty that his hostile laws were allowed to remain dead letters for the few years left of his reign; and he even filled up the ranks of the priestly colleges with members of the Roman aristocracy, who greatly coveted these honours, thus carefully fulfilling his duties as the Pontifex Maximus of the pagan religion, which the first Christian emperors still were. Constantius addressed the nobles in the Senate-house, and the people from the Rostrum, and gave magnificent games. The largely Christian populace was somewhat discontented because of the exile of their bishop (Chapter IV), but Constantius, unlike his father, got on well with the great lords—his new attitude to paganism doubtless oiled the wheels—and the visit was certainly a success. To commemorate it, an obelisk was brought from Thebes in Egypt and set up in the Circus Maximus. It is still to be seen in the Lateran Square. The colossal bronze portrait of Constantius in the Palace of the Conservatori was perhaps the Senate's contribution to the same occasion—a huge statue to rival that of his father. (4)

The last few years of Constantius' reign saw him for the most part engaged in the unremitting military activity on the more troubled frontiers that, as he well recognized, was the price of security. In 354 it had been the Alamanni in Gaul who preoccupied him; then, when this problem was turned over to Julian, he was able to turn his attention to the tribes who threatened the Danube frontier, where a major campaign was fought in 358 and finished off in 359. But by now the Persian danger had reawoken: after abortive peace negotiations in 356–8, in which King Shapur claimed Armenia and Mesopotamia as his ancestral right, the Persians invaded Mesopotamia in force in 359, spurred on and assisted by a well-informed Roman deserter. They captured a number of Roman forts and towns, notably the strongly garrisoned town of Amida (modern Diyarbekir in Turkey) on the Tigris, of whose storming Ammianus gives a thrilling eyewitness account. But Shapur had wasted so much time on the siege of Amida (seventy-three days) that his larger designs—crossing the Euphrates and invading Syria— had to be abandoned. The following season (360) he returned to the attack, and took the city of Singara and the important fortress-town of Bezabde, but was repulsed by another fortress. Constantius tried to recapture Bezabde, but approaching autumn put an end to the siege, and he returned to Antioch. In 361 he marched into Mesopotamia to meet the expected Persian attack, but it failed to materialize because of unfavourable auspices.

The departure of the Persians from the scene enabled Constantius to turn his attention to a menacing situation that was developing to the west. Julian, gaining confidence from his victories over the barbarians, had the year before (360) attempted to persuade his cousin to grant him a greater degree of control over his allotted share of the government of the Empire. He had already been hailed as Augustus by his troops after the battle of Strasbourg, and had won the provincials' hearts by lightening the oppressive tribute. In 360 Constantius sent the notary Decentius to Gaul to detach some of Julian's best troops from his command and bring them to the East as reinforcements for the Persian wars. Decentius ordered the units concerned to march through Paris, where Julian was wintering, whereupon their officers were invited by Julian to a farewell dinner. Dismayed by the prospect of unknown hazards at the other end of the Roman world, and reluctant to leave their homeland and their brave and victorious young leader, the soldiers were in a mutinous mood. After the dinner they surrounded the palace with cries of 'Julianus Augustus', overwhelmed his protestations, and placed a makeshift diadem (a standard-bearer's neck-chain) on his head. Julian responded with the customary promise of largesse, quietened them down, and proceeded to negotiate with Constantius for recognition of his new status, and for the retention of the troops earmarked for the East. He read Constantius' unfavourable reply to the assembled army, was re-acclaimed Augustus, and set out on a final campaign on the Rhine, which brought him to Vienne to pass the winter. His wife Helena died, and he sent her body to Rome to be buried beside her sister in S. Costanza. Then he put the finishing touches to military affairs in Gaul, and marched east against Constantius, hoping by his speed to catch him unprepared. Vain hope! Constantius sent a trusty official to secure the granary province of Africa and, in the lull afforded by the Persian retreat, began to move westwards with his army. Despite Julian's initial successes, winning over much of Illyricum as he marched through it, it would have gone ill with him had he needed to confront the vastly greater forces of Constantius. But an incredible stroke of fortune favoured him: Constantius had scarcely set foot in Asia Minor when a sudden fever carried him off (5 October 361), and on his deathbed he had the statesmanship and generosity to name Julian as his successor. The impending civil war was over almost before it had begun, and Julian, beyond all hope, was the sole legitimate emperor without striking a blow.

The Reign of Julian (361–3)

Julian entered Constantinople in triumph, and proceeded to arrange matters as he thought right. Himself an ascetic who hated pomp and circumstance, he was quick to dismiss the hordes of superfluous cooks, barbers and other servants from the palace, retaining only those who were necessary. It was a clear break with the new, Byzantine, style and a return, but out of tune with the times, to the less expensive and more modest entourage of the earlier emperors. As such, it pleased Julian's supporters, but many felt that he had diminished the majesty of empire. He also greatly decreased the numbers of *agentes in rebus* and notaries, the principal instruments of State control—a universally popular move. Then a tribunal was set up to try certain of the high officials for treason. A number of Constantius' most feared and hated tools were executed, including the chamberlain Eusebius who was behind Gallus' downfall. But there are signs that Julian was not yet in proper control of the East: outmanoeuvred by Arbitio, the powerful Master of the Cavalry, he allowed a heavy over-weighting of the tribunal in favour of the military; and the generals on it seized the opportunity for revenge on a former Count of the Sacred Largesses, Ursulus by name, loved and respected by all for his justice and honesty, who had made a bitter remark about the efficiency of the army on seeing the ruins of Amida, which seven legions had failed to defend. This man's execution was an unfortunate stain on a reign that was otherwise devoted to the highest ideals of government and especially of justice.

Having dealt with these and other matters at Constantinople, Julian left it, never to return, having rejected the idea of waging war on the Goths of the lower Danube in favour of an attack on the Persians. The obvious base for his preparations for this campaign was Antioch, but his nine-month stay in that city was not a happy one (see Chapter V). King Shapur was sufficiently alarmed by the massive preparations to send ambassadors suggesting negotiations, but Julian rejected the overtures, saying that Shapur would soon see him in person. In March 363 he shook the dust of Antioch off his feet and marched forth against the foe, accompanied by the biggest army ever put into the field by the Romans against Persia, some 65,000 men. Constantius at the time of his death had probably been planning some sort of demonstration of strength to deter the Persians from their annual invasions, but Julian, a brilliant and ambitious tactician, with dreams of rivalling Alexander, was not the man to lead it. At first, however, all went well. The great army crossed into northern Mesopotamia, and one division was sent off towards the Tigris, while the bulk of it followed the Euphrates southeast, in conjunction with a fleet of 1,100 ships carrying supplies. Reaching Persian-held Babylonia, they took and destroyed a number of forts and cities. Arriving opposite the great Persian capital of Ctesiphon, they crossed over to the Tigris, taking the fleet along a newly-cleared canal, and managed to gain the further bank, where they won a major victory. This was the last hour of glory of the Persian expedition. Julian decided that it was useless to besiege Ctesiphon, and ambition led him to attempt a march straight into the interior, sacrificing the fleet, which was burnt. But the Persians pursued a scorched earth policy, and they were soon compelled to retreat, harried constantly by the enemy. It was during one of these attacks on the march that Julian, who in haste or because of the heat had failed to put on his breastplate, was mortally wounded by a cavalry spear in the dust and confusion of a rout which he was trying to stem. There was talk afterwards in some quarters of a plot by Christians (one or two such conspiracies had been uncovered in the army while he was at Antioch), but probably his death was an accident. Carried to his tent, Julian consoled his friends, wept for the death of one of his highest officials, his dear friend Anatolius, refused to nominate a successor because of the risk of endangering his life were he not chosen emperor, discoursed at length with his attendant philosophers on the nature of the soul, as did Socrates before his death, and died peacefully. Thus perished the last male scion of the House of Constantine, still only 31 years of age.

Bereft of its leader, the army first offered the throne to the pagan praetorian prefect, Salutius, and then elected the Christian guards-officer Jovian as emperor, to extricate them from their predicament. The Persians, who had suffered huge losses, were also anxious for a respite, and peace was concluded, whereby the Romans gave up their claim to five small provinces beyond the Tigris, and surrendered a tract of Mesopotamia with eighteen strongholds, notably Nisibis, which had thrice repulsed the Persians from its walls. The peace was to last, so to that extent Julian's Persian expedition was successful; but it was a sad end to a glorious enterprise. Julian was buried by his own wish at Tarsus; Ammianus thought he should have been buried at Rome, Libanius, at his beloved Athens. As scholar, soldier, and lawgiver, the lucidity of whose juristic style shows up the bombast of his predecessors' edicts, Julian had achieved much in his short life; but it is as the last pagan emperor of Rome, architect of an important pagan revival, that he is most justly famed (see Chapter V).

Chapter III

The Churches of Constantine and Helena

The Churches in Rome

When Constantine entered Rome in triumph after the battle of the Milvian Bridge, late in 312, one of his most important tasks was the rendering of due thanks, by means of a permanent memorial, to the new God who had given him the victory. He chose to build a magnificent cathedral headquarters for the local chief priest of his new cult, the bishop of Rome. First he handed over to Bishop Sylvester (who succeeded Miltiades in 314) the imperial palace of the Lateran, and then the great new cathedral of Rome, the Basilica Constantiniana *par excellence*, was laid out on the adjoining site of the horse guards' barracks. The completed church was a large basilica (75 by 55 metres (250 by 180 feet)) with a central nave and four side-aisles and western apse; substantial parts of the massive wall foundations survive in the present church of S. Giovanni in Laterano. The interior decoration was exceedingly rich, with a solid silver columned archway leading into the apse, adorned with statues of the teaching Christ flanked by Apostles, facing towards the congregation, and of the risen Christ flanked by angels, facing towards the clergy in the apse, all in solid silver likewise. The roof beams were gilded, the columns dividing the aisles were of red, green and yellow marble, the altars were of gold, and at night the basilica was lit by the lamps and candles of innumerable gold and silver chandeliers and candlesticks, while precious censers wafted incense. The apse at the west end, rather than the east, is a feature of the very earliest churches, an indication that the liturgy was still celebrated by the priest facing towards the people. Attached to this church was a baptistery, distinguishing it as the cathedral church of the city (only the bishop at this date being allowed to baptize). It was a circular building, established on part of the baths of the Lateran palace (the present, octagonal, baptistery is fifth-century). It, too, was lavishly decorated: the walls were covered with porphyry revetments, the font basin was of solid silver, with a porphyry column in its centre surmounted by a massive gold candelabrum, where rare spices were burnt at Easter; a golden lamb spouting water was flanked by life-size statues of Christ and John the Baptist, and seven silver stags formed supplementary fountains. Constantine enriched his foundation with substantial endowments for its upkeep, consisting of 29 estates in Italy, Sicily, Africa and Greece.

These and all the precious ornaments are carefully listed by the *Liber Pontificalis*, the 'Papal Book', which is a mine of information on the early churches of Rome. (13)

Constantine may also have established a private chapel for his own use in the imperial palace on the Palatine hill; but, if so, nothing is known of it. In view of the short time that he spent actually in Rome between 312 and 316, when he left it almost for good, he may have made only a temporary arrangement of a room in his residence. The church that was installed in a pre-existing hall in another imperial palace—the Sessorian—is connected with the name of the empress-mother, Helena, and with the late-fourth-century legend of her finding of the True Cross, in honour of which the church (reconstructed in the eighteenth century) is still called S. Croce in Gerusalemme. The hall concerned was adapted for the purpose of Christian worship by the construction of an apse at one end, and it was divided into three by two rows of arches on double columns running across it, perhaps to mark off an altar sector and places for members of the court and for servants. A lavish provision of gold and silver candlesticks and sacred vessels was made for this church, too, and its finances were made independent of those of the palace by the donation of several estates.

Having made splendid provision for a new cathedral, Constantine proceeded, no doubt at the bishop's suggestion, to the honouring of the principal martyrs of Rome. In the course of this he surrounded the walls with a ring of new churches erected in the cemeteries that began immediately outside the walls, along the great roads leading out of the city. The earliest of these was the *martyrium*-church now called S. Sebastiano, on the Appian Way. It was built above the Catacomb of S. Sebastiano, replacing the *memoria* at the place where the relics of SS. Peter and Paul are thought by some to have been hidden for a time during the mid-third-century persecutions—hence the name it was given: Basilica Apostolorum. The *memoria*, built in about 258 for the holding of a festival of the two Apostles, consisted of an open courtyard with a cult niche and a pillared loggia to shelter those who gathered for the funerary meal that formed the main part of the commemorative festival. The walls are covered with scrawled invocations to SS. Peter and Paul. The basilica, whose foundations sliced the top off this monument, was constructed, perhaps as early as about 312/13, to provide roomier and more comfortable accommodation than its predecessor for the crowds that assembled for the same purpose: memorial liturgy and meal. The central nave is substantially intact behind the seventeenth-century façade and decoration. The other *martyrium*-basilicas of Constantine fulfilled exactly the same function. At the Via Tiburtina grave of St. Lawrence, the heroic deacon who had been roasted to death in the mid third century, he erected another huge basilica beside the rock-cut tomb. A porphyry-clad apsidal *memoria* with solid silver railings, with flights of steps for access, now signalized the tomb itself, and the customary abundance of gold and silver lamp-stands and vessels, together with a silver wreath (the crown of martyrdom) weighing thirty pounds, were bestowed upon the new foundation; eight estates were to provide for its future upkeep. (The present basilica of S. Lorenzo over the tomb itself is of sixth-century origin.) On the Via Labicana, some way outside the walls, a basilica (now disappeared) was built in honour of a pair of martyrs, the priest Marcellinus and the exorcist Peter. The catacomb there was much used for burial in the fourth century, and many fine frescoes were painted (see Chapter VI). Such was the sanctity of the spot that the imperial mausoleum in which the Empress-Mother Helena was buried, a circular edifice of the same type as the mausolea of Augustus and Hadrian, was built close by. Other tombs, from the simplest to the most grandiose, came to be crowded round these funerary basilicas, in people's efforts to obtain the protection in the hereafter that burial near a saint was supposed to afford, and many graves were dug in the church floors. The precious fittings of the Basilica Labicana were particularly grand, in honour of Helena as well as of the martyrs themselves. Lastly, the *martyrium*-basilica of S. Agnese on the Via Nomentana, although attributed to Constantine by the *Liber Pontificalis*, was built by his daughter Constantina in about 350. It was near this church and by her choice that her mausoleum, S. Costanza (Chapter II), was erected, just like that of Helena near SS. Pietro e Marcellino. The same lavish imperial donations and endowments were made to S. Agnese as to the others. (Ruined walls survive near the present, basically seventh-century, basilica.) All these extra-mural *martyrium* and funerary basilicas were very large, being clearly intended to hold huge crowds of people, and a common feature was the porticoed aisle running round all four sides of the nave and forming an ambulatory as in a mausoleum.

The crowning work of this series of edifices was not undertaken until towards the end of Constantine's reign: the great basilica of St. Peter, one of the most important churches of the Christian world. The saint had been buried, according to tradition, in the cemetery on the Vatican hill, and in the second century a small memorial with a columned niche was set up there, in the midst of an area of the cemetery where there were humble graves dug in the ground. In the course of the second and third centuries, a whole street of mainly pagan mausolea grew up enveloping it. Each one belonged to a particular family, whose members and freedmen were laid to rest there, at first in ash-recesses, and then usually in sarcophagi of stone or terracotta. One of these small, square buildings, the Tomb of the Julii, was at first in use for pagan cremation-burials (cremation was an abhorrent practice to the early Christians, who believed very literally in the resurrection of the body), then in about the mid third century the family was converted to Christianity (or else a new family bought the mausoleum) and the mausoleum was beautifully redecorated with mosaics on the walls and vaulted ceiling. The subjects of the wall mosaics are the Good Shepherd, the Fisher of Souls, and Jonah, who is seen falling from the ship into the whale's mouth (for more on these themes, see Chapter VI). The vault depicts a haloed figure standing in a chariot, with his right arm raised and a globe in his left hand. He can be none other than Christ the Sun of Righteousness, for these are the posture and attributes of the Sun-God. He is set amid the spreading branches of a luxuriant vine, an allusion, no doubt, to the Vine who is Christ himself. By the time of Constantine, a few Christian burials had also been made in certain of the other mausolea. (**14, 15**)

This was the site—set, what is more, on the slope of a fairly steep hill—on which Constantine had, perforce, to establish his basilica to honour St. Peter's remains, and the fact that all the obvious difficulties were surmounted, with the expenditure of enormous effort in an age lacking earth-moving machines, shows how strong was the tradition attached to the site. A huge platform had to be created, by cutting into the hillside to the north and west, and by building up a terrace to the south and east. It was in this terrace that the mausolea discovered were incorporated, filled with earth and rubble and in some cases with their roofs dismantled, and were thus preserved. Only an emperor could have obtained the disaffection of so large an area of a well-used and solidly built-up cemetery. Upon the platform was constructed an enormous basilica of unusual plan, preceded by a porticoed court with a monumental entrance. The basilica, whose inner dimensions were a stupendous 112 by 58 metres (368 by 190 feet), had a nave and four side-aisles like the Lateran church, terminated by a vast transept with an apse in the middle of its west side. Just in front of the apse, the top of the second-century shrine of St. Peter rose through the floor, surrounded by a bronze railing and sheltered by a canopy resting on four spiral columns decorated with figured vine-scrolls (brought from Greece). A pure gold cross weighing 150 pounds, dedicated by (or in memory of) Constantine and Helena, was set upon the shrine. The actual relics of the saint would have been enclosed in a casket, probably a jewelled casket of precious metal, and re-buried beneath the centre of the *memoria*; whatever there was must have been stolen by the Saracens, who dug down through the pavement above when they sacked Rome in the ninth century (the bones that have been alleged by the Vatican to be those of St. Peter were found, like other burials, wrapped in purple in a wall near the shrine, and may be the remains of an early bishop of Rome). The furnishings of the basilica were, of course, of exceptional richness, with the usual lavish use of solid gold and silver, and with the patens and chalices, the censer and the altar itself all studded with gems. The chandelier in the form of a martyr's crown that hung before the *memoria* was made of 35 pounds of gold. The estates donated for the basilica's maintenance were all in the East of the Empire, part of the wealth that accrued to Constantine from his victory over Licinius in 324, and including houses, baths, bakeries and gardens at Antioch in Syria (tradition has it that St. Peter was 'bishop' of Antioch before going to Rome), as well as rural estates in Syria, Egypt and Mesopotamia, some of them producing spices and paper (i.e. papyrus). Such were the beginnings of the most prestigious church in western Christendom, completed over many years by the labour of thousands. The mosaic on the triumphal arch leading from the nave into the transept depicted Constantine presenting the church to Christ, with St. Peter standing by, and an inscription recording that 'Because under your leadership the world rose in triumph to the stars, victorious Constantine founded this edifice in your honour'—a very explicit statement of the victory-bond first forged between Constantine and Christ at the Milvian Bridge. The great new church rapidly became the favourite burial-place of the Christian members of the aristocracy of Rome, many of whom were laid to rest either inside the basilica, like the city prefect of 359, Junius Bassus (see Chapter VI for his sarcophagus, a masterpiece of Romano-Christian art), or else in private mausolea close to its walls, like the enormously rich and powerful Anicius family.

The monumental basilica on the Via Ostiensis honouring, in similar fashion, the remains of St. Paul was first built, not by Constantine himself, but by a trio of late-fourth-century emperors. The first Christian emperor built just a small church to mark the spot, enclosing the mausoleum that was either the saint's memorial or his actual burial-place, and had perhaps been erected as early as the first century. The *Liber Pontificalis* has it that the precious furnishings were exactly the same as those in St. Peter's, but they were undoubtedly originally more modest, and then upgraded for the parallel basilica of 385. The endowments included, appropriately enough, property at Paul's home city of Tarsus.

This church completes the tale of Constantine's foundations at Rome, of which a considerable amount is known, from archaeology, from old paintings and drawings, and from the *Liber Pontificalis*. The descriptions create a vivid impression of the richness of the interiors, on which all the decoration was lavished in a riot of colour, of gilding, of precious metals and marbles and jewels that contrasts strongly with the more sober style of classical Graeco-Roman art, and presages that of the high Byzantine period.

Trier Cathedral

The northern capital of the Empire of the West was the city of Trier on the Moselle. Under the Tetrarchy it had been the capital of Constantius Chlorus, and for six years, 306 to 312, was that of Constantine, whose son Constans later had his headquarters there, from about 334. The new, late imperial, role of this small provincial town was emphasized by a series of public buildings of appropriately imposing character, including baths and an imperial palace of which the audience hall, a single-naved basilica of the most perfect internal proportions, once resplendent with revetments of shimmering marble and probably with gilded roof-beams and other adornments, still survives (the *Basilika*, in a restored state incorporating large portions of the original structure, is now a Lutheran church). Not far from the main imperial residence was another palace, that seems to have belonged to Helena. One of its state rooms had a coffered ceiling most beautifully decorated with painted plaster panels, with a motif of pairs of *putti* alternating with portraits of the ladies of the imperial family, of very fine execution. Three of the portraits survive, painstakingly pieced together from tiny fragments of the plaster found in the cellars under the (modern) bishop's palace. They appear to represent Helena herself, Fausta (opinions differ as to which is which), and a young princess who would be one of Fausta's and Constantine's daughters (Constantina or Helena). All are haloed—the prerogative of pagan deities, Christian saints, Christ himself, and the imperial family—and set against a dark blue background. One displays her jewel box, another holds back her veil; the young princess, a wreath in her dark hair, plays the lyre with a plectrum.

The fate of this lovely palace was apparently determined by that of Fausta. After her tragic death in 326, its associations with her were evidently too strong for Helena's comfort: it was demolished and the site given to the Church of Trier for the construction of a grand new cathedral, in keeping with the city's role as a capital of the Christian Empire. In plan it was a double basilica, like the slightly earlier cathedral of Aquileia (Chapter VI), but very much larger (73 by 30/38 metres (240 by 100/125 feet)). Each had a nave and two side-aisles and a square sanctuary at the east end; and they were connected in the middle by a baptistery with a square font, and at the west end by a portico. Each was preceded by its own atrium-court. The South Church (beneath the present Church of Our Lady) was soon finished, helped by the incorporation of existing walls of the demolished palace, but the North Church was not completed until the reign of Constans. Bishop Athanasius of Alexandria, in exile in Trier in 336-7, tells how he attended an Easter Mass in the unfinished church. The plaster of the chancel-rail in the South Church was found covered with graffiti scrawled by the Christians who came to worship there: names, chi-rhos and prayers or salutations on another's behalf (e.g. 'Marcellinus may you live in Christ'). Thus it was that another imposing new church came into being by the benefaction of the emperor or of his mother.

The Churches of the Eastern Capitals

The march of events in the east Mediterranean in mediaeval and modern times has, unfortunately, deprived us of the power to make comparable evocations of the churches built by Constantine in the Eastern half of his empire. The vanishingly small amount known about the churches of Constantinople, the New Rome, has been included with the account of the foundation of that city (Chapter II), and the Church of the Holy Apostles was in any case really an imperial mausoleum of a very special kind rather than a true church. Across the straits, at Nicomedia, Constantine built a magnificent replacement of the church destroyed under Diocletian's eyes at the beginning of the Great Persecution (see Chapter I).

In the most easterly of the imperial capitals, Antioch in Syria, Constantine established a church of octagonal form connected with the palace on the island in the river Orontes, and referred to by Christian writers as the Great Church, on account of its size, or the Golden Church, from its gilded dome. It was set amid courts and dependencies, like most Syrian churches, including a hostel for the lodging of poor strangers. A tiny representation of it is to be seen at the edge of a fifth-century mosaic at Antioch, which has a border depicting many of the more important buildings of the city and of its suburb Daphne. Its octagonal shape is unmistakable; in front of it a man raises veiled hands in a gesture of worship. Begun in 327, the church was not completed until after Constantine's death, and was dedicated by Constantius II in 341 during a synod of the Church specially convened for the occasion; while one Bemarchius, a *pagan* sophist who was a supporter of Constantius, travelled from Syria to Egypt delivering a panegyric of Christ and the Great Church at intervals along the way. It was built on the site of some ruined baths. During the construction work a bronze statue of Poseidon the Earth-shaker, a (rather unsuccessful) charm against earthquakes, was unearthed, and was melted down—Christianity was very strong at Antioch—to make a statue of Constantine. It was this same Great Church that was closed by Julian in retaliation for the burning of the temple of Apollo at Daphne while he was staying at Antioch (see Chapter V). (**16**)

The Churches of the Holy Land

In 326, immediately after the deaths of Crispus and Fausta, Helena left Rome on a pilgrimage to the Holy Places sanctified by the great events of the life of Christ—perhaps in expiation for whatever part she played in the execution of Fausta. It was then that the plan to commemorate by appropriate buildings the Nativity, the Crucifixion and Resurrection, and the Ascension, was formed, and Helena herself oversaw the beginnings of the work and provided the funds from the imperial treasury.

The *pièce de résistance* was the Church of the Holy Sepulchre in Jerusalem. It supposedly marked the site of Golgotha and the Tomb but, over the years since the Crucifixion, local tradition had attached these events to a site in the heart of the city sanctified by much older traditions. The Place of a Skull was identified with the spot where the Jews claimed they had found Adam's skull and tomb, and which formed for them a notional centre of the world like the *omphalos* at Delphi. It was also a pagan cave-sanctuary, dedicated to 'Aphrodite'—probably a Syrian mother-goddess. First every vestige of paganism was cleared away, and then Constantine wrote to Bishop Macarius of Jerusalem, offering workmen and money from the civil administration, imported marble columns of any kind he specified, and all the necessaries for a gilded, coffered ceiling, so that the church might be the most beautiful edifice in the whole Empire. The complexities of the site necessitated a group of buildings rather than a single basilica; their sequence is described by Eusebius. The innermost point, on the west, was occupied by the cave-tomb, sheltered by a circular *martyrium* resting on twelve columns and very richly decorated (a view of it appears on the apse mosaic of S. Pudenziana in Rome (*c.* A.D. 400)). It was set in a porticoed courtyard paved with fine stone, which also enclosed the supposed Rock of Calvary. The east side of the courtyard was closed by the back of the basilica, which had a nave and four side-aisles like the Lateran and St. Peter's, but with the addition of galleries above the aisles. The basilica was terminated at the courtyard end by a highly-developed apse, supported by twelve columns (for the number of the Apostles) adorned with silver bowls, and covered by a semi-dome. This church was preceded by the usual porticoed atrium-court, into which three monumental gateways opened from the street. Passers-by, Christian and non-Christian alike, were astonished by the view which these gates afforded, and the worshippers within were even more dazzled by the marble paving and columns, the gilded ceiling, and the multitude of precious fittings, which must have rivalled, if not surpassed, those of St. Peter's. Begun in 328, the magnificent ensemble was dedicated in

335 during the Council of Tyre, from which the bishops travelled to Jerusalem for the occasion. (**17**)

The exact place of the Saviour's birth at Bethlehem had also been left in uncertainty, and there, too, tradition had fastened upon a pagan sacred grotto, where the local women came each year to lament the dead Adonis, as the setting of the Nativity. It was regarded as a Christian holy place as early as the third century. An octagonal *martyrium* was erected above this, perhaps with an opening in the centre of its roof, like the Pantheon at Rome. Inside, a railing surrounded the grotto, whose top had been cut away to allow the faithful to look down into it (the octagon may, like the Holy Sepulchre, appear on the mosaic of S. Pudenziana). The Constantinian architects attached a basilica to the octagon, again with nave and four side-aisles, roughly 29 metres (100 feet) square. It was preceded by the customary porticoed atrium-court, and this had a forecourt opening on to it, thus providing a long progression in depth towards the holy of holies, as at the Sepulchre.

Yet another sacred cave had, oddly and incongruously, been selected as the place on the Mount of Olives from which Christ disappeared heavenwards at the Ascension. Nothing is known of the plan of this church, but it was probably built to the same scheme as the others, with a basilica and a linked *martyrium*.

Constantine's fourth church in the Holy Land commemorated an incident in the Old Testament: Abraham's entertaining of the three angels at Mamre. Great significance was attached to this by the early Christians as an early appearance of the Saviour and a kind of prefiguration of the Eucharist. The 'oak-tree' (or terebinth) at Mamre where this was supposed to have occurred had become—if indeed it was not so originally—a pagan sanctuary; and when Constantine learned of this from his mother-in-law Eutropia (with whom he had evidently remained on good terms despite the execution of her daughter Fausta), he wrote to the bishops of Palestine, upbraiding them for their negligence, and ordering the immediate destruction of the pagan shrine and the erection of a church by one of his secular officials. The church, a modest basilical structure, was built against the inside of one of the walls of the enclosure surrounding the sacred tree, preceded by a portico that divided the precinct in two. The tree stood in the outer court.

All these basilicas were substantially completed by 333, when a single pilgrim or a small group who had travelled all the way from Bordeaux in far-off Gaul, among the first of a long succession of pilgrims from the West over the centuries, recorded their visit to 'a basilica built on the orders of Constantine' in each of the four places.

Thus Constantine made a worthy repayment to the God of his victory, the God in whose hands he had come to believe the welfare of the

Empire rested, by creating clusters of magnificent churches at the principal Christian holy places and in the imperial capitals. One may quibble at the thousands of pounds of gold and silver, ill spared from the fourth-century treasury, that were lavished on the decoration of these edifices; but there is no denying that these great monuments were a source of immense aesthetic and spiritual enrichment to the people of the time, many of whom must have rejoiced in them as wonderful public buildings even if they were not yet themselves Christians. They undoubtedly helped to swell the tide of conversions, by moving in many a desire to worship amid their splendour, and to associate themselves with the new religion which the emperor was so conspicuously proclaiming as his own. Only faithful pagans must have found them a source of disapproval and lamentation, an honour given to the 'wrong' deity and an attraction to his worship. Yet, being a gift to God from a Roman emperor, they were a fitting atonement for centuries of persecution of the Christian Church.

Chapter IV

The Emperors, the Church and the Pagan Establishment

Privileges for the Church

When Constantine won the battle of the Milvian Bridge with the support of a new God (whom he at first partially identified with his previous patron, the Sun-God), and set his foot upon the road of becoming a Christian, he thereby entered into a relationship with the Christian Church, though he did not, apparently, receive actual instruction in the faith. Although he was but a catechumen and had to withdraw after the opening parts of the Eucharist, he was, by virtue of being emperor, by far the Church's most important layman and patron, a role which he proceeded to fulfil, as far as the monuments and accommodation of Christianity were concerned, by his great church-building programme (described in Chapter III) and by gifts of money for the repair or replacement of other churches ruined in the persecutions. The building and repair of churches had a counterpart in certain privileges granted by Constantine, over and above the restoration of the civil rights, such as the right of assembly, curtailed or removed during the Great Persecution. His victory had instilled into him the certainty that his own fortune, and the fortune of the whole Empire with which that of its emperor was mystically bound up, lay in the power of the Christian God. The deity who had revealed himself as the true guardian of the Empire must at all costs be propitiated and kept favourable towards it—an idea of pagan derivation—and the basic means of achieving this was ensuring the rendering of proper worship. The Church must be helped in its great task by every measure in Constantine's power.

First the Christian clergy must be freed from all extraneous duties that might hinder the performance of their main one. Constantine ordered that all degrees of clergy, even those in the most minor orders (such as readers—the Emperor Julian the Apostate was one in his youth), should be entirely free from the duty of performing any of the compulsory public services that were laid, as a kind of tax, upon both richer and poorer members of the community, making demands on their money, time and labour according to their means: a rich landowner might have to organize and pay for games in the local amphitheatre, procuring beasts and the men to fight them, or go on an embassy to the emperor for his city; other local gentry might be burdened with collecting the taxes for the central government or heating the water in the city's baths, or maintaining the near-by stations of the imperial post; poorer people might have to work on the roads or on a public building site. This clerical exemption was granted as early as 313, and Constantine also made grants of money to all the Churches in the half of the Empire under his control (there was a problem in Africa as to which was the right Church to receive his donations—see below). Further privileges were added in the course of his reign, especially in the legal sphere: a civil suit might be taken before a bishop by the agreement of both parties, instead of to the secular courts, and there would be no appeal from his verdict (318); in 333 it was enacted that even the decision of one party to have recourse to the bishop was sufficient; slaves could be freed before a bishop in church instead of before a magistrate (321); bequests to the Church would have a status in law (321). On account of the honour in which the state of celibacy was held by the Church, Constantine removed the disincentives attached to it and to childlessness by Augustus (320). Christians who were the slaves of Jews were to be freed (336).

Clerical exemption from municipal services was to have grave consequences in the depletion of the *curiae*, the town councils, which were already suffering from illegal desertions by their members (see Chapter V for more about the *curiae*). Numerous *curiales* rushed into holy orders, and Constantine was soon obliged to restrict the exemptions by forbidding the ordination of those who were already members of a *curia*. One of his laws on the subject ends with the enunciation of the principle: 'The rich must shoulder secular obligations, and the poor must be supported by the wealth of the Churches'—an acknowledgement of the dangers inherent in the growing hoard of ecclesiastical riches.

Constantine's son Constantius also found it necessary to legislate on clerical exemption at the end of his reign: *curiales* who enter the clergy are to leave two-thirds of their property to their *curia*, preferably via a near kinsman who would administer it and perform the requisite services (361). Clearly, illegal ordinations of *curiales* were continuing, and this was an attempt to regulate the situation in favour of the *curiae*. Only ex-*curiales* who were bishops were to be allowed to retain their whole property, or lesser clergy by the consent of the *curia* involved. But another law of 361 adds, to the list of the totally exempt, Christians 'of exceptional and extraordinary virtue' who are under a vow—presumably those who had embraced the monastic life—on the rather dangerous grounds that 'we are conscious that our State is supported more by religion than by official duties and physical toil and sweat.' There was no likelihood that Constantius, a devout Christian of a highly superstitious cast of mind, would withdraw any of the privileges granted to the Church by his father; indeed he confirmed and added to them. Bishops were exempted from the necessity of appearing before State courts—cases involving them were to be heard by a tribunal of other bishops (355). (This privilege probably did not extend to criminal trials, where the State jealously guarded its jurisdiction.) And certain privileges of the Church of Rome were confirmed (356). But the Church did not always get its own way: sometimes the statesman in Constantius reasserted himself. At the Council of Rimini in 359 (see below) a decree was passed that land belonging to the Church was to be tax-free: an exorbitant demand that Constantius quickly countermanded, declaring also that the clergy, except for those of very modest means, were to be subject to taxation and municipal services, both as tradesmen and as landowners (360). Under the first Christian emperors, the Church became a very privileged organization—though not State-financed like the main pagan cult—but where its interests encroached too much upon those of the State, especially upon those of its instruments the *curiae*, the claims of the Church were kept within strict bounds by law, though enforcement was not always possible. Nothing, however, could prevent the Church's inexorable increase in power, influence and prestige.

Constantine and the Donatists of Africa

The first requisite for the retention of the favour of the God of the Milvian Bridge was, then, promptly seen to by Constantine, and the clergy had leisure to devote themselves to His worship. But this was not all that was necessary: the whole Church must conduct itself in a manner worthy of its high calling and pleasing to the Almighty. Constantine was greatly distressed to learn of dissensions within the Church, and determined that these should be quickly settled. His motives are illuminated by a letter which he wrote to a Christian official, Aelafius, when he was summoning the Council of Arles in 314 (see below). 'Since I am informed that you also are a worshipper of the Highest God, I confess to your Gravity that I consider it utterly contrary to divine law that we should neglect such quarrels and disputes, by which the Highest Divinity may perhaps be roused to anger not only against the human race but also against me myself, to whose care He has entrusted, by His celestial will, the government of all earthly things; and by which He may be so far moved as to take some untoward step. For I shall not be able to feel truly and fully secure and always to hope for prosperity and every blessing from the ready benevolence of the Most Mighty God, until I see everyone venerating the Most Holy God in the proper cult of the catholic religion with harmonious brotherhood of worship.'

Just as the persecution of Decius, in the mid third century, had raised problems concerning the attitude of the Church towards those who had lapsed, so did the Great Persecution. In most provinces matters were settled satisfactorily by the administration of graded penances, with excommunication reserved just for particularly bad cases. But in North Africa, a split developed that was to dominate the scene for more than a century. The bishop of Carthage under Decius had been the great St. Cyprian, whose uprightness and Christian fervour were respected by all the members of the African Church; and thus reconciliation between those who believed that the repentant lapsed could be readmitted, and the rigorists who insisted on their permanent excommunication, was possible. But Bishop Mensurius in 303 showed himself unduly willing to comply with the orders of the secular authorities that the holy books and Church property should be surrendered; and his archdeacon Caecilianus, who succeeded him as bishop, gained even worse odium from his hostility to martyrs, especially from one incident when he had prevented Christians taking food to a group of their imprisoned fellows, who consequently died of starvation (prisoners awaiting trial were expected to be fed by their families and other members of the community). Thus the see of Carthage was hopelessly compromised in the eyes of the rigorists and their sympathizers, and had totally lost its authority to mediate on the question of the lapsed. The rigorists, outraged by the election of Caecilian as the metropolitan bishop, chose for themselves a rival bishop, first Maiorinus and then the Donatus from whom the sect is named. Thus a rival Church was established, which claimed to be the true Church of Africa, the Church of the Martyrs, while the 'Catholic' Church had fallen away from the straight line of Christianity. So great was the support given to the Donatists by the Christians of Africa, especially in the central province of Numidia where a peasantry inclined to religious fanaticism had been converted in very large numbers during the previous decades, that Donatus and his successor Parmenianus (died 391/2) were effective rulers of the African Church, and it was not until the time of St. Augustine that the initiative passed to the Catholics.

When Constantine installed himself in Rome in 312, the situation was that Caecilian had had himself elected bishop in unseemly haste and without the presence of the Numidian bishops, who regarded his consecration as invalid and had put up Maiorinus in his stead. Caecilian was, however, the titular head of the African Church, and as such it was to him that Constantine's benefactions were addressed. The Donatists, in their struggle to get Caecilian deposed, appealed to Constantine to appoint three Gallic bishops as arbitrators, on the grounds that there had been no persecution under his father in Gaul (and therefore its clergy would not have taken sides over the lapsed)—no mention is made of Constantine's own conversion, of which they were perhaps still unaware. The emperor responded with alacrity, eager to help settle a dispute that would be displeasing to his new God. The three Gauls he appointed were Maternus of Cologne, Marinus of Arles and Reticius of Autun, and he asked Bishop Miltiades of Rome to preside. He in his turn invited fifteen Italian bishops to join the commission, making it into more of a Church council. Caecilian duly arrived, with the ten supporters and ten opponents allowed by Constantine; the case was heard (313) and decided in his favour. But the Donatists appealed against the decision, and a larger council met at Arles in 314. This reached the same conclusion. Meanwhile Constantine had set in motion a judicial enquiry at Carthage as to whether Bishop Felix of Apthungi, who had consecrated Caecilian, was himself a *traditor*, a traitor to his faith who had handed over copies of the Scriptures to be burned, this being the mainstay of the Donatists' case against Caecilian. This, too, turned out in Caecilian's favour, but the Donatists appealed yet again. Constantine, shocked by their rejection of an ecclesiastical judgement in favour of a secular one, had their leaders imprisoned, but later released them. Two bishops sent to Africa to consecrate a replacement for the two rival bishops of Carthage openly sided with Caecilian's party, and provoked Donatist riots. Constantine continued to uphold Caecilian's fitness to be bishop, but took no action against the Donatists until 320, when an internal quarrel produced damaging disclosures (possibly forged) of cowardly and submissive conduct by the Donatist leaders themselves during the Great Persecution. He then banished the leaders and confiscated their churches, but relented after a few months in the face of increasing Donatist fanaticism. Their strength can be gauged from the fact that they seized a basilica being built by Constantine for the Catholics in Cirta, the main capital of Numidia—which he was rebuilding under the new name of Constantina after its destruction during the usurpation of Domitius Alexander: no one was able to secure its return, so Constantine was forced to build another one.

What is remarkable about these episodes is the ease and naturalness with which the Church turned to Constantine to help settle its disputes, accepting his arbitration as that of a superior authority. He was to use that authority also in the more widespread Arian controversy. It was not until the reign of his sons that the alarm bells began to sound audibly in the Church's ears, and it became fully aware of the problems of Church–State relations raised by its emperor's happy conversion to its faith.

At the very end of his reign, Constantine began again to persecute the Donatists. Then the succession troubles occupied the new emperors for a time, and in the meantime social conflicts broke out in Africa, closely linked to Donatism which became the main rallying point of the poor and discontented. Repression of this, under Constans, soon turned into another persecution. Bishop Donatus and others were exiled, and an uneasy peace reigned from 347 until the accession of Julian (361) and his edicts of religious tolerance (for Julian and the Donatists, see Chapter V).

Constantine, Arius, and the Council of Nicaea

Donatism was a schism rather than a heresy, a disciplinary and social problem unconcerned with questions of doctrine. After his victory over Licinius, Constantine was grieved to learn that accusations of grave doctrinal error were being bandied about in the East. The trouble had begun at Alexandria, where one of the senior priests, Arius, a one-time pupil of a Syrian philosopher and theological teacher of the school of Origen (Lucian of Antioch), of views bordering on the heretical, devised a Christological system of logical neatness, subordinating the Son to the Father, and proceeded to popularize his ideas, even going to the length of writing ballads to appeal to the common people. His assertion that the Son was created out of nothing by an indivisible Father was seen as highly derogatory to the dignity of Christ the eternal Word, and scandalized the other clergy of Alexandria. The bishop, Alexander, summoned a council of Egyptian bishops which condemned Arius' doctrine and excommunicated him and his followers.

By a fortunate chance for Arius, a fellow-pupil of Lucian, Eusebius by name (not to be confused with Eusebius of Caesarea, the historian), had become bishop of the imperial capital Nicomedia, an important and influential see, and he took up Arius' cause with warm partisanship. Alexander wrote to the other bishops of the East, explaining why he had excommunicated Arius, and Eusebius replied by summoning his own provincial council of bishops to approve Arius' doctrine. Arius also appealed to the historian, Eusebius of Caesarea (another Origenist), and he, too, held a council, of the bishops of Palestine, who followed the same course, and even directed Arius to return to his parish church at Alexandria and seek reconciliation with Alexander. This last, predictably, was not effected, and the Church of Alexandria was divided into two hostile camps, with the other eastern bishops taking sides for and against Arius and Alexander. The Platonic basis of Arius' ideas was bound to attract the majority of the learned Christians of the East, nurtured as they were on the Dialogues of Plato as well as on the Bible, after the manner of Origen. Many of them held more moderate views than Arius, adopting the logical implications of the terms Father and Son but by no means denying the divinity of Christ, as Arius appeared to do; but they thought it unjust that he should be excommunicated, and were accordingly ready to support him. The battle was on.

It was at this point that Constantine entered upon the scene. He found it more difficult to understand a split over 'extremely trivial' matters of doctrine than a dispute between rival bishops, and showed his irritation in a letter to Alexander and Arius, in which he urged them to desist from idle philosophic speculations and agree to differ. Bishop Hosius of Cordova delivered the letter, but found that the matter was not to be settled so easily. He discovered, too, that the Egyptian Church was also divided by a Donatist-type schism dating back to the Great Persecution, with the rigorist dissidents led by Bishop Melitius of Lycopolis. Although it had nothing like the overwhelming strength of Donatism, the party of Melitius was getting a firm hold in some areas. It was decided that a council should be held to resolve the two conflicts. In the meantime, an anti-Arian council met at Antioch to elect a new bishop for that city, and angered Constantine by an attempt to pre-judge the main issue.

The great ecumenical Council of Nicaea assembled in the emperor's presence (Nicaea was chosen partly for its proximity to Constantinople) in May 325. As the agenda was made up of items that were under current discussion only in the eastern Church, the vast majority of the bishops who attended it, some 270 in number, were from the East, with only a handful from the West—two delegates from the aged bishop of Rome, Sylvester, and one Italian bishop, Caecilian from Carthage, one bishop from Gaul and one from Illyricum, none from Britain and Spain (Hosius was present as the emperor's adviser). Five bishops even came from outside the Empire: from the Crimea, Armenia and Persia. The emperor offered everyone the use of the public post service for his travel. It was in the main audience hall of the palace that the proceed-ings were opened by Constantine himself, arrayed in purple and gold and accompanied by members of his family and some Christian friends instead of his bodyguard. With a humility far removed from the usual imperial pomp, he awaited a signal from the bishops before sitting down in his gilded chair. The bishop on his right—perhaps Eusebius of Caesarea himself—made a speech of welcome. Then Constantine gave his own address, in Latin, the official language of the Empire, stating that in his judgement 'internal strife within the Church of God is far more evil and dangerous than any kind of war or conflict', and once more urging the cause of unity. Then they got down to business. It would seem that a traditional baptismal creed put forward by Eusebius of Caesarea was approved by the bishops as a sound and acceptable statement of the Christian faith, but those strongly opposed to Arius found it insufficiently precise to exclude his views, and proceeded to propose amendments. The dispute became acrimonious. The emperor made matters considerably worse by suggesting, probably on Hosius' advice, the adoption of the formula *homoousios*, 'of the same essence', which was accepted in the West (slightly mistranslated as 'consubstan-tial'—the term should really be 'coessential') but looked on with great disfavour and suspicion in the East, where metaphysical theology was very much more highly developed and subtle. It was only through deference to Constantine that the bishops were prepared to accept the formula, which later became a rallying cry for the orthodox, and insert it in Eusebius' creed. It would certainly prove a stumbling-block to Arians, and as such was pleasing to extreme anti-Arians, among whom was St. Athanasius himself, attending the Council as one of Bishop Alexander's deacons. But it had the great disadvantage of being totally unacceptable to the moderate theologians, men such as Eusebius of Caesarea who were influenced by the thought of Origen and unwilling to be so dogmatic and one-sided about the relationship of the Son to the Father. Eusebius was driven, under pressure, to sign the new version of the creed, but was most unhappy about it, as he makes clear in a letter to his Church concerning the doings of the Council. Arius and two of his closest supporters were excommunicated and their doctrine anathematized. Other dissenters signed, like Eusebius, against their better judgement. Many of the bishops were simple priests unskilled in matters of theology and willing to abide by the majority verdict. Thus Constantine was left under the blissful illusion of having unified the Church on this issue, whereas in reality he had played into the hands of the anti-Arian extremists, and the hardened formulation was bound to be divisive and cause serious trouble in the future.

On the other main issue before the Council of Nicaea, the problem of Bishop Melitius and his schismatic Church in Egypt, a far more moderate line was taken, providing for gradual reunification through the replacement of dead Catholic bishops by their rivals. This plan could have put an end to the schism, given a goodwill that was conspicuously lacking. The Council also settled the date for the celebration of Easter, which was kept at slightly differing times by different Churches. Further canons dealt with a wide range of other matters. The convening of the Council had been arranged to coincide with the celebration of Constantine's *vicennalia*, and in honour of this he entertained the assembled bishops in his own apartments in the palace, as a means of drawing the proceedings to a close of fitting magnificence. It was a triumphant experience for all those concerned, and must have been especially moving for those bishops who, like the Egyptian Paphnutius, had been blinded and maimed or otherwise tortured under the Great Persecution, and now saw God's purposes fulfilled to His glory and the honour of His Church.

The new-found unity of the Church was, however, utterly illusory, for it had only been achieved at the cost of steam-rollering dissenters into line. The peace was soon broken. Constantine had followed up the excommunication of Arius and his two associates by banishing them— to Bithynia, the very province of Asia Minor where the Council had been held. For his purpose of promoting ecclesiastical concord, it was the worst place he could have chosen, for not only was it a great route centre of the eastern Empire, but Bishop Eusebius of Nicomedia, the capital, was one of the moderate, Origenist theologians who, like his namesake of Caesarea, were favourable to Arius' views; as were also the bishops of Nicaea and Chalcedon, two other important Bithynian cities. These three were exiled in their turn, for plotting with Arius. Then, in about 327, after the traumatic events of his visit to Rome, Constantine relented: he summoned Arius to court, accepted a basic creed from him as a profession of the true faith, and attempted to get him reinstated in Alexandria. Meeting opposition from Bishop Alexander, he reassembled the Council of Nicaea, which readmitted Arius to communion and perhaps reaffirmed the Nicene Creed with the omission of the word *homoousios*. The banished Bithynian bishops were recalled, and again there was an appearance of peace, an even more complete peace, with Arius himself reconciled.

In reality, however, attitudes were hardening, with bitter enmity dividing the parties of Alexander and Arius in Egypt, and the returned moderates, under the leadership of Eusebius of Nicomedia, out for the blood of those who had abused the emperor's ignorance of theology to foist upon them a creed which went beyond scriptural evidence and to which they could not conscientiously assent. Their first victim was the extremist Eustathius of Antioch, enemy of Eusebius of Caesarea: he was deposed on a variety of charges (some trumped up), and Eusebius was subsequently elected in his stead, but—perhaps sensibly—declined the offer under pressure from the emperor. The deposition of Eustathius was the beginning of long years of schisms and even riots in the Church of Antioch. The Council of Antioch that chose Eusebius passed some canons restricting the right of recourse and appeal by clergy to the emperor: the Church was beginning to find secular intervention by a Christian sovereign to be a two-edged weapon.

In 328 Bishop Alexander died, and the even more fervently orthodox Athanasius was elected to the see of Alexandria. The great champion of orthodoxy through thick and thin for the next forty-five years, Athanasius was a hard, narrow-minded and self-righteous man, even more disagreeable a personality than his opponent Arius. In contrast to the learned theologians who were disposed to sympathize with Arius' intellectual position, he was an uncultured man of sufficient rather than good education. For the whole of his life he remained in close contact with St. Antony the Great and the monks of the Egyptian desert (about whom see Chapter VI), who were unlettered and strongly orthodox to a man. The subtleties of the Arian controversy were totally beyond their ken and outside their sympathy, and they were entirely ready to embrace the simplistic Nicene formula, like most other illiterate or theologically unsophisticated Christians, and defend it to the death. This was, indeed, the fundamental weakness of the Arian cause at its inception, and a main reason for the ultimate victory of Nicene orthodoxy—namely its over-dependence, despite Arius' popular ballads, on educated understanding. It should have been possible to keep the basic creed free from precise and narrow definitions, leaving the theologians to debate the finer points by themselves, without making any one position an article of faith; but the Council of Nicaea had, with Constantine's unwitting assistance, bungled its opportunity. With the election of Athanasius, rigorist and violently antagonistic fighter that he was, the cause of ecclesiastical peace and harmony was utterly lost.

Athanasius' refusal, following in the steps of Alexander, to reinstate Arius angered Constantine. The early 330s saw the bitter enemies whom the new bishop had made in Egypt, both Arian and Melitian, bring forward accusation after accusation against him: he had collected a tax of lengths of linen (probably imitating the pagan temples of Egypt, where the cult vestments were of linen); he had sent a priest to desecrate a Melitian Eucharist, and murdered a Melitian priest named Arsenius. The first two were at least partly true, the third false. Athanasius had also been foolish enough to try to bribe a high court official. All this did not prevent Constantine, whose irascible temper swayed him first in one direction, then in another, from uttering a sudden condemnation of Arius in 332, but he then summoned him to court, as Athanasius had previously been summoned. This latest change of heart is to be ascribed to the influence of the Arian priest Eutokios, whom Constantine's sister Constantia had recommended to him on her deathbed: Constantine was to be more favourable to the Arians for the remaining years of his life, and would direct all his energies towards a complete healing of the divisions of the eastern Church. A council planned for 334 at Caesarea in Palestine fell through because of the obduracy of Athanasius. The next year was Constantine's *tricennalia*, his thirty-year jubilee, and the Church of the Holy Sepulchre was to be dedicated. First a council would be held at Tyre, to effect the longed-for final reconciliation of the warring factions in the Church. In Constantine's absence, a high official took the chair. The charges against Athanasius were investigated. He was able to produce Arsenius alive to dispose of one charge (though the unfortunate priest had been beaten and left for dead in a burning house by an Athanasian bishop on another occasion). As for the allegedly broken chalice, a commission (composed of his enemies) was sent to Egypt to make enquiries. Athanasius left the Council without waiting for it to report back, and was deposed when it did so, while Arius was admitted to communion. Athanasius took the one course still open to him, and appealed direct to Constantine for a hearing of the charges in the emperor's presence. Constantine, moved by his plight and by his demeanour, wrote an angry letter to the Council ordering it to move to Constantinople and justify its actions to him. But, before it arrived, Athanasius was accused of threatening to cut off the corn supply from Egypt to Constantinople. Constantine immediately exiled him to Trier, where he remained until the emperor's death. He also banished the head of the Melitian Church.

With Athanasius safely out of the way, Arius was summoned to Constantinople, where the orthodox bishop was ordered to admit him to communion. With a true sense of drama the Church historians relate how the bishop prayed that he himself or Arius, whichever was in the wrong, might not live to attend the service. The very day before it, Arius was suddenly attacked by a fatal haemorrhage, and died unceremoniously in the public latrines of the Forum.

The Arian Controversy Continues under the Sons of Constantine

Constantine apparently never took up a doctrinal position of his own on the subject of the Arian controversy: his one aim was to unite the Church round a formula acceptable to all, or at least to the great majority. His sons, brought up as Christians and with more time for reflection, had already taken sides by their accession in 337, Constantine II and Constans as orthodox partisans, Constantius II as a moderate Arian of the same colour of opinion as the two Eusebiuses. Their first actions in the religious sphere were fully characteristic. Constantine II announced to Athanasius that his exile was at an end, and sent him back to Alexandria, pretending that Constantine himself had been about to do this at his death. Constantius arrived at Constantinople and appointed Eusebius of Nicomedia to its bishopric. Bishop Eusebius, leader of the moderate Arians, was well placed to benefit from imperial favour: he had baptized Constantine on his deathbed, and it was probably he who was entrusted with Constantine's will, whereby Constantius received the richest, eastern, part of the Empire. The following year (338) Eusebius had a synod convened at Antioch, in Constantius' presence, which published moderate Arian creeds, condemned Athanasius for an 'unauthorized' return, and appointed an Arian bishop of Alexandria, who was escorted there by 5,000 troops and installed by the local Arians. Athanasius fled to Rome. A new charge had been added to the list of those against him, that he had sold the State corn allowance established by Constantine for the Church to give to the poor.

Bishop Julius of Rome now made himself the champion of Athanasius and of several other expelled orthodox bishops, including Paul of Constantinople, who had sought his protection. After abortive negotiations with the eastern bishops, he summoned a council at Rome (winter 340/1), which cleared Athanasius and asserted the right of appeal to the Roman see. Eusebius of Constantinople's response was the holding of a rival council at Antioch (summer 341), during which the Golden Church was inaugurated. It denied the pre-eminence of the see of Rome, decreed that provincial councils judge without appeal, and produced a new moderate Arian creed. It was the last move of that old campaigner Eusebius, for he died in 342 (his namesake of Caesarea, the historian, had preceded him, a year or two after the death of Constantine), and Bishop Paul was reinstalled at Constantinople, with Macedonius as his Arian rival. Constantius, who was still at Antioch, sent the Master of the Cavalry Hermogenes to expel Paul. Hermogenes was torn to pieces in a riot, whereupon Constantius set out in hot haste from Syria, 'on horseback', and drove out Paul himself. He punished the citizens of Constantinople by halving their corn allowance and by leaving them bishopless for as long as ten years— Macedonius, though Arian, had been ordained without the emperor's consent, and his fight with Paul had caused many deaths.

Paul was now back in Rome, where after further negotiations involving both Constans—who had succeeded his eldest brother as patron of the orthodox—and Constantius, a council was held at Serdica in the Balkans (probably in 343) by their joint authority. The attempt at reconciliation was a total failure. The western bishops were solidly orthodox, while the majority of those from the East were Arian. Charges and counter-charges came so thick and fast, and agreement of any kind was so clearly impossible, that the eastern bishops withdrew from Serdica (where they were lodged in the palace by special favour of Constantius) and held their own council at Philippopolis in Thrace, where they anathematized the term *homoousios*, adopted an extreme Arian position (that the Son is not even of like essence to the Father (as the moderate Arians, including Constantius and the two Eusebiuses, maintained), let alone the same), confirmed the sentences on Athanasius, Paul of Constantinople, and their associates, and even 'deposed' Julius of Rome, Hosius of Cordova, and other champions of orthodoxy. The western bishops, left behind at Serdica, proceeded in their turn to confirm the Nicene Creed, clear Athanasius and his friends, and 'depose' his Arian accusers in the East, including Bishops Ursacius of Singidunum and Valens of Mursa in the Balkans, who appear to have been Constantius' principal ecclesiastical advisers after the death of Eusebius of Constantinople, as Hosius had been to Constantine.

With the Churches of East and West promulgating decrees so utterly opposed to each other, it is scarcely surprising that the immediate consequence of the Council of Serdica was a complete split, for several years, between the two halves of the Empire. Constantius took steps to prevent the orthodox bishops reinstated at Serdica returning to their sees, and there was some kind of persecution of the remaining rigid orthodox in the East. Constans, meanwhile, set himself to effect the execution of the decrees of Serdica. Fanatically orthodox, he was determined to stop at nothing to get his brother to assent: missions, letters, and finally a threat of war if Constantius continued in his refusal to let Athanasius and Paul return to their sees. He would, he said, come himself and restore them in the teeth of his brother's opposition. Threats of war were, of course, very different from the real thing, and they were the best weapon of a junior against a senior Augustus; but Constans' fanaticism stands clearly revealed by this move. So does the statesmanship of Constantius, who set the good of the whole Empire above the furtherance of narrow doctrinal differences: he gave way, and for the next ten years, during the lifetime of Constans and the civil wars after his death, the orthodox leaders were allowed to occupy their sees and carry on as usual. Athanasius returned to Alexandria after reassuring letters from Constantius and leading Christian dignitaries, and an imperial audience; the Arian bishop of Alexandria had conveniently died. Paul was restored to Constantinople, and the Arian bishop Macedonius withdrew to a separate church. Constantius' court bishops Ursacius and Valens went as far as to send a recantation of their Arian views to Julius of Rome and to Athanasius.

Thus, on the surface, all was sweetness and light until after the death of Constans in 350. The imperial brothers held the consulship together in 346, and Libanius, the rhetorician from Antioch, wrote a joint panegyric of them in 348/9. But it was toleration on Constantius' part rather than a real change of heart. Ursacius and Valens, who knew which way the wind was blowing, repudiated their palinode, so damaging to the Arian cause, immediately after the death of the orthodox emperor. Constantius, more prudently, decided to leave the *status quo* behind him when he marched west against the usurper Magnentius, to avoid the risk of religious riots in his absence. He even wrote to Athanasius to assure him of his continuing favour towards him, despite rumours to the contrary. But the orthodox 'honeymoon' was nearly over, and Athanasius' many enemies were gathering like vultures, bringing further charges against him: he had been ordaining outside his diocese, and had been in touch with an envoy of Magnentius.

Constantius was now furthering the Arian cause in the West. During the battle of Mursa in 351 he had left the command to his generals and spent the time in prayer at a martyr's grave near by. Still racked by guilt over the murder of his relatives in 337, he sought victory against Magnentius as a sign of forgiveness from Heaven, a sign that God's favour was with him. His desire was granted, and the person who came with the tidings of victory was none other than Valens, the bishop of the city outside which the battle was fought. This enabled him and his partner Ursacius to reinforce their influence with Constantius. In 353, after the final defeat of Magnentius, a pro-Arian council was held at Arles: Athanasius was condemned once again, and Bishop Paulinus of Trier, metropolitan of Gaul, was exiled for his resistance. Several other leaders of the orthodox resistance in the West were similarly banished two years later, after a council held at Milan, on which Constantius exerted great pressure for conformity to his views. One of these bold dissenters was St. Hilary of Poitiers, subsequently exiled to Phrygia in central Asia Minor. Like Constantine before him, Constantius, freed at last from constraints, was directing all his efforts towards the achievement of unity within the Church, but around formulae of his own choosing, moderate ones that were acceptable to many, but unacceptable to many more principally because of the authority of the Council of Nicaea. Before the year 356 was out, the forces of orthodoxy were—temporarily—broken: Athanasius was on the run and had gone into hiding; Paul of Constantinople had been arrested, and died in prison amid rumours of murder; Bishop Liberius of Rome had joined the ranks of the exiles; and the aged Hosius had been kept at court and sufficiently broken by pressures put upon him, including close confinement, to hold communion with Ursacius and Valens, though he refused to the last to subscribe to the condemnation of Athanasius, and had written a magnificent letter proclaiming the freedom of the Church from control by the State. It was readiness to subscribe against Athanasius, the living embodiment of orthodoxy, that was for Constantius the touchstone of the true man from the false; and there was widespread persecution, fiercest at Alexandria, to achieve universal compliance. The Emperor Julian was later to mention the slaughtering of whole communities of 'heretics' (probably orthodox) in the East, and the sacking of villages.

Although by such measures the orthodox were held in subjection, the difficulty of finding a creed on which all could agree remained. The definitive victory of the moderate Arians whom Constantius supported gave full play to their own 'left wing', the extreme Arians, and the religious history of the last years of his reign is dominated by the struggle with these. The see of Antioch was usurped by an extreme Arian on the death of its moderate bishop in 357, which was the starting point of numerous manoeuvres. The control of all the most important sees was one of the mainstays of Constantius' policy. A series of councils was held, the most important being the double Council of Rimini and Seleucia (in southern Asia Minor), the respective venues for the bishops of West and East, held in 359. The Council of Rimini met first and, predictably, took an orthodox line at first. The 400 delegates were, however, detained until they had subscribed to a moderate Arian creed drawn up by a preliminary commission headed by Ursacius and Valens.

Liberius of Rome, worn down by two years of exile and threats of death, had signed a similar creed the year before, and been allowed to return to his see. The Council of Seleucia was a hotbed of schisms and intrigues between moderate and extreme Arians, with an unexpected boost being given to the orthodox cause by the arrival of St. Hilary from his place of exile in near-by Phrygia. The results were inconclusive, despite the pressure exerted by the chairmanship of a high imperial official, as at Rimini. At a final synod held at Constantinople in 360, the extreme Arians were victorious, deposing numerous bishops, including notable moderate Arians.

Constantius died the following year in the knowledge that he had failed to control the extremists of his own party, and had failed still more to secure unity round a Christological formula acceptable to him. Worse, the confusing welter of councils and creeds had brought the Arian cause into disrepute and made the objectionable orthodox term *homoousios* appear a rock of stability in the quicksand of differing shades of Arian opinion. Arianism was far from dead—there was shortly to be another Arian emperor in the East (Valens, brother of Valentinian I (364–78)), and an Arian regent in the West (Justina, mother of Valentinian II, regent 383–8). But it had lost all chance of becoming the official doctrine of the Church, and by the fifth century was regarded in most quarters as a vile heresy.

One of the reasons for the longevity of Arianism was its adoption by the barbarian Goths, beginning with Arian evangelization during the reign of Constantius. Ulfilas, who sat as bishop of the Goths at the Council of Constantinople in 360, was the descendant of a Cappadocian Christian taken prisoner by the Goths in the third century. He came back into the Empire in the last years of Constantine, perhaps on an embassy, and apparently studied in Asia Minor until about 341, when he was consecrated bishop by Eusebius of Constantinople, and returned on his mission to the Goths. In 348 he was driven out by a persecution— a testimony to the success of his evangelism—and was settled by Constantius with his followers in a little village in Thrace. His most famous achievement was the translation of the Bible into Gothic, for which he had to invent a script, based on Greek and Roman letters, and runes. It was he who was ultimately responsible for the Arian Christianity of the Ostrogoth king Theoderic, who ruled Italy from Ravenna in the late fifth century, and built there an Arian church (S. Apollinare Nuovo) and baptistery that are still standing.

Were the Pagans Persecuted?

The conversion of Constantine to Christianity set an immediate question mark over the status of the pagan cults within the Empire. These ranged from the official, traditional Graeco-Roman cults that had for centuries been thought essential to the maintenance of the *pax deorum*, to the newer oriental mystery religions like Mithraism and the cult of Cybele and Attis, spiritually more satisfying, to which many of the more fervent educated pagans of the fourth century belonged, and the age-old indigenous cults of the provinces, such as Celtic nature-worship, which was still very strong. For some years Constantine seems to have had no idea that adherence to Christianity automatically excluded any pagan attachment, and for this short time there was true liberty of worship for all—except for Christian schismatics. Then the emperor's tone towards the pagans—who still formed the vast majority of his subjects, especially in the West—changes, and becomes condescending and increasingly hostile. After his defeat of Licinius, rumours went round in the East that the practice of paganism was about to be banned. They were soon scotched by an edict proclaiming that the pagans were still free to follow their 'wicked errors', but the contempt in the emperor's language, and his expressed desire that they should be converted to Christianity (he regarded himself, he once told a company of bishops, as bishop of those outside the Church), must have given rise to a profound sense of insecurity.

Worse was to come: in 331 a treasury depleted by the works at Constantinople and by his own extravagant generosity led Constantine to order the making of a general inventory of the goods, and probably revenues, of the pagan temples; and this was made the occasion for stripping them of their gold and silver and of such things as bronze doors and roof-tiles. Earlier emperors, pagans, had laid their hands on temple treasures in their hour of need, but this time there was an intentional element of derision, as gold plating was removed from cult images, and the core and stuffing materials exposed to public scorn. Land belonging to temples was also confiscated, and the more important sanctuaries consequently lost much of their means of support. Many of the statues— including cult statues—taken to decorate Constantinople were probably also plundered at this time. Several major temples were actually closed down: those of the Syrian Aphrodite at Baalbek and at Aphaca in the mountains above, and the famous healing sanctuary of Asklepios at Aegae in Cilicia. Aphaca and the *Aphrodision* at Baalbek were notorious for the immorality of their cult, and its suppression could be viewed as a purge of paganism, part of the duties—liberally interpreted—of the Pontifex Maximus, head of the Empire's religions. But the destruction of Aegae was utterly unwarranted, simply the removal of some too successful competition by an emperor zealous for the honour of Christianity. Two more temples, at the Holy Sepulchre in Jerusalem (Aphrodite again) and at Mamre, were destroyed when the churches were built there.

The imperial cult, especially objectionable to intransigent Christians in times gone by, was purged of all pagan ceremonies, but allowed to continue as a focus of loyalty to the emperor (see Chapter VI). Constantine also forbade the setting up of statues to him in pagan temples. While he was in Rome, either in 315 or 326, he angered the Senate and people by his refusal to take part in a traditional procession of the army up to the Capitol, where sacrifices would be made. He had at first intended to take part, out of fear of the army, which was still pagan at this date, but was dissuaded by Bishop Hosius of Cordova (Chapter II).

All these incidents and enactments were straws, and more than straws, in the wind; and the lavish patronage and favour accorded by Constantine to the Church and its members put pagans in an invidious position. There was no doubt of the best way to the emperor's heart: at least three small communities in the East, which were wholly Christian or virtually so, were made independent of the preponderantly pagan cities to which they were subordinated. Yet paganism was still the official religion of the State; the emperor, by virtue of being Pontifex Maximus, was overseer of all religion, pagan as well as Christian; and most State occasions were still expressed by or accompanied by pagan ceremonies. While forbidding private divination and evil magic, like many an earlier emperor, in laws passed in 319–21, Constantine expressly permitted charms for healing or good weather, and provided for the continuance of the custom of consulting the pagan priestly college of Diviners (*haruspices*) whenever a public building was struck by lightning. The status of paganism was thus left in profound ambiguity at the death of the first Christian emperor.

It is, however, possible that towards the end of his reign Constantine passed a law, which remained a dead letter, actually prohibiting the pagan cult. For in 341 Constans promulgated a law beginning, 'Let superstition cease, let the madness of sacrifices be abolished', and claiming to renew a law of his father's. Some have held that this was directed not against paganism as such, but against magical sacrifices and divination, like the extant laws of Constantine; but in reality it is paganism itself that is under attack. This law was, again, probably a dead letter in most areas, but at Rome, great stronghold of western Christianity, it led to the destruction of a number of temples. This was not intended by the legislator, who passed another law the very next year, declaring that 'Although all superstition is to be utterly eradicated', the temples standing outside the walls of Rome, and connected with the celebration of certain festivals that were popular entertainment, are to be preserved.

The first or second attempt to put an end to paganism yielded, then, discouraging results for its promoters. It is not surprising that for a number of years no more official steps were taken. The emperors were, however, being urged to persecute: a sinister little pamphlet, entitled

On the Error of the Profane Religions, was addressed to them in 346/7 by one Firmicus Maternus, a convert from Neoplatonism who had earlier dedicated a handbook on astrology to a leading pagan. With the narrow fanaticism typical of a certain kind of convert, he turns upon those who were lately his associates, denouncing the mystery religions as Devil-inspired parodies of Christian liturgy, and parading argument after argument in favour of persecution. 'Paganism, most holy emperors, must be utterly destroyed and blotted out, and disciplined by the severest enactments of your edicts, lest the deadly delusion of that presumption continue to stain the Roman world . . .' The pagans must be 'liberated' even against their will, like a doctor curing an uncooperative patient—even in ancient times, it seems, the word 'liberation' was capable of bearing nasty ideological overtones. 'Only a little more effort and the Devil will be completely overthrown by your laws . . . How fortunate you are that God, whose agents you are . . . has reserved for you the destruction of idolatry and the ruin of profane temples.' The advantages of such action, claims Maternus, are numerous, for the crimes of the pagan gods instigate crime among men, and sacrifices attract demons to the images (a good net, this, to catch the superstitious Constantius); while the melting down of pagan statues and ornaments would furnish supplies of metal for the mints and smithies. Firmicus Maternus would have been emboldened by the law of 341 to address his work to the emperors. This was the first public call to use the power of the State to put down its own official religion.

It was not until the mid 350s that the next attacks came, concerted attacks on both paganism and magic. After the fall of Magnentius, his edict permitting night sacrifices, which had been forbidden because of their frequent association with magic, was countermanded by Constantius. This emperor, now master of the whole Empire, turned his attention first to the suppression of orthodox Christianity and then, in 356, to the pagans. He seems to have been pursuing an ideal of the whole of the Roman Empire united in worshipping the Christian God according to the moderate Arian creed. The strongholds of orthodoxy had been reduced, now let the pagans be brought to heel: they had been left too long to continue their ignorant and dangerous practices. A first law, published in February, made capital punishment the penalty for offering sacrifice or worshipping images. This was evidently ineffective, for in December of the same year Constantius ordered the shutting of temples in both town and country, so as to make sacrifices impossible and 'to remove the opportunity of wrongdoing from all the depraved'. Confiscation of property is added to the death penalty, and this is explicitly extended to provincial governors who fail to apply the law. Even now application was very uneven, for those in charge of provinces that were far from the emperor's eye had a great deal of autonomy, and the expanded system of 'secret police', the State couriers, seems to have concentrated on the detection of possible usurpers and traitors rather than on the enforcement of laws. In the East, many urban temples were closed—for example at Antioch in Syria, where we have the vital evidence of Libanius—and some were given to courtiers or to the Church, or even demolished (probably at the instigation of the local bishop); but we know nothing about the rural temples at this date. In general the more secluded the temple, the less likely was it that any attempt was made to keep it shut. In the largely pagan north-west the law may not have been applied at all—certainly there is no archaeological trace of an interruption of activity at the most carefully dug of the flourishing temples of Britain, Gaul and Germany (see Chapter VI).

Nor was it enforced in Rome itself where, three years later, with the law still on the statute-book, the city prefect Tertullus went publicly down to Ostia and sacrificed—successfully—to Castor and Pollux for favourable winds to bring in the corn ships. Law or no law, the ancient State cult, believed by many of the Empire's inhabitants to be a vital necessity for its security, was maintained by State funds and protected by the powerful pagan aristocrats. Constantius' visit to Rome in 357 is very important in this respect, for it confirmed the *status quo*, with the emperor himself admiring the temples and appointing nobles to the pagan priesthoods. The only concession to his now militant Christianity was the temporary removal of the altar that stood before the statue of Victory in the Senate-house, on which it was customary for the senators to offer a pinch of incense when they entered. This altar was destined to be the centre of a doomed struggle of the pagan-dominated Senate against the intransigent Christian government (whose resistance was stiffened by the redoubtable St. Ambrose) in the 380s. The contrast with the situation under Constantius shows clearly that the time for the final showdown between the two religions, the old and the new, was not yet come.

Constantius' attack on paganism was extended to magic in two laws of December 356 and January 357. The connection between the magic arts and the pagan cult was a close one, for divination on behalf either of the State (as under Diocletian: see Chapter I) or of an individual was frequently conducted in a temple by means of or accompanied by a sacrifice, and the practice of magic often involved a sacrifice of some sort. Moreover, the 'highest' and most philosophical variety of paganism, Neoplatonism, was frequently associated with so-called Chaldaean theurgy, which was really nothing more than an exalted and exotic form of magic. It was this combination that was destined to enslave the Emperor Julian in his impressionable adolescence (Chapter V). A typical Chaldaean rite took the form of a secret nocturnal meeting held in the open countryside, with a succession of sacrifices and recitations, hallucinations of light and atmospheric disturbances, very like the practices described in magical papyri. The Chaldaeans themselves sharply divided theurgy (which means literally 'god-working') from ordinary magic: magicians or sorcerers used evil spirits to deceive, while they themselves obtained the favour of good spirits through their asceticism. The distinction, however, is likely to have been lost on Constantius, and indeed on anyone else outside the charmed circle of theurgists. Constantine had expressly permitted public divination, which could not lend itself to sinister enquiries about the life of the emperor and the like, and also 'white' magic. His son Constantius, whose suspiciousness and superstition were among the most exaggerated traits of his personality, condemned and proscribed every form of magic and divination, vainly hoping to silence for ever 'divinandi curiositas'. The results of his laws are described by Ammianus: 'In the emperor's court, on the pretext of protecting his imperial majesty, many wicked acts were perpetrated. For if anyone consulted a soothsayer about the squeaking of a shrew-mouse or a meeting with a weasel or a similar omen, or applied an old wife's charm to soothe pain—which even medical authority permits—he was indicted from an unknown source, dragged into court, and suffered the death penalty.' Even if we allow for some exaggeration, Ammianus relates enough specific cases of treason trials on charges associated with magic or divination to substantiate his accusations. Moreover, a further law passed by Constantius in July 357 deprived even persons of the highest rank of their exemption from torture in cases involving magic at court. This law was to have evil repercussions in 359, when details of answers obtained from a remote oracle in Upper Egypt fell into the hands of Constantius' agents: many of the prominent citizens of Antioch and Alexandria were involved in the trials, facing imprisonment, torture and execution. These were, naturally, pagans—although Christians, too, were not above dabbling in divination—and so the trials came to look like a persecution of paganism, even though they were not so in origin. Again it was the emperor's suspiciousness and superstition that were ultimately responsible. By the fourth century the old, rational certainties of a former age of prosperity had long since evaporated, and superstition touched everyone, from the highest, like Constantius, and the best educated, like Ammianus the historian and Libanius the sophist, to the most ignorant of the common people. Even a calendar addressed to an important Christian layman at Rome contained much astrological detail (see Chapter VI). In these circumstances, it was to be expected that all kinds of magic and divination should be cruelly, and even hysterically, put down. It was to happen again in the later fourth century under the Emperor Valens. It also followed that an accusation of magic was the best stick with which to beat a private enemy. Libanius records several such attempts against himself, and another caused the downfall of Constantine's favourite, the philosopher Sopater.

Christian Emperors and Pagan Men of Letters

While the Christian emperors were increasingly hostile to paganism, their attitude to individual pagans, including convinced and active pagans, forms a most striking contrast. During the years of the foundation of Constantinople, the Neoplatonist philosopher Sopater from Apamea in Syria was one of Constantine's closest friends, seated in public at his right hand, and may even have presided over the inauguration rites of the new capital. He was a pupil of Iamblichus the disciple of Porphyry (whose own master was the fountainhead of Neoplatonism, Plotinus), and was in his day, like them, the leader of the Neoplatonists. Unfortunately little is known about him apart from the manner of his fall and the title of a (lost) philosophical work (*On Providence and the Unjustly Fortunate or Unfortunate*). But as a pupil of Julian's 'god-like Iamblichus', the theurgist and wonder-worker, he probably practised the 'higher' magic exemplified by the *Chaldaean Oracles*. His influence with Constantine made him bitter enemies at court, notably Ablabius, one-time clerk in the governor's office in Crete who had risen to be praetorian prefect of the East, the most powerful man after the emperor (a prophecy to this effect was allegedly given by an Egyptian astrologer at his birth). In 331, when Ablabius was consul (now merely a position of great honour that involved the giving of vastly expensive games) as well as prefect, contrary winds prevented the corn ships from Egypt from entering Constantinople's port. A corn shortage ensued, and the populace manifested its displeasure by thin applause for the emperor when he appeared at the theatre. Ablabius and his co-plotters accused Sopater of fettering the winds by his powers, and the gullible Constantine had him beheaded; he was in any case a convenient scapegoat. His execution was apparently followed by the burning of 'Porphyrian' books—i.e. Neoplatonist works and books of magic like the *Chaldaean Oracles*: a first attack on literature under Christian auspices. As for Ablabius, he was put to death six years later by the young Constantius in connection with the succession crisis (see Chapter II). 'Thus was the "ever-fortunate" Ablabius paid out for the death of Sopater' (Eunapius).

The relations of Constantine's son Constantius with the principal court orator and with the leading teacher of rhetoric in the East are much better documented owing to the survival of their own works. Themistius was a native of Constantinople, born in the old city in about 317 and a witness of its great transformation. He was a steadfast pagan, but wore it lightly and was far from being a fanatic. His speeches in praise of Constantius have sometimes been dismissed as empty bombast, but he was basically a serious philosopher, responsible for a revival of studies and transcriptions of the works of Aristotle. Given the extravagant conventions of classical panegyric, the orations reveal a serious attempt to influence the emperor in the direction of good government. Themistius first met Constantius at Ankara in 350, and delivered before him a discourse entitled *On clemency (philanthropia)*, which he claims is a true tribute from philosophy. The tone of the speech is indeed philosophical and mildly pagan. The orator sets forth the picture of the Neoplatonic ideal ruler, who imitates God by his clemency. Constantius, naturally, is the perfect example. It is interesting that Themistius could get away with likening the virtue of the emperor, as opposed to the outward trappings of empire, to the images in a pagan temple, which *hoi polloi* fail to see because they linger outside dazzled by the stonework and painting of the porch.

The next episode, five years later, was the writing of a long and flowery letter by Constantius—no doubt drafted by the imperial chancellery—to the senators of Constantinople, enrolling Themistius among their number. It is loaded with compliments to Themistius and praises of philosophy. Rather than being honoured by inclusion in the Senate, Themistius will greatly embellish it, for philosophy makes men good private individuals and good citizens. Constantinople has already become a great centre of culture because of Themistius' presence there, and the example he has set by choosing to live in the city and marry and have children is especially valuable because a philosopher's example is much imitated. Constantius might have added that Themistius had tickled his emperor's ears with a most flattering 'philosophical' panegyric. The most remarkable feature of this letter is the fulsome eulogy of philosophy, which was, after all, wholly pagan in origin: the philosopher is 'the judge and knower of all things . . . and the measure of absolutely the whole State . . . , tested and accurate', and his life must be 'as a measure . . . and goal set before everyone else'; philosophy is 'the best of the sciences', 'the first and best art'. The key is to be found in two passages where Constantius emphasizes that the true philosophy of which he is speaking is concerned with human life, available and beneficial to all: a clear rejection of the out-and-out pagan, theurgic type of philosophy, with its atmosphere of a secret society and its preoccupation with initiation rites and 'miracles', in favour of Themistius' virtually secular moral philosophy, which was of obvious usefulness on account of the training in virtue which it offered.

Not to be outdone by his emperor in the exchange of compliments and courtesies, Themistius wrote an answering discourse whose main theme was that Constantius was a better philosopher than Themistius, in that he was a Platonic philosopher-king. Along the way he likens

Constantius to Apollo pronouncing on the wisdom of Socrates, and to Orpheus charming the beasts (this apropos of the deposition of Vetranio (see Chapter II)).

Themistius' next two speeches addressed to Constantius were composed around the time of Constantius' thirty-fifth anniversary in 357. One was written for delivery by him in Rome as the delegate of the Senate of Constantinople. But he never went to Rome, possibly as a demonstration of his disapproval of the recent anti-pagan laws, and the next oration gives, in heavy-handed detail, his excuses for his failure to go to court to celebrate the festival. It begins with a long description, in the present tense, of the Festival of Lamps in Egypt—a reminder to Constantius, perhaps, of the important place still occupied by the pagan cults in the cultural life of the Greek East, despite the spread of Christianity. Themistius also gives, in both speeches, some interesting details of Constantius' building activities at Constantinople, where he added a forum, aqueducts, baths, porticoes and, best of all, a library filled with the works of philosophers, poets and historians. Themistius himself may well have supervised the acquisition of books for the library, by purchase and copying.

The very next year Constantius appointed him proconsul of Constantinople, the equivalent there of the city prefect of Rome, and a very high honour indeed. Themistius was its last proconsul, for Constantius was preparing to raise the new capital to the same status as the old. The senators of Constantinople became *clarissimi*, 'very distinguished', like those of Rome, instead of merely 'distinguished'; and their numbers were increased considerably. It was Themistius who was entrusted with the mission of recruiting the new senators, and in a later speech he boasts of having raised the numbers from 300 to 2,000—perhaps a slight exaggeration, but reflecting none the less a substantial increase in size. A proportion of the new members were drawn from families connected with the *curiae* (town councils) of other eastern cities, and this caused coolness for a time between Themistius and his friend Libanius, the staunch champion of Antioch. The emperor insisted on a reasonable level of culture and some rhetorical education in those who were to grace the enlarged Senate (though the practice was not always as shining as the theory—some were officials of minimal formal education, and some were from the army). The final step was the changing of the title of Themistius' successor, in 359, from proconsul to prefect of Constantinople. It had been from the first almost inevitable that the city that was, from its foundation, the principal residence of the senior or sole emperor (with only one exception, in the later fourth century— Valentinian ruled in the West) should come to be equal in honour with the traditional but superseded heart of the Empire. Its accomplishment took just a generation, and was the joint work of a Christian emperor and a pagan philosopher. In 361 Themistius was accorded the signal honour of a specific mention by name in a law: no quorum for the election of praetors (a Republican office reduced, like the consulship, to the giving of lavish games) would be complete without him.

Libanius of Antioch was less close to Constantius, but was also honoured by him, if less conspicuously. He was a member of a distinguished curial family, but early decided to devote himself to rhetoric, of which he became a highly successful teacher, exponent, and great champion. He, too, was a pagan, deeply attached to the traditional cults of his beloved city and to the gods of pagan literature and eloquence. Born in 314, he studied at Antioch and then at Athens, before teaching first at Athens and then at Constantinople. Forced by the machinations of a rival to leave Constantinople, he resumed his teaching career at Nicomedia for five years, but an imperial summons recalled him to Constantinople, all unwilling, for he disliked the atmosphere of the new capital and the constant need to curry favour to ensure professional survival. While he was there, an official commissioned from him a panegyric of Constantius and Constans (348/9), which praises their achievements and those of their imperial father and grandfather. The almost total absence of anything smacking of paganism and the guarded references to an ambiguous deity who could be either Christian or Neoplatonic, according to taste, make it likely that the man who commissioned the speech was a zealous, not to say fanatical, Christian. The discourse was well received, and Libanius gained the patronage and support of successive proconsuls of Constantinople, and gifts from Constantius and even a grant of the revenues of an imperial estate. But he was longing to escape to peaceful Nicomedia or his native Antioch, and his desire was fulfilled in 353 when, after declining an offer of a job at Athens, he was able to settle permanently at Antioch. The difficulties in leaving Constantinople which he relates in his autobiography show how anxious Constantius was to keep the most talented professors to add their lustre to the capital's new university. Perhaps the loss of Libanius was particularly in his mind when, two years later, he commended Themistius for staying in Constantinople.

Why was it that a Christian emperor like Constantius was positively obsequious in his deference to pagan men of letters, and loaded them with presents and honours? How was it that a pagan philosopher and magician like Sopater could gain such influence with Constantine—not in his initial period of uncertainty after his conversion but when he was fully a Christian—as to arouse the jealousy and hatred of the most powerful official in the Empire? Constantius' attitude to rhetorical culture was to some extent conditioned by his own educational experience: he was a dull student (of Latin oratory) who had tried and failed, and was dazzled by the—for him—unattainable. Part of the secret of Themistius' success with him certainly lay in the philosopher's power to assure him, after all, of his educational superiority. But that was not all, as the large number of examples of men who in the fourth century gained honour and position for little other than their literary activities amply demonstrates. It was, of course, to an emperor's advantage to cultivate the whole body of writers and orators, for it rested with them as to whether his reputation with posterity would stand or fall; and public opinion, in all things secular, was still firmly in the hands of the pagans (we only know of one famous Christian orator at this period, Prohaeresius of Athens, and none of his speeches has survived). Moreover, the classical rhetorical education known as *paideia* was the basic education of the time, and all male (and a few female) members of the middle and upper classes, whether Christian or pagan, were grounded in the study of Homer, Hesiod, and other pagan poets and historians before proceeding to rhetoric itself or to the law schools of Rome or Beirut (rhetoric remained the basic discipline, and law was often combined with it rather than studied in isolation). Thus *paideia* formed a vital common ground of culture between educated Christians and pagans, and smoothed the paths of social life in a multi-religious society.

Yet the appreciation of eloquence was not confined to the educated. Eunapius, in his *Lives of the Philosophers and Sophists*, describes scenes of popular hysteria after public declamations at Athens, and Libanius claims that he was a rival attraction to the racecourse and the theatre (where the usual entertainment was low farces). Here we touch on one of the mainsprings of cultural life in the fourth century. The disasters of the third century had shaken men's confidence in the permanence of the Empire (a new insistence on 'eternity' and 'perpetuity' makes itself heard in the emperor's titles and in coin legends in the fourth century), and this in turn heightened their consciousness of what was most precious and enduring in their civilization: the heritage of Graeco-Roman literary culture. Sophists and orators, poets and philosophers, especially professional ones, were the living embodiment of this heritage. As such, they were extravagantly honoured, not to say fawned upon, by emperor and common people alike. This is not to say that there were not some who rejected classical culture—like the illiterate monks, bane of Libanius and Julian (see Chapter VI)—but this deification of literati was a major tendency of the age.

The Coinage

In a world without newspapers, the devices and legends on coins had been used for centuries, from the time of the first emperor, Augustus, as a means of disseminating information and putting across the ideals and priorities of the government of the day. The coin types of Augustus reveal great virtuosity, and the length of some of their inscriptions (condensed by abbreviation) made considerable demands on the literacy and eyesight of the population at large. Once it was realized that slogans were clearer than posters and remained decipherable for longer, the types were in general simplified. They were often used to convey religious messages, and any emperor who had a particular religious axe to grind would use the coinage as one of his means of propaganda. This might be some special cult of which he was a devoted adherent: Domitian proclaimed himself the son of the goddess Minerva, who received due prominence on his coins; the Syrian Elagabalus used coins to promote the exotic cult of the Baal of Emesa, whose priest he was; and Aurelian, builder of the great temple of the Sun at Rome, almost abdicated in favour of the god on his coins, some of which feature a bust of the Sun on the obverse, in the place of honour normally given to the emperor, and accompanied by the words 'Sol Lord of the Roman Empire'. Other emperors might have a wide-ranging programme of religious restoration and revival, like Augustus, no less than four of whose coin types show temples, and a fifth the altar of the imperial cult at Lyon; or Diocletian, who made sure that the gods of the Tetrarchy received abundant publicity on the major issues of the Empire. Moreover, the vast majority of secular coin types made use of pagan deities and personifications to convey their message in an easily-grasped symbolism: the figure of Fertility would greet an empress and her newborn baby, symbols of pagan apotheosis, such as Jupiter's eagle carrying him to heaven, would surround the death of an emperor, the goddess Victory was virtually inseparable from the announcement of military achievements, and an appeal to Salvation or Apollo the Saviour would be made in the event of a plague. All in all, the coinage perfectly exemplifies the almost inextricable intertwining of the State and public life with the pagan religion (see further, Chapter VI (section on festivals)) that was a leading feature of the Roman world—and caused such headaches for the Christians.

The coinage, then, presented the first Christian emperors with both opportunities and problems: opportunities of advertising and popularizing their new religious adherence, and problems of de-paganizing the traditional stock of types. As it was, the opportunities were almost totally ignored for decades, and the only real impact of Christianity on the coinage was negative: the ejection of the old gods from it. For a time there was little or no change. The Sun-God continued until the 320s to feature as Constantine's personal patron, undergoing the while in Constantine's mind a gradual transformation into Christ the Sun of Righteousness. With the disappearance of Sol from the coinage, the elimination of the pagan gods, never to return, was complete. Only a few minor deities and personifications survived the clean sweep. Victory, for a start, was far too useful, and if she still possessed the odd temple, not to mention the altar in the Senate-house, she was scarcely the object of a fervent or dangerous cult. Peace, Security and Courage (Virtus) also escaped the net, together with a colourless *genius* whose main function was to prop up shields on which Victory inscribes the *vota*—the anniversary prayers for the next five or ten years of the reign. A more important survivor, a personification of a different kind, was the goddess Roma, and to her was added the figure of the New Rome, Constantinople; the city-goddess of Antioch also makes her appearance.

The rejection of the pagan gods created a considerable vacuum in the stock of coin types, the 'survivors' notwithstanding. This can best be appreciated from a glance at the coinage of the Tetrarchy, which was almost entirely devoted to the greater gods—Jupiter, Hercules, Sol and Mars—together with sacrifice scenes (the tetrarchs sacrificing before a camp gate). The age of the Tetrarchy saw the achievement of a unified and highly centralized mint system, with a dozen mints situated in the major cities of the Empire, from London (closed under Constantine) and Trier to Antioch and Alexandria, often striking the same or similar coinages. Each mint stamped all its products with an annually changed mark. Previously there had been a number of local mints in operation, mainly in eastern cities, and these had added greatly to the variety of types, with picturesque local references, again often religious in character, such as those to the cult of Artemis of Ephesus. Moreover, the Tetrarchy's emphasis on the greater gods had led to the final demise of most of the personifications in use earlier. Thus it was that the coinage entered the fourth century with a restricted range of types owing to centralization, and the triumph of Christianity inhibited a whole public language.

Christianity, however, failed almost entirely to fill the gap which it had created. Not only was there no stock of *public* Christian imagery on which to draw, but Christianity still had many of the characteristics of a mystery religion. It would have seemed a profanation to set representations of Christ and Biblical scenes on the common coinage of the realm, to be handled by believers and unbelievers alike. So what we find is the timid introduction, here and there, of tiny Christian symbols into some of the coin types. The first, and most famous, is the chi-rho monogram added as a badge on Constantine's helmet on a few silver medallions struck for presentation to army officers on the occasion of the *decennalia* in 315. Then a die-cutter at Siscia (one of the Balkan mints)—obviously a Christian—added a tiny chi-rho to the emperor's bust on a single die of an issue of 317-20. During the next forty years, more tiny chi-rhos appear incorporated in mint marks, on the sacred military standard, the *labarum*, or as one of several alternative devices decorating the emperor's shield. Their associations, like their origin, were almost exclusively military. It was, indeed, military themes and types that were largely used to fill the vacuum left by the pagan gods, reflecting in this the major preoccupations of the day, in an age that rarely saw a year go by without the emperor himself campaigning on one threatened frontier or another. This is well illustrated by the range of types of the reformed bronze coinage struck from 348 with the legend FEL(*icium*) TEMP(*orum*) REPARATIO, the 'Restoration of Fortunate Times', in honour of the eleven hundredth anniversary of the foundation of Rome. One main type (much imitated by copiers meeting the demand for small change), struck in four different varieties, has Virtus spearing a fallen barbarian horseman. The emperor appears in various attitudes, all military: standing holding the *labarum* on a ship steered by Victory (two varieties); standing and simply holding the *labarum*; on horseback riding down two captives; and spurning a captive with his foot while, again, holding the *labarum* (the emperor's vaunted clemency is sadly lacking in these last two). The only non-military type is that of a phoenix standing on a pyre or a globe. (**18, 7**)

It is one of the paradoxes of the fourth century that the first genuinely and unmistakably Christian coinages were issued not by the legitimate emperors of the House of Constantine but by two usurpers in the early 350s: Vetranio and Magnentius. But on closer examination, the paradox becomes less paradoxical. Usurpers had a desperate need of some legitimation of their claims, and of the support of the army, and both needs would be admirably assisted towards fulfilment by the usurper associating himself with the famous victory-'vision' of Constantine. Vetranio's appeal was the most direct, and provides the first independent evidence of the 'vision' (in its most spectacular form): on bronze coins struck in 350 at Vetranio's mints for both Vetranio himself and Constantius, the emperor stands holding the *labarum* beneath the words HOC SIGNO VICTOR ERIS ('In This Sign You Shall Be Victorious'). Magnentius' Christian coinage was one of his last issues, struck in 353 when he had fallen back on Gaul and was hard pressed. The comparatively big and heavy bronzes have on their reverses a large chi-rho monogram flanked by an alpha and an omega, while the legend asserts that in this lies the SALVS (safety, salvation) of Magnentius and his Caesar Decentius, our Lords (for the political events of these years, see Chapter II). The usurpers were put down and the coinage reverted to its normal range of military and otherwise secular types. Centuries were to pass before the goddess Victory became a Christian angel (on the coins of the Byzantine emperor Justinian II in the early seventh century) and the coinage as a whole came to reflect the status of the emperors as the secular heads of a now fragmented Christendom. (**8, 9**)

The Religion of Court, Government and Army

When Christian evangelists moved outwards from Palestine, and their Gospel began to spread across the Roman world, their converts were drawn substantially from the poorer classes in the towns along the great trade routes. Gradually the Good News of Christ began to filter upwards through society, attracting converts of a higher social status, and also to reach areas of the countryside. Its progress was, naturally, very uneven, and by the end of the third century some provinces, mainly eastern ones, were already Christianized in some depth, while others in the north-west had still scarcely been touched by Christianity. Then, after the storms of the Great Persecution (see Chapters I and II), the whole situation was dramatically changed by the conversion of Constantine. From being the object of persecution, Christianity became, almost overnight, not merely acceptable but even fashionable. As Constantine's certainty and missionary zeal increased, he made efforts to turn those around him to his own newly-embraced religion. Eusebius, bearing witness to this, notes regretfully that his beloved emperor was often taken in by the applause and flattery and fair-weather conversions of his courtiers. Certainly there were many, in all walks of life, who hastened to follow their emperor's lead, beginning with his own mother Helena, who proceeded to outdo her son in conspicuous piety and was canonized for her pains. Thus Constantine's conversion distorted the 'normal' progress of Christianity upwards through society and outwards from the towns to the rural poor, and turned it into something of a pincer movement, as clients and tenants began to follow the lead of their patrons and landlords.

The army, too, soon began to follow the new religion of its emperor, helped on its way by the initial military triumph of Christianity at the Milvian Bridge, and by the victory symbolism and victorious associations of the chi-rho standard that stemmed from it. Eusebius' *Life of Constantine* contains its stories of faithful standard-bearers miraculously saved in battle while those who deserted the *labarum*-standard were slain. There was, of course, a certain time-lag—the army did not become Christian overnight: the soldiers who were discharged after the 'crusade' against Licinius shouted: 'Constantine Augustus, may the gods preserve you for us'. Constantine himself assisted in the good work, by such things as the granting of free leave for Christian soldiers to attend church services, and the prescribing of special prayers to be said on Sundays by the whole army, pagans as well as Christians, assembled specially on a plain outside the city (i.e. Constantinople)—a sort of school assembly for the *comitatenses*, the troops of the central reserve that accompanied the emperor (see Chapter II). Force of example and imperial encouragement may have spread the custom to the legions on the frontiers. Such was the success of his methods, helped by his generosity to, and general popularity with, his troops, that, three decades after the defeat of Licinius, the small army given to Julian when he was made Caesar 'knew only how to pray'. Yet Julian was able to boast to his friend Maximus that the Gallic troops with which he marched against Constantius were now pagan, and the armies of the Empire followed him to Persia. They then, again, supported his Christian successors. The passivity of the army *as a whole* in religious matters is, it seems, to be accounted for by the fact that the individual soldiers, often of pagan peasant or barbarian origin, were men without roots, removed from their natural background and its web of familiar ties and loyalties. Their consequent tendency to follow the herd meant, in religious matters, that any god who could win battles was good enough for their worship, above all if he was the chosen patron of the emperor of the day. It was, indeed, the unwavering support of the army, and the new, victorious, associations of his chosen religion, together with his own immense personal prestige as emperor, that enabled Constantine to fly in the face of tradition as he did, without forfeiting the loyalty of the governing classes and finding a knife in his back.

However, while this was true in general, there were significant exceptions, men who stood out against the prevailing paganism or Christianity of their fellows. Thus, there were Christian soldiers, and even conscientious objectors—like St. Martin later, under Julian in Gaul—in the army of the Tetrarchy (two were put to death in Africa). Then, after a generation of official Christianity, Julian's sudden reversion to paganism found some dissenters among the troops. While he was at Antioch, he mounted a Constantinian-type campaign of propaganda aimed at the army, with a heavy emphasis on the pagan ritual of the imperial cult, and lavish sacrifices and banquets of sacrificial meats laid on for the soldiery in the temples. Ammianus describes the results: gorged and drunken soldiers being carried home on the shoulders of passers-by, bringing the pagan revival into disrepute. Significantly, it was the units of pagan Gauls that had come with Julian from the West who participated most eagerly in these orgies. Zealous Christian soldiers were conspicuous by their absence. A small number of these were executed for gross disobedience or sedition, two of them for restoring the chi-rho to the standards of their units, perhaps as a prelude to mutiny. The army was restive during the preparations for the Persian expedition, and Julian was forced to celebrate his *decennalia*—and distribute the important decennial donative—three years early; but it followed him to Persia, and after his death its officers tried to elect the pagan Salutius as his successor, and then chose and obeyed the Christians Jovian and Valentinian. It was in the early years of Valentinian's reign that officers of the British fleet took part, and perhaps played a leading part, in the building of the pagan temple at Lydney (Chapter V). And although a number of British military Mithraea had been destroyed in the first half of the fourth century, doubtless on the orders of a zealous Christian officer (Chapter VI), at a number of forts in Britain and on the Rhine and Danube pagan temples (including several Mithraea) continued in use until late in the century, while the building of identifiable churches in forts was often delayed until *c.* 400. Thus the overall picture of army religion is an uneven one, of general conformity to the religion of the current emperor, but with a fair number of individual soldiers sufficiently strongly attached to their own religion to be ready to swim against the prevailing tide. In view of the custom of local recruitment, it is no surprise to find the Christian dissenters principally in Africa and the East, and the pagan ones mostly in the northwest, the last region of the Empire to be permeated by Christianity.

Under Constantine, Roman society was still pagan in majority, including a very large majority of the governing classes, and the religion of office-holders reflected this. In the East, the pagan rhetorical education, *paideia*, administered by Libanius and many another sophist, predisposed its pupils to paganism as it spread before them the romance of the pagan past. The members of the town councils, the *curiae*, many of whom were products of *paideia*, were still fairly solidly pagan, as Julian was to realize (see Chapter V); and even at the very end of Constantius' reign the vast majority of the provincial governors were pagans. It was the court offices, the most powerful and the closest to the emperor—those of the praetorian prefects, the masters of the main departments of the civil service, and the chamberlains (generally eunuchs)—that were as often as not, by the mid fourth century, held by Christians. There was perhaps nothing systematic about this, for Constantius promoted talent wherever he found it, educated or uneducated, and many a high official in his reign worked his way up, like Constantine's prefect Ablabius, from the lower echelons of the expanding bureaucracy, that was largely recruited from the humbler, and more Christianized, layers of the population. Yet he may have preferred to have men of his own religion in the offices with whose holders he had most dealings. Even the city prefecture of Rome was coming to be held quite frequently by a Christian, as the new religion began to spread among the senators. Yet it was this same senatorial aristocracy of Rome, whose leading families were for the most part still pagan, and zealously so, that acted as the guardian of the great pagan tradition enshrined in the capital, upholding and upheld by it. And that tradition was strong enough to make even Constantius, fresh from the issuing of his anti-pagan laws, pause in wonder and acquiesce in their non-application. For although the government of the later Roman Empire was apparently an autocracy, the enforcement of particular laws depended to a considerable extent on the consent of the governed and, above all, of the provincial governors who were required to execute imperial enactments. So the anti-pagan laws were largely shipwrecked on the passive resistance of pagan governors, who would have the support of pagan *curiae* in the East and in Africa, of pagan lords in Rome, and of a mostly pagan population in the north-west. The dead weight of this passive resistance acted as a powerful restraint on Constantius and Constans, and *a fortiori* on Constantine himself, if he moved against paganism at the end of his reign. Half a century later much of it would have evaporated, and the laws of Theodosius I in the 380s and 390s succeeded in stamping out much of the remaining pagan cult: by then the tide would have turned, fully and decisively, in Christianity's favour. But first there was an interlude in the new religion's march of progress, with a pagan emperor of energy and resourcefulness on the throne: the Emperor Julian.

Chapter V

The Pagan Revival of Julian the Apostate

Julian's Conversion to Paganism

Flavius Claudius Julianus was born at Constantinople in 332. His mother died soon after his birth, and he was orphaned at the age of five by the political murder of his father, Julius Constantius, at the hands of a mob of soldiers, on the instigation of his cousin Constantius II (see Chapter II). Others of his family were butchered as well—he accuses Constantius of killing seven cousins and two uncles. Julian himself was only spared because of his extreme youth, and his elder brother Gallus because he was ill. Another brother, the eldest of the three, fell victim with his father to the machinations of Constantius.

From then on, Julian led an insecure existence, first at Nicomedia, Diocletian's old capital, where he was under the supervision of Eusebius the Arian bishop, who was a relative of his. He was also in touch with his maternal grandmother and his uncle Julianus, who later became an apostate like his nephew. Here he had the good fortune to be put in the charge of an excellent pedagogue or tutor, the eunuch Mardonius, who inspired the boy with a great love of Greek literature, especially Homer and Hesiod.

Things took a turn for the worse when his guardian Eusebius died in 341: it was probably then that he and Gallus were sent to the isolated villa of Macellum in Cappadocia, in south-east Asia Minor. Here Julian spent six years of what amounted to internment, cut off from the outside world and spied upon by his household. Mardonius had not been allowed to accompany him but, true to his precepts, Julian spent most of his time in study. His and Gallus' education was not, in fact, neglected—neither the secular nor the religious. They were instructed in the Scriptures, partly by George of Cappadocia (who was lynched in Julian's reign while Arian bishop of Alexandria), and both were baptized and became 'readers' in the Church, a minor grade of cleric. George was the possessor of a magnificent library of pagan as well as Christian authors, of which Julian made full use. After George's death Julian claimed the library for himself, partly out of sentiment, for these were the books, including those of the pagan Neoplatonist philosophers Porphyry and Iamblichus, which had sown the seeds of his apostasy.

In 347 came release from 'exile', perhaps after a visit made to Macellum by the Emperor Constantius II. Gallus went to Ephesus, Julian to

Constantinople, where he pursued his education. The next few years saw him in various places in western Asia Minor, but by now his situation had changed in two ways. The promotion of Gallus to the rank of Caesar in 351 and the restoration of Julian's inheritance set him free from much of the constraint under which he had been placed. And he had secretly become a pagan.

It is likely that the first steps of involvement with paganism were taken in Nicomedia, where he was sent again from Constantinople after his return from Macellum, because of Constantius' continuing suspicion. His Christian teachers had forbidden him to attend the lectures of Libanius, the famous pagan sophist from Antioch, but he paid one of Libanius' students to take notes for him. By these means he came into contact with a circle in touch with pagan secret societies which practised the mystical form of magic, theurgy. Strict secrecy was essential because all forms of divination and magic were prohibited under Constantius (see Chapter IV). The leading theurgist of the time was Maximus of Ephesus, whose miracles included making the torches held by a statue of Hecate burst into flame, and the goddess herself smile, while he prayed to her. He regarded himself as a genuine philosopher, but was really more of a magician. A certain emotional streak in Julian's character made him hunger for sensational religious experiences, despite his love of the true Greek intellectual philosophy. Maximus gained such a hold over his imperial pupil that, when Julian became emperor, he summoned Maximus to Constantinople, and rushed out from a meeting of the Senate to greet and embrace him publicly. Maximus seems to have exercised considerable influence on affairs of State, through divination and the oracles he uttered.

One suggestion is that Julian was 'put off' Christianity because of the falsity of the Arian version of it which he was taught. But there is nothing logically wrong with the semi-Arian doctrine which the Emperor Constantius was propagating. Quite the contrary: moderate Arianism is closer than orthodoxy to the Platonic 'theology' of the Form of the Good and the subordinate *demiourgos* or Craftsman. There is also evidence that the Arians drew more support from the intellectually gifted leaders of the eastern Church than did the orthodox. Others have supposed that Julian could not accept the religion of his hated cousin Constantius. But, in that case, all he had to do to dissociate himself from it was to become orthodox instead of Arian. Moreover, he was himself by temperament too much of a religious zealot to be over-much shocked by brutal doings during the Arian-orthodox struggle, if there had been no anterior cause for detachment on his part. The true reasons for his conversion to paganism must be sought elsewhere.

The crucial time in Julian's religious life was the period of exile at

Macellum. He was at an impressionable age and, cut off from teachers of the necessary intellectual calibre, his Christianity stagnated. At the same time, through George's library, he became open to the seductive and romantic influence of late paganism with its Neoplatonic doctrines of the mystical approach of the divine soul in man to the One Supreme Being. Julian was greatly moved, too, by the beauty of nature, especially of the heavenly bodies. 'From my childhood a strange yearning for the rays of the [sun] god sank deep into my soul; and from my earliest years my mind was so completely possessed by the light of heaven that not only did I desire to gaze intently at the sun, but whenever I went forth at night, when the sky was clear and cloudless, I abandoned all else and devoted myself to the beauties of the heavens': so says Julian himself in the opening paragraph of his *Hymn to King Helios*. Here were the gods of the ancient poets and writers whom he loved and admired. Here, too, was a purity that appealed to his adolescent soul as the purity of Manichaeism appealed to the young Augustine. His fate was sealed by the discovery of the religious excitation produced by theurgy, and he was initiated into several mystery cults, including those of Mithras, of Cybele and Attis, of the Eleusinian deities, and doubtless also of Hecate. Paganism and pagan literature still had the power to win converts; nor was Julian the only one, for subsequent emperors found it necessary to promulgate laws against apostasy. Further studies, including some at Athens, the idealized fountainhead of Greek culture, did but confirm Julian in the step which he had taken. For the rest of his short life, he felt himself to be under the special patronage of the 'King Sun' of whom he writes so movingly.

While in Asia Minor and Greece, Julian became the focus of the hopes of a kind of pagan 'party', whose one wish was to see a pagan emperor on the throne once again. Not only the philosophers and theurgists, but also men of affairs who held office in their own towns and in the imperial government, would have been among them. Julian was assured of support for any programme of pagan restoration which he had the opportunity to carry out. The devotion of this band of dedicated men would have made him more determined to reach the throne, for the sake of Helios and the gods of Greece and Rome.

The Pagan 'Church'

When in 361 Julian became sole emperor by the death and will of his late adversary Constantius (see Chapter II), the power to put into action his hopes and plans for reviving paganism was suddenly his. The first step was easy: he declared all temples open, and restored their lands and property which had been confiscated by Constantine. 'From all sides,' says Libanius, 'one could see columns returning to their place, some carried on ships, some on waggons.' But to get these measures enforced was not always easy. Libanius speaks elsewhere of temple columns which a man had built into his house.

These measures, however, did but restore the physical condition of the temples to what it had been before Constantine. If the sacred mission with which Julian felt himself to be entrusted was to have any real success, more positive steps would be needed. It was not merely imperial patronage that had given Christianity its dynamism and ability to win converts. Paganism had to be given the power to fight back. Like the earlier tetrarchic emperor Maximin Daia (see Chapter II), Julian had noticed how the compact, hierarchic structure of the Church gave it combative superiority over the loose-knit and amorphous organization—or rather the lack of any organization—of the pagan cults. So, following in Maximin's footsteps, he appointed a high priest of each province, with wide supervisory powers over all the temples and priests in that province.

He went much further than Maximin, however, in his reorganization. Hitherto, the priesthoods of most pagan cults had really been secular offices, filled by members of the local council, with no demand made upon the holder except that of performing certain sacrifices, especially at festivals, observing ritual purity on these occasions and, often, financing or helping to finance festivals and games in honour of the god whose priest they were. Notorious profligates would have been considered unsuitable for these posts but, short of that, there was no stipulation as to the moral qualifications and conduct of a priest. Julian changed that completely, as he himself makes clear in several pastoral letters written by him as Pontifex Maximus, the supreme priest in the whole of the Empire, to various of the high priests he had appointed. 'I say that the best men in every city, especially those who show most love for the gods, and next those who show most love for their fellow men [must be chosen], whether they are poor or rich.' Even those of humble birth must not be automatically passed over, as they had been in the past, in favour of the local dignitaries of whom the *curia*, or town council, was composed.

Once the priests had been selected by the high priest, they must behave as befits their office: no reading of scandalous matter, like the more scurrilous parts of the Old Comedy of Greece: 'Philosophy alone,' says Julian, 'would be appropriate for us priests, and of philosophers only those who set the gods before them as guides of their intellectual training, like Pythagoras and Plato and Aristotle, and the school of Chrysippus and Zeno'; not, he hastens to add, such impious ones as Epicurus and Pyrrho, whose works have mercifully perished. They must avoid the theatre (which by the late Empire was always coarse and usually obscene) and beast hunts in the arena, and so must their sons.

They must not drink in taverns or engage in sordid trades. And they must only be entertained by men of unimpeachable character. Above all, they must practise *philanthropia*, which Julian interprets along the lines of Christian charity. The Pontifex Maximus outlines their religious duties as well: prayer three times a day, sacrifice at dawn and dusk, and complete ritual and moral purity during and before the allotted period of actual service in the temple. He is anxious, too, to promote the dignity of priests: they must receive high officials of the State in the temple, on their own territory as it were, instead of going to greet them at the city gates, and soldiers must follow them into the temple instead of preceding them. The priest must be regarded 'with respect and reverence as the most honoured possession of the gods.' The great importance attached in the fourth century, as in Byzantine times, to pomp and hieratic dignity is well illustrated here, as in Constantius' visit to Rome (Chapter II).

Julian did not confine his attention to issuing general instructions. We have a letter of his written to an official who had allowed a priest to be assaulted, presumably by Christians. Pointing out that it is sacrilege to strike a priest, he forbids the official 'for three revolutions of the moon to interfere in anything concerning a priest', and says he will pray with him for the gods to pardon him: this is one of the places where Julian's Christian upbringing shows through. The letter also shows the working of the new hierarchy: the high priest of the province—we do not know which one—had appealed to the Pontifex Maximus on behalf of one of the priests in his charge.

In addition to administering the pagan cult, the high priest of each province was to organize large-scale charity, in direct imitation of that of the Christian Church. 'Why do we not notice,' says Julian to Arsacius, high priest of Galatia, 'that it is their benevolence to strangers, their care for the graves of the dead and their feigned holiness of life that have done most to increase atheism [i.e. Christianity]?' Arsacius is to establish hostels in every city for poor pagan and even Christian strangers; and a generous grant of corn and wine is to be made by the imperial exchequer for charitable purposes throughout Galatia. 'For it is disgraceful that, when none of the Jews has to beg, and the impious Galilaeans maintain not only their own poor but ours as well, our people are seen to lack assistance from us.' All pagans were to give alms, in addition to this official generosity. There had been a certain amount of organized charity other than Christian before this, through such channels as the public maintenance of orphans and distributions of presents at the games, but, with the exception of banquets at festivals, they were attached to the civic side of life, rather than to pagan religion. Christian charity, viewed as the showy spending of money for the good of others, was the counterpart of the pagan festivals and games. Under

Julian, who was concerned that his 'church' should lack no advantage, paganism briefly had both.

Theology

By rearranging the structure of paganism, Julian hoped to give it the same advantages as the Church in this respect. But more had to be done if further conversions to Christianity were to be prevented, and more apostates brought back to the pagan 'church'. Another advantage which the Christian Church possessed was that of having a unified theology, even if the details were difficult to settle. Pagans worshipped a multiplicity of gods in a wide variety of rites, which ranged from the refined and sophisticated to the frankly barbaric (e.g. the ritual slaughter of a gladiator in the African cult of Baal-Saturn). In order to attack Christianity and show it up to be thoroughly irrational and such as no sensible man could believe in, a pagan needed to be able to contrast it with the enlightened tenets of his own religion. Thus a body of pagan doctrine began to be developed: such things as the eternity of the world, the immortality and divinity of angels, daimons, heroes, and even of souls, when once delivered from reincarnation at the end of the cycle of metempsychosis; the virtue of the rites of mysteries, and so on. The late-third-century Neoplatonist philosophers Porphyry and Iamblichus, disciples of Plotinus, had begun the work of reducing to order the chaos of the pagan pantheon. Julian clearly saw the need for a pagan theology and devoted some of his literary energies to furnishing it, in his hymns to King Helios and the Mother of the Gods (and to defending it against the Cynics, unorthodox pagan philosophers who condemned civilized society and some aspects of pagan religion (see also Chapter VI)). He based his centralized, solar theology on Iamblichus' work of systematization. The tendency to look upon all the traditional gods as merely different aspects of a single divine power had long been a philosophical refuge for explaining away the large number of different gods and goddesses. The growing importance in the later third century of the cult of Sol Invictus, the Unconquered Sun, with whom were identified Apollo, Mithras, etc., was one part of a general search for simplification that spread to ordinary people, partly, but not necessarily wholly, under the challenge of a monotheistic religion. In Julian's *Hymn to King Helios* are united three different strands of this process: the popular cult of Sol Invictus, the philosophical identification of various gods with him, and the Neoplatonic notion of three worlds, the visible, the intellectual, and the intelligible. The difficulties in the way of the development of a compact pagan theology are well illustrated by the *Hymn to the Mother of the Gods*, in which Julian fits Cybele and her son Attis, the latter very shakily indeed, into the same three-world system. His friend Sallust, praetorian prefect of Gaul, and consul in 363, helped the good work by writing a treatise *On the Gods and the Universe*, also imbued with Neoplatonic ideas, and summarizing the new 'orthodox' pagan theology.

The Paganization of the Government

An emperor has at his disposal considerable means of propagating his beliefs. Julian was not slow to take advantage of these. Modern research has shown the extraordinary vigour of his pagan reaction as revealed in his administration. In 364, when his nominees were still in power, virtually every governor and high official in the eastern provinces was a pagan, in striking contrast to the mixture of Christians and pagans in office before and after his reign. It is obvious that he saw, unlike his predecessors and successors, who may have encouraged Christians but did not cease to appoint pagans, that by unofficially excluding those of the enemy religion from posts in his government he could promote his own religion among all those who were ambitious and had lukewarm beliefs; not that these fair-weather conversions would be of lasting value. A prime example is Domitius Modestus, a Christian (presumably Arian) who was Count of the East under Constantius; apostatized under Julian and was appointed city prefect of Constantinople; and became Arian under Valens and held the office of praetorian prefect of the East. A similar case is that of the Christian sophist Hecebolius, who taught at Constantinople under Constantius and was one of Julian's tutors, became pagan when his pupil was emperor, and after Julian's death lay in front of a church door begging to be trodden upon and moaning that he was salt that had lost its savour!

Julian and the Cities

By giving and withholding office, Julian could spread paganism in the highest section of the governing class. Elsewhere in this class there was a neglected and tottering stronghold of paganism that was badly in need of all possible help and encouragement. Julian did not fail to give it, as far as lay in his power. Graeco-Roman paganism had always been based on the city and was a firmly entrenched part of city life. Sacrifices and prayers accompanied most civic actions, such as the enrolment of a new citizen in the local organization or 'tribe'. All holidays were the festival of one of the gods and goddesses worshipped by the city (see further Chapter VI). Much of the building and upkeep of temples, the provision of sacrifices, the giving of games and theatrical shows and public banquets at festivals, devolved upon the *curia*, the town council. And it was its members who, as we have seen, produced priests for the gods from among their number. Christianity began its work among the lowest strata of society, the slaves and urban poor, and only gradually filtered upwards, except for incidental conversions in the upper classes. By the mid fourth century it was the local aristocracies who were, throughout much of the Empire, the least Christianized element of society (see Chapter IV). These men had been given the rhetorical education of their day, *paideia*, as their fathers and grandfathers before them had had and as they gave their sons. This education, which Julian himself had received, concentrated on the great writers and poets of the classical past: Homer and Demosthenes were its mainstay. It produced quick wits, a good memory, and fluency of speech, and inculcated the virtues of a gentleman. In a sense this curial class was international: Libanius, the main teacher at the 'university' of Antioch, had as his pupils young men of good family from all over the eastern provinces, as we know from his letters to them and their relatives and patrons. A few were Christian, but many were pagan, and there is no reason to suppose that the imbalance was due to most Christians choosing Christian teachers instead of pagan. Here, clearly, was a reservoir of support for Julian.

The city councils were, however, in a parlous state. In the early centuries of the Empire, their members had competed with each other to bestow lavish gifts on their city. But they were gradually burdened with more and more compulsory duties by the State, especially tax collecting, and the spirit of voluntary munificence died. A man might be completely ruined by being chosen to collect taxes, as the lack of coercive power available to councillors—the city watch was quite inadequate and local jurisdiction had virtually ceased—made these difficult to extort from unwilling taxpayers in a bad year, and he had to make up deficits from his personal fortune. Moreover, the role of *curiales* as leaders of local society had passed to the highly privileged and ever more numerous ex-governors and high officials. Thus duties and responsibility, without real powers or compensatory honour, were the councillor's lot in the fourth century. Membership of the council was hereditary, except in the case of loss of one's estate, so a *curialis* was trapped. A long succession of laws was passed to attempt to recall to their duties all those who had tried to escape by loopholes or illegal means. The organization of the whole Empire depended ultimately on local administration, and the councils, diminishing in size and wealth, threatened to collapse; hence the concern of successive emperors. For Julian the problem was all the more acute in that the *curiae* were the chosen instruments of his pagan revival, as well as the main basis of his support. He hoped that under his rule the cities would again prosper, and with encouragement from him the *curiales* would lead their fellow-citizens in a renewal of temples, rites and festivals, spending their new-found wealth gladly on the building and restoration of the cult edifices, and the revival of worship.

The first requisite was to make sure that all who were liable did serve on their council, and to add any more who were financially capable. A clever move which Julian made here was to cancel the immunity from council service given to Christian clergy by his predecessors (see Chapter IV), at one blow harming the Church and helping the councils. Other legal escape routes were cut down and clearly defined: only those who had served in the army for ten years, or had held high office in the State, or were public doctors (or teachers), or had thirteen children(!), were exempt. As for illegal ones, his reduction in the size of the bureaucracy not only returned some deserters but removed one of the most attractive alternatives: it would no longer suck up curial deserters like an ever-growing sponge. At Antioch there was a vigorous recruiting drive, as he tells us himself in the *Misopogon*, and even maternal descent from a decurion was held binding once more.

He also set about improving the financial conditions of decurions. In their private capacity he freed them from liability to pay the tax in gold and silver levied on tradesmen, unless they were engaged in large-scale business. In their public capacity he was concerned that new council members should not be immediately overwhelmed by the existing (municipal) debts of their colleagues and predecessors. Curial debts to the State (incurred in tax-collecting) were in any case remitted. He restored the civic lands, confiscated by Constantine or Constantius, and also the civic taxes, to the use of the city, and he did not exact *aurum coronarium*—the 'crown money' that was 'voluntarily' presented by the rejoicing subjects to their sovereign on his accession and important anniversaries. The public post was reorganized and far fewer people were allowed to use it, thus lightening the load of *curiales* and others who had to furnish personnel, animals and supplies. (The system had been overburdened under Constantius to the point of collapse, because of the 'crowds of bishops scurrying hither and thither to synods' (Ammianus).) The council of Antioch was given 3,000 lots of uncultivated land, so that it could have them reclaimed and enjoy the profits.

Even more important than financial conditions was the status of the *curia* and its members, a vital factor in the hoped-for revival of civic spirit. Julian took good care to honour *curiae* by his attentions. Several he addressed in person—and it was unheard of for a fourth-century emperor even to speak in the Senate of Constantinople. To many others he wrote letters, recalling to some the greatness of their origins. Individual *curiales* were also favoured. Moreover, he encouraged the cities to be responsible for certain aspects of local administration that were beginning to devolve upon the State, in order to increase their importance and independence.

Julian's campaign also included some physical restoration. When he went to Gaul, no fewer than forty-five cities, including Cologne, had been devastated by the invaders. As soon as he could, he set about re-building and fortifying them. He even made a chief of the defeated Alamanni bring building materials and help in the reconstruction of towns destroyed by them (see Chapter II). Later on, when he was at Constantinople, 'he repaired all the cities throughout Thrace, together with the frontier fortifications' (Ammianus). His subordinates were also encouraged to undertake works of restoration and construction. Claudius Hermogenianus Olybrius and Atilius Theodotus, governors of two of the African provinces, carried out various public works, including a new forum at Thubursicu in Numidia, a restored records office at Bulla Regia in Proconsular Africa, and a restored waterworks at Tunis.

Only obdurately Christian cities fared badly under Julian. Nisibis in Mesopotamia was refused help against the Persians. Edessa was avoided in favour of pagan Carrhae on the Persian expedition. Caesarea, capital of Cappadocia, was erased from the roll of cities and taxed as heavily as a village. Maiuma in Palestine was reduced once more to a district of pagan Gaza, from which Constantine had detached it (see Chapter IV).

To separate Julian's work in this sphere from his religious activities, and regard it as a mere attempt to recover a lost ideal state of Greek city life, is to miss the essential cohesion of his policies. He was certainly concerned with this particular side of 'Hellenism' for its own sake, but his very use of this word, which might more properly denote Greek civilization, as the name of his own special brand of paganism shows that he was not unaware of the intimate connection between pagan religion and the State, in Julian's thought almost exclusively at the level of the city. Julian is *philopolis par excellence*, according to Libanius in his great *Funeral Speech* on his beloved emperor, and in his own writings he mentions *theoi poliouchoi*, the gods who look after cities, and connects the city and its gods in letters addressed to Antioch, Athens and Alexandria. A city's religion was just one aspect of its life, the expression of its relationship with the gods, rather than a separate activity. Christianity, for Julian, violated not only the traditional religion but the whole life of the city.

Education

Christianity also violated *paideia*, the true Greek education which Julian and his favoured curial classes in the East had received. How could a Christian professor teach Homer and Aristotle, Plato and Demosthenes, when he regarded as evil demons the gods of whom they spoke with reverence and affection, and treated the mythology as stupid fables? So Julian promulgated a law that the city councils, in nominating a public teacher, should produce a certificate of the candidate's moral worth, to be ratified by the emperor. The accompanying circular made it plain that marks of moral unworthiness included Christianity. Let Christian teachers, he said, cease to be hypocrites, and go and interpret Matthew and Luke in their churches.

This law was revolutionary. Before Julian there had been few hints that there was any incompatibility between Greek (or Latin) literature and Christianity, much less a State enactment separating the two. Education had always been completely free from any such control. What, then, can have motivated so radical a measure? It was not merely an extension of his (unofficial) exclusion of Christians from posts as governors to another series of influential positions, for the vast majority of professors were pagan already. Besides, he specifically laid down that the two most famous Christian teachers—Prohaeresius of Athens and Marius Victorinus of Rome—were to be allowed to retain their posts. From this point of view, the measure would have been wasted effort. But there were two other reasons for it. One was that he wanted to prevent Christians using the reasoning which they had learnt by pagan education against paganism itself. The second was the possible connection between *paideia* and paganism, on which Libanius, for one, insists. *Paideia* had become almost a real religion in itself: dedicated to the gods of learning, Hermes and the Muses, and often carried on in temples or in sanctuaries of the Muses, it would seem that it created an atmosphere that predisposed pupils in favour of paganism. Julian had himself been fired by the romance of the pagan past, and it could inspire others as well. So he probably wished to take advantage of this by preventing the 'defusing' of the pagan content of *paideia* by Christian teachers, who would be bound to play it down, separating out the educational content from pagan associations.

As for the Christians, how did they react to the suggestion that they should confine their teaching to Biblical exegesis? Bishop Gregory of Nazianzus in Cappadocia thundered against Julian's law in the first of his two speeches *Against Julian*, and it clearly aroused his ire to a greater degree than anything else which the apostate emperor did. 'Thus then acted our wise emperor and lawgiver, so that nothing should escape his tyranny, and proclaimed speechlessness over the whole of his empire, exerting his tyranny over words before all else.' 'But I must bring back my speech to the subject of words; for I cannot help coming back to this point again and again, and must try to the best of my ability to plead their cause: for though there are many and weighty reasons why that person deserves to be detested, in no case does he appear to have acted more illegally than in this; and let everyone share my indignation who takes pleasure in words' (Gregory puns on *logoi* meaning both 'words' and 'rhetoric'). Others did what they could to fill what was considered to be a disastrous gap. Two Syrians, both called Apollinaris, father and son, rewrote the Old Testament as epics and tragedies, and put the Gospels into the form of Platonic dialogues, so that the Christian youth could receive some sort of decent education. For it was generally felt, at least in the upper classes, that the rough-and-ready Greek of the Bible was inadequate in this respect. Julian knew the enemy from within, and his attack drew blood.

In the light of subsequent history, however, it was providential that Julian's measure was as short-lived as himself. For though the Church valued and used education and culture, and this facilitated the conversion of the educated classes, there is no question that the Bible would have won the day, if Christians had had to choose between it and *paideia*. If Christianity had been thus artificially cut off from its cultural background, the great work of Clement and Origen and the third-century Alexandrian Fathers in creating a fusion of the highest Christian and Greek thought would have gone for nothing. Worse, as it was the Church that preserved through the Dark Ages almost all that we know of classical civilization, nothing of that great heritage would have been handed down to us. Few measures could have had such devastatingly different consequences from those intended, had Julian lived.

Julian and the Church

This law was published on 17 June 362. Earlier, Julian's relations with the Church had been surprisingly happy. At the same time as the publication of his edicts giving freedom of worship to pagans, and partly in order to create the right conditions for these to be effective, 'he summoned to the palace the dissident bishops of the Christians and the divided people, and courteously advised them to lull to sleep their discords, and each fearlessly and without opposition to follow his own beliefs. He took a firm stand on this, so that, as freedom increased their dissension, he would not afterwards have to fear a united populace, knowing from experience that no wild beasts are so hostile to mankind as are most of the Christians in their savagery towards one another' (Ammianus, a pagan, speaking). He certainly hoped to have the Christians at each other's throats rather than presenting a united opposition to revived paganism. But he may have been acting not from pure cunning, but also from a sincere desire to bring peace to the cities by the removal of the element of force that had caused much bloodshed under Constantius, and from an initial high-minded wish for tolerance after the narrow sectarianism of his predecessor. He seems to have imagined that, when paganism became once again the religion of the court, the Church would lose a large part of its support. Finding that this was not so, he turned to combative measures such as the education edict.

He showed clearly enough where his sympathies lay when, in December 361, the Alexandrians set upon, trampled and killed their

Arian bishop, George of Cappadocia, who had made himself generally unpopular, together with two government officials who had made attacks on pagan worship. The mob burned the three bodies and threw the ashes into the sea, to prevent the appearance of any martyr-cult devoted to their remains. The riot was caused by George's remark, as he passed the temple of the city's Fortune, 'How long shall this sepulchre stand?' The Christians of Alexandria, who could have protected him, according to Ammianus who tells the story, were only too glad to get rid of George, and lifted not a finger to help him.

Julian confined himself to admonishing the citizens of Alexandria, and his letter is a model of how to condemn an action while really, and obviously, approving of it. He speaks as if the whole city were responsible for the murder, and pagan. 'If you do not revere Alexander, your founder, and even more than him the great god, the most holy Serapis, how is it that you took no thought at least for your community, for humanity, for decency? I will add that you took no thought for me either . . . The proper course was for you to reserve for me the decision concerning the wrongdoers. But perhaps your anger and rage led you astray . . .' He then lists George's crimes. 'Your people dare to tear a man in pieces as dogs tear a wolf, and then are not ashamed to lift to the gods their hands still dripping with blood! But, you will say, George deserved this kind of treatment. Yes indeed, and I might even perhaps say that he deserved an even worse and more cruel fate. Yes, you will say, and on your account. With this I too agree; but if you should say by your hands, I no longer agree.' 'It is your good fortune, men of Alexandria, that this offence of yours took place in my reign'— good fortune indeed: in 390, under Theodosius I, three thousand inhabitants of Thessalonica were massacred on the emperor's orders for lynching an official; a terrible contrast with Julian's mild admonition to 'his citizens of Alexandria'.

Yet Julian had no wish to create martyrs: quite the contrary, as he himself states in a number of letters. Thus, to an official: 'I swear by the gods that I do not wish the Galilaeans to be killed or unjustly beaten or suffer any other harm; I do definitely assert, however, that the god-fearing must be preferred to them. For through the folly of the Galilaeans nearly everything has been overturned, but through the favour of the gods are we all preserved. Wherefore we ought to honour the gods and the god-fearing, both men and cities.' Even popular lynchings of Christians must be stopped. Gregory of Nazianzus complains sourly of Julian's refusal to allow Christians the honour of martyrdom. Therefore, apart from the execution of a few Christian soldiers for mutiny, and well-attested lynchings (see also Chapters IV and VI), stories of martyrdom under Julian are to be viewed with scepticism. Reason, said Julian, was the best weapon.

As he was an emperor who had pretensions as a writer, Julian put pen to paper to promote paganism. This was later on in his reign, when he was at Antioch, and his hatred of a Christian Church that refused to die gracefully or even show signs of distress was becoming increasingly bitter. In the manner of learned pagans, such as Celsus and Porphyry, who had attacked Christianity in previous centuries, he wrote a full-scale indictment of Christian beliefs, borrowing many of his arguments from those earlier writers. He called his work *Against the Galilaeans*, this being the name he derisively gave the Christians, implying that they were a sect from a little corner of an unimportant province. He began: 'It is well, I think, to set forth to all mankind the reasons by which I was convinced that the fabrication of the Galilaeans is a fiction of men composed by wickedness.' And he proceeded to compare the doctrines of Plato (in the *Timaeus*) and the Jews (in Genesis) about the Creation, naturally to the detriment of the latter; other beliefs of the Greeks and Jews about God are also compared in the same way. The healing-god Asklepios is put forward, as in the *Hymn to King Helios*, as a pagan saviour parallel (and of course superior) to Christ: 'He sets upright souls that are sinful and bodies that are sick.' Then Julian castigated the Christians for failing to adhere to the ancestral worship of the Jews. Here he shows a very characteristic Roman sentiment, the glorification of *mos maiorum*, ancestral traditions, and utter abhorrence of anything new.

This work, we are told, did succeed in shaking the faith of many Christians, and several Christian writers took it upon themselves to refute it, notably Cyril of Alexandria as late as the fifth century. He wrote a long and detailed answer to it, quoting long passages and summarizing much of the rest. It is to Cyril's refutation that we owe our knowledge of Julian's work, for the original has not survived. That Cyril thought it worth his while to compose an answer, so long after Julian's death, shows how well that emperor, with his inside knowledge of what he was attacking, aimed his shafts at the faith of the intelligent Greek Christians for whom he was writing. Apart from that, we cannot judge the work, since we do not possess it in its entirety, and Cyril is known to have omitted abusive parts and those which he thought especially dangerous.

We can get some idea of these from a cynical misrepresentation of the Christian message to be found in a passage of another of Julian's writings, a satire called *The Caesars*. In this, he caricatures most of the preceding Roman emperors, whom he pictures as invited to a heavenly banquet and then judged by the gods. Julius Caesar is full of overweening ambition, Augustus is like a chameleon, Tiberius is grim and covered with scars from his debauches, Caligula and Nero, together with other wicked emperors, are hurled down to Tartarus, Claudius is lost without his freedmen and his wife Messalina, Hadrian is searching for his beloved boy Antinous, and so on. The gods send for Alexander the Great, and the judgement begins. Alexander, Caesar, Augustus, Trajan and Constantine have to yield the first prize to Marcus Aurelius, the emperor who was a Stoic philosopher, and Julian's hero and pattern. The writer treats Diocletian well, though without giving him any special honours. Constantine he ridicules, particularly at the end, when the emperors who had contended for the prize choose their guardian god. He makes Constantine run to Luxury and Prodigality; 'There too he found Jesus dwelling, proclaiming to all men: "He that is a seducer, he that is a murderer, he that is accursed and infamous, let him approach with confidence! For I shall wash him with this water and shall straightway make him clean. And if he should again fall into those same sins, let him just beat his breast and smite his head, and I shall make him clean again." ' Presumably *Against the Galilaeans* contained passages that were similarly malicious.

Religious Minorities

Side by side with his attacks on the Christians, Julian continued his wooing of possible supporters. There was in the Roman Empire, mainly in the East, an ethnic minority of considerable importance, the Jews, who had every reason to hate the Christians as a breakaway sect that had perverted their ancient doctrines. Around the beginning of 363 Julian accordingly wrote to them granting them permission to rebuild the Temple in Jerusalem, at State expense, and he appointed his friend Alypius to organize the work. The rebuilding would have an important side-effect: it would prove Jesus wrong. For he had predicted that the Temple would be destroyed and remain desolate. Julian had other reasons as well for approving of the Jews, because their 'tribal God' fitted neatly into his system of national gods subordinate to the supreme deity, on which he touches in *Against the Galilaeans*. Furthermore, 'the Jews agree with the pagans, apart from believing that there is only one God ... The rest is in a way common to us both—temples, precincts, altars, purifications, and certain precepts, in which we differ from each other either not at all or only slightly.' The Jews could only sacrifice in the Temple, and he would be churlish, if not impious, not to help them to start sacrifices again. We have a letter of his to the Jewish community, abolishing a levy which they paid. He finishes it with a request to them to pray for him, 'in order that, when I have successfully concluded the war with Persia, I may rebuild by my own efforts the holy city of Jerusalem, which for many years you have longed to see inhabited, and may bring settlers there, and in it may glorify with you the Most High God.'

Julian wrote this letter at about the same time as the Temple rebuilding decree. That project, however, failed miserably. The Jews set about the work with the greatest enthusiasm, adding their private donations to the fund. But a great earthquake shook the area, and some of the builders were crushed beneath a collapsing portico. Such was the panic that the enterprise was abandoned.

To what other minorities could Julian appeal? Was there any chance of an alliance between the pagans and Christian heretics? The Donatists in Africa (see Chapter IV) thought so. The exiled members of the sect, at the beginning of 362, addressed a petition to Julian begging permission to return to their cities, take over their churches, and resume their worship. This we learn from the accusations of St. Augustine and Bishop Optatus, later on. Permission was granted, and the Donatists fell on the Church like ravening wolves to dismember it, according to the highly coloured account of Optatus. There was a little bloodshed in some places when they took over, from the Catholics, the churches that had once been theirs. At Tipasa in Mauretania a number of officials are said to have been present when this happened, including the governor with his insignia. It is just possible that Julian could have directed his African governors and their subordinates to assist the Donatists, but if he had, there would probably have been more than one isolated case.

These were almost the only schismatics or heretics by favouring whom Julian could hope to further his purposes. The Arians had been in the ascendant under Constantius, after all. But the eastern sect of the Novatians, whose church in Constantinople had been moved bodily by its congregation when under threat of destruction in the reign of Constantius, was allowed to take possession of its former site and rebuild it. This would have been popular, for the moving of an entire church would have created a lot of interest and sympathy in the capital city.

Julian's Supporters

The leading pagans who were Julian's natural supporters reacted in different ways to the fulfilment of their hopes. Philosophers and orators flocked to the court, many at Julian's express invitation. Chief among these were Maximus of Ephesus and Priscus the philosopher from Athens; the hierophant of Eleusis, priest of Demeter and Persephone and conductor of the Mysteries, had joined Julian in Gaul, like Priscus. The orator Himerius was another who attached himself to the court. But not all responded to Julian's invitations. Chrysanthius, an associate of Maximus, pleaded contrary omens as an excuse for his refusal. Julian had even written to the man's wife Melitta asking her to urge her husband to accept, but in vain. He 'was suspicious about the refusal of the invitation,' but nevertheless appointed Chrysanthius and Melitta high priest and priestess of Lydia, the province in Asia Minor where they lived. Their behaviour in this office was also very cautious and did little to upset anyone. Clearly this pair had an eye to the future and, rightly as it turned out, were doubtful how long the present state of affairs would last.

Themistius of Constantinople, the court philosopher and panegyrist who had found such favour with Constantius (Chapter IV), also had no intention of jeopardizing his position by over-enthusiasm on Julian's accession. Accordingly he held no office under him, but he wrote a panegyric of him which has perished, and maintained cordial relations with the pagan emperor, with whom he was already in correspondence when Julian was made Caesar. Julian wrote again to Themistius when he became sole emperor, expressing his sense of unfitness for the great task of government laid upon him, and his wish to lead instead the life of a contemplative philosopher, which Plato and Aristotle set above all other lives. Themistius answered and Julian replied, in a letter that has come down to us with his other writings. He begins by stressing again his inequality to the task: 'By your recent letter you have increased my fears, pointing out an enterprise in every way more difficult. You say that God has placed me in the same position as Heracles and Dionysus in olden times who, being both philosophers and kings, purged almost the whole earth and sea of the evils abounding in them.' It is as though, he continues, he were a sailor finding it difficult to cross the Bosphorus, and being told that he would have to sail instead across the Mediterranean and into the Atlantic. The reason for his unwillingness to rule is not fear of work, but his dread of being as totally exposed to the whims of Fortune as the statesman has to be. What Julian says on the subject of Fortune has a grim air of unconscious prophecy. He quotes extensively from the *Laws* of Plato and the *Politics* of Aristotle, the latter 'to show you that I do not altogether neglect his writings'— Aristotle to an Aristotelian philosopher. The main burden of the quotations is that virtually no man is fit to rule his fellow men, and government should therefore be entrusted to demi-gods. 'But ... my dear friend, worthy of every honour I can give, ... you said that you praise a life of action above the philosophic life,' and Julian goes on to restate, with appropriate arguments, his belief that a philosopher confers more benefit on mankind than does a man of action. In conclusion he prays for good fortune and wisdom and for the support of philosophers, and says that whether his reign turns to good or ill, it will be God's doing. Here again his Christian upbringing shows through. It was not in general a pagan tendency to give God the glory.

When Julian moved his headquarters to Antioch in the middle of 362, to prepare on the spot for the Persian expedition, he found there the sophist whose lectures in Nicomedia he had been forbidden to attend— Libanius. It is Libanius himself who tells the story of their relationship in his autobiography. They had, it seems, lost touch in the intervening period, but as Julian rode into Antioch, he caught sight of Libanius in the cortège of welcoming citizens, and said: 'When shall I hear you speak?' But a person unknown, possibly Maximus, persuaded Julian to slight Libanius, and he was not invited to any of the numerous sacrifices made by Julian, daily in the palace gardens, and in various temples. He could have gone uninvited like many another, but hurt pride kept him away. He may, too, have disapproved of the more lurid of Julian's religious practices—his own brand of paganism was far closer to the reasoned worship of earlier centuries, with a strong literary flavour. The good offices of Priscus restored the emperor's favour, and he sent an invitation at last. Thereafter Julian often sent for him— Libanius made it plain that he would not go unsolicited. 'Our fellowship consisted of discussion of oratory, of praise for his successes and criticism of his oversights,' he says. Julian offered him an honorary quaestorship, but Libanius declined it. Libanius wrote a speech asking for the rehabilitation of one Aristophanes of Corinth, a zealous pagan whose fortunes had been shipwrecked under Constantius (he had been involved in the Scythopolis treason trials in 359 (Chapter IV)). This was an instant success with Julian, and Libanius gained his object. When Julian entered on his consulship in 363, Libanius was asked to make a speech in honour of the occasion. During the declamation Julian rose to his feet in his excitement and admiration. In the *Misopogon* (see below) he made a delicate reference to Libanius as an Antiochene 'dear to Hermes and to me, an excellent craftsman of speeches.' After a last dinner at the palace before Julian left for Persia, he told Libanius: 'By your eloquence you are reckoned among the orators, but by your actions you are enrolled among the philosophers'—the highest possible praise from a monarch to whom philosophy was all. Yet, unlike Maximus and Priscus, Libanius seems never to have been one of the innermost circle that helped to dictate Julian's policy. He had every reason, though, to be grateful to the 'crowned sophist'. Nearly all Julian's nominees in office were cultured men, products of *paideia* like himself. Thus education was at a premium, and in his reign Libanius' beloved rhetoric, and philosophy, flourished like the green bay-tree.

One cannot but admire the character of Libanius, marred though it was by certain weaknesses, vanity above all. He had a very grand and noble conception of the role of the sophist in the city and the State. It was the duty of the orator to put his city's case when it presented a petition and to defend it when attacked; to counsel and if necessary reprove the sovereign; to further justice and protest against injustice at all levels, wherever found; and by his eloquence to work for the good of all men. Nor was it just theoretical: again and again, in his voluminous works (64 speeches and over 1,500 letters, together with numerous sophistic works such as declamations), we find him taking up the cause of the oppressed. He was no respecter of persons, and would write a speech on behalf of a baker as readily as a panegyric of a governor. And, although he identified himself completely with the pagan cause, his religious tolerance was such that under Julian he gave asylum in his house to one wronged Christian, and protested against the harrying of others. Thus the rhetorician's role received its most definite shape in a society whose fabric was being revolutionized by Christianity. It was on the bishops, as advocates of their city and advisers of monarchs, that the mantle of the rhetoricians was so soon to fall.

Julian's principal supporter in Rome was a leading senator named Vettius Agorius Praetextatus. He is one of the characters in the *Saturnalia* of Macrobius, in which a group of pagan senators is depicted as meeting in the houses of certain of their number, on the successive days of the winter festival of the Saturnalia, to discuss various aspects of pagan religion. We now know that this work was written well on into the fifth century, so it cannot be relied upon to be accurate in its representation of the characters. But the speech ascribed to Praetextatus in the *Saturnalia* does accord very well with what we know of him from other sources. He discourses on the nature of the Sun-God, whom he calls Apollo, and proceeds to identify with him Liber Pater, Mars, Mercury, Aesculapius, Hercules, Salus, Isis, Serapis, Adonis, Attis, Osiris, Horus, Nemesis, Pan, Saturn, Jupiter, and the Assyrian Adad: a magnificent total of seventeen deities, all assimilated to the Sun! There is no trace of Neoplatonism, but otherwise how close is the thought to that of Julian in his promotion of solar theology. Julian appointed Praetextatus governor of Achaea (the Roman province of Greece), and he spent some time with the emperor in Constantinople. In 364, probably still in his official character of proconsul of Achaea, he appealed successfully against the prohibition, by the Emperors Valentinian and Valens, of nocturnal rites and sacrifices, which prevented the celebration of the great Greek mysteries, including those of Eleusis. He was city prefect of Rome in 367–8, and two of his official actions are connected with paganism. He restored the 'Portico of the Gods Assembled' in the Forum (which can still be seen at the foot of the Capitoline hill): this was clearly an expression of his belief in the unity of the Deity. And he gave orders that secular buildings that were joined on to pagan temples should be pulled down, to restore the dignity of the temples. Praetextatus was leader of the pagan cause and head of the pagan circle in Rome till his death in 384. His example, in holding a large number of priesthoods (including that of priest of the Sun, significantly enough), and in being an initiate of Mithraism, of the cults of Isis and Cybele, and of other oriental religions, was followed by most of the pagan Roman aristocracy. Through the medium of Praetextatus, some of Julian's ideas reached Rome.

When Julian was sent to Gaul as Caesar, he had as mentor in the conduct of affairs of State one Saturninius Secundus Salutius (or Sallustius). It was a particularly happy choice, as Salutius, a native of Gaul, was an experienced statesman and a devout pagan, and the two speedily became great friends. But machinations of Julian's ill-wishers at court effected his recall in 359. Julian was desolate, and 'felt as much anguish as when at home he first left his tutor,' Mardonius. To cheer himself up, he wrote *A Consolation to Himself upon the Departure of the Excellent Sallust,* in which he speaks of their friendship, asking: 'In the future to what friend can I look as well-disposed as you? . . . Who will give me wise advice, criticize me with goodwill, give me strength for noble actions without arrogance and conceit, and use frankness after removing the bitterness from the words?' To console themselves, they must consider the stories of separated friends of olden times, and the precepts of philosophy. The 'ancient history' is somewhat artificial, and curiously suited to the position of two friends apart in Gaul and Constantinople respectively. But the discourse as a whole is far from being artificial. Julian had lost his main confidant and friend, and lamented it sorely. Amid the talk of heroes and impossibly virtuous philosophers he shows, too, a surprisingly modern common sense, for instance: 'Never to give up hope and be worn down by fate, but to play the hero in extremes of toil and danger, does indeed seem to me more than human.' Modern also is his appreciation of the horrors of loneliness (surely a harking back to the years at Macellum): in his panegyric of the Empress Eusebia, also written in Gaul, he classes loneliness with the lack of the necessities of life as the two worst evils that can befall a man. He closes the *Consolation* with a prayer—addressed to Zeus, not by name but under certain of the god's titles—that all will go well with his dear Salutius.

Salutius was not forgotten when Julian came to power as Augustus. In 361 he was made praetorian prefect of the East, the most powerful and prestigious of the three praetorian prefectures. (Julian's other friend Sallust, mentioned above, was appointed prefect of the Gauls and consul for 363.) On Julian's death in Persia, Salutius was even offered the throne, but refused it on the score of ill health and old age. So great was his reputation for justice, moderation, loyalty and good administration that he was allowed to continue as prefect of the East for several years after this. Few men, after refusing a throne, could have escaped with their lives, let alone with the highest office in the land. Julian, it would appear, chose his highest officials well.

The Coinage

Julian was a man who left no stone unturned to further his ends. It is therefore a disappointment to find that his coinage was, in the main, very conservative and stereotyped. This is especially true of the gold and silver. While he was in Gaul after usurping the title Augustus, he briefly continued Constantian types. Later, during his campaign against Constantius, he minted gold coins that flattered the army and were apparently destined for paying it: they depict Courage with a captive and a trophy, and bear the legends VIRTVS EXERC. GALL. and VIRTVS EXERCITVS ROMANI (the Courage of the Gallic and Roman armies respectively). When he became emperor, he continued to strike very similar gold types, still aimed at the army, with the legend VIRTVS EXERCITVS ROMANORVM. Just a few of the *solidi* with this legend, minted in 363 at Antioch only, are consular issues, depicting Julian in consular dress either standing (usually) or enthroned.

His silver (like that of Constantius) displays a preoccupation, that in this case is almost exclusive, with Victory and *vota*. The *vota* coinages are mostly of the type with a wreath enclosing the *vota* inscription, the codified prayer for the next five or ten years of the emperor's reign.

Only in his bronze did Julian break new ground. He issued only two main bronze coinages, both probably in 363. One is a small coin with *vota* inscription in wreath, just as on the silver. The other was struck in a new large bronze denomination that harks back to Diocletian's coinage and also to that of Magnentius, and may have been an attempt to revalue the bronze coinage in the interests of the poorer classes, who were dependent on it. It bears the legend SECVRITAS REIPVB. (the Security of the State), and depicts a bull with two stars above its head. Many are the theories as to the signification of this creature. The traditional view, that it is the Apis bull whose discovery in Egypt was reported to Julian at Antioch in 362, is vitiated by the fact that Julian's bull is not the traditional image of Apis, which was invariably represented on Egyptian coins of the early Empire with a disc between its horns, a crescent on its side, and an altar before it. It is inconceivable that someone as respectful of tradition as Julian should have disregarded it. Moreover, this interpretation violates the convention whereby late Roman coin legends refer to the emperor himself. The most satisfactory explanation yet proposed interprets the device in an astrological sense. Julian was born in May, quite probably under the sign of Taurus, of which the bull, with the two stars symbolizing the constellation, would be a perfectly recognizable representation. Julian himself showed considerable interest in astrology, and so did large numbers of his contemporaries (see Chapters IV and VI). Both the emperor's birthdays, his real one and his 'birthday of empire' (*natalis imperii*), were celebrated by a festival and 'votive games', so the population at large would be well aware of the date of his birthday and, given the prevalence of astrology, of the sign of the zodiac under which he was born. The originality of this coinage, quite unlike any other in the fourth century, makes it likely that it was designed either by Julian himself or by someone close to him, and that it was struck with a purpose. Julian may well have been taking advantage of the popularity of astrology to advertise his pagan revival. It may have seemed to him a more subtle way to begin than by an immediate reversion to the old coin types with pagan deities. The brevity of his reign makes it uncertain whether or not he would have gone on to do this, as one would expect, had he lived, and it certainly deprived the Roman world—and us—of some interesting coins. We do know, however, that Julian began to grasp the possibilities offered by the coinage for pagan propaganda. (**10**)

There are signs, too, that here and there, at a lower level, supporters of his were trying to do the same in their own small way. At the mint of Arles, first a club and then an eagle appeared as part of the bronze mint mark, and only the first mark of Julian's reign had neither. The eagle was also incorporated in the marks used on most of the gold and silver from this mint. At Julian's death they abruptly disappeared, never to occur again. The eagle was the bird of Jupiter, but it also had general associations with Rome (though as Jupiter's bird). On coins it is almost invariably associated with the god. It seems an inescapable conclusion that the eagle on the Arles mint marks was honorific. And as the club used before it, being invariably the attribute of Hercules, was definitely pagan, so must the eagle have been. Both were evidently incorporated in the marks by a pagan mint-master (compare the Christian die-cutter at Siscia (Chapter IV)) who was a supporter of Julian and wished to contribute something, however small, to the promotion of the pagan revival. Is it accidental that the eagle and club were the respective attributes of the two most important deities of the Tetrarchy?

At certain other mints—Siscia, Sirmium, Thessalonica and Constantinople, and perhaps Nicomedia and Antioch—there was an unusually high concentration of palms and wreaths in mint marks on the Julianic bronze. At Siscia especially, there was a positive rash of palms. While these were part of the regular stock of tiny symbols added to mint marks, they were particularly appropriate to Julian, in that they were the attributes of Victory. Such a high incidence does seem suspicious, and may be the work of other supporters of Julian attempting to honour him.

The 'Beard-Hater'

Julian had hoped to make the great Syrian city of Antioch-on-the-Orontes his capital, a pagan capital that would rival the Christian capital of the East, Constantinople. He arrived at Antioch in July 362, and stayed there until the beginning of March 363, when he left to begin the Persian expedition on which he died (see Chapter II). During this period his relationship with the Antiochenes steadily worsened, and he left shaking the dust of Antioch off his feet and stating his intention of settling at Tarsus in Cilicia instead. Before he left, he answered the gibes and mocking verses, which the people of Antioch were composing and repeating about him, in a work entitled *Beard-Hater* (*Misopogon*), in which he started by satirizing himself and went on to attack Antioch for its ungratefulness. No absolute monarch, before or since, has ever done such a thing. If it was a little lowering to his imperial dignity, it says a great deal for his belief in the freedom of speech, when he could so easily have had the worst of his detractors silenced for ever.

What had gone wrong? It is difficult to be sure about apportioning the blame. Certain events had occurred to create friction, and Julian had been foolish in disdaining to court an easy popularity with the masses. He accuses them of frivolity and wanton living and too great love of horse-races and the theatre: he himself only goes to the hippodrome on festival days, and stays for just six races with a look of martyrdom on his face! As for theatres and dancers, 'I care less for such things', says he, 'than for frogs croaking in a pond.' And he upbraids them for flocking to the temples merely to applaud him instead of to pray to the gods.

When Julian arrived in Antioch, 'the populace in the theatre . . . shouted out: "Everything plentiful: everything dear!" ' There was a crisis in the provisioning of the city, but the course that it ran is not entirely clear. There was certainly a corn shortage, caused largely by the failure of that summer's crops after a terrible drought, as Julian himself says. The mustering of the army in the area, in preparation for the Persian campaign, and the arrival of the court, was the other basic cause. The latter would certainly have affected the prices of other commodities besides corn. Julian accused the rich of profiteering (at a meeting of the town council) and begged them to lower prices which they had artificially inflated. Nothing was done—the council in any case had insufficient powers—so Julian sent for large supplies of corn from other parts of Syria and from Egypt, and sold it in the market at a lower price than usual, fixing all other prices as well. This he did, says Ammianus, perhaps unfairly, in a bid for popularity. The result was inevitable: racketeers moved in, bought up much of the cheap corn, and sold it elsewhere for a huge profit. Other foodstuffs disappeared from the market because of the price-fixing. All this was only partly Julian's fault—there had been a similar corn crisis earlier, under his brother Gallus (Chapter II), and were to be others in the 380s. Corrective action must have been very difficult when the laws of economics were little understood. But hungry people are not the most reasonable of beings, and the whole business must have contributed greatly to his unpopularity.

The town council, that favoured nursling of Julian, also came in for some strong criticism in the *Misopogon*. As well as failing him in the matter of the corn supply, the councillors had divided among themselves, for their own profit, 3,000 lots of uncultivated land which Julian had given them at their request. When he decided to increase the numbers of the council by 200 men, he offered them as candidates the richest of the treasury and mint officials resident in Antioch—men who, under other emperors, would have got exemption from council duties. But instead of these they chose people of unsuitable character or inadequate means. They may well have been bribed by those whom Julian intended to serve, to let them off.

These issues set Julian and the city at loggerheads, and religious differences supervened and increased the bitterness. 'I have annoyed . . . many of you,' says Julian, 'I may almost say all, the council, the rich, the common people. The people, indeed, hate me for the most part, or rather all of them hate me because, having chosen "atheism", they see that I am devoted to the ancestral ordinances of the sacred rites; the powerful citizens hate me because they are prevented from selling everything at a high price; but all of you hate me on account of the dancers and the theatres.' From this passage and from the writings of Libanius it appears that the lower classes were almost exclusively Christian, and a goodly section of the upper classes as well, including part of the council. This explains why, when Julian hastened to Daphne, the suburb of Antioch where a famous temple of Apollo stood amid fragrant groves and waterfalls, to join in the celebration of a festival of the god, 'I pictured to myself the procession, as if seeing visions in a dream, sacrificial victims and libations and choruses in honour of the god, and incense, and the youths of the city gathered round the shrine, their souls arrayed with all holiness and they themselves decked out in white and splendid raiment. But when I passed within the precinct I found no incense nor cake nor beast for sacrifice . . . When I began to enquire what sacrifice the city intended to make in celebration of the annual festival in honour of the god, the priest said, "I have brought with me from my house a goose as an offering to the god, but the city this time has made no preparations." ' After this revealing incident, Julian delivered a wrathful harangue in the council, accusing each one of 'allowing his wife to carry everything out of the house to the Galilaeans,' and neglecting the gods.

Another event connected with this same temple at Daphne perhaps did more than anything to cause friction and mutual hatred. Under Gallus, the body of the martyred bishop of Antioch, St. Babylas, had been buried near the temple, and a shrine erected over it. The great temple of Apollo itself had become dilapidated. Julian restored the temple and, in October 362, ordered the removal of the body. The Church of Antioch accordingly took it back to the city, amid a great hymn-singing procession. That very night, the temple of Apollo was completely gutted by fire, and the beautiful gold and ivory statue of the god, the work of the Hellenistic sculptor Bryaxis, was destroyed. Julian drew the obvious conclusion and, while setting on foot a full investigation, ordered the closure of the new Great Church of Antioch, which Constantius had recently dedicated (see Chapter III). It is far from certain, however, whether the Christians really were responsible for the fire. The investigation was inconclusive, and Ammianus suggests that it may have been due to a votive candle which a pagan philosopher left burning. But few things could have been more calculated to arouse Julian's wrath.

Julian leaves an unforgettable picture of himself, as seen by the mocking Antiochenes. 'I will begin with my face. For though it is by nature none too handsome or well-favoured or endowed with the bloom of youth, I myself out of perversity and discontent have added to it this long beard of mine, to punish it, as it would seem, for none other reason than its not being handsome by nature. For the same reason I put up with the lice that run about in it as if it were a thicket for wild beasts . . . But you say that I ought to plait ropes from it. Well, I am ready to furnish them, provided that you are strong enough to pull them and their roughness does not do dreadful damage to your "unworn and tender hands" . . . But, as if the mere length of my beard were not enough for me, my head is dishevelled besides and I rarely have my hair cut or my nails, while my fingers are generally black from using a pen. And if you would like to learn something that is usually a secret, my breast is shaggy and covered with hair, like the breasts of lions who are kings of wild beasts.'

The city which he had grown to hate is also partly described in the same vein. Echoing Plato in the *Republic* (Book VIII), he says: 'Have you not even noticed what great independence there is among the citizens, even down to the asses and camels? The men who hire them out lead even these animals through the porticoes as if they were brides. For the unroofed alleys and the broad highways were not made for the use of pack-asses, I suppose, but they are provided merely for decoration and as an extravagance; and in their independence the asses like to use the porticoes, and no one keeps them out of any of these, lest he should rob them of their independence.'

The sparkling satire, however, is not kept up for long. The *Beard-Hater* is a muddled composition, less well constructed than Julian's other works. It is the outpourings from a deep well of bitterness, as he castigates the city for its ungratefulness. Certainly Antioch was a frivolous city: the Emperor Hadrian in the second century and Bishop John Chrysostom in the fourth reprove it for just the same vices as does Julian. Certainly a large proportion of the population was Christian

and unlikely to appreciate the pagan revival. In particular, the failure
of the *curia* to respond threatened to undermine the social basis of his
city-based programme of revival. But an emperor, however sorely
tried, has no business to fall out with one of his great capital cities. That
Julian did so was a tragic failure on his part. It was an embittered
Julian who left for Persia, while some in Antioch meditated sending an
embassy after him to plead for it, with Libanius as its spokesman. To
Tarsus did Julian indeed return, as he had threatened—but as a corpse.

The Monuments: (i) The Inscriptions

A survey of Julian's reign from the literary sources cannot give a complete picture of the realities of the situation. It is the monuments that
must reveal the physical pagan world of Julian and indicate more about
the reserves of public opinion on which he could draw. Considering the
brevity of Julian's reign, a disproportionately large number of honorific
inscriptions to him have survived. Many of these were inscribed, on
statue-bases or milestones, by the local councils. Antioch (and three
others in the East) apart, these bodies do seem to have responded with
enthusiasm to the pagan emperor with his programme for restoring the
cities and their ancient religion. The largest group comes from North
Africa, the diocese that has yielded the biggest harvest of inscriptions
in the entire Empire, partly for reasons of preservation, but also because
city life flourished there especially. At Casae a dedication described
Julian as 'restorer of liberty and Roman religion', 'abounding in every
kind of virtue'. Another, at Sua, set up a statue to him and his *numen*
or divine self. The council of Thibilis called him 'the restorer of rites',
that of Verecundae 'propagator of the name of Rome, restorer of
liberty'. A milestone in Mauretania even has a radiate crown above the
dedication to Julian, as a kind of counterblast to the chi-rho that was
beginning to be used as a Christian symbol on such inscriptions. (**19**)

Africa was not alone in greeting Julian's advent with enthusiasm.
Similar inscriptions have been found in Arabia, in Syria, at several
places in Asia Minor, in Thrace, at Mursa and elsewhere in Pannonia,
and in northern Italy and the Alps. A Pannonian milestone gives
an idea of the tenor of these. It praises Julian 'for blotting out the evils of
the past'. A very important dedication made by the provincial assembly
of Phoenicia (formed of delegates from the *curiae*) hails Julian as 'restorer of the temples, of the *curiae*, and of the State'. They all confirm
that there was still a great reservoir of paganism which Julian could tap
in the governing classes, all over the Empire.

The Monuments: (ii) Temples in Rome and Arabia

The accession of a pagan emperor to the throne naturally stimulated the building or reconstruction of a number of temples, although the brevity of his reign makes for difficulties in their identification. In the very heart of the Empire, Rome, a temple of unusual design, dedicated to the Syrian gods, was erected in their sanctuary that had been in existence since the first century on the hill of the Janiculum, just outside the city walls across the Tiber. It appears that the walled precinct of Jupiter Heliopolitanus, with its altar and cubicles for ablution, was razed, and the pool of sacred fish filled in, in the middle of the fourth century. It was perhaps one of the temples of Rome that fell victim to the anti-pagan edict of 341 (see Chapter IV): the centre of a strange, foreign, minority cult, it would have been an obvious target for attack by Christians acting under the aegis of the new law and possibly at the instigation of their bishop or of some of his clergy (there would have been no *official* action under pagan city prefects, and it was one of their number who obtained the *de facto* abrogation of the law). The site of the Syrian temple became a public park, adorned with porticoes and a fountain. Stone slabs inscribed with dedications to Jupiter Heliopolitanus (the god of Baalbek) were used as paving-stones. Some years elapsed, and then the reign of Julian would have offered an excellent opportunity for the community of Syrian worshippers to reassert their claim to the site and build a new temple. It was of quite different plan and orientation, forming a long rectangle with projections at each end. The central portion was occupied by an open court separating the temple proper from the 'chapel of the mysteries'. The temple, cut into the hillside on the west, was a small basilica with narthex, nave, and two side-aisles opening on to the nave through doorways in their solid walls: a place of mysterious darkness, penetrated only by shafts of light from the rising sun coming through the door and slit-windows in the narthex and falling on to the statues in three rock-cut niches at the back, emphasizing the solar character of the cult. A statue of Syrian Jupiter looked out from the central niche. At the other end of the court, the diamond-shaped 'chapel of the mysteries' enclosed a large triangular altar. Under and around the altar was a pagan 'reliquary' of sculptures: a Dionysus of gilded marble, an Egyptian Pharaoh of black basalt, and a relief of the Hours. Beneath the centre of the altar, in solitary state, lay the bronze figure of a goddess, her body wreathed by the coils of a snake; seven hens' eggs had been carefully placed between the coils. The bronze goddess—perhaps Atargatis—had been dedicated to the Palmyrene god Iarhibol. The building and furnishing of the temple throws a fascinating light on the diversity of cults that still flourished in mid-fourth-century Rome. (The final fate of the temple was another sack by Christians: before the end of the century it was pillaged and walled up by an official order, perhaps by the Christian city prefect Gracchus who destroyed a number of temples of oriental cults in 377.) (**22**)

Across the Empire in southern Syria (Roman Arabia), the fortunes of the temple of an unknown god at Deir el-Meshkûk followed a strikingly similar pattern. The small classical temple, built in A.D. 124, was actually converted into a church, probably at some time in the first half of the fourth century—Christianity was strong in this area, the Hauran (see Chapter VI). The next chapter in its chequered history is announced by the inscription in Greek carved upon the lintel: 'Under the rule of the Emperor Fl(avius) Cl(audius) Julianus Augustus the rites were restored, and the temple was rebuilt and consecrated in the year 256, on the 5th of Dystrus [i.e. March 362].' An altar, inscribed in similar lettering, seems also to belong to this period of the temple's existence. It was dedicated by one Soraimos or Suraim, freedman of a Julianus who, in the absence of any imperial titles, is probably not the apostate emperor. Beyond these bare facts there is nothing. But the frailty of the pagan revival here was amply demonstrated by the re-conversion of the temple into a church before the end of the fourth century. The front portico was walled up and the columns removed (the Julianic restoration was probably making good similar depredations and alterations). Monastic buildings were added in the sixth century, indicating that the temple given back under Julian to the pagan cult had fallen into the hands of his hated and despised adversaries, the antisocial monks.

The Monuments: (iii) The Corbridge Lanx

The Corbridge *Lanx*, an oblong silver charger 48 by 38 centimetres (19 by 15 inches), was fished out of the river Tyne in the eighteenth century, together with other silver vessels that have since disappeared. (They had perhaps been buried near the river, and were subsequently washed away in a flood.) The *lanx* is engraved with a scene showing figures from the cult of the Aegean island of Delos—Apollo and Artemis, Leto, Athene, and Asteria-Ortygia—with a temple at one side, and various symbolic creatures and objects below (the hound of Artemis and griffin of Apollo, etc.) and between the figures. It was made in the second half of the fourth century. (**20**)

As the scene is not merely a mythological one, but depicts the recipients of cult at a particular sanctuary, it would seem to be a product of Julian's interest in Delos: he sent there to consult the oracle before going on the Persian expedition. The dish was probably made at a centre near Delos, perhaps Ephesus on the coast of Asia Minor. It has been described as a 'commemorative propaganda-work', and was evidently ordered by a supporter of Julian, perhaps from a silversmith who was himself a pagan. It was possibly brought to the far diocese of Britain in the baggage of an official, perhaps by the very supporter of Julian who had it made. This intriguing document of the pagan revival shows how its emanations could reach the farthest corners of the Empire.

The Celtic Pagan Revival

In that same far diocese of Britain, two completely new sanctuaries are known to have been built in the 360s, at Lydney in Gloucestershire and Maiden Castle in Dorset. They were perhaps the latest temples to be built in the Roman Empire. Both were erected inside Iron Age hill-forts. At Maiden Castle, unoccupied from about A.D. 60, a circular, hut-like temple was constructed on the site of a native British hut of the same size and shape, at the head of the main street of what had been the British settlement, in about 360 or a little earlier. A road of approach had been built about 350. The siting and primitive structure of the temple make it a strong possibility that there was continuity of cult, though there is no proof. A little later, after 367, a Romano-Celtic temple of the most common type, with square *cella* or shrine, and a portico or enclosed ambulatory surrounding it on all four sides, was added about 12 metres (40 feet) away from the first temple. A rectangular priest's house completed the sanctuary, which continued to flourish till the fifth century, in the course of which it was abandoned. Large numbers of fourth-century coins, late pottery, and some cult objects were found in the temples.

At Lydney, an imposing temple complex, comprising guest house, baths and a long building (the *abaton*) as well as the temple, was built after A.D. 364. The temple itself was large (19 by 25 metres (60 by 80 feet)) and of unusual plan, with seven projecting chapels round the outside, and a separate and free-standing *cella* with three shrines. It was dedicated to Nodens, a Celtic god with Irish affinities. Soon after construction, most of the temple collapsed into a concealed hole in the limestone, but it was immediately rebuilt, with the addition of a mosaic floor and minor modifications. A strong wall was built round the precinct at some date later than the original construction. The temple was ravaged by fire and the whole site abandoned in about 395. During the mere thirty years of its existence, the sanctuary flowered astonishingly. Vast numbers of votive offerings were found, including 300 bronze bracelets, over 320 pins, many brooches, about 40 bronze spoons, etc., numerous bronze letters from votive inscriptions, as well as three inscriptions on stone, and a number of statuettes including the beautiful 'Lydney dog'. Coins numbering 746, excluding hoards, were found in the excavations by Sir Mortimer Wheeler in 1928, and most if not all of the 4,198 coins of the fourth century at Lydney Park came from the site. The coins, certainly offerings, must have been kept in a box on a shelf or in a niche high up on the wall inside the temple, and were scattered over the floor when the building collapsed in the fire. From the presence of large and elaborate baths and a large guest house it is clear that Lydney was a pilgrim sanctuary, and from the type of offerings it is equally clear that the cult was a healing cult—bracelets, pins and similar feminine offerings generally mean that relief in childbirth is sought or obtained, and a few votives, e.g. a statuette of a woman in childbirth, were directly connected with healing. The baths very likely had a religious significance and were used for ritual washing. The long building was for 'incubation', or sacred sleep in which healing dreams or instructions for a cure were sought. The side-chapels of the temple were also probably for this. (24)

The most anomalous aspect of what would otherwise appear to be an entirely native sanctuary is presented by the inscription on the mosaic floor of the temple, now lost. Paid for from the offerings of worshippers, it was commissioned by an officer in charge of a naval yard apparently in the Bristol Channel, with an official interpreter (into Celtic?) acting as clerk of works. Appropriately enough, the mosaic depicted fish and sea-monsters. In addition, one of the stone inscriptions is a dedication by a soldier who was probably attached to the same Bristol Channel yard. Important dedications made by military personnel give a new slant to the whole proceedings. While they can hardly be said to make the building of the temple an official venture, they do show that it had patrons of greater wealth and status than the run-of-the-mill peasant offerings would suggest. Lydney's status as a water sanctuary overlooking the Severn estuary makes it possible that the initiative for its creation did come from pagans serving in the naval yard there, who looked on it as their own special sanctuary.

Lydney and Maiden Castle stand alone at present in the lateness of their building dates, though discoveries at Rainsborough Camp in Northamptonshire make it highly probable that there was a temple of similar date in that hill-fort as well. But they belong to a series of British temples in Iron Age hill-forts of which the others are Blaise Castle in Gloucestershire, Bow Hill and Chanctonbury Ring in Sussex, Cold Kitchen Hill in Wiltshire, and South Cadbury in Somerset. (Only at Chanctonbury has an actual temple structure been identified: the others are inferred from finds.) South Cadbury and Blaise Castle were built in the first century A.D., Bow Hill a little later. There may have been a continuity of cult from the pre-Roman period at these three temples. Chanctonbury and Cold Kitchen Hill are of the third century and may have been part of the same phenomenon, at an earlier stage, as Lydney and Maiden Castle: namely the Celtic Revival or Celtic Renaissance.

These names indicate the re-emergence of native, pre-Roman art forms and religion, in the later second and third centuries A.D. From the Roman conquest till the mid second century, imported art forms, whether Graeco-Roman or oriental, were dominant in the Celtic lands (Britain, Gaul, Spain, and the Danube provinces), but thereafter there was a reassertion of Celtic styles in isolated regions. In the religious sphere, the Graeco-Roman pantheon began to give way in popularity to native deities like Epona, the goddess of horses and mules; her temples flourished again, and there were more representations of her in art. There may even have been a slight increase in the use of the Celtic language, and more native names and place-names were used in the late Empire.

A main reason for the revival of Celtic art forms was the decline in economic life as a result of the barbarian invasions of the later second and third centuries, when markets, buyers and producers were cut off from each other. People from the towns settled in the country and became customers of the local craftsmen, who had gone on using traditional Celtic designs, and their clientele was augmented also because of the general impoverishment, as fewer people could afford the smarter Romanized wares. These, too, declined in quality as a result, and so offered less competition.

These economic causes, however, will not explain the religious revival, except in so far as the country temples received more worshippers because of the influx of town-dwellers into the countryside. The basic cause of the whole phenomenon was that the great wave of Romanization, which followed the Roman conquest and lasted for well over a century, had spent its force. It was in any case rather superficial, affecting principally the towns and rural upper classes. A reaction against Roman ways was setting in during this period in most parts of the Empire, but in some, for example fourth-century Africa, it was associated with Christianity in the Donatist movement (Chapter IV). The Celtic Renaissance, on the other hand, was very definitely connected with paganism, in its religious manifestation.

It seems likely enough that the third-century foundation of temples inside the hill-forts at Chanctonbury and Cold Kitchen Hill represents a stage in that renaissance, while Lydney and Maiden Castle, where astonishing activity was crammed into a few years, were part of its final flowering. It was all due to a general renewal of interest in hill-forts as strong places, both materially and spiritually, in troubled times. It is significant that several Welsh ones were reoccupied and even refortified in the third and fourth centuries. There were doubtless legends of heroic deeds attached to such forts, perhaps involving divine aid, and

they would also have had their cults in pre-Roman times. Traditions oı
sanctity would not have died out, and there may have been unobtrusive
continuity of cult. Prehistoric barrows, too, began to attract worship,
and the temple of Brean Down was actually built beside one in about
340 (see Chapter VI).

The Celtic Revival had, of course, nothing to do with Julian. Was
the building of Lydney and Maiden Castle, therefore, quite unconnec-
ted with his own religious revival? The establishment of the round
temple at Maiden Castle probably before his reign might suggest that
it was, but the knowledge that a pagan emperor was once again on the
throne, one who actively encouraged paganism, must have given a
certain impetus to the planning of the main foundation. This is especially true of Lydney, where officers of the fleet may well have played
some part. Although they were actually founded in the period of
religious toleration under Julian's successors Valentinian and Valens,
it must be remembered that Julian's main message was to the cities and
city pagans, and there would have been a lapse of time before anything
of its effect reached the countryside. It would, in any case, have taken a
fair time to plan the foundation of a sanctuary like Lydney. So it is
likely that there was some connection between the establishment of these
late temples and the Julianic revival of paganism.

Chapter VI

Christian and Pagan Life and Art

The religious life of the fourth century is remarkable above all for its variety, a natural consequence of the addition of flourishing Christianity to the existing multiplicity of pagan cults. The main feature that had marked out Christianity and prevented it from being regarded as just another of the oriental cults, like Mithraism and the cults of Cybele and Isis, that had become popular over most of the Empire, was its exclusiveness, echoing that of Judaism from which it sprang. But, whereas the Jews had managed to find a *modus vivendi* within the Empire, and were never officially persecuted, it was, as we have seen (in Chapters I and II), different with Christianity, whose missionary character combined with its intransigent rejection of idolatry and its claims to absolute truth to form much more of a threat to the pagan established religious order, the *pax deorum* or 'peace of the gods'. The Christian's claim of unique rightness and thus of superiority over his ignorant pagan brethren must have caused much hostility, both before and especially after the Peace of the Church in 313, when the astonishing turnabout in the fortunes of Christianity added a new and implicitly threatening tone to such claims, now made by the emperor himself.

From then on, the pagans were increasingly on the defensive, subjected in their turn to threats of persecution, both at the imperial level and locally. It was not until later on, at the end of the fourth century, that most of the attacks on temples took place. Some are described in such works as the *Life of St. Martin* of Tours and, from the opposite point of view, in an important discourse addressed by Libanius of Antioch to the Emperor Theodosius, complaining of the destructive activities of bands of monks; and it is sometimes archaeologically possible to discern the probable, if rarely certain, hand of Christian wreckers in the final destruction of a temple, for instance in Gaul and Germany. But some attacks of this kind took place under Constantius or even earlier. In Britain two temples of Mithras on Hadrian's Wall, at Carrawburgh and Rudchester, were carefully destroyed, probably on the orders of a Christian commanding officer, as early as c. 315. Another military Mithraeum, at Caernarvon, was smashed and burnt down when the fort was regarrisoned in about 350. An attack was also made on the richly furnished civilian Mithraeum in London, some time in the early fourth century, forcing the worshippers to hide their most precious images, including beautiful heads of Mithras, Minerva and Serapis, beneath the floor. This attack is unlikely to have had any official character: most probably it was instigated by the local bishop, in the manner of Bishop George's remark about the temple at Alexandria (see Chapter V).

Under Julian, the pagans of Alexandria took their revenge, lynching George and his accomplices. And not only in Alexandria, but in a number of cities of Syria and Palestine too, bloodthirsty attacks on the local Christian community and its places of worship were mounted. Curiously enough, these cities run in a line along the western side of Syria and down into Palestine, revealing the existence of a powerful pagan 'backwater' in these otherwise generally well-Christianized provinces (a phenomenon perhaps connected with the fall of Palmyra in 273 and the subsequent shift of trade-routes to the north, occasioning a certain decline). At Heliopolis in Syria, the great pagan sacred city of Baalbek, and at Askalon and Gaza in Palestine (the latter the citadel of the great god Marnas, whose hold over the population was only loosed with great difficulty by an energetic bishop c. 400), groups of priests and nuns were put to death with horrible savagery, by filling their disembowelled bodies with barley and feeding them to pigs. Unless the sources wrongly attach the same incident to the three cities, the repetition of such bizarre methods would indicate that the pagan rabble of one got the idea from that of another. At Arethusa in Syria it was the aged Bishop Marcus himself who was the victim of vengeful pagans: on his refusal to restore a temple which he had demolished under Constantius and replaced with a church, the pagans tortured him in various recherché ways, pricking him with pens and suspending him in a cage, smeared with honey to attract wasps. Although his tormentors finally let him go, in admiration of his courage, Marcus died as a result of his sufferings. The bishop of the neighbouring city of Epiphania (modern Hama) also died under Julian, apparently of shock on hearing that the local pagans had gone in procession to the sound of flutes and drums to his cathedral church and installed an idol there—perhaps of Cybele or Dionysus, in whose cults the music of the flute was normally used. At Emesa, too (modern Homs), a little further up the river Orontes, the pagans set up an image of Dionysus in the newly-erected great church, and rededicated it to the god (did one city copy the other?). They also set fire to some churches. Another fire-raising incident took place at Berytus (modern Beirut), where one Magnus, a pagan advocate and ex-pupil of Libanius, burned down the church, and was ordered by Julian's Christian successor, Jovian, to rebuild it at his own expense. The apparently single-handed action of this lone pagan contrasts strongly with the mass pagan riots in the other cities mentioned: certainly the cosmopolitan coastal city of Berytus, legal and juristic centre of the Eastern Empire, was much more of a Christian city by this period.

Incidents like these—and there were at least two more in this region, at Sebaste Samaria in Palestine and at Caesarea Paneas on its northern border—reveal a great bitterness of feeling on the part of pagans in at least some parts of the largely Christian provinces of the east Mediterranean, surrounded as they were with flourishing and triumphant Christianity, with its outward and visible signs of multiplying churches, ostentatious processions, and the like. Where they were still strong enough to take avenging action for their past humiliations under Christian emperors, without too much risk of effective resistance on the part of the Christians, they did so, sometimes with a considerable degree of savagery. Yet it is certain that these and other outbreaks of violence between pagans and Christians were isolated incidents in long years of peaceful coexistence. With members of the two religions inextricably intertwined in social life as they were, it could not be otherwise.

For this state of hostility was by no means the norm. Christians and pagans lived together in the same town or village, in the same street, even in the same house, watching and even joining in each other's festival processions through the streets, accepting each other's differing religious views with a good or ill grace. The letters of Libanius, equally courteous to pagan and Christian alike, give an impression of this mutual tolerance at a high level. Libanius, a convinced pagan, was a particularly shining example of tolerance, witness his letters written in defence of Christians when they were being harried under Julian, and his sheltering of one such persecuted Christian, a man called Eusebius, in his own house (as described in Chapter V). He had Christians in his family—cousins—and Christians among his pupils. Innumerable families throughout the Empire at any one time must have been divided in their religion. In the course of this chapter, we shall find that churches sprang up beside temples and worship proceeded at both, that Christians and pagans were buried in the same family catacomb, and that workshops and factories manufactured articles decorated with pagan or secular or Christian motifs, and sometimes a mixture, to display to customers of different faiths and tastes. It is all concrete evidence of the state of coexistence that was the normal condition of religious and social life in the early and mid fourth century. The Christian rejection of the world that took the form of monasticism, and was to add a further element of intransigence to the Christian view of paganism, was only just getting under way in this period, in certain of the eastern provinces (see below).

Temples and Churches

All over the Empire, temples of multifarious kinds—large and small, opulent and simple, urban and rustic—had been built for the purposes of numerous different pagan cults, over a period ranging from three centuries in parts of the West to eight, nine, or ten centuries or even longer in much of the East. They had been paid for in a variety of ways, either by the whole town or village community acting through its council, or by the subscriptions of a confraternity, or by rich individuals from emperors down, or occasionally by the accumulated donations of pilgrims and revenues from sacred lands. Some towns had literally dozens of temples, and not only the large cities—for instance the little town of Dougga (ancient Thugga) in Africa had at least twenty classical temples, while the native sanctuary of the Altbachtal at Trier contained over seventy simpler ones; and many a rural sanctuary in Britain and Gaul boasted two, three or more temples. By the fourth century little but repairs and reconstructions remained to be done to create and embellish the physical context of pagan worship.

For the Christians, on the other hand, as they finally emerged from the Great Persecution into the light of day, almost everything in the way of buildings for public worship had to be created from nothing. Up to this time they had made do with simple house-churches, often adapted from a house already existing, with just one large room fulfilling the function of the church proper, and neighbouring ones devoted to a variety of purposes: baptism, *agape*-meals (meals of fellowship), the teaching of catechumens, storage of clothing and food to be distributed to the poor, lodgings for clergy, and the like. In addition small *martyria* were built over the graves of martyrs in the cemeteries, generally consisting merely of a small enclosure, sometimes with an apse or portico, containing a stone table for commemorative banquets over the actual tomb, like those found at Salonae in Dalmatia. A modest room with a crypt was added to one of these under Constantine. Similar buildings have been found in Spain and Hungary, and numerous *martyrium*-enclosures, of varying dates, in the cemeteries of North African cities such as Tipasa. Some more pretentious structures, based on the architecture of pagan mausolea, were erected over some of the catacombs at Rome, *c.* 300 or later. But the true heyday of the martyr-cult did not begin until the late fourth century, although its roots were already well established.

The best-preserved and most certain example of a pre-Constantinian house-church is the one found at Dura-Europos, an important fort on the Euphrates, and securely dated to the mid third century. It is arranged round a small courtyard, and the baptistery is lavishly if crudely frescoed with Biblical scenes, to impress and instruct the newly converted. A number of the early churches of Rome—e.g. S. Clemente, S. Cecilia in Trastevere and S. Prisca—have Roman houses underneath that may also have been house-churches. (Apart from the Dura house-church, much of the small amount known about these buildings, and the uses to which the various rooms were put, comes from a record of inquisition proceedings made in Africa at the time of the Great Persecution. It is this, for instance, that reveals that quantities of clothing to give to the poor were kept there.) But most of these were humble and inconspicuous buildings, ideally suited to the condition of secrecy in which the pre-Constantinian Churches lived out their lives, but inadequate, both in size and in the lack of any public and monumental character, to meet the new situation. We have already seen, in Chapter III, how Constantine's lavish generosity proceeded to fulfil this need in the imperial capitals and the Holy Places. He also gave instructions for the repair or replacement at State expense, or even enlargement, of churches ruined in the Great Persecution. With this encouragement, the larger and richer Churches, sometimes, no doubt, with the additional patronage of wealthy and important individuals, began to make their own moves towards acquiring more suitable premises for their worship and missionary activity.

It is at Aquileia, important port and route centre on the north-east border of Italy, set on the great highway running at the foot of the Alps where it rounds the head of the Adriatic, that one of the earliest such initiatives of which we have record was made, under the guidance of the energetic Bishop Theodorus, who is commemorated by an inscription on the mosaic floor of the church which he built. It took the form of a double basilica, like the Constantinian cathedral of Trier, with an atrium or open court and perhaps already a baptistery in between, built over the remains of two houses and a street. Each of the two parallel churches measured about 37 by 20 metres (roughly 120 by 65 feet). It is the sheer size of Bishop Theodore's edifice, and the beauty and variety of the huge spread of mosaics that floored it, that are so remarkable at this early date; for his episcopate began in 308 and ended c. 320. It was thus one of the very first churches to be built after the Peace of the Church. The North Church appears to have been constructed first and used as the church proper, for the celebration of the Eucharist, until the South Church was complete. Then it was probably used as the *catechumeneum*, for the crowds of new converts that must have been expected, while the South Church became in its turn the main church. The mosaic floors of both churches are divided into rectangular sections. Those in the North Church are almost entirely decorative, with geometric sections and, in the eastern part, a rich design of animals and birds in panels, including a kid with a basket of eggs, a goat with the shepherd's crook, a family of partridges in a tree, a parrot and a lobster. Sheep and goats were so consistently used in early Christian art to represent faithful Christians that it is possible that some of these panels are symbolic: the goat with the crook, for example, might represent the bishop, and eggs were a very ancient symbol of life and resurrection. One panel is certainly symbolic: it has the picture, unique except for a copy of it added later to the floor of the South Church, of a fight between a cock and a tortoise, with a vase as the prize. The cock was regarded by the ancients as the bird of light, and the tortoise as a creature of darkness, and the scene may allude to the recent triumph of the Church over the evil forces of pagan persecution, or to the struggle against heresy (Arianism?). Several inscriptions are picked out in mosaic, including a salutation of Bishop Theodore, and a donor inscription revealing that one Januarius paid for a considerable area of mosaic.

In the South Church, too, some of the sections of mosaic are purely decorative or just mildly symbolic: geometric designs, portrait busts of donors, various birds and animals, wild and tame—sheep, goats, stags, hares, storks, parrots, etc. But larger figures include a Good Shepherd, and the unique depiction of the Eucharistic Victory. Here Victory holds her normal attributes of wreath and palm, but is accompanied by baskets of bread and grapes, while other figures in surrounding panels may form a procession bringing further Eucharistic offerings, some of them associated with the gathering of the grapes for the wine and the vintage festival. The mosaics at the east end depict Cupids fishing on a sea thronged with fish—a very common genre subject invented in Hellenistic times, which appears in all sorts of settings, secular and religious, and was taken over by the early Christians as decorative and mildly symbolic (the fish could be likened to Christians in the waters of baptism, a simile used by the early-third-century Christian writer Tertullian, while the Cupids could suggest the 'fishers of men' of the Gospels; or the scene could just be a symbol of the joys of paradise, as with pagans). Here it forms a setting for scenes from the story of Jonah: at the left, he is being fed to a delightfully curly whale, and at the right he is being ejected by the whale and then seen lying under the gourd-tree. (This story was widely regarded as an allegory of death and resurrection, hence its frequent appearance in the catacombs at Rome (see below).) In the centre of the east end is the inscription of Theodorus, already mentioned (added later). The congregation in the South Basilica thus had on the floor pictures alluding to the Eucharist, Paradise and resurrection, and perhaps to baptism. Bishop Theodore's imposing complex of churches, apparently carried out without any dominating patronage (which would be mentioned in the inscriptions), speaks volumes of the strength and wealth of the Church of Aquileia already under Constantine. Indeed this busy and cosmopolitan commercial centre is precisely the sort of place which Christianity reached early and where it flourished greatly. A number of Christian rooms, perhaps private chapels, have also been found at Aquileia, and it is possible that one or two of these (small rooms floored with mosaics of the Good Shepherd and the like) may be of approximately the period of the double basilica. (21)

The church of SS. Giovanni e Paolo at Rome is more characteristic of the organic development from house-church to fully fledged church, although the basilica itself was not constructed until *c.* 400. On one side of a steep and narrow street, the *clivus Scauri*, leading up the Caelian hill, were two houses of the second and third centuries, one with a row of shops opening on to the street. In about the middle of the fourth century one of the shops was adapted for Christian use by means of frescoes, one of an Orante-figure with arms spread out in the ancient attitude of prayer; and a special ante-room to it was installed. Upstairs on the first floor the position of the windows may indicate that a large hall was created in the third-century alterations to the building, and this, too, may have been in use for Christian worship in the fourth century and earlier. Later on, towards the end of the fourth century, a frescoed, mezzanine *martyrium* was installed, to house what were probably relics of SS. John and Paul (the tradition that the saints of these names were the owners of the houses, martyred under Julian, is untrustworthy). The process was completed by the erection of the basilica, using some of the upper walls of the houses and leaving the shops and *martyrium* intact beneath it. This church is thus a paradigm case of the progressive adaptation of a house to the needs of a Christian community, ending in the creation of an imposing basilica. The late date at which this development took place—long after the Constantinian period—is instructive: there was no universal rush to replace house-churches by basilicas as soon as the hour of the Peace of the Church had struck, as has sometimes been supposed, and as we might too easily imagine from the single case of Aquileia. (**23**)

On another of the hills of Rome, the Aventine, excavations under the basilica of S. Prisca, constructed in the fifth century, reveal something of the closeness of the coexistence of Christianity and paganism in third- and fourth-century Rome. At the very end of the second century a large and opulent Mithraeum was installed in the basement of a house built about a century earlier. Its frescoed walls depicted processions of Mithraic initiates, and, unusually, the representation of the *suovetaurilia*—the sacrifice of a bull, a sheep, and a pig, always associated with the cult of the emperors—may indicate that this was an imperial temple on imperial property. Not long after its foundation, in the early third century, a Christian oratory was apparently founded in the basement of the house next door to it, and the Mithraeum itself was enlarged. Thus the two arch-enemies—the Mithraic cult was particularly hated by Christians because the sacred meal in its rites appeared to be a 'diabolical parody' of the Eucharist—worshipped side by side for nearly two centuries. During the fourth century the Christians, emboldened by their change of status from being part of a clandestine and persecuted organization to part of a legalized Church that enjoyed imperial patronage, and, no doubt, by the publication of the anti-pagan laws of Constantine and his sons, made attacks on the Mithraeum in the adjoining basement; and the Mithraists, to help protect themselves and their temple, built a makeshift wall across the annexe-room through which the Christian raiding parties made their entrance. So it went on, in a state of lively hostility, to the very end of the fourth century when, as a result of the final proscription of paganism by Theodosius and his sons, the Christians were able to destroy the Mithraeum and fill it with rubble from the demolition of the house above it, which they razed as being a 'den of idolatry'. The fifth-century basilica was built partly over the Mithraeum, to seal its fate and signalize the Christian triumph over the enemies of their faith.

There was another church cheek-by-jowl with a Mithraeum at S. Clemente. This underlines the original affinity between Christianity and Mithraism as oriental mystery cults with certain similar characteristics such as a sacred meal. Being unofficial and secretive they were generally located in private houses, away from the monumental city centre. From Constantine on, different considerations, such as sanctity, dictated the choice of church sites, and caused the erection of new churches over holy tombs and in places made sacred by long years of Christian worship.

A most striking case of this juxtaposition has been brought to light beneath Cologne cathedral. In this north-east corner of the Roman city a temple of Mercury had existed since the first century, and remained in use to the very end of the fourth century. But, some time in the Constantinian period, a church was built behind it, so close to it that the temple jutted slightly into the portico of the atrium-court in front of the church. Certain alterations had to be made to the temple precinct, including the entrances, to adjust them to the new arrangement. The baptistery belonging to the church was a surprisingly long distance in front of the atrium, at a lower level because of the lie of the ground. The separation was imposed by the existence of a late Roman house between the atrium and the baptistery. One suggestion is that this was the premises of a college of priests connected with the temple; but it may have been an ordinary private house, whose owner was unwilling to sell it to the Church. Like St. Peter's at Rome, Cologne's original cathedral church faced west, a characteristic confirming its early date, and although its exact dimensions are unknown, it was clearly a complex of some importance. The oddness of the siting, with the temple interrupting the atrium wall, suggests that it may have been erected on the site of an earlier house-church, which would have lent this position an overriding sanctity in the eyes of the Christian community of Cologne, which was doubtless responsible for the construction of the new cathedral, with or without the financial assistance of a Christian official (such as the governor of Second Germany, whose headquarters were at Cologne) or other rich patron. The two cults, pagan and Christian, were thus carried on side by side for much, or even most, of the fourth century—with what amicability or lack of it can only be imagined. The distance of the baptistery from the cathedral would have necessitated ostentatious processions at Easter and Whitsun (the traditional festivals for baptism), and there may well have been pagan processions on the festival days of Mercury. So it went on until the very end of the fourth century, when, no doubt as a result of the laws of the Emperor Theodosius proscribing paganism (issued from 391 on), the Church took advantage of the disaffection of the temple to demolish it and regularize the south wall of the atrium. No more vivid illustration could be found of the coexistence that must have been the common situation of the two religions in many a town in the West for much of the fourth century, if not necessarily in such close physical proximity as in this quarter of Cologne. The other three Roman churches of Cologne, all extra-mural, funerary basilicas, belong to the later fourth century, thus giving the cathedral a chronological as well as a logical precedence.

While church building was taking place in the capital city of Cologne, in the hilly countryside to the south-west a temple complex was being erected over the ruins of an earlier sanctuary of the Mother-Goddesses, or Matronae, at a little place now called Pesch (*Kreis* Schleiden). The contrast between urban Christianity and rural paganism is characteristic of much of Gaul and Germany, and of other north-western provinces, in this period: it was not that paganism was dying in the towns, but rather that only in them did Christianity make much headway before the end of the fourth century, indeed before the end of the Roman period. Pesch is particularly revealing of the continuing vitality of paganism in the rural Rhineland, because the new sanctuary that was built in the mid fourth century, under the sons of Constantine or under Julian, was not merely a reconstruction of the small sanctuary of the first and second century destroyed in the third-century invasions, but a considerable enlargement of it, to a new and more imposing plan, with several extra buildings. It was laid out on a rectangular plan, with a line of sacred buildings on a low ridge, opposite an L-shaped portico that formed shelter and a setting for the crowds at festival times. The main temple was of the native square Romano-Celtic type, i.e. a rectangular, central shrine or *cella* with solid walls, surrounded on all four sides by a low and narrow portico open to the outside, with its sloping roof against the *cella* wall. In addition to this there was a temple of basilical form, a statue of Jupiter beneath a stone canopy at one side of an open court for the display of votive altars and the like, a priest's house, and another 'secular' building. The basilical temple was the most interesting and unusual building in the complex. It had 'pews' in the central nave, and a square, raised apse over a vaulted crypt, and it may have been a sacred hall for the celebration of the mysteries of Cybele, to whom a dedication was found in the sanctuary, along with those to the Matronae, who at Pesch were given the epithet of Vacallinehae. (25)

This association of the oriental nature-goddess, Cybele, with the Celtic trio of Earth-Mothers is also found in a few places elsewhere in Gaul and Germany. It was a not unnatural development in the great melting-pot of Graeco-Roman, oriental and native cults that was paganism under the Empire, especially in the later Empire with the growth of syncretism, the tendency to identify similar gods as being different aspects of one single, omnipresent Deity. At Pesch it has even been suggested that the cult of Cybele replaced that of the Matronae altogether in the fourth century, but that is far from certain. The 'hall of the mysteries', with seats for the watching of a spectacle—quite different from normal temples, which were thought of as the dwelling of the god, served by his priests, not intended to accommodate the worshippers—can be compared with the earlier theatre of the mysteries, a small, enclosed theatre, at the sanctuary of Cybele in Vienne, on the Rhône below Lyon. No sign has been found, at either Pesch or Vienne, of a pit for the notorious ritual of the *taurobolium* or *criobolium*, one of the more barbaric features of the cult of Cybele, in which the initiate stood below a grating over which a bull or ram was slaughtered, receiving on his body the supposedly life-giving (even eternal life-giving) blood. The series of taurobolic altars found near St. Peter's in Rome reveals that many of the great pagan aristocrats of the fourth century underwent this rite. But at the town of Neuss, in Second Germany (like Pesch), one of the 'pits of blood' necessary for the *taurobolium* was built in the Constantinian period in a sanctuary of the Matronae and Cybele—again like Pesch. Its existence at Neuss, and not at Cologne, where one might suspect the influence of a pagan governor in touch with senatorial circles at Rome, shows that the fourth-century revival of the rite was not confined to those milieux, and may have spread wherever there were groups of worshippers of Cybele and her consort Attis—but not, apparently, to rural Pesch.

The sanctuary at Pesch continued to flourish right to the end of the fourth century, when it was destroyed, possibly by Christian wreckers (or else barbarian invaders). It was a local sanctuary of some importance, and may have attracted unfavourable attention from a zealous Christian landowner or evangelizing priest or bishop. The final fate of the sanctuary at Neuss was similar.

In Britain, too, temples were being built and rebuilt in the fourth century. This was the most solidly pagan diocese of the whole Empire, something it owed to its far-flung situation on the edge of the Empire, furthest from the mainstream of Roman life and thought, and from the currents of Christianity that flowed originally from Palestine. We have seen in the last chapter how, in Britain, it was paganism that was able to draw to itself the full strength of the native revival, the 'Celtic Renaissance', whereas in regions where Christianity had already gained a strong hold, such as North Africa and Egypt, it was the new religion that was associated with the resurgence of the native traditions, leading to the emergence of a popular Christianity. It was also the case that Britain had suffered relatively little in the third-century invasions, and reached its Roman apogee of material prosperity in the Constantinian period. The building activity in the pagan sanctuaries reflects both these factors. There had been an unbroken stream of rebuildings and new foundations throughout the third century, and it continued unabated for much of the fourth. Around the turn of the century, reconstruction work took place at the little town of Springhead in Kent (Roman Vaginacae), where one of the main pair of temples in the multi-temple sanctuary on Watling Street was rebuilt, and a new one was built to replace one that had fallen into ruin; a small temple was erected at the rural sanctuary of Cosgrove (Northamptonshire), perhaps attached to a villa; and a pair of the usual square Romano-Celtic temples was constructed a few hundred metres from the fort at Richborough (Kent; Roman Rutupiae), and was doubtless connected with the creation of the forts of the Saxon Shore, of which Rutupiae was one, under the Tetrarchy. (The activity at Springhead did not prevent the sanctuary becoming disused in the mid fourth century, perhaps as a consequence of strong local Christianity; but such early disuse, even of town temples, was rare. The Richborough temples, too, were demolished before the end of the fourth century, and a church was built in one corner of the fort at this time or a little later.) In the Constantinian period, completely new foundations were made at Chelmsford (the Roman town of Caesaromagus), and in the countryside at Weycock Hill near Maidenhead, Jordon Hill near Weymouth, Worth near Sandwich, and Brean Down near Weston-super-Mare; and the late-third-century temple at Pagans Hill near Chew Stoke (Somerset) was rebuilt after collapsing, and was reconstructed again in the late fourth century. The three temples of Chelmsford, Weycock Hill, and Pagans Hill were all of octagonal Romano-Celtic form, with eight-sided gallery, either open or enclosed, running round the octagonal central shrine; those at Jordon Hill, Worth, and Brean Down were of the more usual square type. Brean Down is particularly interesting: built beside a prehistoric round barrow, it is clearly a product of the Celtic religious revival, like the temples at Lydney and Maiden Castle built around the reign of Julian. Substantial endowments must have been made for its construction, for some of the stone was brought from Bath; and it prospered considerably during its short life, being enlarged and embellished *c.* 355, only about fifteen years after its erection *c.* 340. But its exposed position above the Bristol Channel led to its abandonment *c.* 367/8, as a result of the raids of barbarian pirates. In the small town of Godmanchester in Huntingdonshire (Roman Durovigutum), a square, timber-framed temple of the second and third centuries was replaced by a polygonal one in stone, as late as the late fourth century. Thus there was an amount of temple building going on in Britain in the fourth century that can bear comparison with that in other provinces, such as Gaul and Germany, in the years of prosperity—and the heyday of paganism—before the disasters of the third century. And most of Britain's temples, including those built earlier, were flourishing exceedingly, as is made clear by the large numbers of fourth-century coins, brooches, and other offerings found in their precincts. The Constantinian period and after was the great age of British temples and British paganism, and Christianity had made almost no inroads at all.

The small amount known about Romano-British Christianity would indicate that it was confined, throughout the fourth century, to small urban groups and to the class of villa owners, which was especially susceptible to the influence of the court (see also below, section on mosaics). No church building dateable to the Constantinian period has been found, but the hoard of Christian liturgical silverware discovered at Water Newton in Huntingdonshire in 1975 is almost certainly Constantinian. The treasure consists of nine assorted vessels and eighteen small plaques. No item bears figured decoration (a jug is ornamented with acanthus leaves), but several have inscriptions of major importance, and chi-rho monograms abound. A bowl, beautiful in its simplicity, is inscribed on the base and round the rim with the words: 'Publianus sanctum altare tuum Domine subnixus honoro' ('I, Publianus, honour your holy sanctuary, trusting in you, O Lord'), with a chi-rho with alpha and omega inserted in the word 'Domine'. Another bowl, damaged, also had a dedication inscription, from which the names Innocentia and Viventia and a chi-rho survive. A dish and a strainer also bear a chi-rho monogram. A lovely cup with two handles and a foot, two more bowls, and part of another jug complete the tale of vessels. Seventeen of the plaques are triangles of very thin silver with a leaf or feather rib-pattern, generally with a chi-rho and alpha and omega in the centre; the eighteenth is a small gold disc with a similar chi-rho. Only one of the plaques has an inscription, recording that 'Your handmaid has fulfilled the vow which she promised'. Such dedication plaques are a close parallel of the thousands of pagan plaques, of metal, stone, or pottery, set up in pagan temples all over the Graeco-Roman world for many preceding centuries. They and the inscribed bowls prove beyond all possible doubt that the Water Newton silverware came from a Christian church. This church was quite possibly in Water Newton (Durobrivae) itself, an important cross-roads settlement on Ermine Street, which led from London to Lincoln and York. The inscriptions do not reveal whether the church was a fully public one, or whether it was established in the town house (or villa) of a member of the local gentry, like that in Lullingstone Villa (see section on mosaics); but it clearly had patrons, and probably founders, from this class. The silver may have been buried and abandoned as early as 350 (the date of a hoard of coins and silver plate found at Water Newton in 1974), during the troubled years of Magnentius' usurpation, or under threat of the barbarian raids that characterized the next two decades. (**40**)

It was not only in this farthest corner of the Empire, Britain and Second Germany, that temples were being newly constructed in the fourth century. In south-western Gaul, in the foothills of the Pyrenees, the owner of the villa of Montmaurin (Haute-Garonne) was installing a pagan temple in a prominent position in his luxurious new residence, and building a large and complex pilgrim sanctuary round a sacred spring on another part of his estate. The villa, a 200-roomed mansion fit for the lord of this huge estate, was erected on the site of an earlier villa in the second quarter of the fourth century, and was lavishly decorated with marbles and geometric mosaics. The temple, of elongated hexagonal form with a hexagonal altar, stood at one side of the great semi-circular porticoed court (a quite common feature of late Roman villas) that formed the state entrance. It may have been the main place of worship for the whole estate, where not only the lord and his family but all the workers and villagers would have gathered at certain festival times. A priestess of this temple was cremated and buried near the villa with her cult implements, including a sacrificial knife and libation cups, in a funerary 'well', an ancient form of pagan grave in this part of Gaul. She also took with her shoes, jewellery, door-keys, spinning and weaving equipment, and large numbers of offerings—a hundred pieces of pottery, glassware, a coin of Constantius II, various kinds of food, and the bodies of toads and small mammals considered talismanic. She was certainly a member of the owner's family. To the north of the villa was the spring sanctuary of La Hillère, which was decked out with luxurious baths enclosing the spring, a hexagonal temple, what was probably a pilgrim hostel and, in a later phase, a covered market. Its fortunes closely followed those of the villa, which was sacked and burnt, probably by brigands, not long after its completion, and was rebuilt in a less luxurious form before a final fire and abandonment at the end of the fourth century. In the Middle Ages it was again a pilgrim centre, with chapel and healing spring of Notre-Dame-de-la-Hillère—a clear case of the Christianization of a pagan cult, as happened so often. It is at Montmaurin that the influence of a pagan lord at work on his estate in the Constantinian period is most clearly traceable. Some fifty years later, at the end of the fourth century and the beginning of the fifth, the process would be reversed, and Christian lords would be building churches instead of temples on their estates in this part of Gaul. But that was still two generations away. Christianity was, however, already well established in the important town of St.-Bertrand-de-Comminges near Montmaurin, where a mid-fourth-century funerary basilica, poorly constructed but quite large, has been found. South-western Gaul in general at this period exemplified the contrast between fairly well Christianized towns and still pagan countryside that was characteristic of a certain stage in the spread of Christianity (see Chapter IV).

In Rome itself, a Rome that, despite its long and deep-rooted Christian tradition and its ring of grandiose new churches, was still dominated by the great pagan senatorial aristocracy, the temple of the Syrian gods on the Janiculum was erected under Julian, as we have already seen (Chapter V). And on the other side of Rome, also outside the walls, a mysterious subterranean hall (the 'Hypogeum of Via Livenza') was built in the late Constantinian period, and may have been devoted to the cult of water. It is shaped like a stadium or circus, a narrow rectangle 20 metres (65 feet) long with one curved end. At the square end is a niche beautifully frescoed with Diana the Huntress and a Nymph, and a fountain with birds, with a scene of Cupids fishing near by, and the remains of a mosaic of Moses or St. Peter with the miraculous spring, a common Christian subject of the time (see below) that may have been borrowed by pagans for its suitability for a water sanctuary. Below the niche is a deep basin, carefully railed off with marble slabs.

In Africa, in the great capital city of Carthage, a building of unusual plan on the hill behind the Antonine Baths, while not an actual temple, was apparently the headquarters of a religious guild of some sort, in the second quarter of the fourth century. It comprised a series of small, narrow rooms built into the hillside, a large court with two porticoes and a central basin and an apse at one end, and a large room shaped like a clover-leaf (a popular plan for a dining-room in the fourth century). The central lobe of the trefoil has a most beautiful mosaic floor: four children or dwarfs dance round and decorate with garlands a circular, domed structure with eight columns; it originally had two wings composed of gable-roofed porticoes with a curtained arch at the end; above is a luxuriant vine. The rotunda is certainly a shrine, and the ceremony depicted is the ritual of some cult, perhaps even the dedication ceremony of a temple of Dionysus (hence the vine), newly built in about the reign of Constantius. If so, the building would be the headquarters of a guild placed under the patronage of Dionysus, or even of a Bacchic conventicle devoted to the celebration of the cult of

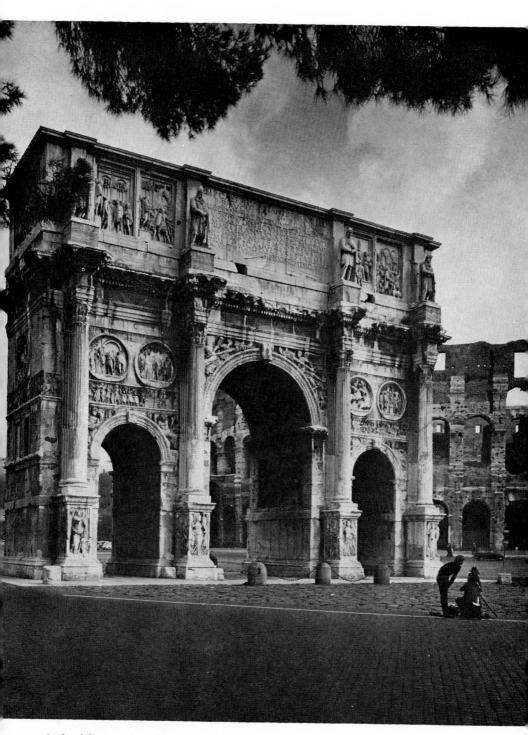

1 Arch of Constantine, Rome

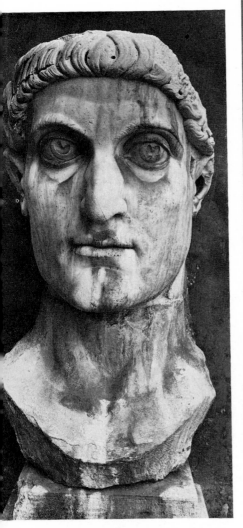

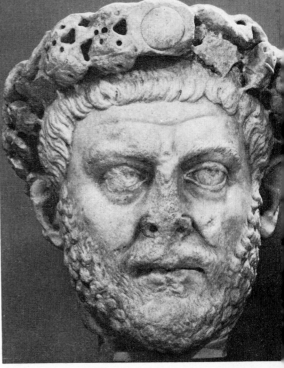

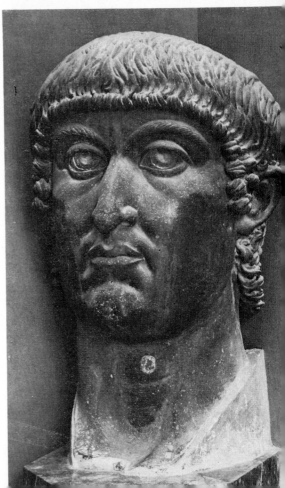

2   *Above* Colossal head of
Constantine. *Rome, Palazzo dei
Conservatori*
3   *Above right* Head of Diocletian
from Nicomedia. *Istanbul,
Archaeological Museum*
4   *Right* Colossal head of
Constantius II. *Rome, Palazzo dei
Conservatori*

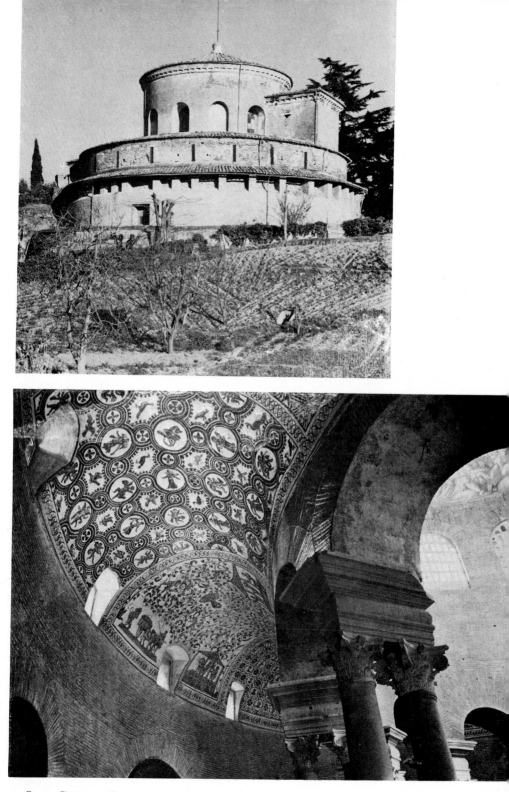

5   Santa Costanza, Rome:
5a *Top* Exterior
5b *Above* Interior, showing part of vault mosaics in ambulatory

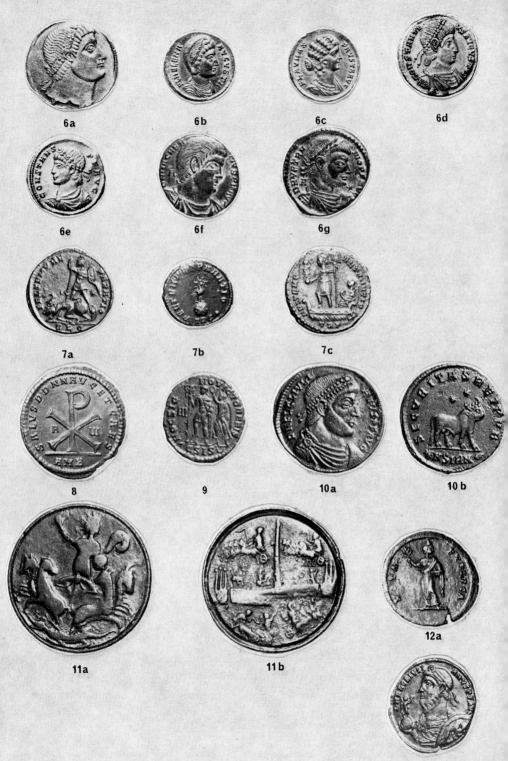

6a   6b   6c   6d

6e   6f   6g

7a   7b   7c

8   9   10a   10b

11a   11b   12a

12b

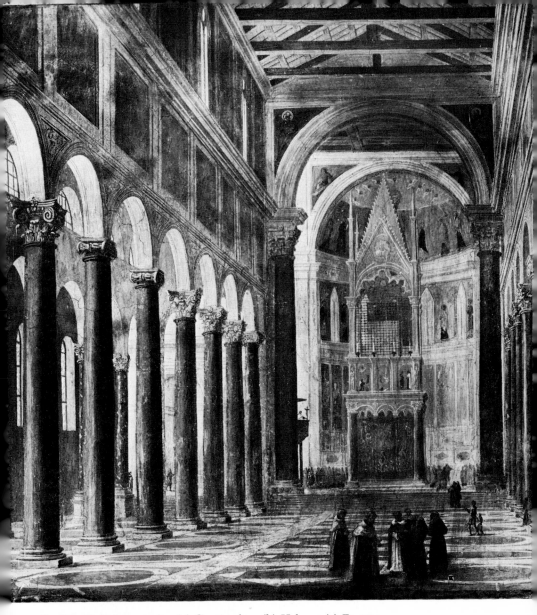

6 *Opposite* Coin portraits: (a) Constantine; (b) Helena; (c) Fausta;
(d) Constantius II; (e) Constans; (f) Magnentius; (g) Vetranio. *Oxford,
Ashmolean Museum*

7 Three reverses of FEL. TEMP. REPARATIO series of Constantius II and
Constans: (a) Virtus spearing falling horseman; (b) Phoenix on globe;
(c) Emperor in galley, holding Victory and *labarum*. *Oxford, Ashmolean
Museum*

8 Chi-rho reverse of Magnentius (SALVS DD. NN. AVG. ET CAES.). *Oxford,
Ashmolean Museum*

9 HOC SIGNO VICTOR ERIS reverse of Vetranio. *Oxford, Ashmolean Museum*

10 Bull coin of Julian (SECVRITAS REIPVB.): (a) obverse; (b) reverse. *Oxford,
Ashmolean Museum*

11 Contorniate reverses: (a) Sol in chariot; (b) Circus Maximus. *Oxford,
Ashmolean Museum*

12 Isis coin: (a) reverse with standing Isis; (b) obverse with portrait of
Julian. *Oxford, Ashmolean Museum*

13 *Above* Fresco attributed to Gaspard Poussin showing interior of St. John
at the Lateran, Rome. *Rome, San Martino ai Monti*

14 *Right* Street of tombs beneath St. Peter's, Rome

15 *Below* Christus-Helios mosaic in Tomb of the Julii beneath St. Peter's, Rome

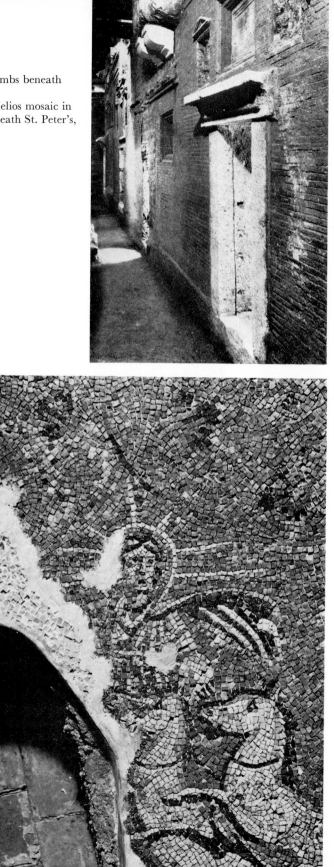

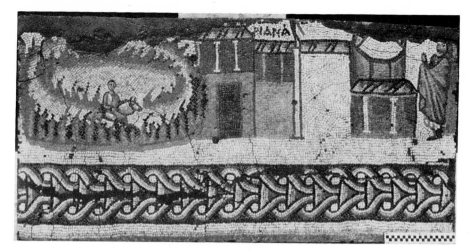

16 *Above* Part of border of Megalopsychia mosaic with Golden Church of Antioch. *Antakya, Archaeological Museum*
17 *Below* Apse mosaic of Santa Pudenziana, Rome, with churches of Holy Sepulchre (left) and Nativity (or Ascension) (right)

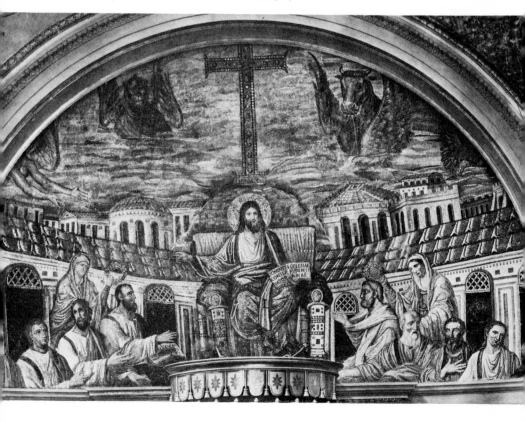

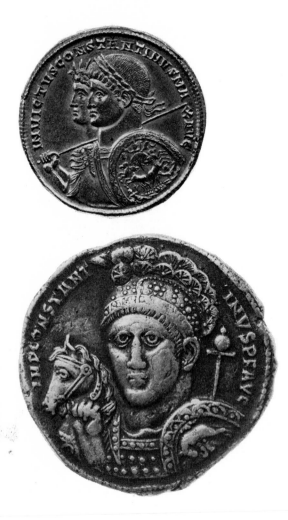

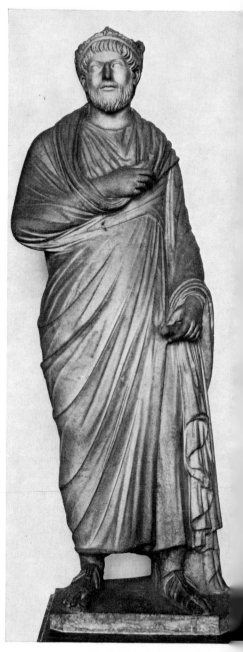

18 Medallions of Constantine:
18a *Top* Obverse with busts of Sol
and Constantine. *Paris, Cabinet des
Médailles*
18b *Above* Obverse with chi-rho
badge on emperor's helmet.
Munich, Staatliche Münzsammlung
19 *Above right* Statue of Julian the
Apostate. *Paris, Musée du Louvre*
20 *Opposite* The Corbridge *Lanx*.
*Collection of His Grace the Duke of
Northumberland*

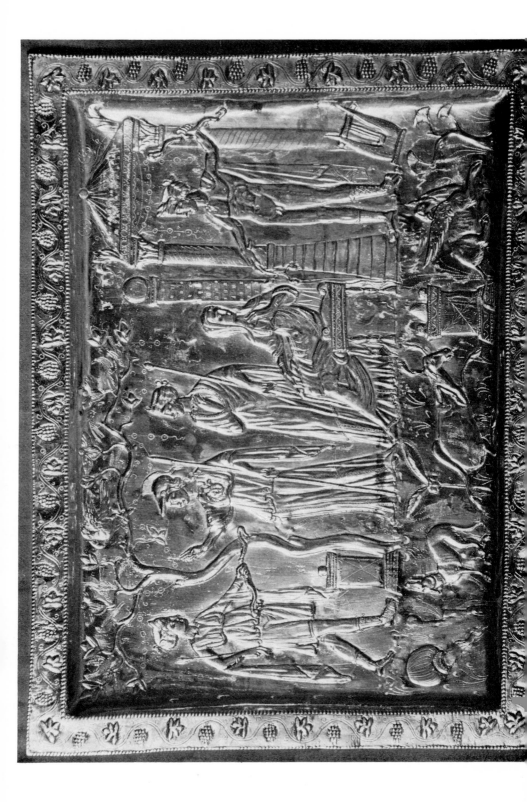

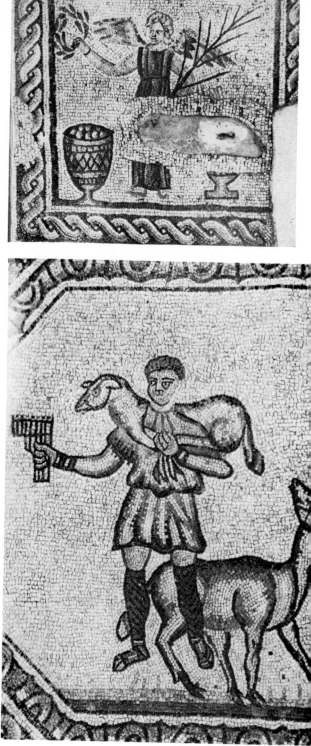

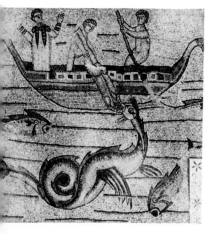

21 Mosaic pavement of
Basilica of Theodorus,
Aquileia:
21a *Above* Jonah and the
Whale
21b *Above right* Eucharistic
Victory
21c *Right* Good Shepherd
22 *Opposite top* Temple of
Syrian gods on Janiculum,
Rome
23 *Opposite bottom* Basilica
of Santi Giovanni e Paolo,
Rome: the Clivus Scauri

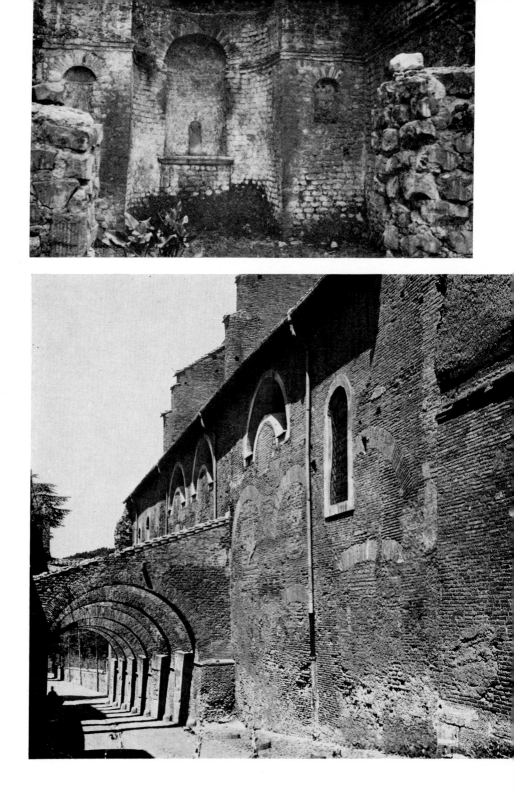

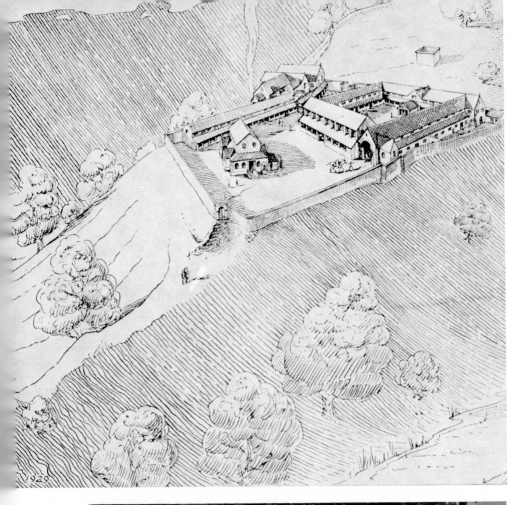

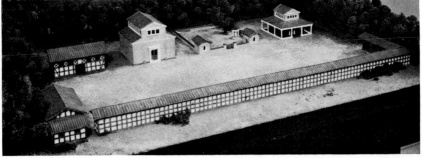

24 *Top* Lydney: reconstruction drawing of the sanctuary
25 *Above* Pesch: reconstruction model of the sanctuary. *Bonn, Rheinisches Landesmuseum*
26 *Opposite top* Church of Qirqbize, south façade
27 *Opposite bottom* House of the Horses, Carthage: mosaic of horse with the she-wolf and Romulus and Remus

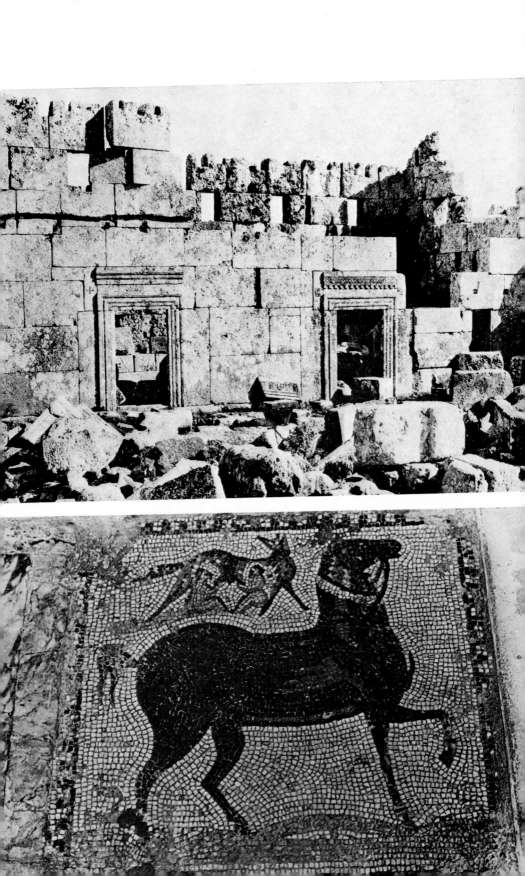

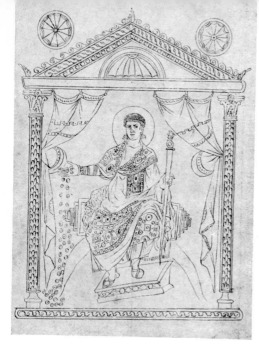

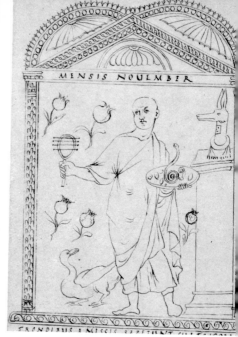

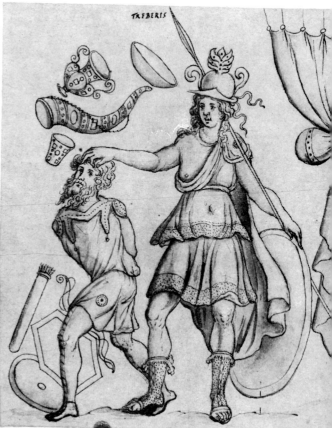

28 *Calendar of 354*:
28a *Above* Constantius II as consul
28b *Above right* November
28c *Right* Trier
29 *Opposite top* Europa mosaic, Lullingstone
30 *Opposite bottom* Hinton St. Mary mosaic pavement (main portion). *London, British Museum*

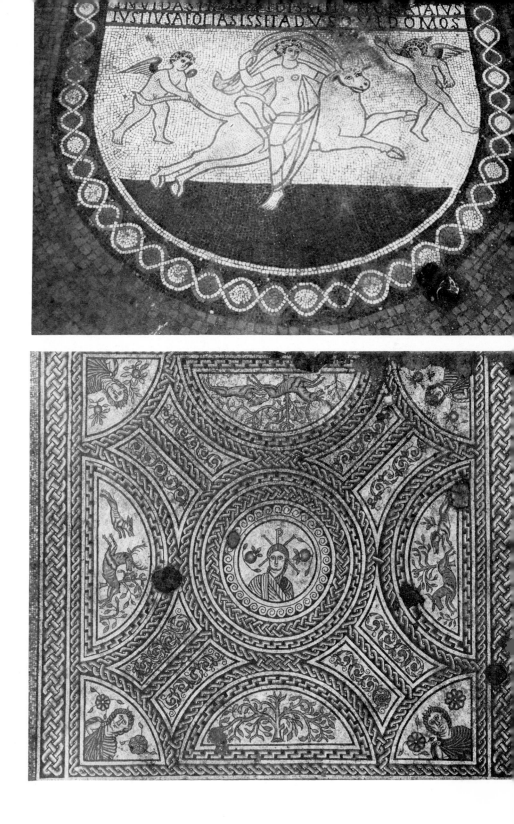

31 *Right* Cock-headed man mosaic, Brading
32 *Below* Detail of Small Hunt pavement, Piazza Armerina
33 *Opposite top left* Winged Seasons mosaic, Carthage: Summer. *Tunis, Musée du Bardo*
34 *Opposite top right* House of the Horses, Carthage: mosaic of sorcerer making sacrifice. *Musée de Carthage*
35 *Opposite below* Coronation of Venus pavement, Ellès. *Tunis, Musée du Bardo*

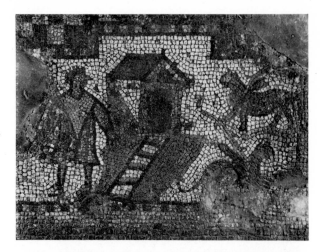

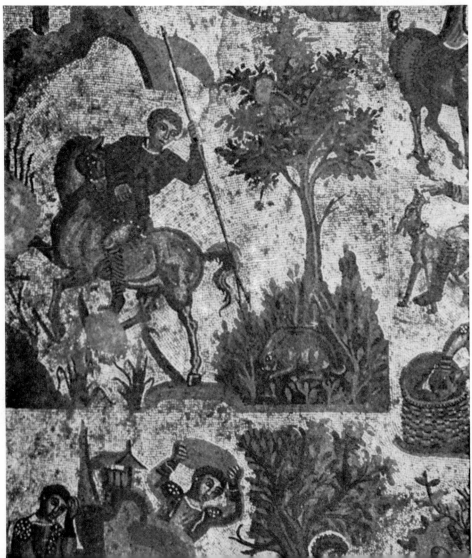

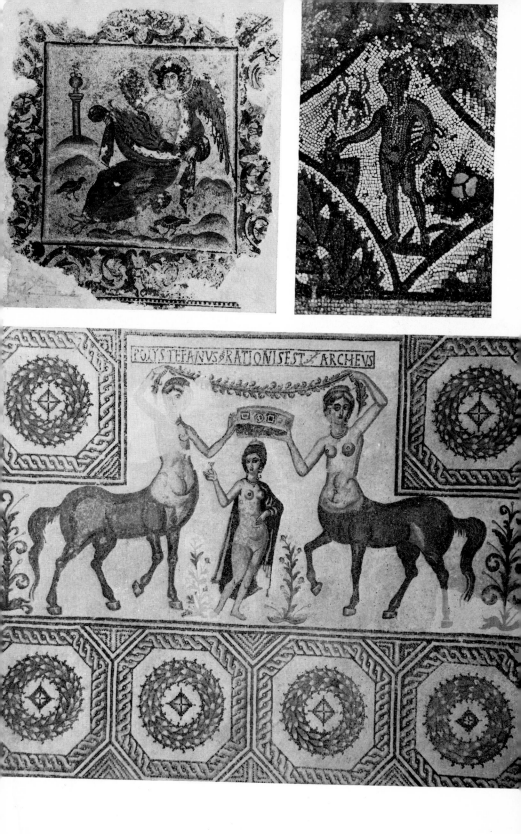

POLYSTEFANVS RATIONIS EST ARCHEVS

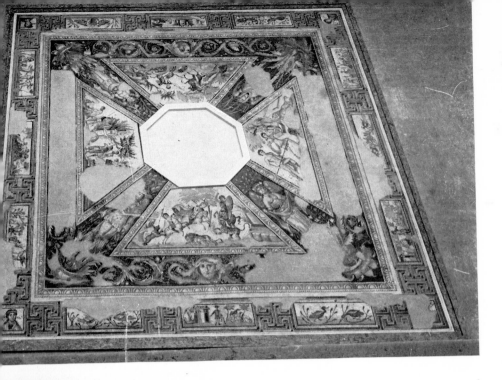

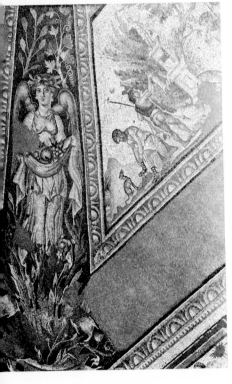

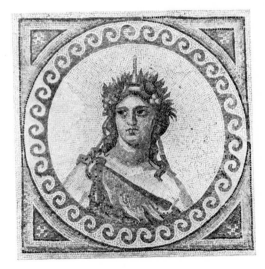

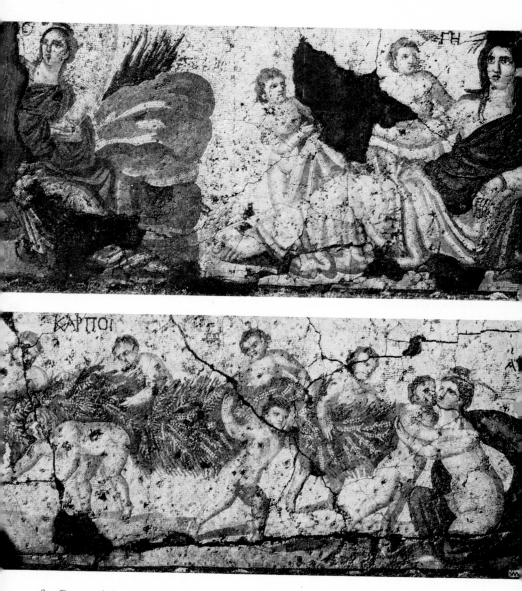

36   Constantinian Villa, Antioch:

36a *Opposite top* General view of main pavement. *Paris, Musée du Louvre*

36b *Opposite left* Detail: Autumn, and part of hunting panel with sacrifice. *Paris, Musée du Louvre*

36c *Opposite right* Bust of Dionysus. *Rhode Island, Museum of Art*

37   Mosaic of Gê and the Karpoi, Antioch:

37a *Top* Gê and Aigyptos

37b *Above* Aroura and *putto* and the Karpoi

Antakya, Archaeological Museum

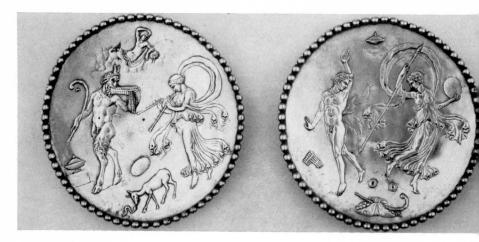

38 Mildenhall Treasure:
38a *Above* Pair of Bacchic platters
38b *Below* Great Dish
London, British Museum

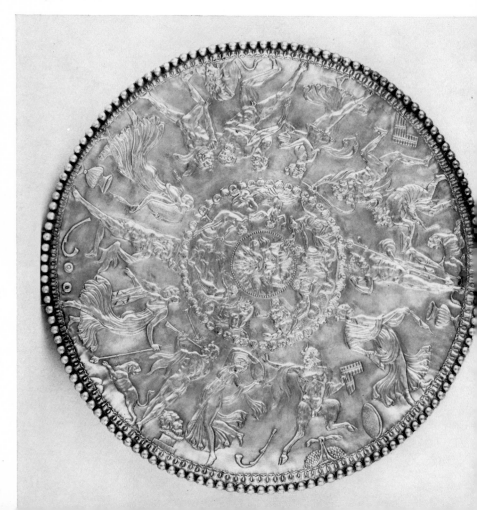

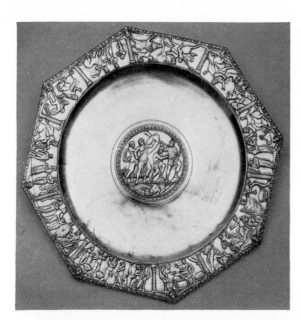

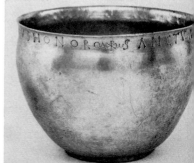

39 Kaiseraugst Treasure:
39a *Left* Achilles Dish (much reduced)
39b *Below left* Ariadne Tray, *Augst, Römermuseum*
40 *Below* Water Newton Treasure: bowl dedicated by Publianus. *London, British Museum*

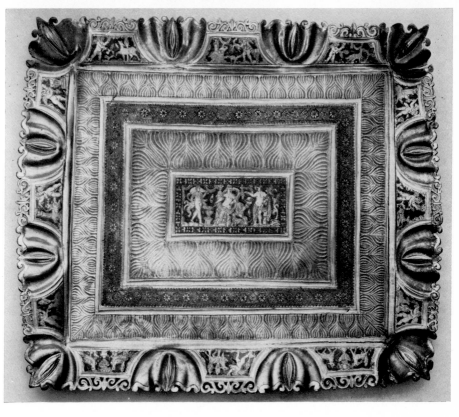

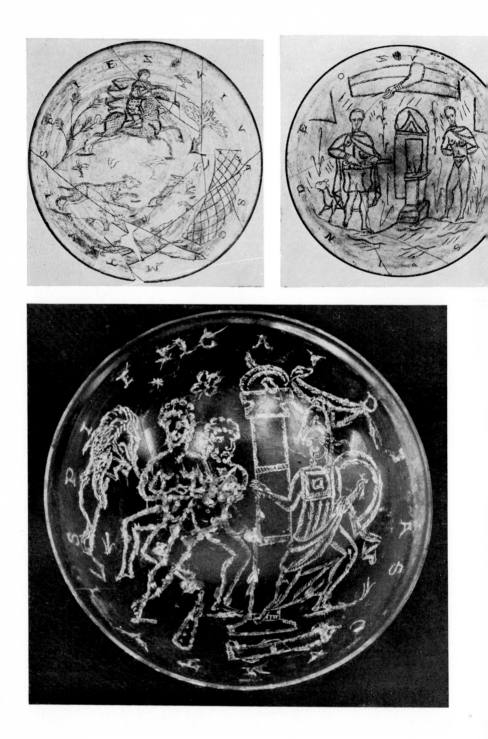

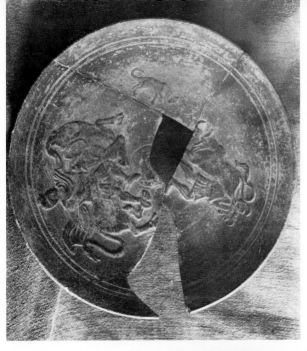

41 Cologne glassware
(workshop using cross-shading):
41a *Opposite left* Wint Hill
hunting-bowl (much reduced).
Oxford, Ashmolean Museum
41b *Opposite right* Bowl with
Sacrifice of Isaac (much
reduced). *Trier, Rheinisches
Landesmuseum*
41c *Opposite below* Hercules
and Antaeus bowl. *Trier,
Rheinisches Landesmuseum*
42 *Left* African light *terra
sigillata* C plate with Mithraic
scenes. *Rome, Museo Nazionale
Romano*
43 *Below* Gold glass
medallion from Rome with
Raising of Lazarus (much
enlarged). *Vatican, Museo
Sacro*

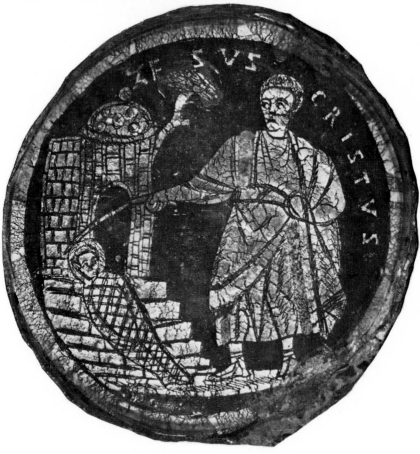

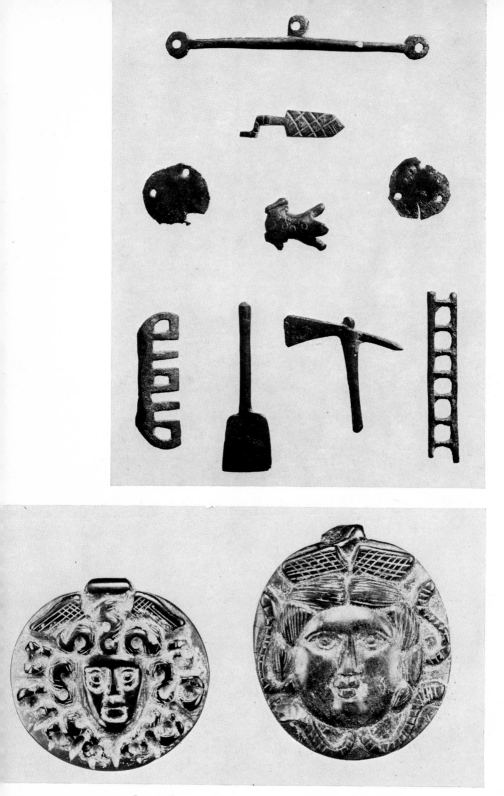

44 Jet pendants and bronze medals found in graves at Cologne. *Cologne, Römisch-germanisches Museum*

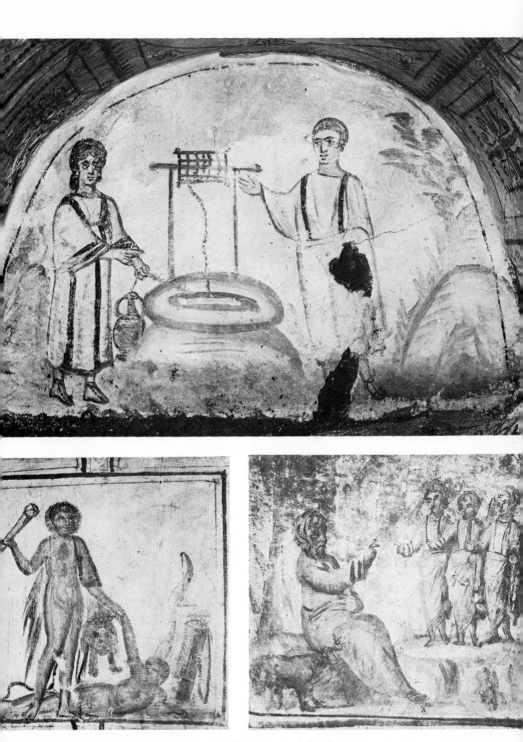

45 Via Latina Catacombs, Rome: (a) *Top* Jesus and the Samaritan woman at the well; (b) *Bottom left* Hercules slaying an enemy; (c) *Bottom right* Vision of Abraham at Mamre

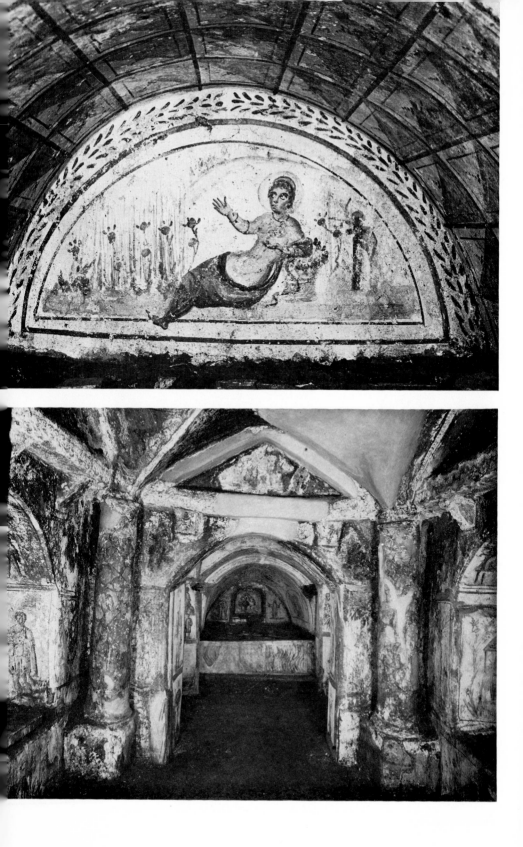

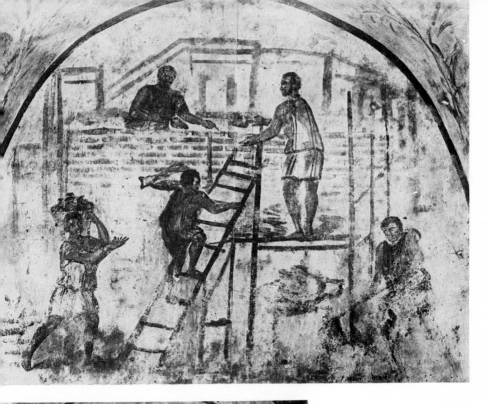

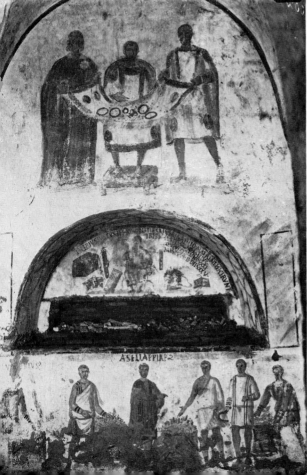

ASELLAPPIA ?

45d *Opposite top* Earth-Goddess (?)
45e *Opposite bottom* View of a funerary chamber
46 Hypogeum of Trebius Justus, Rome:
46a *Above* Building scene
46b *Left* Main wall with offerings scene

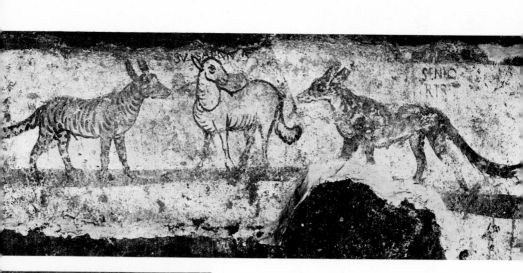

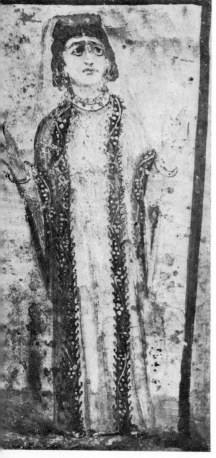

47 Frescoes from public catacombs, Rome:
47a *Above* Allegory of Susanna and the Elders (Catacomb of Praetextatus)
47b *Left* Orante from Catacomb of Thraso

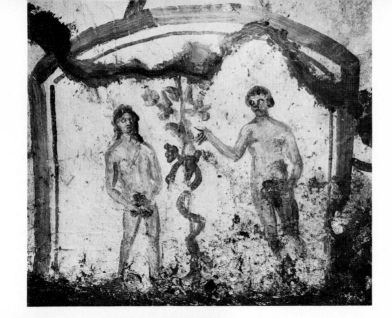

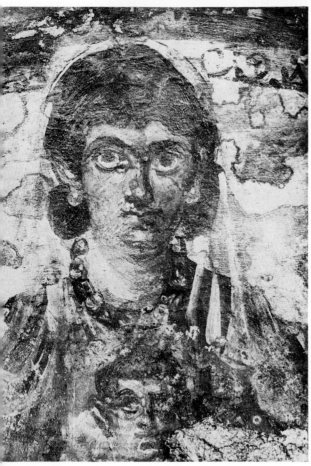

47c *Above* Adam and Eve
(Catacomb of SS. Peter and
Marcellinus)
47d *Left* Virgin and Child
(Coemeterium Maius)

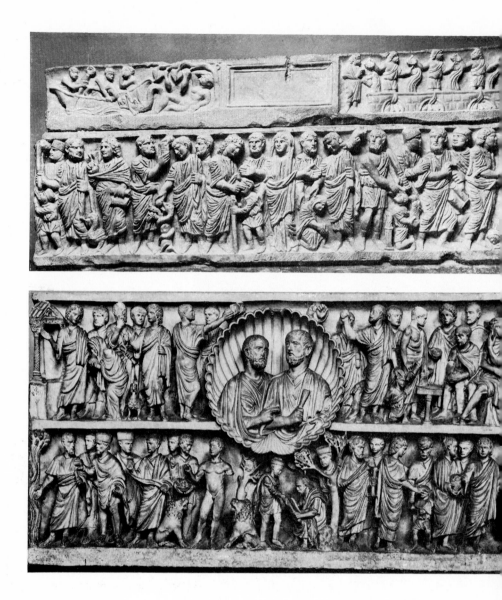

48 *Top* Constantinian frieze sarcophagus found under St. Peter's, Rome.
Vatican Museums
49 *Above* Two Brothers Sarcophagus. *Vatican Museums*

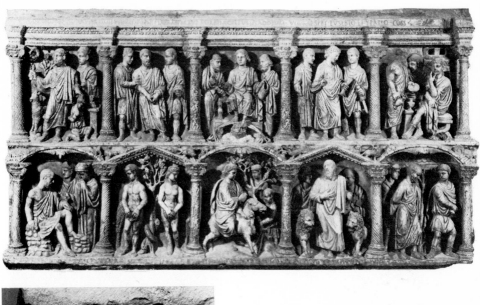

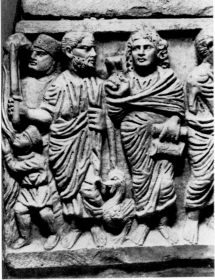

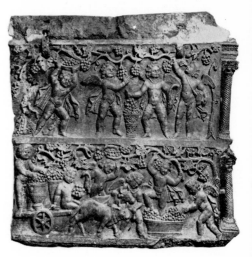

50   Sarcophagus of Junius Bassus:
50a *Top* Front, general view
50b *Above left* Front, detail: Christ and St. Peter
50c *Above right* Side, vintaging Cupids
Vatican, crypt of St. Peter's

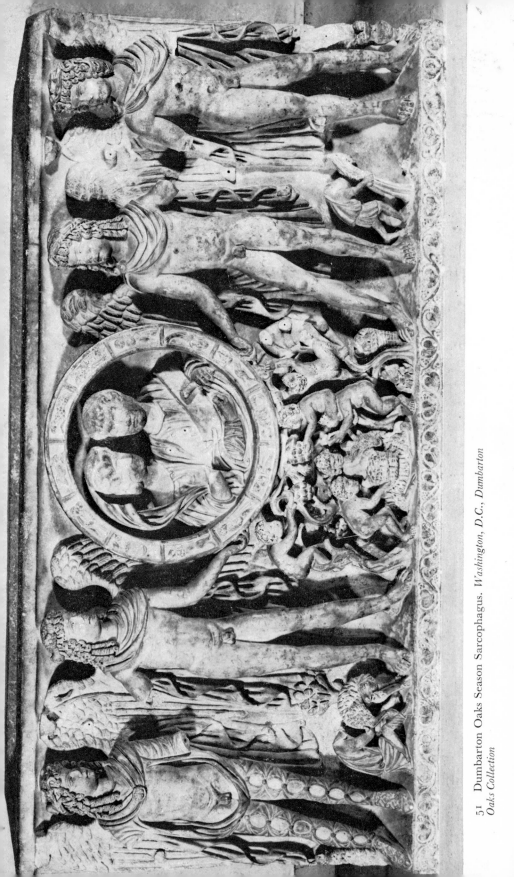

51 Dumbarton Oaks Season Sarcophagus. *Washington, D.C., Dumbarton Oaks Collection*

the god. An alternative theory is that the mosaic represents a ritual of the imperial cult, and the building would then be the premises of a college of the cult of the Second Flavians, which we know to have been established specifically throughout Roman Africa (see also below).

In the eastern half of the Empire, in the province of Arabia, there was not only the Julianic refoundation of Deir el-Meshkûk, discussed in Chapter V, but other late work on temples as well. At the important temple of the god Dusares at Malah es-Sarrar, two towers that flank the temple were demolished and reconstructed in 372, and an inn with a stable was added—this was evidently a pilgrim sanctuary. And at 'Auwas, a shrine of the god Theandrites was built as late as 387. But these manifestations of the vitality of the pagan, native cults were made in the face of strong competition from Christianity: a considerable number of churches were built in the region of the Hauran during the fourth century, some of them, such as those at 'Anz and Sammeh, Nimreh and Tafha, in the early fourth century. They were constructed in the manner typical of the Hauran—an area of black basalt devoid of timber—with a series of semicircular arches spanning the nave(s), to support a roof of basalt slabs. The walls of such churches have often collapsed in the course of the centuries, leaving the beautifully built arches still standing. The church at Tafha, significantly, was erected on the site of a temple, which must already have become disused and probably fallen into ruin. It was not the only one: several other Arabian churches of the fourth century were also built on top of temples, notably the one installed in the main temple of an imposing sanctuary at Qanouat (or Kanawat); and the church in the central court of the fort of Deir el-Kahf, that had been built as a shrine of the imperial cult under the Tetrarchy, and was converted into a church shortly after the Julianic period.

Far to the north of the Hauran, on the Limestone Plateau behind Antioch in Roman Syria, the temple in the height sanctuary of Zeus Koryphaios at El Hosn was restored in 367/8 by the elders of the neighbouring village of Touron, apparently in co-operation with other villages of the neighbourhood. The date and the nature of the enterprise reveal a clear connection with the Julianic revival, for it was precisely through the corporate institutions of cities and smaller communities, as we have seen (Chapter V), that Julian chose to channel his main effort. But it was a rearguard action that was being fought at El Hosn. The Limestone Plateau was already largely conquered for Christianity. In the environs of El Hosn itself, as well as elsewhere on the Plateau, Christians had already been buried in dated tombs beneath inscriptions proclaiming their faith. And all over this region churches were springing up, built in the beautiful limestone architecture that is the glory of the Plateau. One can count no fewer than seven basilicas and a single-naved church of the mid fourth century, and a single-naved church as early as the first third of the century. This last, at Qirqbize, was built beside a villa of the late third century, to which it bears such a close resemblance that it was at first mistaken for another villa. Both have a portico along the south side—a very common feature—and are preceded by a court. The lack of a separate priest's house makes it certain that the church was built by the owner of the villa for his family and peasants, just as John Chrysostom (at Constantinople) was later to urge upon other landowners, taking care to enumerate all the benefits likely to accrue, material as well as spiritual (let them think how much quieter their workers would be, when they were converted and under the rule of the Church!). The basilica of Batuta stands beside a villa dated to the year 363, and these are the two earliest monuments of the village. The other churches, including the basilica of Kharab Shams, were all likewise built in mere villages. The reason for this astonishing flowering of rural Christianity at such an early date—most of the country areas throughout the Empire had to wait until the fifth and sixth centuries, or even later, for their network of church edifices—lies partly in the proximity of the Limestone Plateau to the very Christian city of Antioch, and partly in the nature of the agricultural activity carried on on the Plateau itself. For this was a rich olive-growing region, which needed a large extra workforce at the harvesting season in late autumn, drawn from the cereal-growers of the plains below, at their slack time of year. During the rest of the year, when the olive plantations needed relatively little tending, the peasants of the Plateau were free to work as stonemasons, an occupation in which they necessarily became highly skilled from the simple fact of living on the Plateau, where the creation not just of houses and public buildings, but of the vital cisterns for rain-water, oil-presses, paths, terraces for olives, and tombs—the whole framework of their life and death, in fact—involved stone-cutting. In this capacity they travelled in teams about the Plateau, constructing public buildings, rich villas, temples and churches, and even small villas, making contact at various building sites with specialist teams of mosaicists, carpenters and painters from outside the Plateau, and even themselves travelling down to Antioch and other cities to take part in building there. In October and November, when the olives were being harvested and pressed, the whole Plateau became a hive of activity, with oil merchants thronging in to buy up the produce, and traders of every sort coming to sell their wares to the inhabitants of the Plateau, who would use their new wealth to stock up with necessaries for the year ahead. Thus both the olive-growing and the building activities of the Plateau created to perfection the conditions, namely constant contact with more Christianized places such as Antioch, that favoured the rapid spread of Christianity. In addition, as the oil production of the Plateau was expanding during the late Empire, some of the new inhabitants who moved into it would have been already Christian. (**26**)

Christian and Pagan Saints

This same region, the Limestone Plateau, was one of the cradles of the monastic movement in Roman Syria. Already under Constantius single hermits and small colonies of anchorites were beginning to make their abode on mountainsides above villages, and by the sixth century there were enormous numbers of convents dotted about the area, owning their own estates of olive-groves, just as the more important temples had done before them. The famous monastery of Teleda (modern Deir Tell 'Ade), later to be associated with St. Symeon Stylites, the great saint who came from Cilicia in Asia Minor and spent all his ascetic life on the Plateau, was founded in the mid fourth century. Towards the end of the fourth century the monks of the region of Antioch began to wage war on the pagan temples, demolishing very many of them, and were roundly condemned for this by Libanius in a moving speech composed in 386.

It was Egypt, however, that was the real birthplace of monasticism. The great pioneer was the celebrated St. Antony, whose example, both in his own person and through the medium of his *Life* written by St. Athanasius and subsequently translated into Latin, was widely followed. He was born of a prosperous yeoman family in 251, and was brought up a Christian. After the death of his parents, at about the age of twenty, he resolved to devote himself to the ascetic life, selling the modest estate which he had inherited, for the benefit of the poor, and giving his younger sister into the care of a small community of holy virgins, one of the forerunners of nunneries. He then withdrew to the desert, at first on the fringes of civilization, where he maintained himself by plaiting ropes. He lived to be a centenarian, dying in 356. He was virtually uneducated, and the replies which he made to letters from Constantine and his sons, who wrote begging his attention, must have been dictated. That he should have received letters from the emperors themselves is sufficient indication of his towering influence, derived from his ascetic practices, his struggles with the Devil, his healing miracles, and his wisdom in the lore of God.

It was only natural that a man like Antony should have many disciples and imitators. The reasons why it rapidly became a mass movement, with peasants flocking out into the desert in thousands, were, however, as much social as religious. The prevailing conditions of oppression and over-taxation that had afflicted the province of Egypt, as one of the two main granaries of the Empire (North Africa being the other), since its formation under Augustus (one papyrus records the complaint of a peasant that his crop was taxed twice over *after* it had been eaten by hippopotami!), worsened in the late Empire, as taxation in general became very high. The life of a Christian ascetic offered the oppressed at once a fulfilment of their religious aspirations and a means of escape from their condition, a means, moreover, that was in itself noble and, in the case of exceptional persons, might lead to the acquisition of great holiness and correspondingly great influence. In a world where persecution had ceased, and the supreme crown of martyrdom was no longer to be won, the way of asceticism offered a new means for zealous Christians to become true heroes of the faith, and it replaced martyrdom as the royal road to sainthood. Both dead martyrs and living—and dead—ascetics were greatly honoured, especially from the late fourth century onwards, when the mass of ordinary Christians, many of them converts of convenience, were themselves of far from heroic temper.

However, the influx of large numbers of would-be ascetics into the desert, the majority of them incapable of the tremendous self-discipline necessary for living as a solitary hermit, created a need for organization. The first man to supply this was Pachomius. A man of peasant stock who had been a soldier under Licinius, he founded the first proper monastery, at Tabennisi, a deserted village on the edge of the Libyan desert. It was self-supporting, with monks of the same craft or occupation grouped together in houses, and any surplus was devoted to the relief of the poor, the moving principle behind the monastery. Common buildings included a hospital and a storehouse for provisions. It was a closed monastery surrounded by a wall, and discipline was severe, including corporal punishment. Some of the Rule, written down in Coptic and translated into Greek and Latin, has been preserved, and reveals that illiterate novices were given a rudimentary education, sufficient to enable them to read the Bible and learn it by heart. Other details concern food, a simple but varied vegetarian diet of bread, cheese, fruit and vegetables. There were about 2,500 monks at Tabennisi alone, and other monasteries following the same Rule sprang up around, including a nunnery founded by Pachomius' sister Mary. Pachomius himself died in 345/6.

The monastic movement spread over most of the Eastern Empire during the fourth century. In Asia Minor it was chiefly propagated by the heretical Bishop Eustathius of Sebaste in Armenia, who under Constantius founded monastic communities in the provinces of Armenia, Paphlagonia and Pontus, and laid down rules for them governing food, dress—he himself went about in a philosopher's cloak—and conduct of life. Some of his more extreme views, such as the condemnation of marriage and of married priests (clerical marriage was then lawful throughout the Church), were denounced by a council of bishops that met at Gangra in Paphlagonia in order to depose him from his see. But his outstanding holiness of life and his newly created monasteries were the inspiration of the young St. Basil, Julian's contemporary, who returned to Asia Minor in 356/7 from studying at Athens and, fired by ascetic zeal, undertook on the advice of Eustathius a long journey round Egypt, Palestine, Syria and Mesopotamia, visiting for himself the monasteries and famous hermits. Then in 358 he proceeded to found his own monastery at a place called Annesoi in Pontus, where his family had estates, on which his mother and sister, also devout Christians of an ascetic turn of mind, had already created a small nunnery. His Rule, which came to be widely accepted, was less severe than that of Pachomius. It laid emphasis on the renunciation of worldly wealth and family ties, and obedience to the Superior, prescribing a life spent in meditating on the Bible and in agricultural work.

It was the fundamental failure of late paganism that it was unable to turn to its own account any of this great wave of ascetic idealism. Monasticism was a wholly Christian phenomenon. There were pagan precedents for rejecting human society and living a life of asceticism, notably the Cynic school of philosophy, and Cynic philosophers did exist in the fourth century. They drew down on themselves, however, the wrath of Julian, who saw in them a threat to organized Graeco-Roman society second only to that of the monks, to whom he sneeringly likens them. In Julian's view the contemporary ones were only degenerate Cynics, unworthy of the name of followers of the great Diogenes, who adopted the outward characteristics of Cynicism—long hair, the staff and the philosopher's cloak—and availed themselves of the Cynic's freedom to criticize conventional society, including conventional paganism, but had none of the redeeming inner grace of genuine asceticism and detachment; they were 'drop-outs', who had done badly at their studies, but yet hoped to be honoured as true philosophers. It was, of course, their attacks on paganism, and irreverence towards the gods, that were chiefly responsible for Julian's attitude of condemnation. This made some of them actual allies of the Christians, for whom they furnished anti-pagan propaganda. One Cynic was greatly honoured and praised by St. Gregory of Nazianzus, friend of St. Basil and enemy of Julian. But, despite the superficial resemblance of Cynics to Christian monks, real pagan saints are to be sought elsewhere.

Like the Christians with their martyr-cults, zealous pagans found some of their heroes in the past. Apollonius of Tyana, a first-century sage and wonder-worker, who lived for a time at the temple of Asklepios at Aegae in his native Cilicia and travelled all the way to India where he acquainted himself with the wisdom of the Brahmins, enjoyed a great vogue among all classes and was a kind of Christ-figure for some pagans. The long biography of him, written in the third century in Greek by the writer Philostratus, was translated into Latin in the late fourth century by one of the main leaders of the pagan revival at Rome, Virius Nicomachus Flavianus.

At the very end of the fourth century, the pagan historian Eunapius of Sardis wrote a book called *Lives of the Philosophers and Sophists*, parallel in form to the Lives of Christian saints, both martyrs and ascetics, a form of literary composition that was to remain popular for many centuries. It is in this book that the true equivalents, in the eyes of pious pagans, to the monks and hermits revered by the Christians may be found. But the philosophers described are for the most part a sorry collection of charlatans, and Julian's heroes and high priests of the mysteries, Maximus of Ephesus, Priscus and Chrysanthius, are among the worst, especially Maximus with his carefully contrived 'miracles'. As for the sophists and rhetoricians, it may seem strange to us that they are included at all in a collection of lives of pagan 'saints'. But in the ancient world intellectual life was dominated by the concept of the cult of the Muses, and intellectual activity was held to constitute the most important part of their cult. By the middle and later Empire the practice of Graeco-Roman culture was regarded as one of the main highways to immortality, conferred on the soul in heaven by the Muses whom it had served below. (The idea was taken over by the Christians in the fourth century, in the form of Christ the Sage initiating his disciples into Christian wisdom.) This is why the culture of the dead person features so prominently on numerous sarcophagi, especially of the second and third centuries (see below for a fourth-century example). Rhetorical and philosophical culture had become for its devotees a real religion in itself, and indeed it was often carried on in surroundings of a sacred character, in temples on non-festive days, or even in special sanctuaries of the Muses, *Mouseia*, the most famous being at Alexandria. One such *Mouseion* was created on the Greek island of Aegina in 359/60 by one Ampelius, governor of the Roman province of Greece. An epigram on the base of a statue of Pan gives an allusive description of it: a place shaded by plane-trees, with flowing water in basins and channels, statues of Pan and the Muses and probably a tiny temple of these goddesses, semicircular stone seats, and a small odeon for music and declamation. In the fourth century the consciousness that the Empire was in danger of being overwhelmed by the tides of barbary accentuated the attitude of reverence for culture, widely felt to be the most precious part of the Graeco-Roman heritage (see also Chapter IV). The aura of sanctity surrounding the culture which Libanius was promoting and defending does much to explain the underlying nobility of his life and work, which cannot be interpreted merely in terms of narrow self-interest.

A short biography of Libanius figures in Eunapius' collection, but it is anything but laudatory, and reveals that Eunapius' hagiography was reserved for his special heroes, mainly his own teachers, among whom were rivals of Libanius. One of these is, indeed, the one famous Christian sophist, Prohaeresius, who taught at Athens. In some ways, then, the parallel between Eunapius' *Lives of the Philosophers and Sophists* and Lives of the Christian saints cannot be closely pressed; but it is certainly true that here, if anywhere, are the saints of paganism, among these men of high culture, some of them zealous pagans and fanatical theurgists. Julian certainly looked upon the theurgist Maximus of Ephesus, who initiated him into the Chaldaean mysteries and was his spiritual guide, as a saint; but he was himself, in his heightened consciousness of the presence of the gods, and in his constant and very real sense of his divine mission, much closer to the true ideal of sainthood than was his band of *soi-disant* philosophers. Perhaps some of his closest followers and associates could be counted as pagan saints, too, men like the great Roman aristocrat Praetextatus, who held numerous priesthoods, was initiated into all the mysteries, campaigned actively on behalf of pagan- ism under Christian emperors (see Chapter V), and was the acknow- ledged leader of the pagan aristocracy of Rome.

The difficulty in identifying pagan saints is not accidental. There could not be, in paganism, any real parallel to the mass phenomenon of Christian monasticism, because of the complete renunciation of the world that was central to the latter. Graeco-Roman paganism was, through and through, so entirely wedded to the life of the city or village that such a total rejection of it would have appeared, not as an extreme form of self-denial, but as an unthinkable betrayal. This explains Julian's violent hostility towards monks, and it was also an ingredient in his contempt for the Cynics, who behaved as social outcasts. But even the Cynics haunted the market-place rather than the desert, and their rejection of human society was considerably less total than that of the monks. Many ancient philosophies preached some form of asceticism, including the much maligned Epicurean system that promoted the simple life, and Julian was himself an ascetic. But pagan philosophic self-denial was to be practised 'within the world', not out of it. Perhaps typical is Stoicism, which originally enjoined upon its adherents full participation in the tests and trials of public life and the holding of office. There was thus a basic antagonism between the Christian and the pagan ideals of saintliness, a tension that was never resolved.

Pagan and Christian Festivals

The most important religious form of public life was the festival. The idea of the week-end holiday developed from the Christian Sunday, which became a holy-day/holiday under the Christian Empire (Con- stantine made the first move by forbidding legal business on Sundays).

Throughout the Roman period, however, and to the end of the fourth
century, it was the traditional pagan festivals, such as the Neptunalia
and Saturnalia, and those of the imperial cult, that constituted the real
holidays, and altogether they took up a third of the year. Yet they did
not merely furnish pretexts for rest-days off work. Their true significance
was far greater: it was the festivals and games that provided the occasions for the demonstration of popular solidarity, an essential ingredient
of political life under a system that deprived the common people of
even the show of political power. From time immemorial these demon-
strations had been cast in a religious mould, with everyone in the State
or, in the case of a local festival, everyone in the community, from the
highest to the lowest, making common cause and joining in the celebrations, both solemn and joyful, in honour of the particular deity
whose festival it was.

In the year 354 a Christian notable of Rome, Valentinus by name,
received as a New Year present a magnificently illustrated calendar, the
work of a scribe named Furius Dionysius Filocalus (the last being a most
appropriate Greek name meaning 'lover of beauty'), also a Christian,
who was later to inscribe numerous epigrams written by Pope Damasus,
whose follower he became. This *Calendar of 354* or *Calendar of Filocalus*,
which has come down to us in seventeenth-century copies of a Carolingian manuscript, is divided into two parts, the first being a real pagan
calendar, with the festivals of the Roman religious year, and the seven
days of the week with their astrological properties. Each page of this
part is illustrated, with figures representing the months, the gods of the
week, and the personifications of four great cities of the Empire, and
portraits of the consuls of the year, the Emperor Constantius and Gallus
Caesar. The second part is composed of a series of annexes, four of a
secular character—lists of the consuls and the prefects of Rome, and a
brief description and chronicle of the city of Rome—and five Christian,
namely the cycle of Easter, a list of the bishops of Rome, a Christian
chronicle written by a third-century bishop of Rome and brought up to
date, and lists of the burial dates of bishops and martyrs. These last two
constituted an important calendar of Christian festivals, to set against
the official one of pagan festivals in the first part. So the *Calendar of 354*
contained the outlines of the Christian calendar that was destined to
replace the pagan one; but the relative prominence given to the two
leaves no doubt that it was still the pagan one that had the greater
importance for the everyday life of the people of Rome, while the Christian calendar was still unofficial, celebrated by the Christian majority in
Rome as part of their private lives and worship, not yet as a part of
corporate and official public life. (**28**)

The main part of the *Calendar* presents an intriguing amalgam of
urban pomp and humbler, even rural, celebration, a reminder of the

rustic roots of Rome's power. There are details of the official round of
the Roman aristocrat and gentleman—the meeting days of the Senate,
the swearing-in of the new magistrates (31 December) and the gladiatorial shows they had to give beforehand (on ten days in December),
and the processions and games based on the horse trials of the knights,
once a military necessity. Yet the summer solstice, the vintage, and the
beginning of winter are noted, too, and in the context certainly refer to
pagan festivities. As for the illustrations, some of the representations of
the months are purely secular, and mostly epitomize the rural pursuits
of the season, such as the shepherd with a young goat and vessels of milk
and cheese, the figure for March. Three of them, however, refer to one
of the pagan festivals of the month, echoing in this other calendars, in
mosaic, which also have a mixture of seasonal and religious representations. One of these is January, which shows a local dignitary making the
annual offering of incense on 3 January to the 'household gods' of the
neighbourhood, the Lares Compitales, whose images stood in a shrine
at the cross roads. The figure for April is a male dancer with castanets
before a small statue of Venus (mistakenly drawn as a boy by the modern
copyist) set on an altar, in front of which stands a lighted candle in a
large candlestick, an evident reference to the little-known ceremonies in
honour of Venus that took place on 1 April. November depicts a ton-
sured priest of Isis engaged in the ritual of her festival. The emphasis on
astrology in the *Calendar*, with the appropriate sign of the zodiac on each
page, the days of the week with their supposed properties, and the careful noting of unfavourable days (called 'Egyptian days'), reveals the
degree of interest in this pseudo-science even among the highly educated
—and Christian—members of the Roman nobility in that age of
superstition, and is entirely in tune with what we know from other
sources. The handbook of astrology written by the still-pagan Firmicus
Maternus (see Chapter IV) was also addressed to a member of that
society, and Julian's dream of the death of Constantius was couched in
astrological terms:

> When Jupiter reaches the broad bound of famed Aquarius,
> And Saturn comes to Virgo's twenty-fifth degree,
> Constantius, king of the land of Asia, shall attain
> The hateful and grievous end of sweet life.

A main feature of the catalogue of pagan festivals is the dominance
of the imperial cult which, far from withering away under the Christian
Empire, acquired a new importance from the build-up of the 'sacred
monarchy' dating from the Tetrarchy. This importance can be gauged
from the fact that no fewer than ninety-three days of festivals and games
were devoted to festivals of the imperial cult, mostly those of the Constantinian House. A celebrated inscription from the little Roman town

of Hispellum in Umbria reveals that Constantine confined himself to securalizing the imperial cult, leaving it otherwise untouched or even promoting it, for it was far too useful as a focus of loyalty to the emperor and Empire to be abolished. At Hispellum, owing to local circumstances, there was to be a new centre of the provincial imperial cult, with a 'temple of the Flavian family' (i.e. the Constantinian House, whose family name was Flavius, like that of the Emperor Vespasian and his sons over two centuries earlier), a priest, and games, but with the significant proviso that 'the temple dedicated to our name must not be polluted with the trickeries of foul superstition'. The use of the word *nomen* (name) in place of the normal word *numen* (divinity), for the dedication of the temple, was itself a subtle substitution in the cause of secularization. Henceforth there would be no sacrifices and perhaps no other pagan ritual, and the priest would be chosen merely to give the games and preside at them and at any other celebrations. The reformed, lay cult of the Second Flavians was also instituted throughout the provinces of North Africa (see above for possible guild headquarters at Carthage), and doubtless all over the Empire. There would not have been the difficulty in eliminating the pagan rites from this cult which the Christian emperors were to encounter in attacking other forms of paganism, because it was by its very nature State-orientated rather than truly religious, and the 'worshippers' would be quick to take note of the wishes of the 'divinity' as to the kind of cult he preferred. So the imperial cult continued to flourish, with a simple shift of emphasis from worshipping to honouring the emperor, his family, and the so-called *divi*—former emperors, from Julius Caesar and Augustus onwards, who after their death had been judged worthy of the official process of deification. Constantine's own deification was interpreted by the court as a latter-day Ascent of Elijah, to judge from the commemorative coins issued by his sons, on which an ambiguous hand of God—really a Christian concept, but capable of interpretation by pagans as the hand of Jupiter—receives a chariot-borne Constantine into heaven.

Of the true pagan festivals in the *Calendar of 354*, the longest and most important, in public terms, were those of Cybele (22–28 March and 4–10 April), Ceres (12–19 April), Flora (30 April to 3 May), Apollo (5–13 July), Jupiter Liberator (13–18 October), the Games of the Sun (19–22 October), the festival of Isis (28 October–3 November), and the Saturnalia (17–23 December (only the first day is marked in the *Calendar*)). A little is known of the pagan ritual of some of these festivals, most of which were also signalized by the more secular rejoicings of shows in the theatre and chariot-racing in the circus. The festivities of Cybele included the felling of the pine-tree sacred to Attis (22 March), the washing of the image of Cybele herself in the sea (27 March), and processions of the eunuch priests dancing and gashing themselves in

sacred frenzy, to the music of the flute and tambourine (24 March). The
Saturnalia, which began with sacrifices in front of the temple of Saturn
in the Forum and a public banquet, continued with entertainments
and revelries in private houses; an important feature was the relaxation
of social conventions that permitted slaves to treat their masters as
equals, and even be waited on by them. The great November festival
of Isis, which inspires the illustration for this month in the *Calendar*—a
priest of Isis holding up the sacred rattle and a tray with a rearing snake
on it, before a bust of the jackal-headed god Anubis—was comple-
mented in the spring by the festival of the Voyage of Isis on 5 March, at
which a ship containing the image of Isis was launched on the sea, after
a solemn procession of which Apuleius gives a wonderful description at
the end of the *Metamorphoses* (or *Golden Ass*). This formed the inauguration ceremony of the open season for navigation, and so strong were its
auspicious associations that the images of the Egyptian gods came to be
used almost exclusively on the VOTA PVBLICA coins issued in Rome
for the *vota* ceremony on 3 January, at which prayers were offered for the
safety of the emperor and his family and thus of the State. These coins,
with Isiac scenes and images on the reverse, were issued in the name,
and with the obverse portrait, of all the fourth-century emperors from
the Tetrarchy to the House of Valentinian, including Constantine and
his sons, and Julian. Then, in 379/80, on the accession of the intransigent
Christian emperor Theodosius who was later to initiate the effective
proscription of paganism, a most interesting development took place:
the imperial busts disappeared from the obverse and were replaced by
the busts of Isis and Serapis. From being a semi-official, special-occasion
coinage perhaps authorized by the emperor, the Isis *vota* coins had
become unofficial, evidently issued by the pagan aristocracy of Rome
at their own expense, over a period of about fifteen years, until the
collapse of the pagan party after the defeat of the pro-pagan usurper
Eugenius by Theodosius in 394. The importance attached to the Isis
coins by the pagan nobles shows conclusively how one and the same
festival could mean quite different things to different people. A festive
day that, from the point of view of a Christian emperor and other
Christians, was simply the occasion of the formal expression of loyalty to
the Crown, of an annual donative to the army, and of secular pomp and
amusements, principally games, was to the Roman nobility a festival
of pagan religious character. (**12**)

The day of the *vota*, 3 January, by now formed part of the great New
Year festival of Janus of the *Kalends* of January. This increased considerably in importance in the late Empire, though in 354 it had not
yet achieved official recognition and been inserted in the festival
calendar, hence its absence from our document. Libanius devoted two
short works to a description of the New Year festival and, although these

were written towards the end of his life, the course taken by the celebrations would have been substantially the same in the middle of the century. On New Year's Eve people exchanged presents, and the night of the New Year was kept with feasting, drinking and dancing, and with processions round the town singing bawdy songs. At dawn the doors of the houses were decorated with garlands, and those who were to provide the chariot-races on the third day were escorted to the temples in a torchlight procession, wearing purple and with their slaves scattering money to the crowd. They then sacrificed and prayed for the victory of their horses, and went on to visit the governors where, together with the other members of the *curia*, they gave presents of gold to their staffs, and exchanged greetings with the governors. During the rest of the day some slept, while others accompanied gift-bearing processions through the town. On 2 January, all stayed at home and enjoyed themselves. Master and slaves played dice together, and pupils had no need to fear their pedagogue or teacher. The games, with chariot-races, were held on the third day, the day of the *vota publica*. The rest of the day was spent at the baths and in banqueting and dicing. On 4 January the festival was over, and people returned reluctantly to work.

The games of 3 January were the most magnificent of the year. At Constantinople they were given by the consuls, one of whom was often the emperor himself, and in Rome by the praetors. In other cities, including the Antioch of Libanius, they were given by leading members of the *curia*. The praetorian games at Rome were expected to cost several thousands of pounds of gold, and they thus constituted a kind of surtax on the leading Roman nobles. It was perhaps with these grand games that the curious medallions known as 'contorniates' were connected. The issue of these heavy bronze coins or medals with raised edges began around the time of Constantius' visit to Rome in 357. They were struck in the mint of Rome by the authority of the prefect of the city. The representations they bear are overwhelmingly pagan, with images of numerous pagan gods and scenes from mythology. They reflect with some exactness the whole cultural ambience of the games, and in general the popular culture of Rome, over more than a century. The obverses bear a variety of types of image. One large group has the portraits of Alexander the Great and his mother Olympias, by now figures of romantic legend, or of past emperors (including Julian), especially those who, like Nero and Trajan, had been celebrated for the magnificence of their games; a few, from the end of the fourth century on, have portraits of reigning emperors. Another variety of obverse has figures of charioteers and beast-fighters, or theatrical masks. Pagan gods also appear in the place of honour, on the obverse: the Egyptian god Serapis, Mercury, Apollo, Pan, and especially the goddess Roma. A last group bears figures of famous Greeks and Romans of the past, especially writers: Homer, Solon, Euripides, Socrates, Demosthenes, Terence, Sallust, Horace, Apuleius, Apollonius of Tyana, and others. (The last two both had a popular reputation as magicians.) Men of letters, pagan gods—including the Unconquered Sun, Cybele, Attis, Castor and Pollux, and Wisdom in the form of Athene—and representations from the games (charioteers, beast-fights, the Circus Maximus, actresses playing Venus or the three Graces, etc.) appear also on the reverses, together with themes connected with Alexander or glorifying imperial power (e.g. emperor on horseback with captive barbarian), and mythological figures—Bellerophon, Jason, Scylla, etc. Some of the subjects may have been suggested by tableaux on the stage or paintings exhibited at the games. (11)

Some of the gods were directly connected with festivals and games, notably Cybele and Attis, Apollo, and the Sun, while Castor and Pollux had a temple in the hippodrome at Constantinople, and the Sun-God was almost invariably represented in art as a charioteer. (An elaborate cosmic symbolism for the circus had been worked out by philosophers, in which the circus itself represented the course of the Sun, the four factions were the four Seasons, the twelve gates the Months, etc., but there is no sign that this symbolism meant anything to the people at large.) Festivals signalized by chariot-racing in the circus are marked in the *Calendar of 354* with the letters 'CM' (for *circenses missus*) and the number of races (generally twenty-four). Circuses, which were very costly to produce, were given in connection with most of the imperial festivals, including the last day of games commemorating important victories, such as the Gothic Games, from 4 to 9 February, and the Persian Games, from 13 to 17 May. They also formed part of a number of festivals of the pagan gods, including Jupiter in various aspects, Janus, Hercules, Mars (two festivals), Dionysus, Castor and Pollux, Cybele, Ceres (first and last days of her festival—an unusual honour), Flora, Apollo, probably Neptune, Vulcan and, last but not least, the Sun-God who, like Jupiter, had three such festivals, namely the commemoration of the dedication of the temple of the Sun and Moon on 28 August, the Games of the Sun from 19 to 22 October, with thirty-six chariot-races on the last day, and the Birthday of the Unconquered Sun on 25 December, signalized by thirty races. The unusually high number of races given at festivals of Jupiter and of the Sun reveals the importance of these two cults in the fourth century.

Indeed the 'coincidence' of the Birthday of the Sun, wrongly supposed to have been the date of the winter solstice, falling on what is now Christmas Day points in the same direction. It was, of course, no accident: the Christian holy birthday replaced the pagan one by deliberate design, perhaps from as early as the reign of Constantine. In the East Christmas was long celebrated on 6 January, the date of the pagan festival of Aion, the god of eternity, at Alexandria, and this finally became the feast of the Epiphany or Revelation, a name as well suited to the divine birthday as to the arrival of the Magi and the revealing of Christ to the Gentiles. Many of the pagan festivals, and not only those featuring in the Graeco-Roman calendar, were replaced in the same way by Christian ones, two other notable ones being the setting of the feast of St. John the Baptist on Midsummer Day, and of All Saints' Day on 1 November, the time of the great Celtic festival of the dead, while Mothering Sunday harks back to the spring festival of Cybele, the Mother of the Gods. For the Christian authorities this substitution was one solution to the problem posed by the great strength of popular attachment to the pagan festivals, that had formed such an important part of their way of life, and were still being publicly celebrated. For evidence of this we need look no further than the works of Augustine and John Chrysostom who, at the very end of the fourth century, in provinces as far apart as North Africa and Syria, were still criticizing their respective congregations for attending pagan rites and merry-making. Action of a constructive kind was clearly necessary. As far back as the mid third century St. Gregory Thaumaturgus, or Wonder-worker, the energetic bishop of Neocaesarea in Pontus (the northern-most province in Asia Minor), who had been a pupil of Origen, was initiating the work. After the persecution of the Christians under the Emperor Decius in 250, he had the bodies of the martyrs buried here and there throughout the region, and instituted festivals in their honour, with plenty of jollification. According to his fourth-century biographer St. Gregory of Nyssa, brother of St. Basil, this was prin-cipally responsible for the success of Gregory Thaumaturgus' missionary campaigns in rural Pontus, a success so overwhelming that, when he died, there were only seventeen pagans left in the province, although there had been only seventeen Christians when he arrived! Even allowing for exaggeration, there was a major advance in Christianity in Pontus during this period, and though much was accomplished by Gregory's evangelism and his miracles—exorcizing demons and the like—the institution of the Christian festivals was a deliberate move to attract large numbers of recalcitrant pagans, who were deeply attached to their pagan festivals. Gregory of Nyssa, writing not long after the reign of Julian, may well have witnessed in the Asia Minor of his own day the attraction which they still exercised.

It was one of the new, Christian, festivals, that of the Epiphany, which Julian attended while he was in Gaul in 361, in the city of Vienne, in order to throw dust in the eyes of the court and army, whom he feared might resent his conversion to paganism, as he celebrated his fifth anniversary of power and began his preparations for his march against Constantius. The anniversary was marked by magnificent games, presided over by Julian wearing a splendid, jewelled diadem. On the Epiphany he went to church to pray. We are not told anything further about how the local Church—which was a strong one as elsewhere in south Gaul, especially in the cities of the Rhône valley—celebrated the festival; but the incident, as well as revealing that those whom Julian most needed to impress at this time were mostly Christian, shows how the Christian calendar of festivals was developing, all over the Roman world.

The substitution of Christian festivals for pagan ones was one means of combating the attachment of the common people to them, and was particularly effective when a direct substitution was possible, as with Christmas Day. Another line of attack was the de-paganization of existing festivals. This Constantine was able to effect for the imperial cult, as we have seen, by forbidding all 'taint' of truly pagan ritual, and leaving just the secular rejoicings. The completion of the process is to be seen in the *Calendar of Polemius Silvius*, produced in mid-fifth-century Gaul, in which, to take just one example, the Day of Blood of the cult of Cybele, on which the priests cut themselves and new devotees castrated themselves, has become the 'Birthday of the Chalice', of which the memorial is still continued in Passion Sunday. Constantine even felt free to institute festivals of a semi-pagan character in honour of his new Christian city of Constantinople, as we have seen (Chapter II). The encaenia festival was continued in the same form for most of the fourth century, falling victim at the end of it to the reforming zeal of the Christian emperor Theodosius.

Mosaic Pavements

From considering the conditions and character of religious life in the period of Constantine and Julian, we turn to the physical environment that surrounded Christians and pagans from the cradle to the grave, especially as it throws light on their religious beliefs. Inevitably most of the evidence comes from the houses and tombs of the rich. The poor could not afford to commission expensive mosaic floors or tomb frescoes, or buy silverware or sculptured sarcophagi. So the picture we shall be building up will be a rather one-sided one, although the nature of the figured pottery from Africa suggests that much of the pattern would have been repeated at a humbler level, if there had been enough money available to stimulate popular art in other dioceses. However, we must reckon with the fact that there was a higher proportion of pagans to Christians in the upper echelons of society than lower down.

Certainly paganism is dominant on the figured mosaics with which the principal rooms of the most luxurious houses were often floored. But the use of pagan mythology for decorative purposes presents a problem. For it formed the common cultural background of pagan and

Christian alike, and much of it was quite unexceptionable to Christians, being as innocent of truly pagan content as, for example, the classicizing art of the Renaissance. The proof of this is the existence of monuments with a mixture of Christian and pagan motifs, the most famous being the silver wedding-casket of Secundus and Projecta (really a toilette box destined for the bride), on which a naked Venus, Tritons and Nereids appear together with chi-rho monograms and a Christian inscription (the appropriateness of Venus, the goddess of love and beauty, is obvious, though her presence is none the less surprising—to us—on a work destined for Christians). This casket (in the British Museum) comes from the senatorial milieu of Rome, and was made in about 380. In the Constantinian period, an unknown number of fashion-conscious people at various levels of society followed the emperor's conversion to Christianity without any clear idea of what it involved, especially as regards the exclusiveness of the Christian religion. This led to some degree of confusion—a separate phenomenon from the careful combination of disparate motifs on the Projecta casket and elsewhere—that is manifested in artistic and other expressions of religious sentiment.

The clearest case of this is to be found in some tombs in the Rhineland (see below), but it is possible that some British floor-mosaics may have been commissioned by new converts in a similar state of confusion. They were laid in villas at Frampton and Hinton St. Mary in Dorset, in the reign of Constantine or soon after, by a school of mosaicists established in Dorchester. The one at Frampton, recorded in the eighteenth century and since probably destroyed, presents an engaging mixture of robustly pagan motifs with the Christian symbol of the chi-rho, which is set in the centre of the chord of the apse at one end of the room. The two main panels of the floor, which, like the Hinton St. Mary mosaic, formed the pavement of two adjoining rooms of unequal size, depict respectively Bellerophon and Dionysus with his panther. Four panels round Bellerophon have scenes from the myth of Venus and Adonis, and Cupid and Neptune appear in the border, together with pagan verses in praise of both. Besides the Christogram, the large vase or chalice in the middle of the apse decoration may well be Christian, representing the Christian cup of life rather than the Dionysiac (as in the origin of this motif). The owner who commissioned this mixture must have been either a new convert or a Christian who looked upon the whole of pagan mythology as his cultural treasure-house, irrespective of religious content.

The Hinton St. Mary pavement, on the other hand, is more muted in its paganism, and could even be susceptible of a wholly Christian symbolic interpretation. In the central panel of its main part, where the Frampton mosaic has Bellerophon, there is the head of a young, beardless man who can only be Christ himself, set against a chi-rho monogram that surrounds his head as if with a halo. The depiction of sacred figures, and even the monogram of Christ, on floors where they could be walked upon was later forbidden, and it is certainly no mere chance that this dining-room floor with the portrait of Christ was laid in the most remote of all the dioceses. The smaller portion of the floor has a central Bellerophon slaying the Chimaera, in the position corresponding to the figure of Dionysus at Frampton. Round the borders are hunting scenes with dogs chasing deer, and in the corners of the main part are four uncomfortable-looking figures, Winds without their trumpets, who may be intended to represent the Evangelists. Bellerophon may have been looked upon as a symbol of the triumph of Good over Evil, but he was too conventional a feature of dining-room floors for this to be at all certain. Both this room and the one at Frampton could have been used occasionally as Christian chapels, on Sundays or just on festival days, a use for which the Hinton mosaic would have been particularly suitable; but we cannot be sure of this. (**30**)

Bellerophon appears again on another British floor of the Constantinian period, in the villa at Lullingstone in Kent. This was reoccupied by a pagan family towards the end of the third century, after a period of abandonment. The modifications made at this time included the installation, in a semi-basement room that had previously been a shrine of Water-Nymphs, of two marble portrait busts left behind by the second-century owner, with votive pots containing offerings embedded in the floor in front of them. A little later a temple-mausoleum of square Romano-Celtic plan was built behind the house, and a young man and woman were buried there with rich grave-goods. The mosaic pavements were laid in the reception room and dining-room in the mid fourth century. It is the reception room that has Bellerophon and the Chimaera, and the Four Seasons, the latter being an exceptionally popular subject in rural Britain in the fourth century, suggesting, in the dining-room, the fruits of the earth in their season, and in funerary contexts (generally on the Continent) the harmony and permanence of the rhythm of the universe, and thus immortality. On the Lullingstone dining-room floor are Europa and the Bull, and the two lines of verse that accompany them, on the subject of Juno's jealousy, may indicate that the design of the pavement was, as so often, prophylactic rather than purely decorative—a protection against the Evil Eye. The good state of preservation of the mosaics shows that neither pavement can have been unduly displeasing to the Christians living in the villa, when at least part of the family became converted, not long after the reign of Julian, and the famous chapel (or Christian room), with its frescoes of Orante-figures and ornate chi-rho monograms painted by an artist from the Continent, was installed above the basement room where the portrait busts were still honoured with offerings. The building history of Lullingstone villa during the fourth century, with its temple—disused when the Christian chapel was erected—its pagan mosaics, and later the chapel itself, vividly reflects the religious changes in the life of this one upper-class family, and doubtless exemplifies the gradual progression from paganism to Christianity of many other households of Romano-British landowners as well. (**29**)

The pavements at Lullingstone may have been laid by a Continental mosaicist. Certainly they do not fit into the pattern of local 'schools', or rather workshops, of mosaicists that is beginning to be established for fourth-century Britain. One of these, as we have seen, was based at Dorchester in Dorset. Another, the largest in the country, responsible for about forty known mosaics, was at Cirencester, and its claim to fame is that it invented the special British type of circular Orpheus mosaic, with the divine musician in the centre and the charmed animals arranged in unbroken concentric circles round him. The finest of these is the one at Woodchester (Gloucestershire), that is uncovered every ten years. In this, Orpheus is displaced from the geometric centre by an octagonal mock-basin of mosaic fish, and instead intrudes upon the zone of birds surrounding it, while the animals are disposed in an outer circle, and pairs of Water-Nymphs occupy the corners, inside the wide and richly ornamented border. At least ten Orpheus pavements, spanning the period from *c.* 300 to about the mid fourth century, have been found in Britain, six of them laid by the Cirencester mosaicists in the earlier part of this period. Two more were the work of another local school, based on Brough-on-Humber, in the mid fourth century. The theme of Orpheus charming the beasts had been adopted by the Christians as a parallel and symbol of Christ the Good Shepherd attracting and taming mankind, as early as the second century, as is known from writers and catacomb frescoes. So it is quite possible, indeed likely, that some of the British mosaics are Christian-inspired. On the other hand, the Orpheus myth was much in vogue with fourth-century pagans also, often, it would seem, as a kind of counterpoise to Christ the Good Shepherd. Julian himself calls Orpheus 'the most ancient of the inspired philosophers', while Themistius uses him as a simile for Constantius charming the usurper Vetranio (see Chapters II and IV). More significant still, in North Africa the faces of two mosaic Orpheuses were blanked out or mutilated under the Christian Empire, proving that in one diocese at least he had not lost his pagan associations. One of these, laid in the first half of the fourth century, had a temple behind his head to emphasize his sacred character. It must not be forgotten, however, that the subject of Orpheus and the animals lent itself to a composition of great charm in which the master craftsman could display all his skill, and it was in consequence a very popular genre subject, often associated with pools and running water (note the imitation basin on the Woodchester pavement), so we should not be too quick to read religious significance, either Christian or pagan, into a particular example.

One Orpheus, however, at Brading in the Isle of Wight, is part of a unique group of magico-religious mosaics. A panel on one floor depicts a cock-headed man, perhaps the Gnostic deity Abraxas, two griffins, and what is probably a temple with steps or a ladder leading up to it. This strange scene perhaps represents some kind of initiation, with the neophyte in a bird-mask, the temple and steps symbolizing the soul's ascent to heaven, and the griffins as guardians of the dead. In another room an astronomer is best interpreted as a symbol of the astral mysticism that was such a strong ingredient in late paganism of the Julianic kind (see Chapter V). The rest of this pavement is devoted to a collection of mythological figures fraught with mystical—especially Dionysiac—and philosophical significance: Ceres and Triptolemus (leading figures of the Eleusinian Mysteries of growth and renewal, and symbols of the celestial banquet—'bread of heaven'), Lycurgus and Ambrosia (characters in the cycle of legends of Dionysus, Lycurgus being the Thracian king who attacked the Maenad Ambrosia, who was metamorphosed into a vine and strangled him), Perseus and Andromeda (suggesting the theme of victory over death and evil), Medusa, the Winds that waft the soul to heaven, a Satyr, a shepherd and Maenads, and a sea *thiasos*—a procession of marine Centaurs and other mythological sea-beasts that was supposed to escort the souls of initiates of Dionysus to the Isles of the Blest. The villa owner who commissioned these mosaics must have been a pagan of a fashionably mystical turn of mind, apparently an initiate in various mysteries, including some esoteric, perhaps Gnostic, ones as well as the commoner ones. Many a member of the highest Roman pagan aristocracy was a priest in the cults of Dionysus-Liber and an initiate of Eleusis, as we know from inscriptions at Rome. (31)

The Vergilian pavement from the villa at Low Ham in Somerset forms a complete contrast to the Brading mosaics, for it is a splendid example of 'literary' paganism, the common heritage of both Christian and pagan. Laid in the mid fourth century, it depicts scenes from the *Aeneid*, thought to have been copied from an illustrated book belonging to the villa owner, or else from an imported craftsmen's copy-book. It depicts the story of Dido and Aeneas, dominated by Venus, who stands in the centre with one Cupid holding a reversed torch for Dido, who died as a result of the affair, and another holding a raised torch symbolizing Aeneas, who lived to found Rome. The style is simple and a trifle crude, but lively, and the mosaic is executed in vivid colours, using local materials. The owner of the large villa where this composition floored the cold baths was clearly a man of literary taste and culture, perhaps, even, the proud possessor of an expensive illustrated manuscript. The story of Dido and Aeneas was the most famous romantic 'novel' of the Roman world. At much the same time as the Low Ham pavement was laid, the young Augustine at his studies wept over Dido's fate, as he tells us in his *Confessions*.

Britain, as we have seen, was remarkably prosperous in the Constantinian period, and the great wealth of mosaic pavements laid in and around this time is one of the direct consequences. By contrast, very few figured ones indeed were created in contemporary Gaul, the floors of the great luxury villas of Aquitania and the Moselle valley being exclusively decorated with geometric patterns. An Orpheus pavement in a villa at Blanzy-lès-Fismes (Aisne), arranged round a marble-lined basin, may be compared with the British series of Orpheuses; but, significantly, it does not appear to have been laid by a local team of mosaicists, but probably by one from Italy or even Africa.

It was mosaicists from North Africa, some of them at least from the capital city of Carthage, who were responsible for what is perhaps the most magnificent single complex of mosaics ever discovered, which formed the floors of the great villa near Piazza Armerina in the eastern interior of Sicily. The remains of this extremely large, rich, and luxurious mansion lie in a wooded valley not far from the Roman road from Syracuse to Agrigento, part of the main route between Italy and Africa. The mosaics, which are of an exclusively and triumphantly pagan character, are among the finest products of the Constantinian period (attempts to date them to the tetrarchic period or the late fourth century can be discounted), and must have been laid over a long span of years, extending from *c.* 310/20 to *c.* 360/70, by many teams of mosaicists working at the same time.

The identity of the owner has proved elusive, but the mosaics reveal something about him. For one thing, he was clearly enormously rich. It is certain that he had a big stake in the (probably African) wild beast trade for the amphitheatre, as that is the single subject of the floor of a vast corridor, the Great Hunt Corridor, in which a figure standing and looking on, attended by soldiers, is apparently the proprietor of the villa. The presence of the soldiers makes it likely that he held high office at some point in his career, and indeed the situation of the villa, in charming countryside near an important highway, and certain features of it, such as the basilica for holding audiences, and the picture of the official ceremony of greeting on the vestibule floor, would have made it very suitable for a man of affairs. But, whoever he was, he was a very decided pagan. One room has been identified as a chapel of Aphrodite, while part of the Small Hunt Room, which has lively episodes of a hunt in five bands, shows a sacrifice to Diana. Another room has a large representation of Orpheus charming the animals—yet another testimony to its popularity in late imperial times. Here, as at Brading, he is certainly a pagan Orpheus. (32)

One of the most striking parts of the villa is the great Trifoliate Hall, shaped like a clover-leaf, with three apses. The main subject of the mosaics is Hercules and his deeds. Here, defeated giants worthy of the hand of Michelangelo knot their muscles in an effort to pull out the arrows shot by the hero. There, Diomedes' Thracian riders fall headlong from their horses, surrounded by other vanquished enemies of Hercules and symbols of his labours—the Nemean lion, the Hydra, the river Peneus and the pitchfork that served to cleanse the Augean stables, the bull of Marathon, the serpent that guarded the golden apples of the Hesperides, triple-bodied Geryon, the Erymanthian boar, the Arcadian stag, and the three-headed dog Cerberus brought up from Hades. In the left apse is the apotheosis of the hero, who is crowned by one god and supported by another. The strength and realism of the style of the mosaics are breathtaking indeed. Other mythological subjects as well are represented on this same floor: Apollo; Cyparissus, who killed his pet stag by mistake, and was changed into a cypress-tree; Hesione rescued, like Andromeda, from a sea-monster; Endymion the beloved of the Moon; and Lycurgus (whom we have met before at Brading), the king who tried to kill the Maenad Ambrosia, and was overwhelmed by the luxuriant vine into which she was changed.

Such a riot of paganism would be worthy of a follower of Julian himself, and there has indeed been an attempt to connect it with one of his highest officials. But the main body of the mosaics is earlier, as we have seen. There is, however, a possibility that the name of the estate belonging to the villa was *Philosophiana* and, if this is so, it may give a hint of the owner's favourite pursuits, literary and philosophical-religious. This conjures up a picture of him living the philosophic life at Piazza Armerina in company with a few friends, rather like the Great Tew circle of Lucius Carey Falkland before the English Civil Wars. But this is a little discordant with the indications of his interest in the wild beast trade, though it must be remembered that in the course of the fourth century the villa may have had more than one owner. It is greatly to be hoped that an inscription identifying the man who commissioned the mosaics will come to light in the unexcavated part of the villa.

The Roman art of mosaic pavement laying flourished greatly in the North African provinces throughout the middle and late Empire, and some of the finest of all known mosaics were created there. The prosperous wheat- and olive-growing countryside, and the solid municipal structure of Roman Africa, dotted as it was with hundreds of small towns, provided just the right conditions for a large and skilled artisan class, which produced beautiful buildings and excellent pottery as well as mosaics for their numerous customers, and doubtless more perishable goods, too. There were certainly many different local schools or workshops of mosaic, but these have not yet been studied sufficiently for the pattern to be established.

The burning of Carthage by Maxentius in 311 entailed a great deal of rebuilding under Constantine and, despite the almost total destruction of the city in post-Roman times, an impressive number of mosaic pavements from the fourth century has survived. The so-called House of the Horses has some of the earliest of these, dateable to not long after 300. The house gets its name from the pavement of a large room that opened on to the central part of a courtyard. It is divided into squares, with alternate panels of marble inlay and mosaic. Almost all of the surviving 62 mosaic panels (of an original 98) depict a horse, usually accompanied by a human figure or tiny scene. They are carefully worked in extremely small tesserae, and must have been very expensive to buy. The human figure is frequently a god—Jupiter, Neptune, Mars, Minerva, Mercury or Attis—or a personification such as Victory and the Fortuna of Carthage. A shepherd carrying a sheep is, in this company, almost certainly not a Good Shepherd. The little scenes placed above the horses' backs are mostly mythological: Romulus and Remus with the She-Wolf, Danae, Daedalus with Pasiphae's bull, Icarus, various labours of Hercules, Orpheus, Lycurgus and the vine, and many more. Others feature scenes from everyday life: fishermen, hunters, athletes, a boxer, a dramatic poet, a man reading a book, an augur observing the flight of birds, dice players, etc. It is thought that these scenes and the other figures give the names of the horses in a kind of erudite gloss, for race-horses, as these clearly are, have their names almost invariably written in full on other mosaics. Thus the entire pavement constituted a kind of guessing game for visitors, in addition to its main purpose, which would have been to commemorate circus games given by the owner of the house. The absence of written names may also have been devised as a means of warding off the curses which rivals and their followers so often attempted to put on 'enemy' horses, usually by inserting lead tablets inscribed with magical formulae into the tombs of those cut off in their prime, whose spirits were believed to lend themselves to the accomplishment of such designs. (27)

A wide border surrounding this pavement on three sides depicts eight boys attired as amphitheatre beast-hunters, hunting small animals and birds (lion cub, duck, cock, etc.). It is closely paralleled by one of the mosaics at Piazza Armerina, so closely, in fact, that there can be little doubt that the same workshop was responsible for both. In front of the room with the horses are mosaics with hunting scenes. The central panel shows a big game hunt that is likewise decidedly reminiscent of the two great hunting mosaics at Piazza Armerina. In the courtyard was a semicircular fountain paved with a charming little mosaic of two *putti*, named Navigius and Naccara, fishing from boats.

Opening off one of the short sides of this courtyard was a dining-room that may or may not have belonged to the same house. Certainly the mosaics are some twenty to thirty years later, of the mid-Constantinian period. The main decorative part of the floor is made up of medallions formed by an interlacing wreath of bay, enclosing the busts of the four Seasons, a peacock spreading its tail, and a duck. In between the medallions are other figures: the God of the Year (Genius Saeculi) holding the zodiac (he is often found in company with the Seasons), the toilet of Venus assisted by two attendants labelled Vernaclus and Primitiva, and a nude man sacrificing upon a burning altar. It is clear that the floor was intended to be prophylactic—a very common pre-occupation in Roman Africa, where superstition was especially rife, as it has always been in these countries of the Maghreb—for most of the motifs on it are among those that were believed to promote prosperity or, in one case (the peacock), to protect against the Evil Eye: Apollo's sacred bay, Venus the goddess of luck as well as of love and beauty, the Seasons and God of the Year; and the peacock, Juno's bird, symbol of immortality, with its tail covered with glittering eyes to combat the Evil Eye. The sacrifice, perhaps a magical one (in which nudity was often prescribed), was also in all probability devoted to ensuring prosperity. Although superstition and belief in magic were, as we have seen (in Chapter IV), by no means limited to pagans, the presence of the sacrifice scene on this mosaic guarantees that the owner who commissioned it (whether or not he was the owner of the whole of the House of the Horses) was a pagan. (34)

The Seasons, so often represented as busts crowned with the appropriate attributes, appear in unaccustomed guise on the floor of another grand edifice of the Constantinian period at Carthage, built beside the harbour and overlying part of the Punic tophet, where in pre-Roman times new-born infants were sacrificed to the Carthaginian Baal. The two surviving panels show seated female figures with haloes and long wings, with a look of mediaeval angels about them. Their attributes declare that they are Summer and Autumn respectively. The rest of the floor was strewn with mosaic roses. Remains of frescoes reveal that a marine revel, with Nymphs and Tritons, was painted on the walls. The basilical hall thus decorated, adjoining another large hall, may have been part of an official's residence, or even a public building connected with the export of corn. (33)

The single most popular subject for representation on a mosaic pavement throughout the fourth and early fifth centuries in the North African provinces was the Triumph of Marine Venus. In these compositions great emphasis is placed on the divinity of Venus, by such things as crowns and haloes and the icon-like solemnity of the goddess, who is placed in a central position. As there is no hint, in other sources such as inscriptions, of any increase in devotion to Venus as a pagan cult-figure, it is thought that the phenomenon is rather to be explained by the exigencies of late antique art, which tended to require a strong, central focus for a composition; and also, perhaps, by the ascription of talismanic powers to the image of the goddess of fertility and fortune, surrounded by the teeming life of the sea. From a private house on one of the low hills on which Carthage was built comes one mosaic Coronation of Marine Venus (wrongly called 'Coronation of Ariadne'), of the first half of the fourth century. Venus, enthroned in the centre beneath a domed canopy on an island, sets a crown on her own head. At each side is a boat carrying dwarf dancers and musicians, and fish. One scholar has suggested that such Marine Venus scenes as this may be derived from aquatic tableaux staged in the amphitheatre. That would certainly account for the musicians here. The Coronation of Venus was not, however, invariably marine: on a pavement from Ellès in Tunisia the scene is transposed to dry land, and Venus is being crowned with an enormous, richly-jewelled crown by a pair of busty Centauresses, probably in her role as patroness of the circus faction of the Greens. (35)

A threshold panel from the 'House of Ariadne' at Carthage, where the Coronation of Marine Venus was found, depicts two circus-horses eating palms growing from a central pillar. The palm of victory was one of the more obvious items in the complex of victory symbolism that had come to be strongly associated with the circus, so that representations not only of victorious charioteers but also of single race-horses or of anything to do with the circus were sufficiently redolent of victory in general, and thus of victory over evil forces, to be considered useful as talismans. Hence their use here to protect the threshold, considered one of the most vulnerable parts of the house. North Africa has, indeed, produced an astonishing collection of Roman-period mosaic threshold panels with prophylactic devices for deterring the Evil Eye, many of them obscene—obscenity was regarded as a very powerful charm, because of its connection with fertility. The city of Sousse (ancient Hadrumetum), for example, on the east coast of Tunisia, had a local line in threshold panels featuring male and female sexual organs. The victory symbolism of the circus was another such charm. Talismanic qualities are certainly uppermost in the curious panel from fourth-century Carthage (not, this time, from a threshold) with a design of four horses, representing the four circus factions, arranged like the sails of a windmill, with a single head with staring eyes.

Away from Carthage, with its special reason for rebuilding in the Constantinian period, fewer mosaic pavements were newly laid at this time. Those that have been found display the same preoccupations as at Carthage. Subjects connected with the games were ever popular: for example, a victorious charioteer, and Venus standing naked and haloed in a chariot drawn by four Cupids, from Thuburbo Maius, a town to the south-west of Carthage; and an intriguing pavement from the Great Baths at Tebessa (Roman Theveste), on the border of Algeria and Tunisia, with numbered amphitheatre-animals in medallions and the picture of a galley returning home laden with amphorae, probably commemorating games given by a merchant to celebrate a successful trading venture. There is a Marine Venus pavement of this period from the same baths, and another from a luxurious villa at Hippo, St. Augustine's see (modern Bône-Annaba), a major port on the north coast; while a magnificent Triumph of Neptune and Amphitrite formed a floor at Constantine, the capital of Numidia. Perhaps the most interesting Constantinian mosaic from outside Carthage is a recently discovered floor of a rich villa at Cherchel (Roman Caesarea, capital of Mauretania Caesariensis), another north coast port, that vied with Hippo for the honour of being the second city in Africa. It has two juxtaposed central panels, one with drunken Silenus asleep, being tied with garlands by Cupids, surrounded by vintaging Cupids and other figures; the other with two scenes of the Marriage of Peleus and the Sea-Nymph Thetis, the parents of Achilles. One shows the marine cortège bringing Thetis to Peleus, the other, which is imbued with an impressively religious atmosphere, is of the actual wedding ceremony. Several deities attend: Mercury, Hymenaeus the god of marriage with his torch, and two Fates or Muses, as well as figures like Silenus, Nereids and Maenads.

Apart from the subjects with some degree of religious interest, on which we have concentrated, hunting mosaics and scenes from rural life were also popular, both at Carthage and elsewhere in Africa. Hunting was, indeed, in great vogue among the upper classes in late Roman Africa; they themselves went out hunting the lion, boar, hare, and other animals on their country estates, and provided the lower classes with vicarious enjoyment of such pursuits by laying on beast-fights in the amphitheatre.

Antioch-on-the-Orontes (modern Antakya in Turkey), capital of Roman Syria and great city of the Eastern Empire, was another major centre of the manufacture of mosaic pavements, in both the early and the late Empire. The most sumptuous of the fourth-century mosaics are those of the so-called Constantinian Villa, of the second quarter of the fourth century. The larger portion of the floor of the principal room has an octagonal basin in the centre, and the mosaics surrounding it imitate a ceiling with groin vaulting, as if it were reflected in the water of a larger pool. Along the four diagonally-placed 'groins' are set winged figures of the Seasons. They spring from clumps of acanthus, and hold appropriate flowers and fruits in their laps. Spring and Autumn are crowned with garlands, Summer wears a shady hat, and Winter is hooded. They are among the most beautiful and iconographically complete representations of the Seasons ever found. They are to be counted among the ancestors of the Christian angels in mosaic on the spandrels of the ceiling of the chapel of the Archbishop's Palace at Ravenna, built *c.* 500. Whereas these angels have the four Evangelical Beasts in the triangular spaces between them, in between the Seasons at Antioch are trapezoidal panels with hunting scenes. The one seen first, from the entrance, depicts preparations for the hunt and the sacrifice of a hare to Artemis—so the owner who commissioned these mosaics was a pagan. An attendant holds up the hare before the statue of the goddess in her sacred grove (suggested by a tree and a bush of large leaves). Two of the other panels show the hunting of lions, tiger, leopard and bear by men on horseback. The fourth panel departs from the plane of realism, and presents a scene from mythology: Meleager and Atalanta hunting the Calydonian boar and a lion. To underline the heroic character of this panel, Meleager is naked and Atalanta wears a radiate crown. This attribute of the Sun-God passed in the third century into imperial iconography, was dropped by the sons of Constantine, and taken up again by Julian, that devotee of the Sun. Legend has it that he objected so strongly to its assumption by the Christian Constantine, that he threw down the famous statue of that emperor set on a porphyry column at Constantinople (see Chapter II), because of the radiate crown it bore. (**36**)

The smaller, rectangular, part of the floor of this same room in the villa is quite differently arranged, with a meander pattern enclosing a series of round and almond-shaped medallions, with figures of the Bacchic cortège. The three almond-shaped ones frame, respectively, a dancing Satyr, a dancing Maenad, and Hercules resting. The round ones enclose busts, of a Satyr, two Maenads, Silenus, and Dionysus himself. The bust of Dionysus is quite extraordinarily beautiful and majestic, with its high head-dress and imperious look of command. In its central position, it dominated the whole floor. This is no mere figure of mythology, but a divine image of majesty and power.

Even the border of this superb pavement is figured rather than being purely geometric. The small panels set in it are of no fewer than four different kinds. In the corners and at each end of the band dividing the two portions of the floor are six busts of abstract personifications. The four extant ones embody the Stoic virtues of Euandria (manliness), Dynamis (strength of character), Ktisis (the virtue of a founder) and Ananeosis (renewal). The personifications of these and other rather abstruse philosophical concepts, such as Soteria (safety, salvation) and

Chresis (the right use of possessions), were very popular as adornments of the floors of rich houses in fourth- and fifth-century Antioch. Iconographically these female busts are so similar that, without their labels, we should be unable to identify them. Three long panels depict Cupids respectively dancing, feasting, and weaving garlands. The other two types of border panels exchange the realms of fantasy and personification for a more realistic vein. Several have facing pairs of peacocks, ducks, and other birds. But the most interesting are a set of four with scenes of rural life, charming little pastoral idylls. In two, shepherds are minding their flocks near little farms; one is blowing his horn. A third shepherd is milking a goat beneath a tree, near a farmhouse or villa of some elaboration. In the fourth scene a lady sits weaving garlands, and a shepherd or other countryman pulls one of them from a large basket. Finally, the 'vault' part of the pavement has an inner border, really part of the decoration of the imitation ceiling, composed of a luxuriant acanthus scroll. Some of the scrolls contain curious heads, with the leaf arranged to form hair.

I have elaborated at some length on these mosaics of the Constantinian Villa in order to give some idea of the tremendous wealth of artistic invention and craftsmanship that could go into the creation of the floor of a single room, albeit the principal reception room of the villa, which this undoubtedly was. Even this does not exhaust the tale of the mosaics found at this level in the villa. A corridor is paved with a scene of wrestling, and may evoke the celebration of the Antiochene Olympic Games, which were founded by the Hellenistic kings of Syria and continued to be given by rich members of the *curia* of Antioch, generally if not exclusively pagans, at four-yearly intervals throughout the fourth century and beyond. A convinced pagan of considerable wealth, as the first owner of the Constantinian Villa demonstrably was, would have been just the sort of man to be chosen to shoulder this immensely costly and prestigious burden.

A small but well-built set of public baths (Bath E) furnishes the other group of elaborate mosaics of the late Constantinian period so far found at Antioch. The main ones paved the central social hall, where bathers could meet and talk to their friends. One very long panel, almost a frieze, depicts an allegory of the fertility of the earth. The principal earth-goddess (Gê, or Terra Mater) reclines on a sphinx-shaped seat in the centre, while behind her a row of *putti* labelled *Karpoi*, the fruits of the earth, carry along an enormous garland plaited from wheat. The *putto* at the further end is being embraced by a subsidiary earth-goddess labelled *Aroura*, the personification of arable land. The embracing arms of these two figures exemplify the tendency, in late antique art, to concentrate on conveying surface appearances at the expense of a proper rendering of the structure, which is almost non-existent in these elbowless and nearly shoulderless arms; even the remarkably fine head of Dionysus from the Constantinian Villa shows traces of this tendency. On the other side of Gê is another lady, personifying the land of Egypt, that great granary of the Eastern Empire. A number of shorter panels from the pavement of this same hall display the *dramatis personae* of one of the marine revels so popular in Africa, a theme of obvious appropriateness in these baths. Here they are grouped in pairs, with two Tritons or sea-Centaurs carrying two Nereids on each panel. The corners of the hall were decorated with panels containing, each one, the personification of a province and its principal river, the only one preserved being Lacedaemon (Sparta) and its river Eurotas. An octagonal pool from another baths (Bath F), built at much the same time, was lined with mosaics depicting a rather heavy bust of Thetis (labelled *Tethys*) amid fish of all sorts and sizes. All these bath decorations are of the most anodyne type of paganism—neutral personifications, which appeared in profusion on the coinages of the Christian emperors, and harmless creatures of mythology—that formed part of the common cultural background of pagan and Christian alike; quite different from the mosaics of the Constantinian Villa, with their very positive pagan content. The proof of this, at Antioch, is the continuing use of these figures to adorn the floors of both public buildings and private houses during the fifth and sixth centuries, when all remnants of real paganism had been driven underground, and virtually everyone was at least nominally Christian. (**37**)

Tableware Exalted and Humble

The religious beliefs and atmosphere of the period were reflected not only in the designs of the floors of people's houses but also in the decoration of some of their best tableware. Owing to its relatively imperishable nature, considerable quantities of this have survived, so that it is sometimes possible to attribute individual pieces to a particular workshop, with significant consequences, as we shall see. This is not, unfortunately, possible in the case of silverware, the majority of pieces having been melted down in subsequent ages. However, some of the most important hoards of it are of late Roman work, including items of the Constantinian period. The Mildenhall Treasure, found at Mildenhall in Suffolk and now in the British Museum, comprises the stock of silver plate belonging to a Roman official, or else to a very rich Romano-British family (no doubt with official connections), in the mid or later fourth century. The finest pieces are of Constantinian date, and are entirely pagan. The figured ornamentation of the Great Dish, 60 centimetres (2 feet) in diameter and weighing over 8 kilograms (18¼ pounds), combines three elements that occur together so frequently on sarcophagi and other funerary monuments that it is thought by some that their presence here, transposed to a different medium, may be symbolic rather than purely decorative. In the centre is the head of the god Oceanus, with beard of seaweed and dolphins emerging from his hair. Round this is an inner frieze of a marine revel, with Nereids astride curly-tailed sea-beasts. The outer frieze, occupying the largest portion of the dish, depicts the drinking contest between Bacchus and Hercules, and in general a Bacchic revel with Pan, Satyrs, and Maenads. In funerary art Oceanus symbolizes the Isles of the Blest, Nereids on marine beasts the soul's journey thither, and the Bacchic revel was a common allegory of the bliss of Paradise. It is possible that the Great Dish was no piece of secular tableware, but a sacred vessel used in some semi-private mystery cult, with myths of salvation in the hereafter for its initiates. A pair of beautiful silver platters, one with Pan playing his pipes and a Maenad playing the double flute, the other with dancing Satyr and Maenad, are from the same (Mediterranean) workshop and apparently form a set with the Great Dish. They could have been used as accessory vessels in a cult, but, on the other hand, decorative Bacchic figures were so common that the platters (and even the Great Dish) may well have been in entirely secular use or display. (**38**)

The rest of the silverware in the Mildenhall Treasure—another large dish, a covered bowl with a frieze of Centaurs and Bacchic heads, seven other bowls, a pair of goblets, five ladles, and eight spoons (some pieces probably of Gallic or even British workmanship)—is more difficult to date within the fourth century. Some of it is Christian. Three spoons have the chi-rho monogram with alpha and omega engraved on the bowl, and two others inscribed with the salutations 'Papittedo, may you live!' and 'Pascentia, may you live!' were perhaps Christening spoons (though the absence of the words 'in God' or 'in Christ' leaves open the possibility that they were gifts of secular intent on some worldly joyous occasion). By the time of the burial of the hoard, then, the owner or at least part of his family were Christian, but free from a fanaticism that would have led them (or him) to reject or refuse the pagan dishes. They kept them for their magnificence, for their aesthetic and perhaps sentimental value, or even reinterpreted the after-life symbolism in Christian terms. The two platters have the name of their owner, Eutherius, scratched on the back in Greek, and this may give a clue to the ownership of the whole treasure. Wealth of this order would have been restricted to the highest circles, and, while Julian was in Gaul, he had as his Lord High Chamberlain a pagan eunuch named Eutherius, a man in whom he had the highest confidence, using him for delicate missions to Constantius. It has been conjectured that Eutherius might have given the platters and Great Dish to the (notoriously covetous) Christian Lupicinus, Master of the Cavalry, whom Julian sent to

Britain in 360 to deal with raids by the Picts and Scots. Lupicinus' career was jeopardized, while he was still in Britain, by Julian's proclamation as Augustus, and he was arrested on his return to Gaul.

It was at first thought that the Kaiseraugst Treasure, brought to light in that late Roman fort on the upper Rhine by a mechanical excavator in the early 1960s, could have belonged to Julian himself. But the large number of silver coins and three bars of stamped bullion included in the hoard indicate that it can only have been buried in 350/1, not long after the usurpation of Magnentius. The coins, 185 of them in all, range from the reign of Diocletian to that of Constantius, struck in the years 294–350, and all are in mint condition. The silver bars bear the stamp of Magnentius of A.D. 350. At the time of burial they must have been in the possession of a high official with access to the imperial treasury of the Western Empire, now in the hands of Magnentius. It is not possible, unfortunately, to identify this official, though he was presumably one of Magnentius' highest officers of State. The table and household silverware in the hoard would have come from his private possessions or those of his family. He was probably a Christian, for one small eating-utensil incorporates the chi-rho monogram. The other sixty-seven items comprise numerous silver dishes, bowls, cups, spoons, and strainers, a beautifully chased candlestick over one metre high, and a statuette of Venus with gilded hair, holding a mirror. Three of the most magnificent dishes are also pagan. The Achilles Dish is a fine example of Constantinian silver workmanship from Thessalonica (an inscription on the back gives its place of origin), with scenes from the life of Achilles in the centre and round the octagonal border. It is quite difficult to recognize the Achilles of the *Iliad* in this late cycle, for most of the details, such as the proverbial Achilles' heel, were added many centuries after Homer. The Seaside-city Dish has a central medallion depicting a walled city with towers, temples, and porticoes, beside a sea thronged with fish and fishing Cupids. Round the edge are hunting scenes worked, like the centre, in niello with gilding. The Ariadne Tray is a rectangular dish with Ariadne, Dionysus, and a Satyr in a central panel worked in the same technique of niello and gilt. The two dishes each weigh nearly 5 kilograms (10 pounds), the tray nearly 3 kilograms (6 pounds). These four pagan articles in the Kaiseraugst Treasure are more conventional than the Great Dish of the Mildenhall Treasure, which may have had actual religious significance. Achilles and Ariadne were figures of mythology; temples, whether in use or disaffected, were still very much part of the urban landscape of the fourth century; and even Venus, as we have seen, was acceptable to many Christians as the personification of love and beauty. There is a world of difference between the bust of Dionysus in the Constantinian Villa at Antioch, charged with religious power, and the anodyne mythological personage on the Ariadne Tray. This silverware could easily have been bought by someone who was already Christian; although, given the slow progress of Christianity among the governing classes in the Constantinian period (see Chapter IV), it is equally likely that the Venus, for example, was bought before the owner's conversion. Perhaps the chief interest of the pagan pieces from Kaiseraugst, some of them with the precise place of manufacture noted, lies in the indication that there was a clientele in the first half of the fourth century ready to purchase or commission them, in the more Christianized East as well as in the West. (**39**)

Germany, with its copious supplies of fine sand, owes its origin as an important centre of glass production to the Romans, who introduced the manufacture of glass and the technique of glass-blowing from Syria. By the fourth century the Rhineland was producing more glassware than anywhere else in the whole Empire. Most of it came from the workshops or factories of Cologne. Levels of extraordinary technical virtuosity had been reached, the peak of this being represented by the *vasa diatreta* or 'pierced' glasses, in which the cup is enclosed in a second layer of glass, laboriously cut away to form a layer of glass filigree. They must have been extremely expensive, and fewer than half a dozen are known, found in sarcophagi in the Rhineland, where they were protected from damage. While much of the other glass was plain, some of the finer pieces were engraved or gilded by workshops that specialized in the manufacture of this type of glassware. The engraved ones, many of which date from the Constantinian period, have been preserved in sufficient quantities to make possible the isolation of several different workshop-groups. Religious themes were common in this type of glassware, though their great preponderance may be partly due to the frequent choice of a religious piece from among the dead person's possessions—or indeed the special purchase of such a piece—for inclusion in the grave; and it is in a funerary context, especially where protection was afforded to fragile articles by the strong stone walls of a sarcophagus, that the vast majority of the glasses have been found. They reveal, as one would expect, that there was a mixed pagan and Christian clientele. It was less predictable that the workshop-groups would prove that there were at least two workshops or factories producing both pagan and Christian decoration.

One of these workshops, in production during the Constantinian period, specialized in the manufacture of shallow bowls with engraved design, all but one of the twenty-six known pieces being of this type. The engraving, like that of other workshops, was rather crudely done with a flint burin, and the most striking characteristic, the use of cross-shading to emphasize the outlines, is unique to the products of this workshop. The designs on them fall into three categories. Nine of them depict hunts of different animals—boar, hare, stag, bear—on foot or on horseback. One with a hare hunt was found in the Roman villa at Wint Hill in Dorset, and is in the Ashmolean Museum in Oxford. At least six others are pagan, with mythological scenes: Neptune between a sea lion and a sea leopard; Hercules wrestling with the giant Antaeus, while Athena gives him advice; Apollo and Diana in hunting garb; Venus flanked by two Cupids; Dionysus dancing, with Pan and a Satyr; and the contest between Apollo, playing the lyre, and Marsyas, playing the double flute (the competition ended with the flaying of the unfortunate Marsyas by Apollo, whose victory was held to symbolize the superiority of divine reason to the earthly forces of unreason and emotion, and, in Pythagorean thought, the winning of souls from the earthly to the heavenly sphere). The only one that does not depict an actual pagan deity is a cup decorated with a scene of Cupids harvesting grapes. The seven Christian bowls depict Old and New Testament scenes familiar from sarcophagi and other forms of early Christian art. The finest of the whole group has a chi-rho monogram in the centre and tiny scenes round the edge, with each of the figures composing them set in one of the spaces of a palm-tree arcade. We find Adam and Eve with the Serpent, Susanna and the Elders, and Daniel between two lions and, in an apocryphal story, feeding a poisoned cake to the sacred snake of the Babylonians. Adam and Eve with the Serpent appear by themselves on another of the bowls, inscribed round the edge (inscriptions inviting to good cheer or Christian life occur on most of the bowls) 'Rejoice in God, drink and live', in an interesting mixture of Latin and Greek and of sacred with secular ideas. Two bowls, very similar to each other, show the Sacrifice of Isaac. The hand of God emerges from the clouds above the lighted altar, as Abraham, knife in hand, prepares to kill his son; the ram is near by. One of these glasses was found at Trier, the other at Boulogne. The other three Christian glasses represent, respectively, Susanna, naked except for a fig-leaf, between the accusing Elders; Daniel in the Lions' Den; and the Raising of Lazarus, with Christ, holding the magician's staff which fourth-century art always gives him as an attribute when he is working miracles, calling forth a mummy-like Lazarus from a temple-like mausoleum with columned porch and conical roof. The great interest of these bowls lies in the choice of both pagan and Christian themes for representation on different glasses manufactured in the same workshop and, in one case at least, actually by the same craftsman, whose hand can be traced in the Cupids harvesting grapes, the Adam and Eve bowl, and a fragment with what is perhaps Bellerophon. The glasses were in considerable demand, and were exported to various parts of northern and central Gaul (these were often Christian pieces, much prized by those among the gentry who followed that religion), and even to Britain. It is tempting to draw conclusions from the numerical balance between the types of glasses, especially between pagan and Christian ones, but this may be partly due to accidents of preservation. What is clear, however, is that there was sufficient demand from Christians to stimulate the creation of a mass-produced supply of designs that were completely new to the centuries-old glassworks of Cologne. They may have been invented by the craftsmen themselves under Christian direction, or taken from copy-books of Christian designs that may have begun to circulate under Constantine. (41)

The other certain Christian-pagan workshop, operating in about the mid fourth century, specialized in making engraved beakers, either rounded or conical. Several of these are Christian, mostly adorned with a selection of the familiar Biblical scenes: Adam and Eve, the Sacrifice of Isaac, Moses striking water from the rock, the Raising of Lazarus, and the Feeding of the Five Thousand. One is more original: it has engraved on it a wooden bridge, a fisherman with a fish he has caught, and the Feeding of the Five Thousand. Fish symbolism was common in Christian thought and art from New Testament times: Christ himself had used fish in the Feeding of the Five Thousand, generally regarded as a forerunner of the Eucharist, and had called the disciples to be fishers of men (both of these strands are present on the beaker). The widespread oriental belief that the fish was talismanic (we have already met this apropos of the African mosaics) or even sacred (the great pools full of sacred fish of the cult of the Syrian goddess Atargatis are there to this day in Edessa (modern Urfa in Mesopotamia)) contributed to this, and the early Christians soon discovered that the letters of the Greek word for fish, *ichthys*, could stand for 'Jesus Christ, Son of God, Saviour'. The beaker alludes to the role of Christ as the Fisher of Souls.

The pagan glasses of this group are more ambiguous, the dominant motif being figures, often dancing, holding curious plants with trailing roots, or sometimes branches. A similar motif on a beaker found in a drain under the temple of Cybele at Vienne (ancient Vienna, on the Rhône below Lyon) has been interpreted as a Bacchic dance, and the place where it was found does help to corroborate the attribution of a sacred signification to the other glasses with this motif. One beaker of this group, with five men in tunic and toga with outstretched right hands, divided by cypress-trees, would also seem to have ritual conno-tations, perhaps of a more specifically funerary character than the ritual dances, for the cypress, tree of the dark Apollo, was already a symbol of death in Roman times, and was planted beside graves as it still is in Mediterranean cemeteries today. There are no hunting scenes decorating glasses of this group, but two beakers with secular ornament are known, each with four busts in medallions.

Another group of glasses, less homogeneous in date, is closely related to these beakers, somewhat similar in style and with repetition of some of the motifs. Perhaps the two groups were turned out by independent units of the same factory. This seems more likely than that two quite different motifs were copied by or from a rival establishment, and stylistic differences rule out the moving of a craftsman from one workshop to another. The motif of figures with trailing plants occurs on the beaker from Vienne, and on another beaker, where the figures are Cupids. And a third glass with busts in medallions belongs to this group. Pagan glasses are preponderant, almost to the exclusion of Christian ones, and some of the paganism is more full-blooded than in the previous group.

The lone Christian piece depicts four members of the emperor's bodyguard between standards bearing eight-pointed stars, a motif common to many of the Cologne glasses, but here representing the chi-rho monogram. The only secular glass in this group, apart from the bowl with busts, has a picture of a hare hunt. One of the pagan glasses, a shallow bowl with a two-scene version of the Apollo and Marsyas myth, is as late as *c.* 380. Others are more difficult to date precisely. One of the two glasses with Bacchic revels was found at the small villa of Colliton Park near Dorchester (Dorset) (now in Dorchester Museum). A tall, conical beaker depicts Venus and Cupid in a tavern. One bowl has in the centre an engraving of the bust of the Sun-God, wearing a radiate crown and holding a charioteer's whip, surrounded by chariot-teams racing round the Circus Maximus. This is a clear allusion to the cosmic symbolism of the circus, as representing the course of the Sun (see above, section on festivals).

The circus bowl, which dates from the first half of the fourth century, was found in the sarcophagus in which one of the owners of a Roman villa near Cologne (Cologne-Braunsfeld) was buried. At least one owner of this villa was a Christian, for another sarcophagus yielded the blue bowl decorated with gilded medallions depicting Moses striking water from the rock, Noah's Ark with the returning dove, Jonah and the Whale and Jonah lying beneath the gourd-tree, and Daniel in the Lions' Den, that is dated to the jubilee year 325/6 by the four busts of Constantine's sons—Crispus, Constantine II, Constantius II and Constans—round the edge. This is the most important known piece of gilded glass from the workshops of Cologne. All the other examples so far found are Christian, too, and it may be that the workshops that produced them specialized in Christian themes, although it is difficult to understand why pagans should not have wished to buy glasses so attractively decorated. Accidents of preservation may, of course, have something to do with it, especially as there are only nine certain examples, but the contrast with the fairly evenly divided Christian and pagan engraved glass is striking.

Gold glass was very popular with fourth-century Christians at Rome, too, for numerous products of the Rome factories have come to light in the catacombs. A few of these, however, are secular, with portraits, or even pagan, with mythological scenes. Insufficient work has been done on them for the bulk of them to be dated even generally, to the third, fourth or fifth centuries, but it is certain that the techniques of gilding glass and of putting a layer of gold leaf between two layers of glass originated in the third century, and that the majority of the gold glasses are of the fourth century, many, doubtless, of the Constantinian period. The actual pieces that accompanied the burials in the catacombs were usually just the medallions from the bases of cups or dishes, with saints (especially SS. Peter and Paul) or Biblical scenes. (**43**)

The third kind of tableware that is decorated with a mixture of pagan and Christian themes is a red earthenware pottery made in North Africa, destined for a humbler clientele than the silverware or even the glass, mass-produced as that was. Indeed the most characteristic form of the very late type of this pottery, known as light *terra sigillata* D, of which production did not begin until the last quarter of the fourth century, was a large rectangular dish in imitation of silverware, made for presentation on special occasions by those who could not afford silver. The only pagan themes on these dishes were of the most innocuous kind, such as the grooming of Pegasus by two Nymphs and scenes from the life of Achilles. Christian motifs such as Jonah, scenes from the games, and representations of high officials (for presentation on State occasions) were also used to decorate this very late pottery.

The paganism on the earlier light *terra sigillata* C, which began to be made during the first half of the fourth century and continued in production for the rest of the century, is, by contrast, much more robust, with scenes of actual pagan religion as well as mythology. Significantly, these religious scenes are mostly connected with the oriental cults which, as we have seen (Chapters IV, V), constituted one of the most vital strands of late paganism. One bowl has two Mithraic scenes: Mithras carrying the bull over his shoulders, and killing the bull to release the forces of life and fertility. The dog that, together with the snake and the scorpion, is an invariable accompaniment of larger representations of the bull-slaying appears on the bowl as a separate motif between the two scenes. It is perhaps significant that none of this Mithraic pottery has yet been found in Africa itself. The bowl is from near Rome, and most of the few fragments known are also from this area. In view of the very limited spread of Mithraism in Roman Africa, where it was largely confined to the foreign communities in the ports and army camps, it appears that the Mithraic pottery, almost certainly made for use in the Mithraic cult, may have been manufactured with an eye to the export market. Motifs on other pottery were associated with the cult of Isis, which was more widespread in Africa itself. One fragment depicts the bust of a priestess of Isis, another has a ship carrying Isis-Demeter and

Bacchus and two musicians. It is, unfortunately, not known where either piece was found. Of the more strictly mythological subjects, the dominant themes are the Labours of Hercules and Leda and the Swan. Hercules' struggles with the Nemean lion and the Hydra, separated by detached elements of landscape—a tree and a curiously shaped rock—adorn one bowl found in Spain. Others of the twelve Labours decorated companion pieces, including plates, probably forming the complete cycle. It is more than likely that this treatment was also accorded to other episodic myths, including the full Mithras legend, beginning with the birth of the god from a rock. Not all the representations of Hercules on the light *sigillata* C, however, fitted into the cycle of Labours. A fragment from Egypt shows him sacrificing at a small, portable altar. The myth of Leda and the Swan was arranged in similar fashion on a pair of plates. One depicts the bird advancing towards Leda, while two Cupids bearing hymeneal torches fly overhead. The other, of which only fragments are known, shows the altar on which, in one version of the legend, the egg was laid to keep it warm, with the triplets—Castor, Pollux and Helen—hatching out. Exemplars of both have been found in Africa. The potters' repertoire of stamps with mythological scenes was doubtless much larger, but other surviving pieces are ambiguous or fragmentary or both. (42)

It is no mere coincidence that a larger quantity of the Christian products of these potteries has been found in the country of origin, for the African provinces were already Christian in majority in the time of Constantine, in striking contrast with Britain and most of Gaul. The commonest theme is the Sacrifice of Isaac, which seems to have been made up of two scenes arranged either on one platter or on two. A complete one, found in a grave in Spain, depicts Abraham and his son setting off up the mountain, with the landscape suggested by a pine-tree, and the symbolic content of the scene by a large libation-vase. The best-preserved example of the actual sacrifice scene, which was among the rubble thrown into the S. Prisca Mithraeum in Rome (see above), also had on it another episode of the same story, with Abraham holding the sacrificial knife; the rest has disappeared. Other pottery depicted the story of Jonah, again in episodic form on one or more pieces. The decoration of a complete bowl, found not far from the probable site of the potteries, in central Tunisia, is devoted to the second scene of the story, with a large sea dragon spewing up Jonah, amid fishes, sea stags, and another sea dragon. On one small fragment (from Djemila in Algeria) can be detected the throwing of Jonah into the sea from the ship, while two others, found in Rome, have Jonah lying under the gourd-tree, the third episode of the cycle; a sea dragon appearing on one of these indicates that one or both of the marine episodes also adorned the platter. A fragment from Carthage also has a sea dragon on it. A third certain Biblical subject is Adam and Eve, who adorn a bowl at Constantine in Algeria. Other possibilities are Daniel in the Lions' Den and the three young men in the fiery furnace, while one fragment has an Orante.

Not all the embossed decoration of this pottery was of religious character, however. Some of it depicted amphitheatre scenes, with wild animals attacking beast-fighters and condemned criminals. These last, some of which are complete, might possibly be scenes of Christian martyrdom. A series of scattered motifs on a bowl found in the mortar of a temple wall in Morocco suggests a rural scene: two rabbits, a hunting-dog with its prey, a tree, and a basket of fruit. Fragments from Sicily and Egypt depict what is probably a potters' oven. All this gives some idea of the great variety of motif used to decorate this pottery, and of the large number of different provinces, in both the west and east Mediterranean, to which so much of it was exported. Throughout the late Empire, North Africa was the principal producer and exporter of fine figured pottery in the whole Empire.

Tomb Furniture

The provisions made by people in the fourth century, especially but by no means exclusively the better-off, for the housing of their dead bodies furnish a mine of information about their beliefs and modes of life. They were following a tradition that attached great importance to the physical context of death and the ceremonies surrounding it, and which went back many centuries in Graeco-Roman culture. The tombs of the kings at Mycenae, the great funeral pyres and ceremonial described by Homer, the frescoed subterranean tombs of the Etruscans at Tarquinia and elsewhere, the classical Greek *stelae*, the Mausoleum of Halicarnassus, and the monumental sarcophagi, of Hellenistic kings in Istanbul Archaeological Museum, are among the most spectacular of the earlier manifestations of this tendency. In the Roman period, provision for the dead took four main forms: family mausolea were built by those who could afford them, and decorated with frescoes and mosaic; urns and, when in the course of the second century inhumation took over from cremation, sarcophagi, of varying degrees of elaboration, were put in mausolea or buried in the ground; gravestones with epitaphs marked many burials; and grave-goods of various kinds, few or many, rich or humble, were laid beside the remains of the dead, to give them food and drink and occasionally pastimes (e.g. a gaming-board) for their journey to the after-life, 'obols of Charon' to pay their passage over the river Styx, talismans to ward off evil spirits, and sometimes favourite possessions, such as a child's toys, to take with them. By the fourth century the once numerous and solidly prosperous freedman class, that was responsible for so many of the mausolea at a place like Ostia, had almost died out, and the middle classes were greatly reduced in size and prosperity, which meant that there were far fewer families who could afford a mausoleum. These were, in fact, very few and far between in the fourth century, now largely the prerogative of royalty and great landed families, should they choose to build one. Many did not: Christian members of the senatorial aristocracy at Rome, for example, might be buried in ornate sarcophagi in the new extra-mural churches built by Constantine, especially St. Peter's, rather than build their own funerary chapel. So the emphasis shifted to the smaller tomb furnishings—gravestones, sarcophagi and grave-goods. Even gravestones were greatly reduced in number, as compared with the early Empire, because of the general impoverishment of the lower strata of the population. Those that have been found, for example in the Rhône cities of Lyon and Vienne as well as at Rome itself, are almost exclusively Christian, which would seem to point to some sort of burial-fund or other organization established by the local Churches, that enabled people to purchase them at low cost, or even have them free, if they were poor. And, of course, the rapidly expanding catacombs, dug out of the rock wherever it was soft enough for easy tunnelling, permitted the burial of the Christian poor in more opulent surroundings than would have been possible with a humble plot of earth, and provided ample scope for frescoes. The sculptured sarcophagi, too, were almost exclusively Christian, but the reasons for this cannot have been of a financial order. The death of the tradition represented by the wonderful mythological sarcophagi of earlier centuries points towards a shift in beliefs about the nature of the after-life, away from the materialistic towards the uncompromisingly spiritual. Only grave-goods continued for a while to be placed, often in considerable profusion, in pagan tombs—and in Christian ones too, for the custom of giving the dead objects of use and beauty to take with them took some time to disappear. Dozens of cemeteries of pagan town and country folk have been excavated in the north-west of the Empire, in which even the poorest were given a vessel or two of coarse pottery. Yet here, too, changes were taking place. The great majority of these well-furnished cemeteries of the late Roman period in Britain and Gaul belong to the end of the third and the first half of the fourth century. Thereafter the only grave-goods were usually coins, frequently put in the mouth or hand as 'obols of Charon'. It would seem that, by the second half of the century, Christian influence had been brought to bear on the still largely pagan populations, making them doubt the value of burying food and possessions with the dead, and, in general, question their too-materialistic ideas of the after-life.

In the Constantinian period, however, this influence had yet to operate. In fact the situation was almost the reverse, with newly converted Christians still attached to pagan burial customs. Some striking examples of this have been found in the Rhineland. An appliqué bronze plate from a wooden box, depicting the three young men in the fiery furnace, was found in a richly furnished tomb at Cologne, together with a dish once heaped with joints of poultry, six shellfish, a Medusa head medallion (a charm against evil spirits), 39 coins down to the sons of Constantine, jewellery, and a number of pottery and glass vessels. And the glass bowl engraved with Adam and Eve (mentioned above) had been put in the plain stone sarcophagus of another citizen of Cologne, together with 178 coins of the second and third centuries, eight other glass vessels, a jet pendant with Medusa's head, and a small bronze ladder and balance that belong to a group of pagan cult-symbols. These symbols, found in a number of graves in a restricted area of the Rhineland (principally Cologne), fall into two groups: small models of implements of various kinds, the commonest being rakes, balances, ladders, yokes, shovels, mattocks and keys, and of various small animals associated in ancient times with the Underworld and its deities— lizards, snakes, frogs, toads, and the like. The link between the two groups is the fertility of the earth, upon which the agricultural implements acted directly, and which the powers of the Underworld had in their keeping. It was natural for ancient peoples to connect the growth of the crops from the earth with the dark spaces beneath it reserved, in their lore, for the souls of the dead, and to suppose them in the keeping of one and the same god or group of deities, such as the all-powerful Saturn in Africa, the Phoenician and Carthaginian Baal, lord of the great corn-growing lands and of the Underworld; the Greek myth of Persephone was another expression of this same connection. In view of the very limited geographical distribution of the little bronze models, it is probable that they were the hallmark of an esoteric sect with religious beliefs of this kind, that flourished in the Cologne area in the second half of the third century and the first half of the fourth, the period to which nearly all the burials belong. Presumably the owner of the Adam and Eve bowl, or his next of kin, was a newly converted Christian who had been a member of this sect, and sought to include in the grave everything that might give protection in the Hereafter. The occupants of this and of the other 'mixed' tomb were probably members of the local gentry who followed the court in religious matters, and had embraced Christianity when Constantine did, without any clear idea of what it involved, just as it was long before that emperor came to realize the exclusiveness of Christianity (see Chapter II). (44)

Another Christian-pagan mixture, but of a different kind, is revealed by the Via Latina Catacombs of Rome, one of the most beautiful and fascinating monuments of the fourth century. This was not one of the large, public catacombs organized by the Church, but a group of private mausolea, dug out of the tufa on a preconceived plan and lavishly decorated with beautiful frescoes. It was only discovered in the 1950s, and access is, unfortunately, very difficult to obtain, as the original entrance comes to the surface under the bedroom of a modern house, and the newly created one descends through a manhole in the pavement, necessitating the presence of several workmen. The impression it creates is of a picture gallery of fourth-century art, in a wonderful state of preservation. It was apparently built by a single, large family, each of whose branches decorated their own mausoleum according to their beliefs. The members of the family were predominantly Christian, but some were still uncompromisingly pagan, to judge from the careful separation of Christian and pagan frescoes into different mausolea. Two of them are wholly pagan. One is frescoed with a series of scenes involving Hercules: Hercules and the goddess Athena, Hercules slaying an enemy, taking the golden apples of the Hesperides from the serpent-guarded tree, killing the Hydra, and bringing back Alcestis, the wife of Admetus, from Hades, and the death of Admetus. (It is worth remembering that the god Hercules was given prominence by Julian as a pagan parallel to Christ.) The other mausoleum, less aggressively pagan, has as its chief ornament a picture of a reclining, half-naked, haloed lady who is best interpreted as the Earth-Goddess (or possibly as a dead woman in Paradise). The snake beside her is a symbol of fertility (or of the realm of the dead). In addition to these two pagan mausolea, there is a passage and a vestibule that have entirely secular decoration, forming neutral ground, as it were. The wide range of neutral motifs, that occur also in the Christian and pagan mausolea, is mainly pastoral and idyllic. (45)

The remaining seven mausolea and another vestibule are Christian, frescoed with an amazing range of Biblical scenes, in which the emphasis on the symbolism of salvation that dominated earlier Christian funerary art, and led to the frequent appearance of themes like the Raising of Lazarus and the story of Jonah, has given way to an interest in narrative for its own sake. A large proportion of the scenes was completely new to the Christian funerary repertoire, e.g. Adam and Eve with Cain and Abel, the three angels appearing to Abraham at Mamre, Isaac's meal and his blessing of Jacob and Esau, episodes from the life of Joseph, Moses being saved from the bulrushes, Samson with the lion, foxes, and ass's jawbone, Absalom hanging from the oak-tree by his hair, and the casting of lots for Jesus' robe. And there are many, many other scenes that were already part of the repertoire, including Adam and Eve, Noah in the Ark, the Sacrifice of Isaac, Jacob's Ladder, the Crossing of the Red Sea, Moses striking water from the rock and receiving the Law, the Ascent of Elijah, the story of Jonah, the three young men in the fiery furnace, Daniel in the Lions' Den, and Susanna and the Elders;

and, from the New Testament, the Three Wise Men, Jesus and the Samaritan woman at the well, the Feeding of the Five Thousand, the Raising of Lazarus, and Jesus teaching, with the Twelve Disciples, and between SS. Peter and Paul. This gives some idea of the virtuosity of the artists and the wealth of ideas of artists or patrons. The dominant colour used in the frescoes was reddish brown, together with lighter, yellower shades, brownish violet to black, green, and light blue. The impression of richness is further strengthened by the presence of marble column-bases and capitals, garnishing the tufa-cut columns. The dating of this lavish ensemble within the fourth century is, unfortunately, not entirely secure. It was excavated and decorated over a period of several decades, that were at first thought to fall squarely within the Constantinian period, from *c*. 320 to *c*. 360. But the style of the paintings suggests that it may be later, from *c*. 340/50 to *c*. 380/90, and this later dating has in its favour the fact that the great preponderance of Christian over pagan mausolea reflects the known pattern of conversion among the upper classes in the second half of the fourth century more closely than that of the first half of the century, when there were at least as many pagans as Christians. The extent of the Christian repertoire, which could only have been built up since the Peace of the Church, is also more easily explicable with the later dating, especially if, as seems likely, the artists were deriving their inspiration from an illustrated Bible in the possession of one member of the family.

The flavour of originality is also present in two other private funerary monuments in Rome, the hypogea (or underground mausolea) of Trebius Justus and of Vibia. Here there is no clear division into Christian and pagan but, instead, a syncretism of the two religions, an infiltration of ideas from one into the other, in the minds of the people buried there. Those responsible for the frescoes of the Hypogeum of Trebius Justus were apparently Christians, yet the paintings lack any incontrovertible sign of Christian inspiration, while some features are actually pagan. The vaulted ceiling, it is true, depicts a shepherd and sheep, and he is almost certainly a Good Shepherd, but it is nevertheless the case that the notion of a pastoral paradise was common to pagans and Christians. The main frescoed wall has at the top a picture of offerings being made to the dead man, after the pagan fashion. A man and a woman hold before him a rich piece of cloth, containing bracelets, a jewelled ring, and a vase. The chair on which he is supposedly seated is incomplete, with only the top painted in. Below this, in the arched recess containing the sarcophagus, is another portrait of Trebius Justus, surrounded this time with books and writing materials, and a painted inscription, cast in the normal pagan mould of a dedication to the dead man, by his sorrowing parents, revealing that he died at the age of twenty-one. The books and writing materials indicate that he was

—at least in his parents' estimation—an accomplished scholar, and the picture is in the pagan tradition of viewing learning as a high road to immortality (see above). The fresco below this depicts Trebius Justus' father ordering the presentation of baskets of flowers and fruit for his son, either as further offerings, or as a sign of the dead youth's interest in horticulture. On the other walls of the hypogeum are scenes illustrating the construction of a monument that may be the mausoleum itself. The standard of painting is high, despite the omission of part of the chair, and the result is a very attractive ensemble. But the riddle of the precise religious affiliation of the family remains. A number of Christian and semi-Christian graffiti were inscribed on the walls of the mausoleum and its vestibules. They include one with a chi-rho, and another invoking the wrath of God upon a person unknown who had harmed someone's mother and daughter. This call for vengeance is, like the frescoes, more pagan than Christian. This monument of the Constantinian period probably reveals a family of newly converted, or rather half-converted, Christians still steeped in their pagan ways. (46)

The Hypogeum of Vibia is the reverse: here, Christian ideas and iconography had to some extent affected the beliefs of a pagan family about the details of the after-life, and especially the artistic expression of it on the walls of their burial-place. In the arched recess above the tomb of Vibia and her husband Vincentius is a fresco depicting Vibia being led into Paradise by an Angelus Bonus, a scene that partakes of the ancient pagan tradition of Hermes the conductor of souls to the Underworld, of Christian, Jewish and Gnostic angels (and of Roman *genii* or soul-guardians), and of pictures in the Christian catacombs such as St. Petronilla receiving Veneranda into heaven (see below). The Good Angel leads Vibia towards a table at which she now appears seated in the centre of the banquet of the just; flowers reveal that the setting is the Elysian Fields. These two scenes combined in one are the crowning episodes of a narrative of which the preceding parts are painted under the arch. First we see the dead Vibia being snatched away by Pluto in his chariot, in a second Rape of Persephone. At the head of the team of horses is none other than Hermes Psychopompos, Guide of Souls, in person. Next we have a judgement scene: on a tribunal sit Pluto and Persephone (under their ancient Roman names of Dispater and Aeracura); on their right are the three Fates while, to their left, Mercury-Hermes brings Vibia for judgement. She is accompanied by Alcestis, the heroic, self-sacrificing wife of Greek mythology whom we have already encountered in the Via Latina Catacombs. She fulfils exactly the same role of support and welcome as many a Christian saint pictured with a dead person in the catacombs. On the other side of this scene is the banquet of the 'Seven Pious Priests', among whom is Vincentius. An inscription on the front of the tomb reveals that he was a priest of Jupiter Sabazios (i.e. Sabaoth), a Thracian mystery-god in whose cult Jewish influences had been at work. The two banquet scenes are very similar to frescoes of the Christian *agape*-meal in the catacombs. It is very likely that the artist was familiar with these and other Christian works, or had even himself painted some, or that Vibia and Vincentius had themselves visited the catacombs.

In comparison with the private catacombs, especially those of the Via Latina where Christian themes are dominant, the paintings of the Constantinian period in the public catacombs seem rather repetitive and conventional, preoccupied as they are with the theme of salvation. Other inhibiting factors were the conservatism of the clergy and the communal character of the public catacombs, which developed in the early third century from private or semi-private family burial-galleries and mausolea—the predecessors of the Via Latina Catacombs and Hypogeum of Trebius Justus—into the beginnings of the huge complexes which can be seen nowadays, burial-places for the poor and not-so-poor of the Christian community, under the surveillance of the Church. The catacombs also formed a convenient place for the annual celebrations of the cult of the martyrs who were buried there during the persecutions, and whose festal days are listed in the *Calendar of 354* (see above). Most of the frescoes adorned the arched tombs or the walls and ceilings of funerary chapels of richer Christians, whose families would have commissioned them. The two catacombs that were the scene of the most artistic activity in this period were those of Domitilla and of SS. Peter and Marcellinus, while those of St. Callistus, of Vigna Massimo, and the Major Cemetery are also well represented. The commonest themes are those that, having been chosen and become popular for their suitability to funerary symbolism, were endlessly repeated throughout the life of the catacombs. Good Shepherds and Orante-figures (representing the soul of the dead person) abound, as do allegories of rescue from death and life in Paradise: the story of Jonah in three episodes—being thrown to the whale, spewed up by it, and lying under the gourd-tree; Moses striking water from the rock and the Raising of Lazarus, very frequent as a pair of corresponding scenes; Noah in the Ark, Daniel in the Lions' Den, the three young men in the fiery furnace, the Feeding of the Five Thousand, and the Christian *agape*-meal. This last also belongs to a further group of themes, exemplifying new life in Christ, and including a number of miracles—the healing of blind Bartimaeus, of the paralytic, and of the woman with the issue of blood, and the Marriage at Cana—the Epiphany, and Christ with the Twelve, with SS. Peter and Paul, or with saints. Other subjects are related generally to the theme of salvation: Adam and Eve, the Sacrifice of Isaac, Susanna and the Elders. In one instance, in the Catacombs of Praetextatus, Susanna is represented allegorically as a lamb between two wolves, all carefully labelled to prevent anyone missing the point. In the Major Cemetery there is an impressive example of the subject that was to become one of the most popular in the whole of Christian art: a solemn and rather fleshy Virgin with the Child centrally placed, in Byzantine fashion, on her lap, flanked by chi-rho monograms. Christ commonly appears as a Teacher—for example in a scene of Christ and the Apostles in an arch above a tomb in the Catacombs of Domitilla—this being the most characteristic representation of the Divine Master in an age that regarded him as being, above all, the embodiment of Holy Wisdom. A more unusual fresco in these same catacombs depicts the martyr St. Petronilla receiving the lady buried beneath, named Veneranda, into heaven. The haloed Sun-God who appears between two Jonah scenes in the Catacombs of SS. Peter and Marcellinus is doubtless the same Christ the Sun of Righteousness who adorns the ceiling of the third-century Christian mausoleum under the Vatican (see Chapter III). The Seasons and their attributes, found in the same catacombs and elsewhere, are the familiar symbol of eternity, taken over from the pagans. Few truly secular subjects appear. A baker buried in the Catacombs of Domitilla saw fit, however, to have his tomb-chamber frescoed, after the centuries-old pagan custom, with scenes relating to his trade: corn being unloaded from ships, officials of the public corn-supply, a baker, and corn being carried to the bakeries.(47)

The subjects that figure most prominently in the catacomb paintings appear again, carved in stone, on the sarcophagi of the Constantinian period. The mid third century had seen the beginnings of Christian sarcophagus art in the workshops of Rome, but the themes were heavily symbolic and the Christianity usually veiled, by means of subjects such as the Good Shepherd and the pastoral paradise, Orante-figures (current in pagan art as a symbol of piety), the philosopher, and the Mystic Fisherman. Later, in the tetrarchic period, the introduction of Biblical scenes began in earnest. Jonah was a particular favourite, and one very beautiful sarcophagus has as its centrepiece two representations of Leviathan, arranged tail to tail, forming part of the swallowing and the spewing-up episodes, respectively. The fluid arrangement of this work, which has some smaller scenes above but is only partially divided into two registers, was to disappear from the Christian sarcophagus art of the fourth century, which tended towards formality and symmetry of organization.

With the advent of Constantine and the Peace of the Church this art form flowered, with a greatly extended repertoire and a new and fitting emphasis on the kingship and majesty of Christ. The most characteristic early Constantinian sarcophagi were carved with a continuous frieze of Old and New Testament scenes, some of them apparently—and intriguingly—by the same workshop that produced the set of reliefs depicting the emperor and his people for the Arch of Constantine (Chapter II). The compressed but quite recognizable little scenes are mostly the familiar ones of the catacomb repertoire. Some of the newer ones concern St. Peter: the Denial of Peter, indicated by Christ's warning gesture and the presence of the cock, Peter's arrest, and Peter creating a miraculous spring, like Moses (an episode from the apocryphal life of the saint). The range of scenes from the life of Christ himself is widened by the inclusion of such scenes as the Nativity, Christ before Caiaphas, Zacchaeus, and the Entry into Jerusalem. There is often an Orante placed in the centre of the frieze, representing, as usual, the soul of the dead person. The most striking stylistic feature of these sarcophagi is the deeply scored and rigid parallel folds of the drapery, carved with the help of the drill rather than with the chisel. Plate 48 shows a typical frieze sarcophagus which has, from left to right: a curious conflation of the two scenes of Peter's miraculous spring, and his Denial, with one and the same figure of Peter taking part in both; Moses receiving the Law from the hand of God; Daniel giving a poisoned cake to the Babylonian sacred serpent (as on one of the Cologne glass dishes—see above); Christ with blind Bartimaeus; the central Orante flanked by two Apostles; Christ healing the woman with the issue of blood; the Sacrifice of Isaac; Peter's arrest; and the Raising of Lazarus. The lid has, on either side of a tablet that may once have held a painted inscription, Jonah being thrown to the whale and lying under the gourd-tree, and the three young men in the fiery furnace. On top of the lid is carved a chi-rho monogram. This sarcophagus was found under the floor of Constantinian St. Peter's (for which, see Chapter III).

A less over-decorated—to modern taste—form of fourth-century sarcophagus was a direct successor of both pagan and Christian works of the third century. Isolated motifs in the centre and at the corners (the latter sometimes replaced by columns) were divided by two large panels of so-called strigilations, parallel straight or frequently S-shaped flutings, producing a pleasingly harmonious effect. It would also, of course, be cheaper than all-over figured decoration. A central Orante was popular, with, for example, two Good Shepherds at the corners. A more elaborate sarcophagus has the Denial of Peter in the centre, and the Raising of Lazarus and Peter's miraculous spring (which now replaces, more and more, the similar scene with Moses) at the corners. The lid has a tiny series of miracles—the Marriage at Cana, Blind Bartimaeus, the Feeding of the Five Thousand, and the Raising of the Widow's Son of Nain—set between the central tablet (held by *genii*) and the large heads that form the corners. Not until about 330 onwards was there any real innovation, with the manufacture of strigilated sarcophagi in two registers, with four smaller panels of strigilations separating six little scenes. A particularly interesting one has in the centre, occupying almost the whole depth of the sarcophagus front so that it dominates the design, the representation of the wedding ceremony of the couple who lay buried inside, presided over by Juno Pronuba, the goddess of marriage. The wedding scene, with or without Juno, was a common feature of pagan funerary monuments of earlier centuries, and the Christian pair took it over without more ado, regarding Juno as simply the personification of marriage. Underneath the Juno scene is a tiny fantasy scene of Cupid and Psyche with fighting-cocks. At the corners are two pairs of Biblical subjects, one above the other: the Creation of Eve and Christ healing blind Bartimaeus on the left, and the Raising of Lazarus and Peter's miraculous spring on the right.

The division of the front of a sarcophagus into two registers was one of the leading tendencies of Constantinian funerary art. One type is a development of the ordinary frieze sarcophagus, and the centre of the upper register is occupied by the portrait or portraits of the deceased set in a medallion. Perhaps the finest of them, dateable to *c.* 340, is the so-called Sarcophagus of the Two Brothers, with the busts of two bearded men in a central shell-medallion. The upper frieze depicts, from left to right: the Raising of Lazarus, Peter's Denial, Moses receiving the Law, the Sacrifice of Isaac, and Pilate washing his hands. In the lower register, from left to right, are: Peter's miraculous spring, the arrest of a person who is probably Moses, Daniel in the Lions' Den, Peter sitting beneath a tree and reading in the presence of two soldiers, Christ with blind Bartimaeus, and the Feeding of the Five Thousand. All the numerous figures are exquisitely carved, with the heads conforming to the highest standards of Roman portrait and idealized portrait sculpture, and there is a sense of spaciousness that is usually conspicuously absent from the crowded scenarios of frieze sarcophagi. (**49**)

The acknowledged masterpiece of all the Roman Christian sarcophagi is that of Junius Bassus the Younger, who died in 359 at the age of forty-two while city prefect of Rome, having been baptized on his deathbed, as was the custom. He was buried in the great new church of St. Peter's, where his sarcophagus is still to be seen. It, too, is in two registers, but the scenes that adorn it, instead of flowing one into the other in an uninterrupted frieze, are each framed between the columns of an arcade. The two central scenes lay emphasis on Christ in triumph. Above is the *Traditio legis*, a very common scene on later sarcophagi, with Christ, enthroned above a pagan figure representing the Heavens, handing the scrolls with the New Law to SS. Peter and Paul; below is the more human triumph of the Entry into Jerusalem. The other four scenes of the upper register are, from left to right: the Sacrifice of Isaac, the arrest of St. Peter, Christ before Pilate, and Pilate washing his hands. Those of the lower register, in the same order, are: Job on his dunghill, Adam and Eve, Daniel in the Lions' Den (much restored), and St. Paul being led away to execution. Each subject was carefully chosen to illustrate the themes of redemption and triumph through sacrifice and suffering. The short sides of the Sarcophagus of Junius Bassus are also decorated, unusually. At one end are two registers of Cupids gathering and treading the vintage, representing Autumn. The upper register of the other end depicts three Cupids tying up sheaves of corn, the activity characteristic of Summer. The prominence given to the two activities is a clear allusion to the bread and wine of the Eucharist. Underneath is a group of *putti* with the attributes of the other two Seasons. Every detail of the sculpture of the sarcophagus is perfect, even down to the ornate architectural surround that comes from the Greek taste, and the carving of some of the heads makes it likely that the master-craftsman was trained, appropriately enough, in the workshop that produced the Sarcophagus of the Two Brothers. A work of such quality would have been a fitting ornament to the new Basilica of St. Peter, and the family of Junius Bassus must have found consolation in contemplating such a noble monument to their illustrious dead. (50)

The architectural division of the front of a sarcophagus was to have a long run, both in the workshops of Rome and in those that were founded, towards the end of the century, in the two great Christian centres of southern Gaul, Arles and Marseille. One favourite design, that originated in Rome in the mid fourth century and of which exemplars were later exported to Arles, was the *Anastasis* or 'Resurrection' sarcophagus. Of the five spaces delineated by spirally fluted columns the central one is occupied by a symbolic representation of the Mystery of the Resurrection, indicated by the Cross surmounted by a chi-rho monogram in a wreath on which two birds, representing Christian souls, are feeding; two soldiers sleep at the foot of the Cross. To the right are Christ before Pilate, and Pilate washing his hands (over a typical Roman tripod-table with lion masks and lion feet—examples have been found at Pompeii and elsewhere). To the left a soldier sets a wreath on Christ's head, and Simon of Cyrene carries his cross. The flanking scenes of other *Anastasis* sarcophagi were different, often including the arrests of SS. Peter and Paul, and sometimes they were divided up by trees instead of columns, an attractive device invented in mid-fourth-century Rome and later adopted by the school of Arles on its own account.

A sarcophagus of a different kind that is very interesting for its mixture of Christianity and paganism was made in Rome in the Constantinian period and exported to Arles. The front is divided into four by columns, and in the outer spaces stand the two Dioscuri, Castor and Pollux, with their horses, flanking the scenes of the marriage and farewells of the dead person. The Dioscuri, demi-gods who according to pagan mythology changed places with each other, one in heaven and the other in the Underworld, every six months (and symbolized the dark and light hemispheres of the earth), had for long centuries been looked on as guardians of the dead and symbols of immortality. It was in this latter role that they were used by Christian artists, appearing on a number of indubitably Christian monuments, including a terracotta plate of the late fifth century exported from Africa to Marseille, on which they flank a Latin cross. On this Sarcophagus of the Dioscuri the indications of Christianity, apart from some ambiguous doves (Venus' birds, as well as symbols of Christian love and of the Holy Spirit), are relegated to the short sides, where they take the form of the Feeding of the Five Thousand and a (damaged) scene from the life of St. Peter.

There is little to be found by way of a pagan counterpart to this magnificent series of inventive and highly decorative Christian sarcophagi, a fact that cannot fail to surprise anyone familiar with the beautiful products of the pagan workshops of the second and third centuries, in many parts of the Empire. The great tradition of pagan sarcophagus sculpture seems to have died out by *c.* 340 at the latest. What is more, the character of the last few pagan works was almost totally anodyne, emptied of virtually all truly religious content. The best products of the workshops of Rome in the third century were the mythological sarcophagi, usually featuring some hero who had met an untimely death, and the production of these just overlapped into the fourth century. Two depicting the story of the hunting-hero Meleager, two with Theseus' doomed son Hippolytus, one with the flute-playing demi-god Marsyas who was killed by Apollo (as on Cologne glassware—see above), one with Venus' beloved Adonis who was slain by a boar, and two with Nereids may belong to the early years of the fourth century, but only two of them—one Hippolytus sarcophagus and one with Nereids— are later than 320. Neither subject would have been at all offensive to Christians: Nereids even make their appearance on a Christian pewter cup from Ely in Britain. Whether the artists who made the mythological sarcophagi moved to Constantinople (none of the new capital's art of the early decades has survived), or simply died out, is not known, but it is certain that patrons in Rome must have ceased to order such works.

The other main type of late sarcophagi that were not specifically Christian were decorated with representations of the Seasons, a theme that was entirely neutral ground between pagans and Christians. Seasons make their appearance, as we have seen, on the ends of the Sarcophagus of Junius Bassus, and also on catacomb frescoes. Most of the Season sarcophagi were 'popular' and fairly mass-produced works, with chubby *putti* personifying the four Seasons, turned out by workshops whose artists were employed on purely secular monuments as well, including, perhaps, the Basilica of Maxentius (Chapter II). One variant incorporates Victories flanking the central portrait of the deceased, and these may emanate from the workshops that produced such imperial monuments as the *Decennalia* Base (Chapter I), the Arch of Constantine (Chapter II), and the Baths of Helena (of A.D. 324). Like the mythological sarcophagi, the bulk of these 'popular' Season sarcophagi belong to the first two decades of the fourth century, and only one or two are as late as 320–30. One fairly good piece was found in Carthage, to which it was apparently exported from Rome. The Season *genii* flank the portrait of a boy who has a scroll and writing-tablets to denote his learning, and a diadem on his head to signify the immortality gained by its means.

A few Season sarcophagi, of finer quality than most, are closely connected stylistically with the best of the Christian frieze sarcophagi produced during the twenties and early thirties of the fourth century, and it is thought that one of them, which has naked Dionysus and a Satyr in the centre, was made in the same workshop as the Christian sarcophagus of Claudianus, a lively work with a central Orante. Moreover, this same workshop may have been responsible for a statue of the goddess Artemis. So here again we find a workshop executing both pagan and Christian pieces, although in this case it is not possible to decide whether the same artist was engaged on both, as in the one glass factory at Cologne. What is striking, however, is the contrast between the crowded and vital, if rather awkward, figures of the Christian sarcophagi and the cold and lifeless pagan abstractions of the Season sarcophagi, repetitions of an outworn convention. These strictures apply even to the one exceptional item among the latter, namely the Barberini Season Sarcophagus (now in Dumbarton Oaks in America), a work of superior dimensions and style that was clearly a special commission by an aristocratic patron, and is dateable as late as 330–40. It is sculptured in the Constantinian classicizing style, and certain details make it probable that the artist was apprenticed to the same master as the sculptor of the most beautiful of the Christian frieze sarcophagi, which is of the same period and exhibits the same classicizing tendency, but with differences. The Dumbarton Oaks Sarcophagus, unlike most of the 'neutral' Season sarcophagi, is definitely pagan, for the winged *genius* who personifies Winter is dressed in the garb of Attis, the god who was Cybele's consort and a major abomination to the Christians. The other three Seasons are naked; all have a look of Christian angels about them. They are interspersed with animal attributes and tiny scenes, such as the boar accompanying Winter, the Dionysiac panther at the side of Autumn, and the shepherd milking a goat who exemplifies the activities of Spring. In the centre is a medallion edged by the signs of the zodiac—yet another testimony to the spread of astrology—enclosing the portrait busts of the dead husband

and wife, which have a warmth and character lacking in the Seasons themselves. Underneath the medallion is a little scene of vintaging *putti*. (51)

This sarcophagus would have held the remains of a pagan lord and lady of Constantinian Rome. But it was almost the last pagan sarcophagus made in Rome, and thereafter there is little indication as to how the numerous upper-class pagans were buried, apart, perhaps, from the pagan mausolea in the Via Latina Catacombs and the Hypogeum of Vibia. The reasons for the dying-out of pagan sarcophagi must be sought in the shift in pagan beliefs about the after-life that led to the almost complete cessation, from about the middle of the fourth century, of the age-old custom of providing the dead with grave-goods for their use and consolation and protection in the world beyond the tomb. Pagan intellectuals of Julian's stamp, now more strongly spiritual in their religion than ever before, may have felt that mythological sarcophagi were too worldly, and that even the symbolism of the Season sarcophagi was not altogether suitable for their exalted beliefs about union with the Deity after death; while ordinary people, becoming more familiar with the lack of materialism of Christian beliefs about the resurrection-life, and in general affected by the increasing spirituality of the age, began to doubt the value of giving grave-goods. Yet we have seen elsewhere in this chapter how in other spheres, floor-mosaics for example, pagan themes and motifs continued to flourish for up to another hundred years; and the building of temples, even in Rome itself, and the continuity of pagan worship are sufficient proof, should we need it, that paganism was still a living entity.

*　　*　　*

In the course of this chapter there has emerged a striking degree of parallelism between the monuments and practices of Christians and pagans at this period, the early and mid fourth century. This parallelism was not exact in all respects, as became clear in the section on Christian and pagan saints, but it was genuine, as far as it went; and the existence of Christian activities closely analogous to many in the multifarious world of Graeco-Roman and native paganisms is the main characteristic of religious life in an age that saw the last real liberty of worship for many centuries. This was, however, only true of this particular period when, taking one part of the Empire with another, the two religions were in approximate balance, a position achieved prematurely by Christianity because of the conversion of Constantine. For the Christian religion—more suited, as we have seen in Chapter I, to the heightened spirituality of a shaken society, and its need for authority—was in the ascendant, while paganism was nearing the end of its course; and one further generation would see the definitive proscription of paganism. Thus the manifestations of Christian life described were destined to supplant the parallel pagan ones; and though the use of pagan ideas by Christians, and of Christian ideas by pagans might seem to be a genuinely two-way process, the former was really a residual use by Christians of elements from the common cultural background, as they built up their own systems of iconography and ritual, while the adoption of Christian motifs by pagans, though natural to a religion that had shown an exceptional capacity for the absorption of ideas from outside, was also a symptom of approaching poverty of inspiration. Julian himself bore unwitting witness to this when he created a hierarchic structure for paganism in direct imitation of that of the Christian Church; and in his somewhat defiant promotion of pagan 'saviours' as a substitute for Christ. The failure of pagan self-confidence in an important part of the funerary sphere is another indication that all was not well with paganism, that it had suffered a certain loss of vitality. Despite the energy and partial success of Julian and his followers, and the enormous amount of residual paganism in so much of private, and especially public, life, before another century had passed the Roman world was effectively Christian, a process hastened in the West by the trauma of the great invasions and the collapse of Roman rule. The signs of the triumph were already there in the flourishing Christianity of the Constantinian period.

Bibliography and Notes

*The bibliography and notes represent the principal sources the author has used,
together with some suggestions for further reading*

Ancient Sources The middle fifty years of the third century, from about A.D. 235
to 284, form a kind of dark age in Roman history. The inscriptions, which
were a major source of information about the early Empire, peter out. Only
fragments survive from the works of the contemporary historian Dexippus
(F. Jacoby, *Die Fragmente der griechischen Historiker*, no. 100 (vol. IIA)). The
only connected narratives are provided by the 'breviaries' of Aurelius Victor,
Festus, and Eutropius—brief histories in which a whole reign is covered in a
few sentences giving salient facts, chiefly wars and usurpations; by the twelfth
book of the *Annals* of Zonaras, of similar content; by the relevant part of
Zosimus' *New History*, which is scarcely fuller than the breviaries except on
certain military matters; and by the *Historia Augusta*, a set of imperial
biographies apparently compiled by a late-fourth-century writer more interest-
ed in producing a good story than in historical accuracy. Gradually we
emerge into the light of day, around the beginning of the fourth century. The
reign of Diocletian is a twilight area: without the few hints contained in
Lactantius' work *On the Deaths of the Persecutors* we should know little for
certain of the character and scale of his reforms (Zosimus' account of these
years is lost). Several of the *Latin Panegyrics* are addressed to tetrarchs, and
some, a little later, to the young Constantine; florid rhetorical works, they
add little solid information. The *Acts* or *Passions* of certain martyrs, and an
invaluable record of requisition proceedings in Africa, help fill out the history
of the Great Persecution.

We are on much firmer ground with the events of the break-up of the
Tetrarchy: the two basic accounts are those of Lactantius, the Christian
rhetorician who came from North Africa to Nicomedia and was eventually
appointed tutor to Constantine's son Crispus (A.D. 318), and of Eusebius,
bishop of Caesarea in Palestine, in the concluding books of his *Church
History*. This last is supplemented by passages in another work of Eusebius, of
a different kind: *On the Life of Constantine*, a laudatory account of that emperor's triumphs and Christian actions that is far more closely related to
panegyric than to sober historiography, and needs to be used with appropriate caution. Yet, for all its limitations, the *Life of Constantine* is an invaluable
contemporary source for the years of his sole reign. The strongly Christian
slant of the information is counterbalanced to some extent by the rather
sketchy but none the less valuable account of Zosimus, a convinced pagan
who wrote in the late fifth or early sixth century and drew on the lost *History*
of Eunapius of Sardis, an admirer of Julian. Aurelius Victor, an active
supporter of Julian, under whom he was governor of Second Pannonia, adds

a little more information on the pagan side in his short *Book on the Caesars*, which finishes at the end of Constantius II's reign. (An epitomist working in parallel from the same source carries the story down to the reign of Theodosius.) The breviarists Festus and Eutropius, who wrote and held high office in the late fourth century, were also pagans. And a secular fragment known as the *Anonymus Valesianus* (first part) is a minor source for the early part of Constantine's reign. But the Christian bias of the Constantinian sources is confirmed by the existence of the works of three fifth-century Church historians—Socrates, Sozomen and Theodoret—and, in a fragmentary state, that of the Arian Philostorgius; all of them begin their ecclesiastical histories with the reign of Constantine. They were preceded, *c.* 400, by Sulpicius Severus and Rufinus, but their accounts, though useful in some details, were much less full. (Theodoret also wrote a *Religious History* about the monastic movement in Syria, and Palladius' *Lausiac History* fulfils the same function for Egypt.) Minor Christian sources that cover the whole of the period include four Byzantine chronicles: the seventh-century *Chronicon Paschale*, and the works of the sixth-century Antiochene John Malalas and of the late Byzantine Zonaras and Georgius Codinus.

The first part of the reign of the sons of Constantine is a relatively dark area, covered mainly by Zosimus, by the three breviarists Aurelius Victor, Festus and Eutropius, and by the three Church historians Socrates, Sozomen and Theodoret, who concentrate almost exclusively on internal ecclesiastical affairs. The works of St. Athanasius, especially the *History of the Arians*, are a new, vivid, and very biased source for these, and a little is added in the same vein by the polemics of St. Hilary of Poitiers. Sulpicius Severus, disciple of St. Martin and friend of St. Paulinus of Nola, apparently received information from Hilary about certain events of the 350s for his *Chronica* (or *Historia sacra*), and the preserved fragments of Philostorgius' Church history are of obvious interest for the reign of his fellow-Arian Constantius. Then, in the 350s, new and extremely valuable sources begin to make their contribution, turning the next quarter-century into the most floodlit part of the fourth century. Chief among these is the *History* of Ammianus Marcellinus, which for all its convoluted style is one of the major achievements of ancient historiography, the work of a historian as great as Tacitus—and some would say greater. Ammianus was a Greek-speaking army officer from Antioch, a member of the curial classes, who served in the Persian wars, in Gaul, and on Julian's Persian expedition. He supplements his own eyewitness accounts with carefully assembled material gathered from competent observers, written up towards the end of the fourth century in a Latin whose grammar he had laboriously mastered but whose conciseness and elegance eluded him. He was a pagan and a devoted admirer of Julian, but disapproved of that emperor's religious excesses and was quite prepared to criticize certain of his policies. In Ammianus we have at last a detailed and reliable source of secular history as a counterweight to the Christian writers. The speeches of Themistius, philosopher and orator of Constantinople, and the speeches and letters of Libanius, sophist of Antioch, also begin around 350. They shed light, respectively, on Constantius' relations with the leading intellectuals of his day, and on many aspects of life and government in the Greek East.

The Emperor Julian's own works begin in 355, and are of inestimable value in revealing to us the spirit that animated his pagan revival. Although he was not an original thinker, most of his philosophy being derived from the Neoplatonist Iamblichus, he was no mean writer in Greek, and much of his writing is infused with a human warmth and vividness and immediacy that make Julian one of the most sympathetic characters in the fourth century, if a rather tragic and sometimes misguided one. The other three literary corner-stones of his exceptionally well-documented reign are Ammianus, Libanius (especially his series of Julianic speeches), and a new source: Eunapius of Sardis. The *History* written by this fanatical pagan at the very end of the fourth century is lost, but survived long enough to be used extensively by Zosimus. His *Lives of the Philosophers and Sophists* is, however, extant, and the biographies of the mages and philosophers who surrounded Julian, written by one who was enjoying higher education in Athens while Julian was on the throne, give valuable information and insights. A contrasting, hostile, witness is St. Gregory of Nazianzus, who wrote two speeches *Against Julian* shortly after the emperor's death. A few additional, minor, sources for the Julianic period and earlier are mentioned in the notes.

The fifth cornerstone of the Julianic sources introduces us to a new kind of source: the laws. A large proportion of the public legislation of the fourth-century emperors, from 312 on, is collected in the mid-fifth-century *Theodosian Code*, and many of these laws, and a few extra ones, are included in the sixth-century *Code of Justinian*. They need to be used with some caution, for we know that some of them remained a dead letter and that others were geographically restricted in their application or only partially enforced. This is especially to be suspected whenever a particular prohibition is repeatedly enacted, at intervals of a few years, by the same or successive emperors (e.g. the laws forbidding the flight of *curiales*). Again, many, if not most, were issued in response to a particular situation, usually when a senior official requested a ruling on some problem he had encountered: they did not all originate in the emperor's mind as spontaneous policy. Yet the body of an emperor's legislation will indicate the main areas of his concern, and something of the originality and effectiveness of his solutions to problems. This is especially important in the case of a great reformer like Constantine or Julian, and it is most unfortunate that virtually none of Diocletian's political legislation has survived, only legislation concerned with civil law. Even the literary style can tell us something. The brevity and directness of Julian's laws contrasts with the more longwinded, elaborate and ambiguous style of his predecessors' legislation. The chancellery may have taken over most of the drafting of imperial letters and laws under the bureaucratically-inclined Constantius, but Julian, who spent much of the day in official business and administered justice in person, reverted to the earlier practice in this sphere, too, and probably drafted many such documents himself (he certainly wrote important letters). There is also a certain amount of secondary information to be gleaned: the place and date of the issue of individual laws reveal the emperor's movements; and groups of laws addressed to a particular official—often a praetorian prefect or city prefect—can reveal his own policies and spheres of activity through his soliciting of imperial responses, for the Empire was no monolith, and powerful men of good or evil intent could carve out their own empires of influence within it.

Some laws and other administrative documents, such as imperial letters, have survived outside the codes, by being quoted in a literary source. This is the case with both the Palinode of Galerius and the Edict of Milan, which are quoted in full by both Lactantius and Eusebius (the latter translated them into Greek). Ammianus also quotes the occasional document. Eusebius is outstanding in this respect, quoting numerous Constantinian edicts and letters verbatim, something normally studiously avoided by ancient writers. In addition, a body of valuable documents relating to the Donatist controversy in Africa was annexed by Optatus to his history of it. One important administrative document, the *Notitia dignitatum* ('List of Dignities'), has come down to us on its own, from an illustrated manuscript copied in the Carolingian period and again in mediaeval times. Compiled in about 400, it lists the dispositions of officials and troops throughout the Empire, sometimes amalgamating two successive states of affairs in a single province. It is a vital source for the military reforms of both Diocletian and Constantine. The *Calendar of 354* survived in a similar manner, though we have only third-hand copies of the illustrations. The collected canons of certain Christian councils are also extant.

Inscriptions are very scarce, in a sad contrast with the early Empire, for which they are one of the richest sources. There were few new buildings, and therefore few building-inscriptions. Money was lacking for the frequent putting up of statues to local worthies, patrons and officials. Epitaphs are brief and uninformative, again, no doubt, for financial reasons, together with a Christian or Christian-influenced disregard for the details of an earthly life. Only the rich and important still had the resources and taste for epitaphs detailing their glorious careers, and only emperors and high officials were still likely to receive statues and dedicatory inscriptions from the cities and from wealthy individuals. The great majority of imperial dedications were brief acclamations engraved on milestones—often ones already in existence, with the name of the earlier emperor erased. The very large series of dedications to Julian is of the first importance, revealing as it does the wave of enthusiasm that greeted his reign in many quarters. A handful of pagan dedications made by Roman aristocrats is extant. There are also a few military inscriptions that shed light on the organization of the army under Diocletian and Constantine, and Diocletian's Price Edict is extant in several copies from market-places in Asia Minor.

Coins, as sources, have something in common with inscriptions. They differ chiefly in their centralized, imperial origin, and especially in the completeness of our knowledge of them, a consequence of the huge quantities in which even quite minor issues were struck. Something of their value as evidence can be seen in Chapters II, IV and V.

Coins are also of immense value in dating the archaeology of the ancient monuments, the last category of ancient evidence. From the interpretation of carefully excavated Roman buildings and the surviving monuments it is possible to reconstruct much of the ancient physical environment, no mean achievement in itself. But that is not all: in studying a period of rapid religious change, an enormous amount of information can be gleaned from the archaeology of dying, disused, destroyed, restored, or even flourishing temples, and of the new churches. The artistic objects found in the course of excavation can also give us unique insights into the prevailing religious, artistic and economic climate (see Chapter VI). Archaeology, if carefully evaluated, is thus a very rich source, and a continually expanding one, an advantage that otherwise applies only to epigraphy (and papyri).

Note: Translations Most of the major literary sources have been translated into English: Zosimus, *Historia Nova*, trans. J. J. Buchanan and H. T. Davis (Texas, 1967); Eusebius, *The History of the Church*, trans. G. A. Williamson (Harmondsworth, Penguin Classics, 1965); Eusebius' *Vita Constantini*, together with the *Church History*, is translated in volume I of *The Nicene and Post-Nicene Fathers* (second series); Lactantius' *On the Deaths of the Persecutors* is in volume XXII of *The Ante-Nicene Christian Library*, and volume LIV of *The Fathers of the Church*, trans. MacDonald, (1965); volume II of *The Nicene and Post-Nicene Fathers* (second series) contains the Church histories of Socrates and Sozomen, and volume III that of Theodoret; while volume IV contains works of Athanasius, volume VII, of Gregory of Nazianzus, and volume XI, of Sulpicius Severus; the works of Ammianus, Julian and Eunapius, and the Julianic speeches of Libanius, are all published in the *Loeb Classical Library* (text and translation); Libanius' *Autobiography* is edited and translated by A. F. Norman (Oxford, 1965); Gregory of Nazianzus' two speeches *Against Julian* are translated by C. W. King in *Julian the Emperor* (London, 1888) (see also above); Sallust, *On the Gods and the World* is edited and translated by A. D. Nock (1926) (see also below); lastly, the *Theodosian Code* is translated by C. Pharr (Princeton, 1952). Several other works have been translated into French (together with some of the above) in the Budé series (text and translation): *Latin Panegyrics*, ed. Galletier (1949); Firmicus Maternus, *On the Error of the Profane Religions*, ed. Heuten (1938); and Sallust, *On the Gods and the World*, ed. Rochefort (1960); while the *Exposition of the Whole World*, a curious little work apparently written in 359 by a merchant from Tyre, is in the *Sources chrétiennes* series, ed. Rougé (1966).

A Selection of Modern Treatments The best modern, general account of the period in English is in A. H. M. Jones, *The Later Roman Empire, 284–602* (Oxford, 1964), vol. I. The accounts in the last volume of *The Cambridge Ancient History* (1939) and the first volume of *The Cambridge Mediaeval History* (1911) are useful, but rather out of date. The best history of the fourth century is in French: A. Piganiol, *L'Empire chrétien (325–395)* (Paris, 1947; second edition, Paris, 1972). E. Stein, *Histoire du Bas-Empire*, vol. I, translated from the German with additional notes by J.-R. Palanque (Paris, 1959), is also useful. There are two excellent biographies of Constantine in English: A. H. M. Jones, *Constantine and the Conversion of Europe* (London, 1949), and R. MacMullen, *Constantine* (in U.S.A., 1969; London, 1970); to which may be added the fine essay by N. H. Baynes, *Constantine the Great and the Christian Church* in *Proceedings of the British Academy* XV (1929) (and published separately). There is now at last a biography of Julian—and a good one—in English: R. Browning, *The Emperor Julian* (1976), which appeared after this book was completed. But the French biography by J. Bidez, *La vie de l'Empereur Julien* (second edition, Paris, 1965), remains fundamental. (Gore Vidal's novel *Julian* (1964) is worth reading for its vivid reconstruction of the events of his life, though some characters are distorted (notably the philosopher Priscus), the account of Gallus, already exaggerated in Ammianus, is made even more lurid, and a distinctly superfluous sex-life is conjured up for the devoutly ascetic Julian.) Seven other books of interest are: *The Conflict between Paganism and Christianity in the Fourth Century*, ed. A. Momigliano (Oxford, 1963)—a valuable collection of essays; R. Markus, *Christianity in the Roman World* (1974); E. R. Dodds, *Pagan and Christian in an Age of Anxiety*, (Cambridge, 1965); H. P. L'Orange, *Art Forms and Civic Life in the Later Roman Empire* (Princeton, 1965)—the contrast between the early and late Empire is somewhat overstated, but was none the less real; R. MacMullen, *Soldier and Civilian in the Later Roman Empire* (Cambridge, Mass., 1963)—an interesting discussion of the growing influence of the military element; and two books by Peter Brown: *The World of Late Antiquity* (London, 1971); and *Augustine of Hippo* (London, 1967) which, though not of precisely this period, gives brilliant insights into the life of the time. Finally, no list would be complete without Gibbon's *Decline and Fall of the Roman Empire* (best read in J. B. Bury's edition (London, 1896–7)); but see the remarks by Jones in *Constantine and the Conversion of Europe*, p. 260 (p. 242 in the paperback edition).

Chapters I–II The third-century anarchy: A. H. M. Jones, *The Later Roman Empire, 284–602* (Oxford, 1964) vol. I, pp. 21–36; for a detailed narrative, see H. M. D. Parker, *A History of the Roman World from A.D. 138 to 337* (2nd edition, London, 1958), parts III–IV. The army: Jones, op. cit., pp. 52–60, 649–54; D. van Berchem, *L'armée de Dioclétien et la réforme constantinienne* (Paris, 1952). The Tetrarchy: Lactantius, *De mortibus persecutorum* 7; Jones, op. cit., ch. II; Stein-Palanque, *Histoire du Bas-Empire* I, pp. 65–82; W. Seston, *Dioclétien et la Tétrarchie I: Guerres et réformes (284–300)* (Paris, 1946)—out of date on some points. Britain under Carausius and the Tetrarchy: I. A. Richmond, *Roman Britain* (2nd edition, Harmondsworth, 1963), pp. 60–2; S. S. Frere, *Britannia* (London, 1967), pp. 335–45. Constantius Chlorus and Autun: Eumenius, *Pro instaurandis scholis* (= *Panegyrici Latini* IV, ed. Galletier). Tetrarchic art and architecture: L'Orange, *Art Forms and Civic Life*; D. E. Strong, *Roman Imperial Sculpture* (London, 1961), pp. 72–4 and plates 131–5; K. F. Kinch, *L'arc de triomphe de Salonique* (Paris, 1890); C. C. Vermeule, *Roman Imperial Art in Greece and Asia Minor* (Cambridge, Mass., 1968), pp. 336–50; L'Orange, 'Ein tetrarchisches Ehrendenkmal auf dem Forum Romanum' in *Mitteilungen des Deutschen Archäologischen Instituts, Römische Abteilung*, LIII (1938), pp. 1–34; H. Kähler, *Das Fünfsäulendenkmal für die Tetrarchen auf dem Forum Romanum* (Cologne, 1964) (not readily available); R. Delbrueck, *Antike Porphyrwerke* (Berlin, 1932), pp. 84–92, plates 31–7; G. Niemann, *Der Palast Diokletians in Spalato* (Vienna, 1910) (also difficult to obtain). Price Edict: text with English translation in *Economic Survey of Ancient Rome*, ed. Tenney Frank, vol. V (Baltimore, 1940), pp. 305–421. Taxation: A. Déléage, *La capitation du Bas-Empire* (1945). The Great Persecution: Lactantius, *De mort. persec.* 10ff.; Eusebius, *Historia ecclesiastica* VIII–IX; A. Musurillo, *Acts of the Christian Martyrs* (Oxford, 1972), pp. 244–59; *Gesta apud Zenophilum*, in Optatus, *De schismate Donatis-*

tarum, Appendix I; W. H. C. Frend, *Martyrdom and Persecution in the Early Church* (Oxford, 1965), chs. XIV and XV; Jones, op. cit., pp. 71–6. Events of Second and Third Tetrarchies and battle of the Milvian Bridge: Lactantius, *De mort. persec.* 17ff.; Eusebius, *Hist. eccles.* VIII.13–IX.11; *Vita Constantini* I.18ff.; *Pan. Lat.* VIII–X; Zosimus II.8ff. Maxentius and Africa: Zosimus II.12, 14; Aurelius Victor XL.19, 28; G.-C. Picard, *La Carthage de saint Augustin* (Paris, 1965), pp. 36–49; P. Romanelli, *Storia delle province romane dell' Africa* (Rome, 1959), pp. 534–40. Pagan policies of Maximin: Eusebius, *Hist. eccles.* VIII.14.8–9; Lactantius, *De mort. persec.* 26.4. Basilica of Maxentius and Arch of Constantine: E. Nash, *Illustrated Dictionary of Ancient Rome* (1961–2) I, pp. 104–12, 180–2 (with full bibliography); L'Orange and von Gerkan, *Der spätantike Bildschmuck des Konstantinsbogens* (Berlin, 1939); Strong, *Roman Imperial Sculpture*, pp. 75–8. Colossal portrait of Constantine: R. Delbrueck, *Spätantike Kaiserporträts* (Berlin-Leipzig, 1933), p. 121 and plates 37–9; L'Orange, *Studien zur Geschichte des spätantiken Porträts* (1933), p. 63 and fig. 163; Eusebius, *Hist. eccles.* IX.9.10–11; *Vita Const.* I.40. Sol Invictus on the coins of Constantine: P. Bruun in *Arctos*, II (1958), pp. 15–37. Constantine, Licinius and Maximin (A.D. 313): Lactantius, *De mort. persec.* 45ff.; Eusebius, *Hist. eccles.* IX.9ff.; *Vita Constantini* I.41–7, 58–9; Zosimus II.17. Constantine and Licinius (313–24): Eusebius, *Hist. eccles.* X; *Vita Const.* I.48–56, II.1–18; Zosimus II.18–28; *Anonymus Valesianus, pars prior* 5; Libanius, *Oratio* XXX.6. Constantine sole emperor: Zosimus II.29–38; Eusebius, *Vita Const.* II.19–IV.75; Piganiol, *L'Empire chrétien*, chs. I–II. Foundation of Constantinople: Zosimus II.30–2, 35–7; Eusebius, *Vita Const.* III.48–9, IV.58–60; Codinus, *De antiquitatibus Constantinopolitanis*, especially 7Bff., 22C–23C, 25A, 25C, 26D, 28C–D, 32C–D, 34C, 34D–35A, 37D–38B, 51B, 91D, 98D–99A; Malalas, *Chronographia* XIII.319–24; *Chronicon Paschale* I, pp. 528–30 (Bonn); Zonaras, *Epitome historiarum* XIII.3; Socrates, *Hist. eccles.* I.16; Sozomen, *Hist. eccles.* II.3; *Codex Theodosianus* V.xiv.36, XIV.xvi.2; *Novellae Theodosii* (to be found at end of *Cod. Theod.*) V.1; Piganiol, op. cit., pp. 53–6; W. Amelung, 'Kybele-Orans' in *Römische Mitteilungen* (for full title, see above), XIV (1899), pp. 8–12; T. Preger, 'Konstantinos-Helios' in *Hermes*, XXXVI (1901), pp. 457–69; A. Frolow, 'La dédicace de Constantinople dans la tradition byzantine' in *Revue de l'Histoire des Religions*, CXXVII (1944), pp. 61–85; G. Downey, 'The Builder of the Original Church of the Apostles at Constantinople' in *Dumbarton Oaks Papers*, VI (1951), pp. 53–80; J. Vogt, 'Der Erbauer der Apostelkirche in Konstantinopel' in *Hermes*, LXXXI (1953), pp. 111–17; R. Krautheimer, *Early Christian and Byzantine Architecture* (Harmondsworth, 1965), pp. 46–9; C. Mango, 'Antique Statuary and the Byzantine Beholder' in *Dumbarton Oaks Papers*, XVII (1963), pp. 53–75; Carson, Hill, and Kent, *Late Roman Bronze Coinage* (London, 1965), I nos. 51–2, 58–9 and *passim*. Visit to Rome in 326: Zosimus II.29; Philostorgius, *Hist. eccles.* II.4; cf. Julian, *The Caesars* 336A–B; Piganiol, op. cit., pp. 37–40. Constantine and Persia: Eusebius, *Vita* IV.8–13; Ammianus XVIII.ix.1, XXV.iv.23; Cedrenus, *Chron. anno XXI Constantini*, P.295A–B (= I, pp. 516–17, Bonn); Piganiol, op. cit., pp. 62–3. Reforms of Constantine: Zosimus II.32–4; Jones, *Later Roman Empire*, pp. 97–110; Piganiol, pp. 70–7; J.-R. Palanque, *Essai sur la préfec-*

ture du prétoire du Bas-Empire (Paris, 1933); A. Chastagnol, 'Observations sur le consulat suffect et la préture du Bas-Empire' in *Revue Historique*, CCXIX (1958), pp. 221–53; Ammianus XXI.x.8, xii.25; S. Mazzarino, *Aspetti sociali del quarto secolo* (Richerche di storia tardo-romana) (Rome, 1951), especially chs. I–II (but the *De rebus bellicis* was written under Valentinian, not under Constantius: see E. A. Thompson, *A Roman Reformer and Inventor* (Oxford, 1952), pp. 1–2); *Cod. Theod.* I.xxii.2 (widows and orphans), XI.xxvii.1 (poor relief), II.xxv.1 (slaves: cf. IX.xii.1, IX.ix.1, IV.x.1), III.xvi.1 (divorce), IV.vi.2–3 (illegitimate children), VII.xxii.1–2 and 4–5, XIII.v.1–3, vi.1, XII.i.7, V.xvii.1, VII.xxii.3 (heredity of condition), I.xvi.7 (corruption); Eusebius, *Vita* IV.31 (clemency); *Cod. Theod.* XV.xii.1; G. Ville in *Mélanges d'Archéologie et d'Histoire*, LXXII (1960), pp. 273–335 (gladiators); Sozomen I.8 (crucifixion); *Cod. Theod.* IX.xl.2 (branding), IX.iii.1 (prisoners). The succession crisis: Julian, *Epistula* 20 (ed. Bidez-Cumont) (= Loeb, frag. 3); *Epistula ad Athenienses* 270C–D; Ausonius, *Commemoratio Professorum Burdigalensium* XVIII; Zosimus II.39–40; Socrates II.25, III.1; Sozomen V.2; *Epitome de Caesaribus* XLI.15–20; *Anon. Vales.*, *pars prior* 35; A. H. M. Jones, J. R. Martindale and J. Morris, *The Prosopography of the Later Roman Empire* I (Cambridge, 1971), s.v. Dalmatius 6 and 7, (Julius) Constantius 7, Hannibalianus 2, etc.; Piganiol, op. cit., pp. 60–1, 81–3. Character of Constantius II: Ammianus XXI.xvi; Athanasius, *Historia Arianorum* 70; Eunapius, *Vitae philosophorum* VI.iii.8–13 (= Loeb, pp. 388–91) (Ablabius); M. K. Hopkins in *Proceedings of the Cambridge Philological Society*, new series, XI (1963), pp. 62–80 (eunuchs). Death of Constantine II: Zosimus II.41 (confused); *Epitome de Caesaribus* XLI.21; Eutropius X.9; Socrates II.5; Piganiol, p. 84. Reign of Constantius II and Constans (340–50): Julian, *Or.* I.17C–30A; Libanius, *Or.* LIX.59ff.; *Chron. Pasch.*, pp. 536–9 (Bonn); Ammianus XX.i.1, XXV.ix.3, XXVIII.iii.8; Eutropius X.9; Piganiol, pp. 83–9; J. P. C. Kent, '*Fel. temp. reparatio*' in *Numismatic Chronicle*, seventh series, VII (1967), pp. 83–90. Usurpations of Magnentius, Vetranio and Nepotianus (350–3): Zosimus II.42–54; Julian, *Or.* I.26B–D, 30B–40B; II.74C; Themistius, *Or.* II.37c; Eutropius X.12; Ammianus XV.vi.4 (Trier); Socrates II.32; Sozomen IV.7; Piganiol, pp. 94–9; Kent in *Num. Chron.*, sixth series, XIX (1959), pp. 105–8 (Trier). Sole rule of Constantius II (353–61): Ammianus XIV–XXI; Zosimus II.55; Piganiol, pp. 101–21. Fall of Gallus: Ammianus XIV.i.1–4, 7, 9, 11; Julian, *Ep. ad Athen.* 270C–272D; Zosimus II.45, 55; Socrates II.33–4; Sozomen II.7; E. A. Thompson, *The Historical Work of Ammianus Marcellinus* (Cambridge, 1947), ch. 4; Piganiol, pp. 102–3. S. Costanza: W. F. Volbach and M. Hirmer, *Early Christian Art* (London, 1961), p. 319 (with bibliography), plates 29–35 and figs. 12–13; Krautheimer, *Early Christian and Byzantine Architecture*, pp. 43–4. Julian Caesar (355–60): Ammianus XV.viii, XVI.i–v, vii.1–3, xi–xii (battle of Strasbourg), XVII.i–iii, viii–xi, XVIII.i–ii, XX.i; Zosimus III.3–8; Julian, *Ep. ad Athen.* 274C–282C; J. Bidez, *Vie de l'empereur Julien*, pp. 123–76; Piganiol, pp. 128, 133–6. Constantius' visit to Rome: Ammianus XVI.xx, XVII.iv; Symmachus, *Relatio* III.7; Theodoret, *Hist. eccles.* II.14; cf. *Expositio totius mundi* 55 (of just this period). Siege of Amida: Ammianus XIX.i–viii. Usurpation of Julian (360–1): Ammianus XX.iv–v, viii–x, XXI.i–xv, XXII.i–ii; Julian, *Ep. ad Athen.*, especially 282Cff.; *Ep.* 9 (Loeb) (= Bidez-Cumont no. 28); Zosimus III 8–11; Libanius, *Or.* XII.57–65, XIII.33–40, XVIII.90–118; Bidez, op. cit., pp. 177–99; Piganiol, pp. 137–41. Reign of Julian (political events): Ammianus XXII.ii–XXV.iv; Zosimus III.11ff.; Julian, *Misopogon*; Libanius, *Or.* XII–XVIII; Bidez, op. cit., pp. 203–331; Piganiol, pp. 143–51, 157–62. Clean-up of palace: Ammianus XXII.iv; Socrates III.1. Chalcedon trials: Ammianus XXII.iii, XX.xi.5; cf. Thompson, *Historical Work of Ammianus*, pp. 73–9. The Persian expedition: Ammianus XXII.xii, XXIII.ii–XXV.ix; Zosimus III.12–29; Julian, *Ep.* 58 (Loeb) (= Bidez-Cumont no. 98); Libanius, *Or.* XVIII.204–80; Piganiol, pp. 157–64; Bidez, op. cit., pp. 315–31; L. Dillemann, *Haute Mésopotamie orientale et pays adjacentes* (Paris, 1962), pp. 216–23, 299–312; id. in *Syria*, XXXVIII (1961), pp. 87–158.

Chapter III: Churches of Rome: *Liber Pontificalis*, ed. Duchesne (Paris, 1955), XXXIV; F. W. Deichmann, *Frühchristliche Kirchen in Rom* (Basle, 1948), pp. 11–35; R. Krautheimer, *Corpus basilicarum christianarum Romae* I (Vatican, 1937), pp. 14–39, 165–94; II (1959), pp. 1–144, 191–204; IV (1970), pp. 99–147; id., *Early Christian and Byzantine Architecture*, (Harmondsworth, 1965) pp. 17–36, 63; G. Matthiae, *Le chiese di Roma dal IV al X secolo* (Bologna, 1962), pp. 35–53; F. Tolotti, *Memorie degli Apostoli in Catacumbas* (Vatican, 1953); A. Ferrua, *S. Sebastiano fuori le mura e la sua catacomba* (Rome, 1968); A. P. Frutaz, *Il complesso monumentale di S. Agnese e di S. Costanza* (Vatican, 1960) (not readily available); J. M. C. Toynbee and J. Ward Perkins, *The Shrine of St. Peter and the Vatican Excavations* (London, 1956); G. Downey, *A History of Antioch in Syria from Seleucus to the Arab Conquest* (1961), pp. 281–4, 583–6. Trier: *Frühchristliche Zeugnisse im Einzugsgebiet von Rhein und Mosel*, ed. W. Reusch (Trier, 1965), pp. 144–50 (Basilika), 236–46 (paintings), 223–30 (graffiti); T. Kempf in *Neue Ausgrabungen in Deutschland* (Berlin, 1958), pp. 368–74 (cathedral); Krautheimer, *Early Christian and Byzantine Architecture*, p. 27. Nicomedia: Eusebius, *Vita Constantini* III.50. Antioch: Eusebius, *Vita* III.50; Malalas XIII.318; G. Downey, *A History of Antioch in Syria from Seleucus to the Arab Conquest* (Princeton, 1961), pp. 342–9, 661–3; W. Eltester in *Zeitschrift für die neutestamentliche Wissenschaft*, XXXVI (1937), pp. 254–70; A. Grabar, *Martyrium* (Paris, 1943–6) I, pp. 214–27; J. Lassus, *Sanctuaires chrétiens de Syrie* (Paris, 1947), p. 109; Lassus in *Antioch-on-the-Orontes I: The Excavations of 1932* (ed. G. W. Elderkin) (Princeton, 1934), p. 145; cf. D. Levi, *Antioch Mosaic Pavements* (Princeton, 1947), pp. 332–3; Socrates II.8; Sozomen III.5; Libanius, *Oratio* I.39 (Bemarchius). Holy Land: Eusebius, *Vita* III.25–43, 51–3, IV.43–7; *Itinerarium Burdigalense* (in *Corpus Scriptorum Ecclesiasticorum Latinorum* XXXIX, or *Corpus Christianorum, series Latina*, CLXXV); Krautheimer, *Early Christian and Byzantine Architecture*, pp. 36–41, with bibliography; Piganiol, op. cit., pp. 40–4, with bibliography; C. Coüasnon, *The Church of the Holy Sepulchre, Jerusalem* (Oxford, British Academy, 1974); J. Wilkinson, *Egeria's Travels* (London, 1971), especially pp. 36–53.

Chapter IV: Privileges for the Church: *Codex Theodosianus* XVI.ii.1–16, ix.1–2; Eusebius, *Historia ecclesiastica* X.6–7; *Vita* I.42, II.20–43, 45–6, IV.26–8, 38–9. The Donatists: Optatus, *De schismate Donatistarum* (*Liber contra Parmenianum*), with Appendix (collected documents); Eusebius, *Hist. eccles.* X.5–7; W. H. C. Frend, *The Donatist Church* (Oxford, 1952), chs. 1–12; for modifications to the central thesis of this seminal book, see A. H. M. Jones in *Journal of Theological Studies*, new series, X (1959), pp. 280–95; E. Tengström, *Donatisten und Katholiken* (1964); Peter Brown in *Journal of Roman Studies*, LVIII (1968), pp. 85–95; Fergus Millar, ibid., pp. 126–34; see also J.-P. Brisson, *Autonomisme et christianisme dans l'Afrique romaine* (Paris, 1958). Arianism under Constantine: Eusebius, *Vita* II.61–73, III.4–23, 59–62, IV.41–2; H. G. Opitz, *Athanasius Werke* III (Berlin, 1935) (collected documents); Athanasius, *De decretis Nicaeni synodi*; Socrates I.5–15, 23–38; Sozomen I.15–17, 19–25, II.16–23, 25, 27–33; Theodoret, *Hist. eccles.* I.2–13, 18–21, 25–9; Philostorgius, *Hist. eccles.* I–II; Canons of Councils of Arles and Nicaea, ed. J.-D. Mansi, II, pp. 470–4, 667–77; Piganiol, op. cit., pp. 34–5, 44–9, 63–7; *Histoire de l'Église depuis les origines jusqu'à nos jours*, ed. Fliche and Martin, III (Paris, 1936), pp. 69–115. Arianism under Constantius II: Athanasius, *Historia Arianorum, Apologia contra Arianos, Apologia ad Constantium, Apologia de fuga, Epistula ad Serapionem de morte Arii, De synodis* 1–14; Socrates II; Sozomen III–IV; Canons of Council of Serdica, ed. Mansi, III, pp. 5–21; Sulpicius Severus, *Chronica* II.37–45; Julian, *Ep.* 41 (Loeb) (= Bidez-Cumont no. 114); Piganiol, op. cit., pp. 90–3, 105–8, 113–18; Fliche-Martin III, pp. 115–76. For an illuminating summary of the ideas behind Arianism, see Peter Brown, *The World of Late Antiquity* (London, 1971), p. 90. Ulfilas and the Goths: Letter of Auxentius of Durostorum (from *Dissertatio Maximini contra Ambrosium*); Philostorgius II.5; Socrates II.41, IV.33; Sozomen IV.24, VI.37; Theodoret, *Hist. eccles.* IV.37; these and other sources are conveniently collected in the introduction to *Die gotische Bibel*, ed. W. Streitberg (fifth edition, Heidelberg, 1965); E. A. Thompson, *The Visigoths in the Time of Ulfila* (Oxford, 1966), especially pp. xiii–xxiii; Piganiol, op. cit., pp. 423–4. Constantine and paganism: Eusebius, *Vita* II.47–60 (edict); III.54; Libanius, *Oratio* XXX.6, LXII.8; Piganiol, op. cit., pp. 57–8 (inventory); Eusebius, *Vita* III.55–6, 58, 26–7, 51–3; Socrates I.18; Sozomen II.5 (Baalbek etc.); Dessau, *Inscriptiones latinae selectae* 705 (imperial cult); Eusebius, *Vita* IV.16 (statues in temples); Zosimus II.29 (procession to Capitol); Eusebius, *Vita* IV.38–9; Sozomen V.3; Dessau, *ILS* 6091 (new Christian 'cities'); *Cod. Theod.* IX.xvi.1–3, XVI.x.1 (divination). Constantius and Constans and paganism: *Cod. Theod.* XVI.x.2–6; F. Martroye in *Revue Historique de Droit Français et Étranger*, 1930, pp. 669–701; Piganiol, op. cit., p. 88 (anti-pagan legislation); Firmicus Maternus, *Mathesis*; id., *De errore profanarum religionum* (a call to persecute); Libanius, *Or.* XVII.7; *Ep.* 685 (closure of temples); Libanius, *Or.* I.27, XIV.41, XVII.7, XXX.7; *Ep.* 1338, 1351 (prohibition of sacrifices); *Or.* VII.10, XVII.7, XXX.38; Ammianus XXII.iv.3 (temples given to courtiers); Sozomen III.17 (to the Church); Libanius, *Or.* XV.53, XVII.7, LXII.8 (demolition); Ammianus XIX.x (sacrifice at Ostia); Libanius, *Or.* XXX.33–4 (cf. 35–6) (necessity of cult); Ammianus XVI.x.14; Symmachus, *Relatio* III.7 (pagan side of visit to Rome); Symm., *Rel.* III (especially s. 5); Ambrose, *Ep.* 17–18 (altar of Victory); *Cod. Theod.* IX.xvi.4–6; H. Lewy, *Chaldaean Oracles and Theurgy. Mysticism, magic and Platonism in the later Roman Empire* (Cairo, 1956), and review by E. R. Dodds in *Harvard Theological Review*, LIV (1961), pp. 263–73; Ammianus XVI.viii.1–2 (magic); Ammianus XIX.xii; Libanius, *Or.* XIV.15–20, *Ep.* 37, 112 (Scythopolis trials of 359); Ammianus XXI.xiv.1–xv.2, XVI.viii.2; Libanius, *Or.* XXXVI; J. Maurice in *Revue Hist. de Droit Fr. et Étr.*, 1927, pp. 108–20; A. A. Barb in *The Conflict between Paganism and Christianity* ..., ed. Momigliano, pp. 100–25 (superstition); Ammianus XXIX.i–ii; Maurice, op. cit.; Barb, op. cit. (treason trials under Valens); Libanius, *Or.* I.44, 62–4, 159, 194; Eunapius, *Vitae philosophorum* VI.ii (= 462–3) (magic and private enemies). Constantine, Sopater and Ablabius: Eunapius, *Vit. phil.* VI.ii–iii (= 462–4); A. H. M. Jones, J. R. Martindale and J. Morris, *The Prosopography of the Later Roman Empire* I (Cambridge, 1971), pp. 3–4, 846. Constantius and Themistius: Themistius, *Or.* I–IV (with the *Oratio Constantii* prefacing *Or.* II (in Dindorf's edition)); Jones *et al.*, *Prosopography* I, pp. 889–94. Senate of Constantinople: Themistius, *Or.* XXXIV.13; Zonaras XIII.11 p. 22d; Libanius, *Or.* I.76, XLII; *Ep.* 62, 77, 1452, 667; *Cod. Theod.* VI.iv.12; F. Bouchéry, *Themistius in Libanius' Brieven* (Antwerp—Paris—The Hague, 1936); P. Petit, *Libanius et la vie municipale à Antioche au IVe siècle après J.-C.* (Paris, 1955), p. 168; Piganiol, op. cit., p. 117. Constantius and Libanius: Libanius, *Or.* I.1–100, LIX; Jones *et al.*, *Prosopography*, pp. 505–7; Petit, op. cit., pp. 191–7 (religion of L.). Constantius' education: Ammianus XXI.xvi.4; Libanius, *Or.* LIX.34; Aurelius Victor, *Liber de Caesaribus* XLII.23; *Epitome de Caesaribus* XLII.18; Julian, *Or.* I.10c–16c. Literati in high office: Jones *et al.*, *Prosopography* I, s.v. Eumenius 1, Aurelius Victor, Eutropius 2, Ausonius, as well as Themistius himself and, to some extent, Libanius (honorary offices); O. Seeck, *Geschichte des Untergangs der antiken Welt* (Stuttgart, 1897–1921), vol. IV (1911), pp. 191–4. *Paideia*: H.-I. Marrou, *Histoire de l'éducation dans l'antiquité* (6th edition, Paris, 1965), pp. 441–71; W. Jaeger, *Early Christianity and Greek Paideia* (Cambridge, Mass., and London, 1962); R. A. Markus in *Latin Literature of the Fourth Century*, ed. J. W. Binns (London–Boston, 1974), pp. 1–21; Peter Brown, *Augustine of Hippo* (London, 1967), especially pp. 35–43; P. Petit, *Les étudiants de Libanius* (Paris, 1956); A. J. Festugière, *Antioche païenne et chrétienne* (Paris, 1959), pp. 91–240, 403–511. Popular hysteria: Eunapius, *Vit. phil.* X.iii.11–13 (= 487), X.v.1–6 (= 489), cf. X.vii.1–5 (= 492); Libanius, *Or.* I.37. The coinage: C. H. V. Sutherland, *Coinage in Roman Imperial Policy 31 B.C. to A.D. 68* (Oxford, 1951), pp. 1–52; ed. Mattingly, Sutherland and Carson, *The Roman Imperial Coinage* (London, 1923–), especially vol. VII (Constantine) by P. Bruun (London, 1966); Carson, Hill and Kent, *Late Roman Bronze Coinage (A.D. 324–498)* (London, 1965); H. Cohen, *Description historique des médailles impériales* VII–VIII (2nd edition, Paris–London, 1888, 1892); H. Mattingly, *Roman Coins, from the earliest times to the fall of the Western Empire* (1st edition, London, 1928); Bruun in *Arctos*, II (1958), pp. 15–37 (Sol); Kent, 'Fel. Temp. Reparatio' in *Numismatic Chronicle*, 1967, pp. 83–90; P. Bastien, *Le monnayage de Magnence* (Wetteren, 1964); W. Kellner, *Libertas und Christogramm* (Karlsruhe, 1968) (Magnentius); J. D. Breckenridge, *The Numismatic Iconography of Justinian II (685–95, 705–11 A.D.)* (Numismatic Notes and Monographs No. 144) (New York, 1959), especially pp. 1, 33–5. Progress of Christianity: Eusebius, *Hist. eccles.*; A. Harnack,

Mission und Ausbreitung des Christentums in den ersten drei Jahrhunderten (4th edition, Leipzig, 1924); G. Boissier, *La fin du paganisme* (Paris, 1891); J. Geffcken, *Der Ausgang des griechisch-römischen Heidentums* (2nd edition, Heidelberg, 1929); P. de Labriolle, *La réaction païenne* (10th edition, Paris, 1950); Jones in *The Conflict* . . . , ed. Momigliano, pp. 17–37. Constantine and flatterers: Eusebius, *Vita* IV.54–5. Religion in the army: Eusebius, *Vita* II.7–9, IV.18–20; *Cod. Theod.* VII.xx.2 (cf. *Codex Justinianus* XII.xlvi.1); Julian, *Or.* I.8A; *Ep.* 8 (Loeb) (= Bidez-Cumont no. 26); Zosimus III.3; Jones, loc. cit. (pp. 23–6); Musurillo, *Acts of the Christian Martyrs*, pp. 244ff. (also in G. Krüger, *Ausgewählte Märtyrerakten* (4th edition, Tübingen, 1965), nos. 19–20). Julian and the army: Zosimus III.3; Julian, *Ep.* 8 (Loeb) (= Bidez-Cumont no. 26); Gregory Nazianzen, *Or.* IV.66, 82–4; Sozomen V.17; Ammianus XXII.xi.2, xii.3, 6; Libanius, *Or.* XII.84, XV.43, XVI.19; Theodoret, *Hist. eccles.* III.15; John Chrysostom, *In Iuventinum et Maximinum martyres* (in Migne, *Patrologia Graeca*, L); Kent in *Num. Chron.*, series 6, XIX (1959), p. 116. Military temples and churches on Rhine (see chapter VI for Britain): H. Lehner and W. Bader in *Bonner Jahrbücher*, CXXXV (1930), pp. 1–48; CXXXVI–VII (1932), pp. 1–216; H. von Petrikovits in *Kölner Jahrbücher*, IX (1967–8), pp. 112–19 (Bonn); F. Sprater, *Die Pfalz unter den Römern* II (Spire, 1930), pp. 73–4 (Rockenhausen Mithraeum); R. Laur-Belart, *Die frühchristliche Kirche mit Baptisterium und Bad in Kaiseraugst, Aargau* (Basle, 1967); *Römer am Rhein*, ed. O. Doppelfeld (Cologne, 1967), nos. 64, 71; H. Bürgin-Kreis in *Ur-Schweiz*, XXVI (1962), pp. 57–66 (Boppard, Zurzach). Danubian Mithraea: M. J. Vermaseren, *Corpus Inscriptionum et Monumentorum Religionis Mithriacae* II (The Hague, 1960), pp. 154–7, nos. 1409–12, 1414–21; pp. 192–9, nos. 1578–1612; pp. 203–5, nos. 1636–47; pp. 229–31, nos. 1750–7. Religion of officials in 360: Petit, *Libanius et la vie municipale* . . . , p. 202. Prefects of Rome: A. Chastagnol, *La préfecture urbaine à Rome sous le Bas-Empire* (Paris, 1960), especially pp. 137–78, 400–27; id., *Les fastes de la préfecture de Rome au Bas-Empire* (Paris, 1962), especially pp. 63–159. Senatorial aristocracy: H. Bloch in *Harvard Theological Review*, XXXVIII (1945), pp. 99–244; id. in *The Conflict* . . . , ed. Momigliano, pp. 193–218; Chastagnol in *Revue des Études Anciennes*, LVIII (1956), pp. 241–53; id. in *Latomus*, XX (1961), pp. 744–58; Brown in *Journal of Roman Studies*, LI (1961), pp. 1–11. Laws of Theodosius: *Cod. Theod.* XVI.x.7–12.

Chapter V: Main sources: Julian's own works (Loeb, 3 vols.); Bidez and Cumont, *Iuliani imperatoris epistulae leges poematia fragmenta varia* (Paris, 1922) is a most valuable chronological arrangement of the letters and legislation; Ammianus XXII–XXV; Libanius, *Oratio* XII–XVIII (especially XVIII), I.118–35; Gregory Nazianzen, *Or.* IV and V *Contra Julianum*; Eunapius, *Vitae philosophorum*; Zosimus III; *Panegyrici Latini* XI (III); Socrates III; Sozomen V–VI; Theodoret, *Historia ecclesiastica* III. Biography with detailed references: J. Bidez, *Vie de l'Empereur Julien* (2nd edition, 1965). Special topics: Leading Arian intellectuals: e.g. Eusebius of Caesarea, and 5 of the 7 most eloquent bishops of Sozomen's list (III.14). Laws against apostasy: *Codex Theodosianus* XVI.vii. Pagan 'party' under Constantius: Petit, *Libanius et la vie municipale*, pp. 204–6. Temple columns built into houses: Julian, *Epistula* 29 (Loeb) (= Bidez-Cumont no. 80); Libanius, *Or.* XVIII.126,

Ep. 724. Maximin Daia's high priests: Eusebius, *Hist. eccles.* IX.4; Lactantius, *De mortibus persecutorum* 26.4. Julian's high priests: Julian, *Fragment of a Letter to a Priest*; *Ep.* 22 (Loeb) (= Bidez-Cumont no. 84a), 18 (= Bidez-Cumont no. 88), 20 (cf. 16) (= 89, 30). Paganization of government: Petit, *Libanius* . . . , pp. 202–3. Modestus and Hecebolius: A. H. M. Jones, J. R. Martindale and J. Morris, *The Prosopography of the Later Roman Empire* I (Cambridge, 1971), pp. 605–8, 409. *Paideia*: see notes to ch. IV. The cities: *Cod. Theod.* XII.i, XII.xiii.1; Petit, *Libanius* . . .; R. Ganghoffer, *L'évolution des institutions municipales en Occident et en Orient au Bas-Empire* (Paris, 1963); A. H. M. Jones, *The Greek City from Alexander to Justinian* (Oxford, 1940); J. H. W. G. Liebeschuetz, *Antioch* (Oxford, 1972); Libanius, *Or.* XVIII.146–9, 163, 193; Julian, *Misopogon* 367D, 370D. Civic lands: *Cod. Theod.* X.iii.1; *Codex Justinianus* XI.lxx.2; Ammianus XXV. iv.15; Libanius, *Or.* XIII.45, XXXI; *Ep.* 828; Sozomen V.3; Liebeschuetz in *Byzantinische Zeitschriften*, LII (1959), pp. 344–56; id., *Antioch*, pp. 151–5. Public post: *Cod. Theod.* VIII.v.12–16; Libanius, *Or.* XVIII.143–5; Ammianus XXI.xvi.18. Attentions to cities and *curiales*: Socrates III.7; Libanius, *Or.* XVIII.154–6; Ammianus XXI.xii.23, XXII.vii.3; Julian, *Misopogon* 362B–363C, 347A; *Ep.* 58 (= Bidez-Cumont no. 98), 21, 24, 47–8 (= Bidez-Cumont nos. 60, 110–11, 59), 39 (= 54), 41 (= 114), Bidez-Cumont nos. 20–1, 55, 91, 115; *Epistula ad Athenienses*; Zosimus III.10; Mazzarino, *Aspetti sociali del quarto secolo*, pp. 131–2, 271–80, 297, 323–6. Rebuilding in Gaul and Thrace: Libanius, *Or.* XII 48–51; Ammianus XVI.xi.11, XVII.i.11–13, ix–x; XXII.v.7. Public works in Africa: *Inscriptions latines de l'Algérie* I.1229, 1247, 1274, 1276, 1285, 1286; *Corpus Inscriptionum Latinarum* VIII.25521; *Année Épigraphique*, 1955, no. 55; Jones et al., *Prosopography* . . . I, pp. 640–2, 905–6. Christian cities: Sozomen V.3–4, 11, VI.1; Libanius, *Or.* XVI.14, XVIII. 129; Bidez-Cumont, nos. 56, 125; cf. Eusebius, *Vita Constantini* IV.38. Rescript on Christian teachers: *Cod. Theod.* XIII.iii.5; Julian, *Ep.* 36; Bidez-Cumont, no. 61; Gregory Nazianzen, *Or.* IV.4–6, 100–110. Apollinares: Socrates III.16; Sozomen V.18. Martyrs: Julian, *Ep.* 37, 40, 41 (= Bidez-Cumont nos. 83, 115, 114); Gregory Nazianzen, *Or.* IV.27, 58. Donatists: Optatus, *De schismate Donatistarum* II.16–18; Frend, *Donatist Church*, pp. 187–92. Novatians: Sozomen IV.20. Philosopher friends: Eunapius, *Vitae philosophorum*; Jones et al., *Prosopography* . . . I, s.v. Maximus 21, Priscus 5, Himerius. Praetextatus: *Prosopography* . . . I, pp. 722–4; Macrobius, *Saturnalia* I; A. D. E. Cameron in *Journal of Roman Studies*, LVI, 1966, pp. 25–38; Bloch in *Harvard Theological Review*, 1945, pp. 199–244. Secundus Salutius: Jones et al., *Prosopography* . . . I, pp. 814–17. Coinage: Carson, Hill and Kent, *Late Roman Bronze Coinage (A.D. 324–498)* (1965); H. Cohen, *Description historique des médailles impériales* VIII, pp. 41–64; Kent in *Num. Chron.*, 1959, p. 109–17; ibid., 1954, p. 216–17; F. D. Gilliard in *Journal of Roman Studies*, LIV (1964), pp. 135–41. Antioch: Julian, *Misopogon*; Libanius, *Or.* XV–XVI; G. Downey, *A History of Antioch in Syria from Seleucus to the Arab Conquest* (Princeton, 1961), pp. 380–96; Petit, *Libanius* . . . , pp. 109–18 (corn shortage, with bibliography), 200–2 (Christianity); Festugière, *Antioche païenne et chrétienne*, pp. 63–89; Liebeschuetz, *Antioch*, pp. 126–32 (corn shortage). St. Babylas and the burning of Daphne:

The Pagan Revival of Julian the Apostate

Socrates III.18; Sozomen V.19–20; Theodoret, *Hist. eccles.* III. 6–8; Julian, *Misopogon* 361B–C; Ammianus XXII.xiii.1–3; Libanius, *Or.* LX; *Ep.* 1376; John Chrysostom, *De S. Babyla* (Migne, *Patrologia Graeca*, L). Inscriptions: these are scattered throughout the main collections, notably *CIL* (especially vol. VIII, Africa); the second largest source, is the annual harvest of new inscriptions published in *L'Année Épigraphique*; and other periodicals. A few are republished together as nos. 749–55 in Dessau, *Inscriptiones Latinae Selectae*. Bidez assembles references to some of the more obscure sources in note 12, p. 393. Casae: *CIL* VIII.4326, 18529. Sua: *CIL* VIII.25849. Thibilis: *Ann. Ép.*, 1893, no. 87. Verecundae: *Ann. Ép.*, 1937, no. 145. Radiate crown: information from P. Salama of Algiers University. Pannonian milestone: *CIL* III.10648b. Phoenician provincial assembly: *Ann. Ép.*, 1969–70, no. 631. Also specifically from *curiae*: *CIL* VIII.2387, 4771, 11805; *ILS* 750; *Ann. Ép.*, 1916, nos. 10–11, no. 20; *Inscriptions latines de l'Algérie* I 253 (= *CIL* VIII.5338) —all from Africa; *Orientis Graeci Inscriptiones Selectae* 520 (Iasos in Caria); Dittenberger, *Sylloge Inscriptionum Graecarum* II³.906A (Miletus), 906B (Magnesia); *CIL* IX.417 and XI.6658 (both from Italy). Syrian temple on Janiculum: P. Gauckler, *Le sanctuaire syrien du Janicule* (Paris, 1912) (collection of the following articles, plus an unpublished paper); id. in *Comptes-Rendus de l'Académie des Inscriptions*, 1907, pp. 135–59; 1908, pp. 510–29; 1909, pp. 617–47; 1910, pp. 378–408; id. in *Mélanges d'Archéologie et d'Histoire de l'École Française de Rome*, 1908, pp. 283–336; 1909, pp. 232–68; G. Nicole and G. Darier, ibid., pp. 3–86. Deir el-Meshkuk: *Syria: Publications of the Princeton University Archaeological Expeditions to Syria in 1904–5 and 1909*, division IIA (by H. C. Butler) (Leyden, 1919), pp. 129–31; IIIA, nos. 186–7. Corbridge *Lanx*: O. Brendel in *Journal of Roman Studies*, XXXI (1941), pp. 100–27; J. M. C. Toynbee, *Art in Roman Britain* (London, 1962), p. 172; Theodoret, *Hist. eccles.* III.16. Maiden Castle: R. E. M. Wheeler, *Maiden Castle, Dorset* (Oxford, 1943), pp. 72–8, 131–5; K. W. Muckelroy in *Britannia*, VII (1976), p. 179. Lydney: R. E. M. and T. V. Wheeler, *Report on the Excavation of the Prehistoric, Roman and Post-Roman Site in Lydney Park, Glos.* (Oxford, 1932), pp. 22–68, 76–93, 96–131; G. C. Boon in *Numismatic Chronicle*, 7th series, I (1961), pp. 191–7 (dating of *minimissimi* coins); M. J. T. Lewis, *Temples in Roman Britain* (Cambridge, 1965), pp. 91–2; Collingwood and Wright, *The Roman Inscriptions of Britain* I (1965), pp. 305–8; *CIL* VII.137. Rainsborough Camp: *Journal of Roman Studies*, LVI (1966), pp. 207–8. Other hill-fort temples: Lewis, op. cit., pp. 1–56 (*passim*), 125–7; Wheeler in *Antiquaries' Journal*, VIII (1928), pp. 318–19. Celtic Renaissance: R. MacMullen in *Historia*, XIV (1965), pp. 93–104. Reoccupation of Welsh hill-forts: S. S. Frere, *Britannia* (London, 1967), p. 274; *Journal of Roman Studies*, LVII (1967), p. 174; *Britannia*, I (1970), p. 269; III (1972), pp. 299–300. Barrows: A. Ross, *Pagan Celtic Britain* (London and New York, 1967), p. 44.

Chapter VI: Attacks on temples: Sulpicius Severus, *Vita S. Martini*; Libanius, *Oratio XXX, Pro templis* (French translation in *Byzantion* VIII (1933), pp. 7–39); cf. Socrates V.16, Sozomen VII.15, Theodoret, *Historia ecclesiastica* V 21–2; J. Moreau in *Rome et le christianisme dans la région rhénane* (*Colloque du Centre de recherches d'histoire des religions de l'Université de Strasbourg, 1960*) (Paris, 1963), pp. 109–26 (end of fourth century); Lewis, *Temples in Roman Britain*, pp. 99–106; W. F. Grimes, *The Excavation of Roman and Mediaeval Londou* (1968), pp. 92–117 (Mithraea). Attacks on Christians: Sozomen V.10 (cf. 9); Theodoret, *Hist. eccles.* III.3 (cf. Mark the Deacon, *Life of Porphyry*, ed. Grégoire and Kugener (with French translation)); *Chronicon Paschale*, pp. 546–7 (Bonn); Julian, *Misopogon* 357C; Theodoret, *Hist. eccles.* IV.22, with A. H. M. Jones, J. R. Martindale and J. Morris, *The Prosopography of the Later Roman Empire* I, s.v. Magnus 12; Philostorgius VII.3. Libanius and Eusebius: Libanius, *Epistula* 1411. Pre-Constantinian Christian buildings: Krautheimer, *Early Christian and Byzantine Architecture*, pp. 1–15; M. Gough, *The Early Christians* (London, 1961), pp. 58–79. Dura-Europos: *The Excavations at Dura-Europos (conducted by Yale University and the French Academy of Inscriptions and Letters): Final Report VIII, Part II*, ed. C. Bradford Weller (New Haven, 1967): Kraeling, C. H., *The Christian Building*. Constantine's letter on church repairs: Eusebius, *Vita* II.45–6. Aquileia: G. Brusin and P. L. Zovatto, *Monumenti paleocristiani di Aquileia e di Grado* (Udine, 1957), pp. 17–140, 189–230; Brusin, *Due nuovi sacelli cristiani di Aquileia* (Aquileia, 1961). SS. Giovanni e Paolo: Krautheimer, *Corpus basilicarum christianarum Romae* I, pp. 265–300; A. Prandi, *Il complesso monumentale della basilica celimontana dei SS. G. e P.* (Vatican, 1953); B. M. Margarucci Italiani, *Il titolo di Pammachio, SS. G. e P.* (Rome, 1967); Matthiae, *Le chiese di Roma*, pp. 21–4, 58. S. Prisca: M. J. Vermaseren and C. C. van Essen, *The Excavations in the Mithraeum of the Church of S. Prisca in Rome* (Leyden, 1965). S. Clemente: E. Junyent, *Il titolo di S. Clemente in Roma* (Rome, 1932); Matthiae, op. cit., p. 18. Cologne: W. Weyres in *Kölner Domblatt*, XXX (1969), pp. 121–36. Pesch: H. Lehner in *Bonner Jahrbücher*, CXXV (1919), pp. 74–162; id. in *Germania*, IV (1920), pp. 63–6; résumé in A. Grenier, *Manuel d'archéologie gallo-romaine*, IV (Paris, 1960), pp. 907–16. Vienne theatre of mysteries: C. Picard in *Revue Archéologique*, 1955, i, pp. 59–62; *Comptes-Rendus de l'Académie des Inscriptions*, 1955, pp. 229–48; *Gallia*, XVI (1958), pp. 376–7; XXIX (1971), pp. 425; H. Graillot, *Le culte de Cybèle* (Paris, 1912), pp. 107–42. Vatican taurobolic altars: Bloch in *Harvard Theological Review*, 1945, pp. 199–244. Neuss: H. von Petrikovits, *Das römische Rheinland* (Cologne and Opladen, 1960), pp. 125, 127–31. For most British temples, see: M. J. T. Lewis, *Temples in Roman Britain*; K. W. Muckelroy, 'Enclosed ambulatories in Romano-Celtic temples in Britain' in *Britannia*, VII (1976), pp. 173–91; see also: *Britannia*, I (1970), p. 288 (Cosgrove); *Journal of Roman Studies*, LVII (1967), pp. 200–2; LVIII (1968), p. 205; *Britannia*, II (1971), p. 288; III (1972), p. 351; IV (1973), p. 323 (Springhead); II (1971), pp. 225–31 (Richborough church); pp. 271–2 (Chelmsford); III (1972), p. 320 (Godmanchester); A. M. ApSimon in *Proceedings of the University of Bristol Spelaeological Society*, X (1962–5), pp. 195–258 (Brean Down). Water Newton Treasure: K. S. Painter, *The Water Newton Early Christian Silver* (London, 1977) (*non vidi*); *Wealth of the Roman World*, ed. Kent and Painter (London, British Museum, 1977), pp. 29–33; *Britannia*, VII (1976), pp. 385–6. Christianity in Britain: J. M. C. Toynbee in *Journal of the British Archaeological Association*, 3rd series, XVI (1953), pp. 1–24; Frend, ibid., 3rd series, XVIII (1955), pp. 1–18; Painter in *Actas del VIII Congreso internacional de Arqueologia cristiana, Barcelona 1969* (Vatican-Barcelona, 1972), pp. 149–66. Montmaurin:

G. Fouet, *La villa gallo-romaine de Montmaurin (Haute-Garonne)* (Paris, 1969); id., in *Gallia*, XVI (1958), pp. 158–96 (funerary well); XXX (1972), pp. 83–126 (La Hillère); cf. temple in villa at Arnesp (excavations not yet published): H.-P. Eydoux, *La résurrection de la Gaule* (Paris, 1961), pp. 333–60, especially pp. 346–8 (but Nymfius epitaph is fifth-century); Gallia, XVII (1959), pp. 430–3. St.-Bertrand-de-Comminges: R. Lizop, *Histoire de deux cités gallo-romaines: les Convenae et les Consoranni* (Toulouse-Paris, 1931), pp. 338–40, 428–37. Hypogeum of Via Livenza: C. Cecchelli, *Monumenti cristiano-eretici di Roma* (Rome, 1944), pp. 201–8. Carthage, guild headquarters: G. C. Picard in *Karthago*, III (1952), pp. 169–91; (summary in his *La Carthage de St. Augustin*, pp. 173–82); forthcoming book on African mosaics by K. Dunbabin (see pp. 251–4 of her D. Phil. thesis in the Bodleian Library, Oxford); Aurelius Victor, *Caesares* XL.28. Arabian temples: *Syria: Publications of the Princeton University Archaeological Expeditions to Syria in 1904–5 and 1909*, IIA, pp. 333–4; IIIA, nos. 689, 696, 706, 693. Arabian churches: ibid., IIA, pp. 132–5, 172–3, 145–8, 344–5, etc.; *Publications of an American Archaeological Expedition to Syria*, II (1903), pp. 357–61, 402–8; H. C. Butler, *Early Churches in Syria* (Princeton, 1929), pp. 19–24. El Hosn: Jalabert and Mouterde, *Inscriptions grecques et latines de la Syrie* 652. Qirqbize: G. Tchalenko, *Villages antiques de la Syrie du nord* (Paris, 1953), pp. 325–39. Mid-fourth-century churches of Limestone Plateau (Batuta, Bankusa, Burdj Heidar, Kharab Shams, Kherbet Muqa, Kafr Nabo, Simkhar—all basilicas—and Ishruq (single-naved)): Tchalenko, op. cit.; *Publications of American ... Expedition ...* II, pp. 88–90; *Publications of Princeton ... Expeditions ...* IIB (Leyden, 1920), pp. 288–90, 294–5, 323–5, 330, 334–6; Butler, *Early Churches ...*, pp. 29–31, 76; see also J. Lassus, *Sanctuaires chrétiens de Syrie*. Economic life of Plateau: Tchalenko, op. cit. For a third area of Syria where Christianity flourished early, see: Mouterde and Poidebard, *Le limes de Chalcis: Organisation de la steppe en haute Syrie romaine* (Paris, 1945), especially pp. 163–6 (basilica at Zebed). Monasticism: Athanasius, *Vita S. Antonii*; Theodoret, *Historia religiosa*; Libanius, *Or.* XXX, *Pro templis*; Sozomen III.14; S. Schiwietz, *Das morgenländische Mönchtum* (Vienna, 1904–38); Petit, 'Sur la date du *Pro templis* ...' in *Byzantion*, XXI (1951), pp. 285–309; Palladius, *Historia lausiaca*; W. H. C. Frend, *Martyrdom and Persecution in the Early Church* (1965), especially pp. 546–50; Brown, *World of Late Antiquity*, ch. 8; E. Amand, *L'ascèse monastique de St. Basile* (Maredsous, 1950). Eustathius of Sebaste: Socrates II.43; Sozomen III.14; Canons of Council of Gangra (ed. Mansi, II, pp. 1101–5). Pagan saints: Philostratus, *Vita Apollonii*; Jones *et al.*, *Prosopography ...* I, s.v. Flavianus 15; Eunapius, *Vitae philosophorum*; Jones *et al.*, *Prosopography ...* I, s.v. Maximus 21, Priscus 5, Praetextatus 1, etc. *Paideia* as a religion: H.-I. Marrou, MOYCIKOC ANHP (2nd edition, Rome, 1964); Philostratus, *Vitae sophistarum* 618 (teaching in temples); P. M. Fraser, *Ptolemaic Alexandria* (Oxford, 1972), pp. 312–19 (*Mouseion* of Alexandria); L. Robert, *Hellenica IV: Épigrammes du Bas-Empire* (Paris, 1948), pp. 30–4 (*Mouseion* of Ampelius). Festivals: *Codex Theodosianus* II.viii.1 (Sunday); *Corpus Inscriptionum Latinarum* I (2nd edition), pp. 256–78; *Monumenta Germaniae Historica, Auctores Antiquissimi* IX, pp. 511–54; H. Stern, *Le Calendrier de 354* (Paris, 1953); Ammianus XXI.ii.2 (Julian's dream);

Bibliography and Notes

Dessau, *Inscriptiones Latinae Selectae* 705 (Hispellum); Carson, Hill, and Kent, *Late Roman Bronze Coinage (A.D. 324–498)* (1965) I, nos. 106, 114, 245, 943, 1041, etc. (consecration coin); A. Alföldi, *A Festival of Isis in Rome under the Christian Emperors of the Fourth Century* (Budapest, 1936); Libanius, *Or.* IX and *Descriptio* V; M. Meslin, *La fête des Kalendes de janvier dans l'Empire romain* (Brussels, 1970); Chastagnol in *Revue Historique*, CCXIX (1958), pp. 237–53 (praetorship); Alföldi, *Die Kontorniaten* (Budapest-Leipzig, 1942–3; second edition, Berlin, 1976–); review by J. M. C. Toynbee in *Journal of Roman Studies*, XXXV (1945), pp. 115–21; S. Mazzarino in *Doxa*, IV (1951), pp. 121–48; id. in *Enciclopedia dell' arte antica*, II (Rome, 1959), pp. 784–91, s.v. *Contorniati*; G. M. A. Hanfmann, *The Season Sarcophagus in Dumbarton Oaks* (Cambridge, Mass., 1951), pp. 159–63 (circus symbolism); Piganiol, *L'Empire chrétien*, p. 413, with bibliography (Christmas and Epiphany); Gregory of Nyssa, *Vita S. Gregorii Thaumaturgi*, in *Patrologia Graeca* XLVI, especially col. 953; Ammianus XXI.ii.4–5 (Julian at Vienne); *CIL* I (2nd edition), pp. 257–79 (*Calendar of Polemius Silvius*). Projecta casket: Volbach and Hirmer, *Early Christian Art*, p. 333 and plates 116–17. Frampton and Hinton St. Mary mosaics: D. J. Smith, 'The Mosaic Pavements' in *The Roman Villa in Britain*, ed. A. L. F. Rivet (London, 1969), pp. 109–10; id., 'Three 4th-century Schools of Mosaic in Roman Britain' in *La mosaïque gréco-romaine* (Paris, 1965), pp. 99–101; Toynbee, *Art in Roman Britain*, no. 199; id., *Art in Britain under the Romans* (Oxford, 1964), pp. 250–2; id. in *Journal of Roman Studies*, LIV (1964), pp. 7–14; H. Brandenburg in *Römische Quartalschriften*, LXIII (1968), pp. 51–86; K. S. Painter in *British Museum Quarterly*, XXXII (Autumn 1967), pp. 15–31. Lullingstone: G. W. Meates, *Lullingstone Roman Villa* (H.M.S.O. 1963); Toynbee, *Art in Britain under the Romans*, pp. 262–5; Frend in *Journal of the British Archaeological Association*, 3rd series, XVIII (1955), pp. 14–15. British mosaic schools: Smith, works cited above. Orpheus mosaics: ibid.; Toynbee, *Art in Britain under the Romans*, pp. 247–8, 253–83; id. in *Christianity in Britain, 300–700*, ed. M. W. Barley and R. P. C. Hanson (Leicester, 1968), pp. 188–9; Stern, 'La mosaïque d'Orphée de Blanzy-lès-Fismes' in *Gallia*, XIII (1955), pp. 41–77; R. M. Harrison in *Journal of Roman Studies*, LII (1962), pp. 13–18. Christian Orpheus: *Dictionnaire d'archéologie chrétienne et de liturgie*, ed. Cabrol and Leclercq, XII.ii, col. 2735–55. Pagan Orpheus: Julian, *Or.* VII.215B, 217C; VIII.240B; cf. Themistius, *Or.* II.37c. Orpheus mutilated in Africa: P. Gauckler in *Monuments Piot* III, 1896, pp. 219–20; J. Thirion in *Mélanges d'Archéologie et d'Histoire de l'École Française de Rome*, LXVII (1955), pp. 149–79. Brading: Toynbee, *Art in Roman Britain*, nos. 196–7; id., *Art in Britain under the Romans*, pp. 254–8. Low Ham: Toynbee, *Art in Roman Britain*, no. 200; id., *Art in Britain under the Romans*, pp. 241–6; Smith in ed. Rivet, op. cit., p. 80 (dating); cf. Augustine, *Confessions* I.xiii. Piazza Armerina: G. V. Gentili, *The Imperial Villa of Piazza Armerina* (3rd edition, Rome, 1966); B. Pace, *I mosaici di P. A.* (Rome, 1955); A. Ragona, *Il proprietario della villa romana di P. A.* (1962); A. Carandini in *Studi Miscellanei*, VII (1961–2); for other literature, see refs. in these. Roman Africa: B. H. Warmington, *The North African Provinces from Diocletian to the Vandal Conquest* (Cambridge, 1954); G. C. Picard, *La civilisation de l'Afrique romaine* (Paris, 1959); id., *Les religions de l'Afrique antique* (Paris, 1954); P. Romanelli, *Storia delle province romane dell' Africa*. African mosaics: forthcoming book by K. Dunbabin (see above); J. W. Salomonson, *La mosaïque aux chevaux de l'Antiquarium de Carthage* (The Hague, 1965); Picard, *La Carthage de saint Augustin*, pp. 49–54; id. in *Bulletin Archéologique* 1943–5, pp. 360–2 (Seasons); Poinssot and Lantier in *Monuments Piot*, XXVII (1924), pp. 69–86 (Coronation of Venus, misdescribed as Ariadne); Picard in *Mélanges . . . de l'École Française de Rome*, LVIII (1941–6), pp. 43–108 (Ellès Venus); L. Foucher, *Inventaire des mosaïques: Sousse* (Tunis, 1960); P. Gauckler, *Inventaire des mosaïques de la Gaule et de l'Afrique, II: Afrique Proconsulaire (Tunisie)* (1910), no. 694; Picard, *La Carthage . . .* , pp. 22, 24 (horses like windmill); cf. also Merlin and Poinssot in *Monuments Piot*, XXXIV (1934), pp. 129–54 (House of the Peacock); M. Yacoub, *Le Musée du Bardo* (Tunis, 1969), p. 85, inv. 3014 (Thuburbo Venus; some of the Carthaginian mosaics are also catalogued in this); G. de Pachtère, *Inventaire des mosaïques de la Gaule et de l'Afrique III (Algérie)* (1911), nos. 2–3; S. Gsell, *Musée de Tébessa* (Paris, 1902), pp. 64–70; E. Marec, *Hippone-la-Royale, antique Hippo Regius* (1954), p. 45 and fig. 20; W. Dorigo, *Pittura tardo-romana* (Milan, 1966), p. 186; de Pachtère, *Inventaire . . . (Algérie)* no. 226 (Constantine); J. Lassus in *Bulletin d'Archéologie Algérienne*, I (1962–5), pp. 75–105 (Cherchel). Antioch mosaics: D. Levi, *Antioch Mosaic Pavements* (1947), pp. 226–77. Silverware: J. W. Brailsford, *The Mildenhall Treasure* (London, 1955); Toynbee, *Art in Roman Britain*, no. 106; R. P. Wright in *Journal of Roman Studies*, XXXVIII (1948), pp. 102–3 and n. 17; K. S. Painter, *The Mildenhall Treasure* (London, 1977) (*non vidi*); *Wealth of the Roman World*, ed. Kent and Painter, pp. 33–43; R. Laur-Belart, *Der spätrömische Silberschatz von Kaiseraugst* (1963). Glassware: D. B. Harden in *Journal of Glass Studies*, II (1960), pp. 44–81; W. Haberey in *Kölner Jahrbücher*, IX (1967–8), pp. 31–3; F. Fremersdorf, *Die Denkmäler des römischen Köln, VIII: Die römischen Gläser mit Schliff, Bemalung und Goldauflagen aus Köln* (Cologne, 1967); A. Pelletier in *Gallia*, XXV (1967), pp. 169–73 (Vienne); Haberey in *Bonner Jahrbücher*, CXLIX (1949), pp. 94–104 (Marsyas); C. R. Morey, *The Gold-Glass Collection of the Vatican Library* (1959). African pottery: Salomonson in *Oudheidkundige Mededelingen uit het Rijksmuseum van Oudheden te Leiden*, XLIII (1962), pp. 53–95; id. in *Bulletin van de Vereeniging tot Bevorderung der Kennis van de Antieke Beschaving te 'S-Gravenhage*, XLIV (1969), pp. 4–109. Pagan cemeteries in north-west: see annual reports of excavations in *Journal of Roman Studies, Britannia, Gallia* and *Bonner Jahrbücher, passim*; A. van Doorselaer, *Les nécropoles d'époque romaine en Gaule septentrionale* (Bruges, 1967). Dying-out of grave-goods: L. P. Wenham, *The Romano-British Cemetery at Trentholme Drive, York* (London, 1968), pp. 45–7; M. R. Hull, *Roman Colchester* (Oxford, 1958), pp. 252, 256–7; G. Clarke in *Antiquaries' Journal*, L (1970), pp. 294–5 (Winchester); R. Pirling, *Das römisch-fränkische Gräberfeld von Krefeld-Gellep* (Berlin, 1966) I–II. Mixed pagan-Christian graves: *Frühchristliches Köln*, ed. Doppelfeld (Cologne, 1965), pp. 73ff., nos. 10, 14. Pagan cult symbols: H. Lehner in *Bonner Jahrbücher*, CXXIX (1924), pp. 63–4, 89–90, nos. 286–95; Haberey, ibid., 1949, pp. 94–104, especially p. 104; H. von Petrikovits, *Das römische Rheinland* (Cologne and Opladen, 1960), pp. 134–5. Catacombs: A. Ferrua, *Le pitture della nuova catacomba di Via Latina* (Vatican,

1960); C. Cecchelli, *Monumenti cristiano-eretici di Roma*, pp. 135–46 (Trebius Justus), 167–80 (Vibia); C. Casalone in *Cahiers Archéologiques*, XII (1962), pp. 53–64 (Trebius Justus); P. Testini, *Le catacombe e gli antichi cimiteri cristiani in Roma* (Bologna, 1966); J. Wilpert, *Die Malereien der Katakomben Roms* (Freiburg, 1903). Christian sarcophagi: F. W. Deichmann, G. Bovini and H. Brandenburg, *Repertorium der christlich-antiken Sarkophage, I: Rom und Ostia* (Wiesbaden, 1967); Testini, *Le catacombe . . .*, pp. 311–40; Gough, *The Early Christians*, pp. 172–7; F. Benoit, *Sarcophages paléochrétiens d'Arles et de Marseille* (Paris, 1954), p. 33, no. 1 (Dioscuri), etc.; G. Wilpert, *I sarcofagi antichi cristiani* (Vatican, 1929–36). Dioscuri plate: Benoit in *Bulletin de la Société Nationale des Antiquaires de France*, 1945–7, pp. 245–50. Pagan sarcophagi: Hanfmann, *The Season Sarcophagus in Dumbarton Oaks*; H. Fournet-Pilipenko in *Karthago*, XI (1961–2), pp. 92–6, no. 22; Picard, *La Carthage de saint Augustin*, pp. 163–5. Ely pewter cup: Toynbee, *Art in Roman Britain*, no. 121.

Addenda

Page 39, sixth line of new section, after 'frontiers':
The Emperor Gallienus (260–8), in the darkest time of the third century, had begun to accumulate detachments of troops round the person of the emperor, and paved the way for the victories of the Illyrian soldier-emperors who succeeded him, but these were only small beginnings.

Page 113, ten lines from foot, after 'action':
This had been axiomatic from the time of Plato; it is Themistius' position that is the more interesting.

Page 205, five lines from foot, after 'topics':
Julian's conversion: Bidez, op. cit., pp. 82–9; Festugière, *Antioche païenne et chrétienne*, pp. 69–73; Brown, *The World of Late Antiquity*, pp. 78–80.

Page 207, line 9, before 'Casae':
References to all Julianic dedications known to me are collected in my D.Phil. thesis in the Bodleian Library, Oxford (vol. II, p. 691, n. 116).

Another biography of Julian in English has appeared since this work went to press: G. W. Bowerstock, *Julian the Apostate* (London, 1978).

Appendix I

The House of Constantine

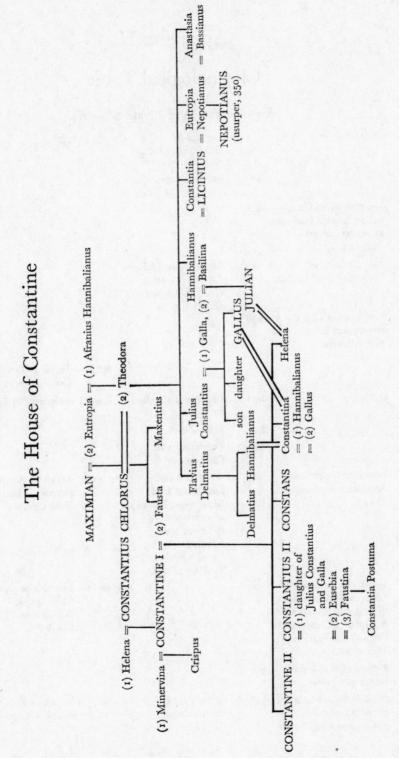

Appendix II

Chronological Table

Emperors and Major Events, 284–363

West		General		East
	284	DIOCLETIAN (284–305).		
	285	MAXIMIAN co-emperor (West).		
Usurpation of Carausius in Britain (temporarily recognized Augustus).	286			
Assassination of Carausius by Allectus.	293	Constantius Chlorus Caesar (West), Galerius Caesar (East).		
Constantius Chlorus reconquers Britain and kills Allectus.	296			
			297/8	Revolt of Domitius Domitianus in Egypt.
	298	Christians expelled from army.	298	Galerius' Persian war.
	301	Price Edict.		
	303–4	Persecution of Christians.		
CONSTANTIUS CHLORUS Augustus, Severus Caesar.	305	Abdication of Diocletian and Maximian. Elevation of CONSTANTIUS CHLORUS and GALERIUS. New Caesars Severus and Maximin Daia.	305	GALERIUS Augustus (senior), Maximin Daia Caesar.
Death of Constantius Chlorus. Proclamation of Constantine. SEVERUS Augustus, Constantine Caesar. Usurpation of Maxentius.	306		306–11	Persecution of Christians by Galerius and Maximin.
Return of Maximian. Death of Severus.	307			
CONSTANTINE Augustus, LICINIUS Augustus. Maxentius and Maxi-	308	Conference of Carnuntum.	308	GALERIUS Augustus, MAXIMIN Augustus.

214

Appendix II

West	General		East
mian self-proclaimed Augusti. Revolt of Domitius Alexander in Africa. Spain goes over to Constantine.			
Death of Maximian. 310			
Maxentius reconquers Africa. 311		311	Palinode and death of Galerius. Maximin and Licinius occupy his dominions.
Constantine defeats and kills Maxentius at ⚔ Milvian Bridge (28 October). 312	Alliance of Constantine and Licinius.	312	Renewed persecution of Christians by Maximin.
CONSTANTINE emperor of West. 313	Conference and Edict of Milan (Constantine and Licinius).	313	Licinius defeats and kills Maximin. LICINIUS emperor of East.
	314 Constantine gains Licinius' European territory (except Thrace).		
	317 Crispus, Constantine II and Licinianus made Caesars.		
Constantine campaigns on lower Danube. 322–3			
	324 CONSTANTINE defeats and kills Licinius and becomes sole emperor. Byzantium chosen as capital. Constantius II made Caesar.		
	325 Council of Nicaea.		
	326 Constantine puts Crispus and Fausta to death during visit to Rome.		
Constantine campaigns on Danube. 326–9			
	328 St. Athanasius bishop of Alexandria.		
	330 Inauguration of Constantinople (11 May).		
	331 Confiscation of temple treasures.		

West		General		East
Gothic war.	332			
	333	Constans made Caesar.		
	333–7	Arrangements made for succession.	333–7	Beginning of trouble with Persia under Shapur II (310–79).
			335	Councils of Tyre and Jerusalem. Exile of Athanasius.
	337	Death of Constantine (May) and succession crisis.		
	337–40	CONSTANTINE II, CONSTANTIUS II and CONSTANS Augusti.	338	First siege of Nisibis by Shapur.
	340	Constans eliminates Constantine II. CONSTANS emperor of West (337–50), CONSTANTIUS II emperor of East (337–61) and senior Augustus.		
Constans reorganizes Hadrian's Wall system in Britain. Campaigns on Rhine and Danube.	341–3	Arian crisis. Council of Antioch (341). Council of Serdica (343).	341	Ulfilas bishop of Goths.
			343	Constantius invades Adiabene.
Donatist troubles in Africa (346–7).	346	Victory of orthodoxy.	346	Second siege of Nisibis.
	348	Eleventh centenary of Rome. Reform of coinage.	348	✗ Singara. Persecution of Christian Goths. Ulfilas flees to Thrace.
Usurpation of Magnentius at Autun and death of Constans. Ephemeral usurpations of Vetranio at Mursa and Nepotianus at Rome.	350		350	Third siege of Nisibis. Shapur withdraws to deal with internal troubles.
Campaign of Constantius against Magnentius (351–3). ✗ Mursa (351). Alamannic and Frankish invasions of Gaul (352). Final defeat and death of Magnentius (353).	351	Gallus made Caesar in East.	351–4	Gallus' troubled and unsuccessful rule.
	353–61	CONSTANTIUS II sole emperor.		

Appendix II

West		General	East	
	354	Gallus recalled and put to death.		
Further invasions of Gaul by Franks and Alamans.	355	Julian made Caesar at Milan and sent to Gaul.		
	355–6	Victory of Arianism. Anti-pagan edicts.		
Campaigns of Julian in Gaul.	356–61			
✂ Strasbourg.	357	Constantius visits Rome.		
Constantius campaigns on Danube.	358–9			
	359	Double council of Rimini and Seleucia.	359–61	Renewal of war with Persia. Fall of Amida (359).
JULIAN proclaimed Augustus at Paris.	360	Council of Constantinople.		
Julian marches against Constantius.	361	Constantius returns from Syria and dies on way to meet Julian's attack.		
	361–3	JULIAN sole emperor. At Constantinople (December 361–May 362), at Antioch (July 362–March 363). Restoration of paganism.		
	363			Julian's Persian expedition (March to June). Death of Julian. JOVIAN elected emperor and leads army back after making peace with Persia.

Note: For convenience, events on the Danube have all been set in the West, although in reality split between West and East (the line of division was in any case not constant).

Index

Individual people are listed under the name by which they are usually known (and referred to in this book)

Ablabius, praetorian prefect 44, 85, 95
Achaea 115, 148. *See also* Greece
Achilles 167, 177; Achilles Dish 172
Adam and Eve 174, 175, 179, 181, 182, 185, 189, cf. 188
administration, the imperial 4, 23, 44, 95, 105; Diocletian's reform of 8; Julian's paganization of 103
Aegae 80, 147
Africa *passim*; Donatists, *s.v.*; figured pottery 157, 177–9, 190; mosaics 163–7, 170, 175
after-life 57, 171, 179, 180, 181, 184, 192. *See also* immortality, Isles of the Blest, Paradise, Underworld
agape-meal 132, 185, cf. 56
agentes in rebus 48, 53, 83
agriculture xi-xii, 2, 8, 9, 21, 38, 41, 45, 59, 144–5, 145–6, 147, 163, 169–70, 181, cf.189
Alamanni xi, 50, 51, 106
Alban, St. 14
Alexander, bishop of Alexandria 70–4 *passim*
Alexander Severus, the Emperor 1
Alexandria 60, 70, 73, 75, 77, 78, 84, 91, 97, 106, 108–9, 110, 130, 148, 156
altar, Christian 55, 56, 58, cf. 140; of imperial cult 90; Jewish 111, 174; pagan 83, 91, 111, 117, 123, 124, 137, 138, 141, 151, 165, 178
Amida 39, 51–2, 53
Ammianus Marcellinus, the historian 30, 48–9, 51, 52, 54, 84, 94, 105, 106, 108, 109, 119, 121, 195, 196, 197
amphitheatre 13, 65, 100, 162, 164, 166, 167, 179. *See also* beast-fight, gladiator
angel 29, 55, 63, 92, 102, 165, 168, 184, 191
anniversary, imperial 22, 87, 91, 105 (*see also decennalia, quinquennalia, tricennalia, vicennalia*); eleven-hundredth anniversary of Rome 45–6, 92
Antioch *passim*; Great (Golden) Church 61, 76, 121; Julian at 53, 54, 61, 94, 110, 118–22; mosaics of 167–70, 172
Antony, St. 73, 145
Apamea 35, 85
Apis bull 117
Apollo 2, 12, 22, 25, 26, 37, 61, 87, 90, 102, 115, 124, 152, 154, 155, 163, 165, 175; temple of at Daphne 120–1; Apollo and Marsyas myth 174, 176, 190
Apollonius of Tyana 38, 147–8, 155
apostate 10, 18, 97, 99, 102, 103; Julian xiv, 19, 65, 97–9, 107, 124
Apostles 36, 50, 55, 62, 183, 185, 186, 187; Church of the Holy Apostles 36, 61
appeal, to emperor 68, 69, 73, 74, cf. 115; to see of Rome 76
apse, in Christian basilica 49, 55, 56, 57, 58, 62, 132; in secular building 24, 138, 142, 158, 163; western apse 55, 58, 62, cf. 136
Aquileia 33, 44, 60; church 133–4, 135
Arabia 122, 123, 124, 143
arch; chancel (triumphal) arch in churches 55, 59; Constantine 24–8, 187, 191; of Galerius 5
archaeology as source xiii, 59, 197–8
Arethusa, in Syria 130
Arianism, Arians 69, 70–9, 97, 98, 103, 109, 112, 134, 195; Constantius II as patron of 75–9, 82, 98, 112
aristocracy, *see* Senate
Arius, priest of Alexandria 70–5
Arles 17, 31, 48, 69, 78, 118, 189; Council of Arles 67, 69
Armenia 5, 39, 51, 71, 146
army 1–2, 9, 13, 16, 17, 21–2, 29–30, 31, 38, 41, 43–4, 49, 53, 75, 87, 91, 92, 97, 105, 117, 119, 153, 177, 195, 197; barbarians in 38, 40; of Constantine 22, 23, 25, 27, 32, 39; Danube 47; under Diocletian 3; dynastic loyalty of 15, 16, 46, 47; indiscipline in 1, 45; of Julian's Persian expedition 53–4; reforms of Constantine 39–40; religion in 12, 23, 34, 50, 54, 81, 93–5, cf. 156; Rhine 18, 39, 47, 50; in recognition of emperor and usurpers 15–16, 17, 46, 52, 54. *See also* cavalry, *comitatenses, dux,* fort, frontier, legion, *limitanei,* military campaign, officer, *ripenses,* soldier
art xi, xiii, 59, 127, 169, 182, 190, 198, cf. 86; of Arch of Constantine 25–8; Byzantine 27, 59; plundered for Constantinople 36–7; of S. Costanza 49–50; of Tetrarchy 5–6, 27. *See also* Christian art, pagan art
artist, craftsman 6, 25, 27, 125, 127, 144, 158, 159–60, 161, 162, 163–4, 169, 174, 176, 178, 183, 189, 190, 191, cf. xi
ascetic, asceticism, Christian 145–7, 148; pagan 53, 84, 147, 149. *See also* monasticism
Askalon 130
Asklepios (Aesculapius) 80, 110, 115, 147
astrology 27, 82, 84, 85, 117–18, 150–1, 165, 191
Athanasius, St. 44, 60, 72, 73–8, 145, 195

Index

Athens 50, 54, 88, 89, 99, 106, 107, 112, 147, 149, 196, cf. 32
Attis, *see* Cybele
Augustine, St. xiii, 11, 36, 68, 99, 112, 156, 162, 167
Augustus, the Emperor 57, 66, 89–90, 110, 111, 145, 152
Augustus, Senior 4, 14, 15, 28, 44, 77, 87; proclamation as 4, 15–16, 43, 52, 117, 172
Aurelian, the Emperor 1, 3, 7, 16, 26, 90
Autun 5, 6, 46, 69

Baal, *see* Saturn
Baalbek (Heliopolis) 80, 123, 130
Bacchic motifs and figures 49–50, 158, 161, 163, 167, 168, 171, 172, 174, 175, 176, 191, cf. 165; Bacchus, *see* Dionysus
Bagaudae, the 2, 4, 5
baptism 55, 71, 97, 132, 134, 137, 171; on deathbed 39, 75, 188
Baptist, John the 55, 156
baptistery 55, 60, 79, 132, 133, 136–7
barbarians xi, 1, 2, 12, 22, 39, 45, 46, 50, 52, 79, 92, 127, 138, 140, 141, 148, 155; as allies 38; in army 38, 40, 94; in consulship 40; migrations xi, 1; settled in Empire 38, 40. *See also* Alamanni, Franks, Germans, Goths, Huns, Sarmatians, Saxons, Vandals
Basil, St. 147, 156
basilica, Christian 24, 36, 49, 55–60, 62–3, 69, 133–4, 135, 136, 137, 142, 143–4, 189; pagan 123, 137–8; secular (law-court, etc.) 7, 24, 60, 162, 165, 190; double 60–1, 133–4
beast-fight, beast-fighter 13, 42, 65, 100, 154, 155, 162, 163, 164, 167, 179
Beirut (Berytus) 89, 130
Bellerophon 155, 158–9, 174
Bethlehem, Church of the Nativity 63
Bible 12, 32, 36, 68, 69, 70, 91, 97, 107–8, 134, 146, 147, 183; Gothic 79; Biblical scenes 132, 177, 178, 182, 186, 188; Old Testament scenes 35, 50, 63, 142, 152, 174, 175, 176, 179, 181, 182, 185, 186, 187, 188, 189, *see also* Adam and Eve, Daniel in the Lions' Den, Jonah, Moses, sacrifice, Susanna and the Elders; New Testament scenes 55, 156, 174, 175, 182, 183, 186, 187, 188–9, *see also* Feeding of the Five Thousand, Jerusalem, miracle, Raising of Lazarus
bishop *passim*; as heir to sophist 115; as instigator of attacks on temples 83, 109, 123, 130, 138; bishopric, *s.v.* see; Constantine as 'bishop of those outside the Church' 80
bodyguard, imperial 3, 8, 14, 40, 71, 176, cf. 49, 54; of high priest 19
book (manuscript) 85, 87, 150, 161–2, 164, 183, 197; craftsmen's copy-book 161, 175; Sibylline 22. *See also* library
Brading, villa of 161, 163
Brahmins 38, 147
Brean Down, temple of 128, 139–40
Britain 4–5, 6, 8, 9, 13, 14, 16, 17, 28, 39,

40, 43, 45, 48, 71, 83, 94–5, 124–8, 129, 132, 170–2, 174, 178, 180, 190; Celtic Revival in 125–8, 139–40; Christianity in 140–1, 158–60, 171; mosaics 158–62; temples 125–8, 138–41
building xi, 5, 6, 49, 50, 61, 90, 106, 111–12, 144, 163, 164, 166, 169, 197; of churches, *s.v.*; of Constantinople 32–3, 34–6, 37, 80, 87; by Maxentius 24; of temples, *s.v.*; tetrarchic 6–7
Bulla Regia 106
Byzantium 29, 32–3, 34, 35. *See also* Constantinople

Caecilianus, bishop of Carthage 68–9, 71
Caerleon 14
Caernarvon 129
Caesar, creation of 4, 14, 15, 31, 32, 43, 48, 50, 94, 98, 113; *The Caesars* of Julian 110–11
Caesarea in Cappadocia 39, 106
Caesarea in Palestine 18, 70, 71, 72, 73, 74, 76, 194
calendar 150–7; *Polemius Silvius* 157; *of 354* 84, 150–5, 185, 197
canons (of Church councils) 72, 73, 197, cf. 77
Capitol 24, 34, 81; hill of 115
Cappadocia 30, 39, 43, 79, 97, 106, 107, 109
Caracalla, the Emperor 11
Carausius, emperor of Britain 4
Carnuntum, conference of 17
Carrhae (Harran) 106
Carthage 18, 68, 69, 71, 142–3, 152, 162, 164, 167, 178, 181, 191; mosaics of 164–6, 167
Castor and Pollux, *see* Dioscuri
catacomb 6, 49, 56, 57, 131, 132, 134, 160, 177, 180, 181–3, 184, 185–6, 187, 190, 192
catechumen 65, 132, 133
cathedral 55, 56, 60–1, 130, 133–4, 136–7. *See also* basilica, church, house-church
Catholic 67–9, 72, 112
cavalry 3, 32, 51, 54, 55, cf. 92. *See also magister equitum*
Celtic Renaissance 127, 139; Celtic pagan revival 125–8, 139; Celtic religion 80, 127, 138, 156
cemetery 56, 57, 58, 132, 175, 180; Coemeterium Maius (Major Cemetery), *s.v.*
Chalcedon 73; trials of 53
Chaldaeans, Chaldaean oracles 83–4, 85, 149
chamberlain 8, 44, 53, 95, 171
chancellery, the imperial 86, 196
Chanctonbury Ring 126–7
chapel, Christian 56, 134, 135, 141, 159–60, 168, 180, 185; pagan 123, 125–6, 162
chariot, charioteer, chariot-races 26, 35, 36, 51, 58, 152, 154, 155, 166, 167, 176; Sun-God as charioteer 155
charity, Christian 61, 101, 132, 133; pagan 101–2, cf. 153
charm 61, 81, 84, 166, 181. *See also* talisman
Charon, obols of 179, 180

Chelmsford (Caesaromagus) 139
Cherchel (Caesarea) 167
chi-rho monogram, origin 22–3; symbolism 23–4, 93; use of motif 23, 24, 27, 61, 91–2, 94, 122, 140, 158–9, 171, 172, 174, 176, 184, 186, 187, 189. *See also* labarum
Christ *passim*; in art 49, 55, 58, 60, 158–9, 174, 183, 185–9 *passim*; as Holy Wisdom, Sage 36, 148, 186, *and see* teacher; as patron of Constantine 22–3, 26, 27, 33, 59, 90; as Sun of Righteousness 58, 90, 186; Christology 70–3, 76, 79
Christian(s) *passim*; attacks on by pagans 108–9, 130–1; attacks on temples by 83, 94, 109, 123–4, 129–30, 136, 138; cities 36, 106, 130, 144, cf. 81, 120, 121; exclusion from office by Julian 103, 107; Great Persecution, *s.v.*; men of letters 89, 98, 103, 104, 107–8, 149, 194, *and see* Christian writers; other individual 79, 91, 143, 145–6, 150; plots against Julian by 54, 94, 109; soldiers 93–5, 109, 129; upper class (and educated) 37, 44, 54, 59, 70, 71, 77, 84, 88, 89, 95, 103, 107–8, 115, 131, 136, 138, 142, 147, 150, 157, 158–60, 171, 172, 174, 176, 180, 181, 182, 183, 184, 185. *See also* Christian art, Christian Empire, Church, Galilaeans, monasticism, persecution, saint, Senate, etc.
Christian art 49–50, 58, 59, 129, 133–4, 158–9, 173, 174–9, 180, 182–90
Christian Empire xii, 50, 60, 149, 151, 160, cf. 83; Church-State relations in 69, 73; inauguration of 22–3; Christian emperor 35, 36, 41, 51, 59, 67, 81, 85–9, 90, 94, 131, 149, 152, 153, 157, 170
Christian writers xiii, 61, 97, 110, 134, 160, 195. *See also* Athanasius, Eusebius, Lactantius
Christianity, Christian religion *passim*; in army 93–5, 109; in Britain, *s.v.*; coexistence with paganism 131, 135–7; and coinage 90–2; of Constantine xii, xiii, 26, 33–4, 42, 79, 80; of Constantinople 35–6, 38, 157; exclusiveness of xii, 80, 129, 158, 181; Great Persecution, *s.v.*; growth in third century xii, 2, 93, cf. 134; of Julian 97–9, 101, 113; opposition to 10, 108–11, 130–1; and *paideia* 106–8; popular 127, 139; progress of 93–6, 101, 103–4, 130, 134, 137, 139, 140, 142, 143, 144, 156, 173, 178, 180, 192–3; strength of 61, 81, 87, 93, 100, 124, 129, 131, 134, 139, 143–4, 157, 178, 192–3; triumph of xiii 23, 26, 28–31, 91, 93, 131, 136, 193; urban Christianity, rural paganism 137, 142. *See also* conversion, evangelization
Christianization, of pagan cult 141, 155–6, 157; of population 93–6, 104–5, 142, 144, 173. *See also* Christianity, evangelization
Christmas Day 43, 155, 157
Christogram, *signum Christi, see* chi-rho monogram
Chrysanthius, philosopher 112, 148
Church, the (Christian) *passim*; Arian

heresy, *s.v.*; historians 195, *and see* Christian writers, Eusebius of Caesarea; Church-State relations 69, 73, 78; Constantine as patron of 26, 33, 64, 65, 69, 81; Donatist schism, *s.v.*; eastern 70–9, 98; Great Persecution, *s.v.*; Julian and 108–11; local Churches and Christian communities 29, 31, 60, 66, 67, 70, 72, 73, 120–1, 130, 133, 134, 135, 136–7, 157, 180; Peace of, *s.v.*; privileges for 65–7; western 71, 76, 78; pagan 'Church' 99–102
church xiii, 20, 21, 29, 30, 66, 69, 70, 103, 107, 112, 130, 141; attacks on 130; building of 18, 55–64, 65, 69, 95, 112, 130, 131, 132–7, 139, 142, 143–4, 159–60, 198; of Constantine and Helena 55–64, 65, 69, 80, 180; of Constantinople 33, 36, cf. 77; demolition of 12, 13, 20, 32, 61, 112; pre-Constantinian 132–3; services 20, 32, 56, 75, 82, 93, 157, cf. 35, *and see* Eucharist, worship; temples into churches 124, 130, 141, 143. *See also* basilica, cathedral, house-church, Sant...
Church of the Holy Apostles 36, 61
Church of the Holy Sepulchre 62–3, 74, 80
Church of the Nativity 63
Cilicia 38, 80, 119, 145, 147
circus (hippodrome, race-course) 7, 33, 35, 37, 89, 119, 142, 152, 155, 164, 166; cosmic symbolism of 155, 176; victory symbolism of 166 (*and s.v.*)
Circus Maximus 22, 51, 155, 176
Cirencester 160
cities, towns *passim*; Christian 36 (cf. 81), 106, 120–2, 144, 189; civic lands 105; institutions, councils, *see curia*; Julian and 103–6, 128, 143; pagan 81, 130, cf. 109; urban Christianity, rural paganism 137, 142, cf. 140
city prefect 196; of Constantinople 87, 103; of Rome 37, 59, 83, 87, 95, 115, 123, 124, 150, 154, 188
civil service 2, 41–2, 85, 95, 105. *See also* chancellery, notary, official
Claudius Gothicus, the Emperor 4, 18
clergy, (Christian) 13, 55, 65, 68, 70, 73, 97, 123, 132, 146, 185; clerical exemption from liturgies 66, 67, 105. *See also* bishop, deacon, exorcist, priest
clivus Scauri 135
Coemeterium Maius (Major Cemetery) 185, 186
coin, coinage xii, xiii, 2, 7, 8–9, 26, 27, 34, 37, 89–92, 125, 140, 141, 170, 172, 179, 180, 181, 197; Christian 47, 91–2, cf. 152; contorniates 154–5; Isis coins 153; of Julian 116–18; reform of Constantine 40–1; reform of Diocletian 9, 117; reform of 348 (FEL. TEMP. REPARATIO) 45–6, 92; as sources 197
college, priestly 51, 136; of imperial cult 143
Cologne 50, 69, 105, 176, 181; cathedral 136–7; glass factories 173–6, 187, 190, 191

Index

column, of Constantine 35, 168; of Helena
34; removed from temples 99–100, 124
comitatenses 39, 93
conspiracy 32, 46, 49, 53 (cf. 2, 4, 13); in
army under Julian 54, 94, 109. *See also*
usurper
Constans, the Emperor 60, 145, 168;
Caesar 43, 176; Augustus xii, 43–6, 48,
60, 69, 81, 88, 96, 136, 137, 152, 153, 195;
orthodoxy of 75–7
Constantia, sister of Constantine 21, 28, 31,
42, 74
Constantina, daughter of Constantine 43,
46, 48, 49–50, 52, 57, 60
Constantina (Constantine), capital of Numidia 69, 167, 179
Constantine (I), the Emperor *passim*;
youth 4; coming to power 15–18, 21–4,
194; Caesar 15–17; created Augustus
17; conversion xii, 22–3, 33–4, 65, 68, 79,
88, 90, 92, 93, 158, 181, 186, 192; in
Rome 24, 33–4, 56, 73, 81; Arch of 24–8,
187, 191; emperor of West 24, 28–32,
195; sole emperor 32–43, 44, 45, 105,
194; foundation of Constantinople 32–3,
34–8, 85, 157, 168; baptism 39; deification 152, cf. 36; succession 42–3; and
Arians 70–5, 78; and the army 15–16,
17–18, 21–2, 23, 25, 27, 32, 39, 45, 47, 93–4,
and see Milvian Bridge; and the Church
xiii, 65–6, 76, cf. 93–4, 145; churches of
55–64, 65, 133, 180, 186, 187; civil
reforms 38, 40–2, 45, 48, 196; and the
coinage 26, 40–1, 90–1, cf. 152; and
Donatists 67–9; military reforms 3, 39–
40, 197; as missionary 80–1, 93–4, 106;
and the pagans 80–1, 84, 85, 88, 95, 99–
100, 136, 152, 157; as seen by Julian 111;
sources for reign of 13, 21, 22–3, 24, 30,
31, 33, 34, 35, 39, 194–5, 197. *See also*
Eusebius of Caesarea, Lactantius, Zosimus
Constantine II, the Emperor, 181; Caesar
31, 34, 38, 43, 153, 176; Augustus xii,
43–4, 75–6, 152, 168, 195
Constantinople 43, 44, 47, 53, 71, 75, 76,
77, 79, 80, 86, 87, 88, 91, 93, 97, 98, 103,
105, 106, 113, 115, 116, 118, 144, 154,
155, 190, 195; foundation of 7, 32–3,
34–8, 85, cf. 87; dedication ceremony 24,
34, 35–6, 85, 157; Christianity of 35–6;
118; churches of 33, 36, 61, cf. 77, 112;
Senate of, *s.v.*
Constantius Chlorus, tetrarch 25, 26, 60,
68, 88; Caesar 4, 5, 6, 13, 16; Augustus
14, 15
Constantius II, the Emperor, xii, xiii, 36,
53, 87, 95, 103, 112, 117, 129, 137, 141,
145, 153, 168, 181, 195; Caesar 32, 39,
176; in succession crisis 42–3, 69, 85, 97;
Augustus 43ff., 61, 92, 97, 98, 105, 142,
146, 152, 160, 196; sole emperor 47–53,
94, 99, 103, 150, 151, 156, 171; visit to
Rome 50–1, 83, 101, 154; character 44,
47–8, 53, 66, 77, 84; and Arianism 75–9,
98, 108, 112, 195; and the Church 66–7,

122; and magic 83–4, 98; and pagan men
of letters 85–9, 113, 195; and paganism
82–4, 96, 114, 136
consul, consulship 43, 77, 85, 88, 102, 114,
116, 117, 150, 154; Constantine's reform
of 40
contorniate 154–5
conversion, convert, of Constantine xii,
22–3, 33–4, 65, 68, 69, 79, 88, 93, 158,
192; in general to Christianity xiii, 58,
64, 68, 80, 82, 93, 100, 102, 104, 132, 133,
144, 146, 158, 159–60, 173, 180–1, 183,
184; to paganism xiii, 94, 97–9, 102, 103,
156. *See also* apostate, Christianization,
evangelization
Corbridge *Lanx* 124–5
corn 21, 38, 181, cf. 59, 115; dole 37, 76,
cf. 75, 101; shortage 2, 21, 38, 48, 49, 50,
85, 119; supply 16–17, 22, 41–2, 50, 52,
75, 83, 85, 119–20, 145, 165, 169–70,
186, cf. 181
council of the Church 69, 70, 71, 74, 75, 76,
78, 79, 146, 197; of Antioch 73; of Arles 67;
69; of Constantinople 79; of Nicaea 33,
70, 71–2, 73, 74, 78; of Rimini and Seleucia 67, 78–9; of Serdica 76–7; of Tyre
63, 74. *See also* synod
court, the imperial, 4, 15, 23, 33, 37, 44, 47,
56, 73, 74, 77, 78, 83, 84, 85, 87, 93, 95,
108, 112, 113, 116, 119, 140, 152, 156,
181; law-court, *s.v.* . *See also* palace
craftsman, *see* artist
creed 71–2, 73, 74, 75, 76, 78, 79, 82;
Nicene Creed 73, 76
cremation 57–8, 141, 179
Crispus, son of Constantine 7, 16, 31, 33,
34, 49, 62, 153, 176, 194
Cross, the 22, 24, 35, 56, 58, 189, 190
cult 11, 26, 29, 129; Christian 19, 28, 55, 56,
67, 136, 137; imperial, *s.v.*; of martyrs 109,
132, 147, 156, 185; native xii, 127–8, 138,
143, 192; oriental 80, 99, 115, 123, 124,
129, 135, 136, 138, 157, 161, 175, 177, cf.
82, 102; pagan xii, xiii, 74, 79–80, 81, 83,
87, 88, 90, 91, 96, 100, 101, 102, 104,
124, 125–6, 129, 130, 131, 137, 138, 141,
142, 148, 155, 161, 166, 171, 185; pagan
cult-symbols 181; pagano-Christian 35.
See also Christianity, god, mystery
religion, paganism
culture 31, 73, 86, 87, 88, 89, 99, 108, 114,
148–9, 161–2, 179; the common cultural
heritage 37, 89, 108, 148, 157–8, 161, 170,
193; popular 154–5. *See also* education,
Greek, *paideia*
Cupids, *putti* 49, 60, 158, 161, 167, 169,
174, 176, 178, 188, 189, 190; fishing 134,
142, 165, 172; vintaging 49–50, 167, 174,
189, 192, cf. 142
curia, curiales xiii, 8, 19, 20–1, 31, 34, 37,
41–2, 66, 87, 88, 95–6, 99, 100, 103–6,
119–22, 132, 143, 154, 169, 195, 196;
Julian and *curiae* 103–6, 122; ordination
of *curiales* and clerical exemption 65–6,
67; paganism of *curiae* 20–1, 122. *See also*
cities

Index

Cybele 34, 102, 130, 155, 156, 175, 191; Attis 115, 155, 164, 191; cult of Cybele (and Attis) 80, 99, 102, 115, 129, 138, 152–3, 157, cf. 175
Cynic, Cynicism 102, 147, 149
Cyprus 38, 43

Dacia 4, 8, 43
Dalmatia 132
Dalmatius, half-brother of Constantine 43
Dalmatius the Younger, nephew of Constantine 43
Daniel, in Lions' Den 174, 176, 179, 182, 185, 188, 189; and serpent 174, 187
Danube, river xi, 1, 4, 5, 17, 31, 32, 34, 38, 43, 45, 51, 53, 95, 127; army of 47
Daphne, suburb of Antioch 61, 120–1
deacon 56, 72; archdeacon 68
decennalia 25, 91, 94; Base 6, 191
Decentius, brother of Magnentius 47, 92
Decius, the Emperor 11, 12, 14, 67–8, 156
dedication, to Christian God 140; of church 62–3; of Constantinople, *s.v.*; to dead 183; to emperor 27, 197; to Julian 122, 197; to pagan god 37, 126, 140, 197; of temple 142, 155, cf. 130. *See also* inscription, votive offering
Deir el-Meshkûk 124, 143
deputy-prefect, or 'vicar' 8, 17, 40
diocese (administrative area) 4, 5, 6, 16, 17, 39, 40, 43, 122, 125, 138, 157, 159, 160; creation of 8
diocese (ecclesiastical) 77. *See also* see
Diocletian, the Emperor xi, 30, 32, 33, 39, 43, 45, 83, 90, 97, 111; reign of 1–14, 194, 196; creation of Tetrarchy 3–4, of Second Tetrarchy 15, 16; abdication 14; building activities 6–7, 27; civil reforms 7–9, 15, 40, 41, 117, 194, 197; conference of Carnuntum 17; Great Persecution 10–14, 61 (*and s.v.*); military reforms 3, 197
Dionysus 113, 123, 130, 142, 155, 158–9, 161, 168, 170, 172, 174, 191; Bacchic conventicle 142; Bacchus 171, 178; Liber Pater 115, 161. *See also* Bacchic motifs
Dioscuri 35, 83, 155, 178, 189–90
divi, deification 11, 152
divination xii, 12, 46, 52, 81, 83, 84, 98, 164
Divinity, the 25, 27, 28–9, 67, 88, 115; Neoplatonic 86, 88, 99, 102, 111, 138, 192
divorce 4, 16, 41
Djemila 178
Domitian, the Emperor 90
Domitilla, catacomb of 185, 186
Domitius Alexander, usurper 17, 18, 69
Domitius Domitianus, usurper 5
Domitius Modestus, praetorian prefect, etc. 103
Donatists, the 11, 67–70, 71, 112, 127, 197
Donatus, bishop of Carthage (Donatist) 68, 69
Dorchester (Dorset) 158, 160, 176
Dougga (ancient Thugga) 132
dream xii, 22, 29, 30, 120, 126; dream-vision of Constantine xii, 22–3, 25, 27. *See also* vision

Dura-Europos 132
dux, duces 3, 5, 8, 12, 40

Earth-Goddess 138, 169–70, 182. *See also* Matronae
Easter 55, 61, 72, 137, 150
economy, of Roman Empire 1–2, 8–9, 31, 38, 40–1, 45–6, 119, 127, 197, 198. *See also* agriculture, coinage, factory, industry, inflation, taxation, trade
Edessa (Urfa) 14, 106, 175
edict 33, 54, 70, 80, 82, 108, 123, 197; of Great Persecution 12, 13, 14, 18, 19–20; of Milan 28–9, 30, 31, 197; Price Edict 9. *See also* law, letter
education xii, 37, 70, 80, 84, 87, 88, 89, 95, 97, 98, 104, 145, 146, 147, 151, 162, 191, 196; and Arianism 73–4, 98; Julian and 106–8, 114. *See also* paideia
Egypt *passim*
Elagabalus, the Emperor 90
Eleusis, Eleusinian Mysteries 99, 112, 115, 161, 181, 184
Ellès, mosaic from 166
Ely, Nereid cup from 190
Emesa (Homs) 90, 130
emperor, the, and his advisers 85–8, 114–15, *and s.v.* Hosius, Maximus of Ephesus, Priscus, Secundus Salutius, Urascius, Valens of Mursa; as arbitrator and patron of Church 67–79; on Arch of Constantine, *see* arch; on coins 45, 91–2, 155, cf. 117; cosmic powers of 27; by Grace of God 24, 65; 'good' emperors 25; *natalis imperii* 117; sacred monarchy 7–8, 44, 151; and safety of Empire 23, 65, 67, 153; virtues of 26, 86, cf. 122
Ephesus 91, 97, 98, 112, 124, 148, 149
epidemic 2, 11, 21, 38, 41, 90
Epiphania (Hama) 130
Epiphany 156, 183, 185; Julian attends service on 156–7
epitaph 143, 179, 197
equites, see knights
Ermine Street 141
estate, imperial, *see* imperial lands; monastic 145; private xii, 141–2, 145, 147, 163, 167. *See also* landowner
eternity 186; of Christ 70; of Empire xi, 89; eternal life 138; god of (Aion) 156; of world 102. *See also* after-life, immortality, paradise, resurrection
Eucharist 61, 63, 65, 74, 133, 134, 135, 175, 189; Eucharistic Victory 134; readmittance to communion, *see* excommunication
Eunapius, historian 30, 85, 148–9, 194, 196
eunuch 8, 13, 44, 95, 97, 152, 171; political importance of 44
Euphrates, river 51, 52, 54, 132
Eusebia, wife of Constantius II 50, 116
Eusebius, a Christian of Antioch 115, 131
Eusebius, bishop of Nicomedia, then of Constantinople 70, 73, 75–6, 79, 97
Eusebius, Lord High Chamberlain 53

Index

Eusebius of Caesarea, Church historian 13, 18, 19, 20, 21, 22–3, 24, 35, 36, 42, 62, 70, 71–2, 73, 75, 76, 93, 194, 197
Eustathius, bishop of Sebaste 146–7
Eutropia, half-sister of Constantine 46
Eutropia, mother-in-law of Constantine 63
Eutropius, historian 47, 194
evangelization 12, 79, 93, 103–4, 129, 133, 138, 156; Evangelists 50, 159, 168
Evil Eye, the 159, 165, 166
excommunication 68, 70, 72; readmittance to communion 73, 74, 75, 78
exorcist, exorcism, 57, 156

Factory, workshop 6, 170, 173, 176–7, 178, 179, 186, 189, 190–1; State arms and uniform factories 2, 3, 7, 9; with mixed pagan and Christian production 131, 173–6, 177–9, 186–7, 191. See also mint
Fausta, (second) wife of Constantine 16, 32, 33, 60, 62, 63
Feeding of the Five Thousand, the 175, 183, 185, 187, 190
FEL. TEMP. REPARATIO 45–6, 92
festival, festival day 90, 131, 149–57; Christian 56, 137, 149, 150, 155–7, 159, 185; imperial 13, 33, 87, 117, 150, 151–2, 155; pagan 12, 34, 81, 87, 100, 101, 103, 104, 119, 120, 134, 137, 141, 148, 149–57, 176; eleventh centenary of Rome 45; encaenia of Constantinople, see Constantinople; political importance of pagan 150. See also anniversary, Christmas, decennalia, Easter, Epiphany, New Year, quinquennalia, tricennalia, vicennalia
Filocalus, Furius Dionysius, scribe 150; Calendar of Filocalus, see Calendar of 354
Firmicus Maternus, pagan, then Christian, writer 82, 151
fort, fortification, 3, 4, 5, 6, 16, 30, 50, 51–2, 54, 94–5, 106, 127, 129, 132, 139, 143, 172
Fortune 113; of Alexandria 109; of Carthage 164; of Constantinople 34–5, 37, cf. 91; of Rome 34, and see Roma
Forum, of Constantinople 33, 35, 75, cf. 87; Romanum 5–6, 24, 27, 51, 115, 153
Frampton, mosaic of 158–9
Franks xi, 17, 50
freedman 41, 57, 110, 124, 179–80
frescoes xi, xiii, 6, 57, 60, 132, 135, 142, 157, 159, 160, 165, 179, 180, 182–6, 190
frontier xi, 1, 3, 4, 5, 22, 33, 34, 38, 39, 40, 51, 92, 94, 106. See also Danube, Rhine

Galerius Maximianus, tetrarch, as Caesar 4, 5, 6, 11, 12, 13; as Augustus 14–20; Palinode and death 19–20, 23, 197
Galilaeans (Julian's name for Christians) 101, 109, 110, 111, 120
Gallienus, the Emperor 1, 212
Gallus, (Constantius), half-brother of Julian 43, 44, 50, 97; Caesar 47, 48–9, 53, 98, 119, 120, 150
games 35, 48, 51, 65, 85, 88, 100, 101, 103, 117, 150–7, 164, 167, 177; Olympic 169;

political importance 150. See also amphitheatre, beast-fight, charioteer, cricus, gladiator
Gangra 146
Gaul passim; Julian in 50, 52, 94, 105–6, 112, 116, 117
Gaza 106 (cf. 81), 130
Gê and Karpoi, mosaic of 169–70
genius 91, 184, 187, 191; Saeculi 165. See also Cupids
George, Arian bishop of Alexandria 97, 99, 108–9, 130
Germans 5, 22, 40, 50; in imperial bodyguard 40. See also Alamanni, Franks
Germany 83, 129, 137, 140; Second 136–8, 141, 173–6; free 34
gladiator 42, 102, 151
glassware xii, xiii, 141, 173–7, 181, 187, 190, 191
Gnosticism 161, 184
God, of the Christians (and Jews) passim; Neoplatonic 86, 99, 110, 113; as patron of Constantine 22–3, 26, 27, 54, 63–4, 65, 67, 69, 152; as protector of Empire xiii, 23, 24, 25, 28, 30, 63–4, 65, 67
god(s), pagan passim; Neoplatonic, see above; of paideia, see Hermes, Muses; pax deorum, see pax; removal from coinage 90–1. See also Apollo, Asklepios, Cybele, Dionysus, Dioscuri, Earth-Goddess, Fortune, Hercules, Isis, Jupiter, Mars, Matronae, Mercury, Mother-Goddess, Neptune, Orpheus, Saturn, Serapis, Sol Invictus, Sun-God
Good Shepherd 58, 134, 160, 164, 183, 185, 186, 187
Goths xi, 1, 11, 34, 38, 53, 79, 155; Gothic Bible 79
governing classes, religion of 95–6, 103–6, 122, 173, 181, 183, cf. 99, 120, 123, 124, 131, 174
governor, provincial passim; religion of 95, 103, 107, 138, 194
grave xii, 57, 58, 77, 101, 132, 157, 173, 175, 177, 179ff.; burial ad sanctos 57; funerary well 141. See also tomb
grave-goods 159, 179, 180, 181, 192
gravestone 179, 180; mostly Christian in fourth century 180. See also epitaph
Great Persecution, the xii, 3, 7, 10–14, 18–21, 23, 28–31, 31–2, 61, 65, 68, 69, 71, 72, 93, 132, 133, 194
Greece 29, 31, 36, 37, 55, 58, 99, 100, 148. See also Achaea
Greek, culture, literature, etc. xiii, 87, 97, 98, 99, 106, 107, 108, 110, 115, 154–5, 179, 181, 184, 189, 195; language 22, 79, 108, 124, 146, 147, 171, 174, 175, 195, 196, 197. See also 'Hellenism'
Gregory of Nazianzus, St. 107, 109, 147, 196
Gregory of Nyssa, St. 156
Gregory Thaumaturgus, St. 156

Hadrian, the Emperor 25–6, 57, 110–11, 121
Hadrian's Wall 45, 129

Index

halo 45, 58, 60, 159, 165, 166, 167, 182, 186; uses in art 60
Hannibalianus, nephew of Constantine 39, 43, 46, 48
Hauran, the 124, 143
Helena, daughter of Constantine, wife of Julian 50, 52, 60
Helena, mother of Constantine 4, 33, 34, 42, 56, 57, 58, 60, 61, 62, 93, 191; churches of Constantine and Helena 55-64
Heliopolis, see Baalbek
Helios, see Sun-God
'Hellenism' 106
Hercules 4, 10, 25, 26, 91, 113, 115, 118, 155, 163, 164, 168, 171, 174, 178, 182; Herculius 4, 7
heredity of calling xi-xii, 41-2, 104
heresy 70, 78, 79, 112, 134, 146. See also Arianism, Novatians, schism, sect
Hermes 107, 114, 184
hero 116; Christian 146; pagan 33, 63, 102, 116, 147-9, 158, 163, 168, 190, and see Achilles, Bellerophon, Hercules, mythology
high priest, of Julian 100-1, 112, 193; of Maximin 19, 100
Hilary, St., of Poitiers 78, 79, 195
hill-fort temples 125-8
Hinton St. Mary, mosaic of 158-9
Hippo (Bône-Annaba) 167
hippodrome, see circus
Hispellum 151-2
Holy Land, the 33; churches of 62-3, 133. See also Palestine
homoousios 71, 73, 76, 79
Hosius (Ossius), bishop of Cordova 33-4, 71, 76, 78, 81
House of the Horses, Carthage 164-5
house-church 12, 132-3, 135, 136
Huns xi, 1
hunting 25-7, 46, 100, 159, 162, 164, 167-8, 172, 173-4, 175, 176, 179, 190; importance of 167; symbolism of 26. See also beast-fights
hymn, Christian 20, 121; of Julian 99, 102, 110
hypogeum, of Trebius Justus 183-4, 185; of Via Livenza 142; of Vibia 183, 184-5, 192

Iamblichus, philosopher 85, 97, 102, 196
iconography, Christian 184, 193; imperial 168; of Seasons 168
Illyricum 4, 18, 40, 46-7, 52, 71
immortality 102, 159, 165, 190, cf. 174; through courage 26; through culture 148, 184, 191. See also after-life, eternity, Paradise, Underworld
immunity, see clergy, liturgy
imperial cult 2, 10, 13, 33, 81, 90, 94, 135, 142-3, 150, 151-2, 157
imperial lands 37, 41, 55, 56, 57, 59, 88
incense 10, 55, 83, 120, 151, cf. 59
India 38, 147
industry 2, 6, 9, 18, 20, 37, 38, 41, 59, 82, 144, 163-4, 173ff., cf. 146. See also artist, factory

inflation 2, 8, 9, 41
initiation 99, 115, 161, 171, cf. 148
inscription 6, 9, 25, 59, 90, 117, 124, 125-6, 133-4, 140-1, 143, 151-2, 158, 161, 163, 164, 166, 172, 183, 184, 187, 194, 197; graffiti 61, 184; in honour of Julian 122
invasion, barbarian xi, 1-2, 6, 11, 39, 50, 105-6, 127, 137, 138, 139, 193, cf. 140, 141, 172; Persian 5, 53
Ireland 125
Isis 115, 129, 151, 152, 153, 177-8; Anubis 153; coins 153; Osiris, Horus 115. See also Apis, Serapis
Isle of White 4, 161
Isles of the Blest 161, 171. See also Paradise

Janiculum 123, 142
Jerusalem 62-3, 80, 111-12; Entry into 187, 188
Jews 10, 48, 62, 66, 101, 110, 111-12, 129, 184, 185
John Chrysostom, St. 121, 144, 156
Jonah scenes 58, 134, 176, 177, 178, 182, 185, 186, 187
Jovian, the Emperor 54, 94, 130
Julian the Apostate, the Emperor xiii, 30, 33, 35, 40, 41, 43, 44, 48, 78, 143, 147, 153, 154, 157, 159, 192, 196; youth 44, 50, 97-9; Caesar 50, 51, 94, 113, 116, 171-2; Augustus (and usurpation) 52-4, 117, 151, 156-7, 172; reign of 53-4, 113, 116, 117-18, 137, 140, 197; and the army 50, 52-4, 94, 117; and the Church 65, 70, 89, 97, 108-12, 120-1; coinage of 116-18; conversion to paganism 83, 85, 94, 97-9, cf. 148-9, 161, 163, 168; literary works 33, 45, 99, 102, 113, 121, 147, 160, 196, and see hymn, letter, Misopogon; revival of paganism xii, 19, 94, 95, 96, 97-128, 142, 143, 147, 149, 156, 160, 182, 193, 196, cf. 130-1; supporters of 112-16, 118, 125, 193, 194-6, 197
Julius, bishop of Rome 75, 76, 77
Julius Constantius, half-brother of Constantine, father of Julian 43, 44, 48, 97
Junius Bassus, city prefect of Rome, sarcophagus of 59, 188-9, 190
Jupiter 4, 10, 14, 26, 29, 90, 91, 115, 118, 137, 151, 152, 155, 164; Heliopolitanus 123; Jovius 4, 7; Sabazios 185; Zeus 116, 143
justice, administration of 11, 32, 41, 42, 48, 53, 67, 68, 84, 104, 114, 130, 149, 196. See also law, law-court, prison, tribunal
Justinian II, the Emperor 92

Kaiseraugst Treasure 172-3
Kharab Shams 144
knights 34, 151

Labarum 23, 45, 91-2, 93
Lactantius, Christian writer 7, 8, 12, 13, 18, 20, 21, 22, 28, 30, 194, 197
landowner 65, 67, 93, 138, 141-2, 144, 160, 162-3, 180
Lateran 51, 55; St. John at the 55-6, 58, 62

Index

Latin 71, 88, 107, 145, 146, 147, 174, 195, cf. 190

aw 4, 13, 14, 28, 31, 32, 33, 44, 54, 83, 95; as academic subject 89; individual 41–2, 46, 66, 88, 104, 106–8; Jewish and Christian 49, 182, 187, 188; re magic 81, 83–4; re paganism xiii, 42, 51, 81–3, 87, 95–6, 99, 123, 136, 137; as source 196–7; unevenness of application 82–3, 196. *See also* edict, justice, law-court, letter

law-court 42, 66, 67, 84, cf. 130

legion 3, 14, 39, 53, 94

letter, rescript, of Constantine 33, 38, 67, 70, 74, 145, 197; of Julian 100, 101, 105, 106, 109, 111, 112, 113, 196; of other emperors 21, 42, 77, 86, 145, 196–7; of private persons 77, 78, 104, 113, 114, 131, 195

Libanius, sophist 31, 49, 54, 77, 83, 84, 87, 88, 89, 95, 98, 99–100, 104, 106, 107, 113–14, 120, 122, 129, 130, 131, 145, 148–9, 153–4, 195, 196; paganism of 114–15

libation 19, 49, 120, 141, 178. *See also* sacrifice

Liber Pontificalis 56, 57, 59

Liberius, bishop of Rome 78, 79

library 87, 97, 99. *See also* book

Licinius, tetrarch 17–18, 20, 21, 25–7, 28–32, 33, 38, 39, 40, 42, 59, 70, 80, 93, 94, 146

Limestone Plateau (Massif Calcaire), the 143–5

limitanei 3, 39

liturgy, *munus* (compulsory public service) 65–6, 67, 105; clerical exemption from 66, 67, 105; other exemption from 120

London 91, 129–30, 141

Low Ham, mosaic of 161–2

Lullingstone Villa 141, 159–60

Lydney 94, 125–8, 139

Lyon 11, 47, 90, 138, 175, 180

Macedonia 8, 31, 38, 43

Macedonius, Arian bishop of Constantinople 76, 77

Macellum 97, 98, 99, 116

Macrobius, pagan writer 115

magic 23, 25, 30, 37, 81, 82, 83–5, 98, 161, 164–6; and paganism 83–4, 165. *See also* theurgy

magician 84, 88, 98, 155, 174, cf. 196

magister equitum (Master of the Cavalry) 39–40, 48–9, 53, 76, 171–2

magister peditum (Master of the Infantry) 39–40, 46

magistrate 13, 37, 66, 151

Magentius, usurper 46–7, 48, 50, 77–8, 82, 92, 117, 141, 172

Maiden Castle 125–8, 139

Maiuma 106, cf. 81

Major Cemetery (Coemeterium Maius) 185, 186

Mamre 63, 80, 182

Manichaeism 99

Marcus, bishop of Arethusa 130

Marcus Aurelius, the Emperor xi, 11, 25, 111

Mardonius, tutor of Julian 97, 116

Marius Victorinus, Christian Neoplatonist 107

market 18, 119, 141, cf. 177; shops 135. *See also* trade

Mars 26, 91, 115, 155, 164

Marseille 17, 189, 190

Martin, St. 94, 129, 195

martyr 13, 14, 18–19, 21, 23, 36, 56, 57, 68, 77, 109, 120, 132, 135, 146, 147, 148, 150, 156, 179, 185, 186, 194

martyrium 36, 56, 57, 62, 63, 120, 132, 135

Matronae 137–8. *See also* mother-goddess

Mauretania 112, 122, 167

mausoleum, imperial 14, 36, 49–50, 57, 61, 180, *and see* Church of the Holy Apostles, S. Costanza; private 57–8, 59, 132, 159, 174, 179, 180, 181–5, 186, 192, *and see* hypogeum

Maxentius, usurper 15–18, 21–4, 27, 28, 29, 39, 164, 190

Maximian, tetrarch 4, 5, 6, 7, 13, 14, 16–18, 32, 42

Maximin Daia, tetrarch, Caesar 14, 17; Augustus 17–21, 28, 29–31; anti-Christian policies 18–19, 20–1, 29, 30–1, 100, 100

Maximus of Ephesus, philosopher 94, 98, 112, 114, 148, 149

Medusa 161; as talisman 181

Melitius, bishop of Lycopolis 71; Melitian schism 71, 72, 74, 75

Mercury 115, 136–7, 154, 164, 167, 184

Mesopotamia 3, 5, 14, 39, 45, 51–2, 54, 59, 106, 147, 175

Milan 5, 28–9, 50, 78; Edict of 28–9, 30, 31, 197

Mildenhall Treasure 170–2

military campaign xi, 3, 4, 5, 12, 22, 27, 31, 32, 34, 38, 45, 47, 50, 51, 52, 53, 90, 92; Julian's against Constantius II 52–3, 117; military espionage 45. *See also* war

Milvian Bridge, battle of 22–3, 24, 25, 26, 27, 30, 54, 59, 65, 93

Minervina, first wife of Constantine 16, 31

mint 7, 26, 33, 37, 82, 91, 92, 117, 118, 120, 154

miracle Christian 25, 30, 145, 156, 174–5, 185, 187, 188; pagan 26, 86, 98, 148

Misopogon (Beard-Hater) 105, 114, 118–22

Mithras, Mithraism, Mithraeum 80, 94–5, 99, 102, 115, 129–30, 135–6, 177, 178

monasticism, monasteries, monks 66, 73, 89, 124, 129, 131, 145–9, 195

monotheism 29; Christian 102; solar xii, 102, 115

Montmaurin 141–2; La Hillère 141

mosaics xi, xiii, 6, 49–50, 58, 59, 61, 62, 63, 125, 126, 133–4, 140, 141, 142–3, 144, 151, 157–70, 175, 179, 192

Moselle, river 5, 60, 162

Moses 182, 188; and the miraculous spring 35, 142, 175, 176, 182, 185, 187; receiving Law 182, 187, 188

Index

mother-goddess 62, 137-8, *and see* Matronae; Mother of Gods, *see* Cybele
Mursa 76, 122; battle of 47, 77
Muses, *Mouseion* 107, 148, 167
mystery religion 80, 82, 99, 102, 112, 115, 123, 136, 138, 148, 149, 161, 171, 185. *See also* Eleusis
mysticism 99, 161. *See also* mystery religion
mythology 106, 154, 172, 180, 181, 184, 190, 191; figures from 33, 37, 124, 142, 155, 158-78 *passim*, 180, 181, 182, 184, 190; sarcophagi 180, 190-1, 192; use of by Christians 157-9, 160, 170, 189-90. *See also* Bacchic motifs, hero, Nereid

Naissus (Nish) 47
navy, fleet 4, 32, 33, 47, 54, 94, 128; naval yard 126
Neoplatonism, Neoplatonist 12, 35, 82, 83, 85, 86, 97, 99, 102, 103, 115, 196
Nepotianus, nephew of Constantine, usurper 46
Neptune 155, 158, 164, 167, 174; Neptunalia festival 150, 155; Poseidon 61
Nereid 158, 167, 170, 171, 190; on Christian casket and cup 158, 190; symbolism of 171; Thetis 167, 170
Nero, the Emperor 10, 36, 110, 154
New Testament 32, 107-8, 134; scenes from, *see* Bible
New Year (Kalends) festival 150, 153-4
Nicaea 73; Council of 33, 70, 71-2, 73
Nicomedia 7, 12, 13, 14, 21, 28, 30, 32, 33, 37, 61, 70, 73, 88, 97, 98, 113, 118, 194
Nisibis 5, 45, 54, 106
notary (State secretary) 5, 48, 52, 53
Novations 112
Numidia 68, 69, 106, 167
nun, nunnery 130, 145, 146, 147

Obelisk, of Constantius II 51
officer, of army 12, 14, 39, 46, 48, 52, 54, 77, 87, 91, 128, 129, 195
official(s) *passim, and see* city prefect, deputy-prefect, praetorian prefect, provincial governor, etc.; minor 2, 41-2, 85, 154
official monument 5-6, 24-8, 49-50, 51, 186-7, 197
Old Testament, *see* Bible
oracle 12, 22, 84, 98, 124. *See also* Chaldaeans
Orante 34, 135, 159, 179, 185, 186, 187, 191
oratory, orator 5, 18, 27, 31, 47, 85-9, 104, 107, 112, 114, 115, 116, 120, 129, 145, 195, 196; political role of 114-15. *See also* rhetoric, sophist
Origen 70, 72, 73, 108, 156
Orontes, river 61, 118, 130, 167
Orpheus 47, 87, 160, 162-3, 164; and Christianity 160; pagan 160, 161 163
orthodox, orthodoxy 72-9, 82, 98; Constantine II and Constans as patrons of 75-7; pagan 102, 103
Ostia 83, 180

Pachomius, monastic founder 146, 147

pagan(s) *passim*; attacks on Christians by 108-9, 130-1; 'Church' 99-102; cities of pagan 'backwater' 130-1; men of letters 30, 33, 61, 85-9, 97, 98, 102, 104, 107, 108, 112-15, 121, 131, 148-9, 194-6, cf. 192; other upper class (and educated) 11, 25, 29, 37, 54, 89, 95-6, 102, 103, 114, 115, 116, 123, 131, 141-2, 153, 159, 161, 162, 165, 168, 169, 171, 182, 183, 191-2; paganization of government by Julian 103, 107; 'party' 99, 153; saints 147-9, 192; soldiers 93-5, 126; supporters of Julian 112-16, 118, 125, 194-6
pagan art 25-8, 49-50, 124-5, 157-79, 182-5, 186, 187, 188, 190-2; acceptable to Christians 49-50, 157-8, 160-1, 161-2, 170, 171, 172, 177, 189-90, cf. 183-4, *and see* mythology
pagan revival, Celtic, *see* Celtic Renaissance; of Julian xii, xiii, 19, 54, 94, 97-128, 143, 196; late fourth century 148; of Maximin 19, 21. *See also* high priest
paganism, pagan religion *passim*; in army 93-5; coexistence with Christianity 131, 135-7; of *curiae* 20-1, 95-6, 103-6; decline of 3, 19, 96, 193; extinction of xiii, 26, 96, 193; finances of 19, 38, 40, 67, 80, 132, *and see* temple lands; of Julian xiii, 97-9, 114, 161, 163; late xii, 80, 83-4, 99, 97-128 *passim*, 138, 147, 161, 177; official at Constantinople 36; persecution of 79-85; proscription of xii, xiii, 42, 51, 80, 81, 82, 87, 95-6, 123, 136, 137, 149, 153, 193, cf. 170; reserves of xii, 23, 80, 83, 95-6, 99, 103-6, 107, 122, 137, 138-40, 142, 157, 180, 192. *See also* altar, cult, god, monotheism, mystery religion, pagan art, pagan revival, pagano-Christian, priest, sacrifice, temple, etc.
pagano-Christian, catacombs 181-5; cult 35; mixed production 131, 173-6, 177-9, 186-7, 191; mixture of themes 49-50, 158-9, 189-90; tombs 158, 180-1
pageantry, pomp and circumstance 8, 51, 53, 71, 101, 150, 153; Byzantine love of 51, 101, cf. 8
paideia 89, 95, 104, 106-8; Julian and 106-8, 114; as a religion 107, 148, 184, *and see* immortality. *See also* culture, education, Greek, Libanius, oratory, rhetoric, sophist
palace (and imperial household) 6, 12, 13, 14, 27, 31, 33, 35, 37, 49, 52, 55, 56, 60, 61, 71, 72, 76, 108, 114, 168; Julian's purge of 53. *See also* court
Palestine 18, 48, 63, 70, 74, 93, 106, 130, 131, 139, 147, 194. *See also* Holy Land
Palmyra 1, 3, 123, 130
(Caesarea) Paneas 131
panegyric 5, 7, 18, 22, 23, 45, 61, 77, 86, 88, 113, 115, 116, 194
Pannonia 17, 31, 43, 122, 194, cf. 132
papyrus 59, 84, 145, 198
Paradise 50, 134, 171, 182, 183, 184, 185, 186; Elysian Fields 184; heaven 152, 161, 186. *See also* Isles of the Blest

Paris 52
patronage 93, 104; of the arts 5–6, 88, 126, 157–73 *passim*, 182–92 *passim* (*especially* 190, 191); of cult or Church 26, 65, 81, 100, 126, 133, 134, 135–7, 141; gods as patrons 35, 90, 94, 142, 166; in public life 19, 42, 103, 197; of sect 75–9
Paul, bishop of Constantinople 75, 76, 77, 78
Paulus Catena (Paul 'the Chain'), notary 48
pax, deorum 10, 80, 129; *romana* 1
Peace of the Church, the 28–31, 129, 133, 134, 135, 183, 186
peasant xi, 2, 4, 31, 41, 68, 94, 144, 145–6
persecution, of Christian dissenters 69, 76, 78; of Christians 10, 11, 12, 14, 29, 31–2, 56, 64, 65, 67, 79, 93, 129, 134, 135, 146, 185; under Decius 11–12, 14, 67, 156; of pagans 79–85, 129. *See also* Great Persecution
Persia, Persians 1, 5, 8, 32, 37, 38–9, 45, 46, 48, 51–2, 71, 155, 195; Julian's Persian expedition 53–4, 94, 106, 111, 113, 114, 116, 118, 119, 122, 124, 195
personification 2, 19, 111, 172, 188, 191; of cities 37, 91, 150, *and see* Fortune, Roma; on coins 45, 90, 91–2, 117; on mosaics 168–9, 170. *See also* salvation, Seasons
Pesch 137–8
philosopher, philosophy 12, 35, 36, 38, 54, 70, 71, 83, 85–9, 97, 98, 99, 100, 102, 111, 112, 113, 114, 116, 121, 146, 147, 155, 160, 161, 163, 168–9, 195, 196; Epicurean 100, 149; as saints 148–9. *See also* Cynic, Pythagoras, Stoicism
Phoenicia 13, 21, 122, 165, 181
Phrygia 34, 78, 79
Piazza Armerina 162–3, 164
Picts and Scots 172
pilgrim, pilgrimage, Chritian 62, 63; pagan 126, 132, 141, 143
Pliny the Younger 10–11
Plotinus 12, 85, 102
Pola 33, 49
Pontifex Maximus 51, 80, 81, 100, 101
Pontus 32, 43, 146, 147, 156
poor, poverty xi, xii, 6, 41, 42, 46, 61, 65–6, 69, 75, 93, 100, 101, 103, 117, 127, 132, 133, 145–6, 157, 179, 180, 185
Porphyry, philosopher 12, 85, 97, 102, 110
portico 34, 35, 87, 121, 172, etc.; of the Gods Assembled 115
portrait 5, 6, 11, 23, 49, 51, 60, 134, 150, 153, 154, 159, 177, 183, 188, 191
pottery xii, 125, 141, 159, 163, 180, 181; African figured 157, 177–9, 190
Praetextatus, Vettius Agorius 115, 149
Praetextatus (Pretestato), catacomb of 185–6
praetor 88, 154
praetorian guard 12, 28, 39
praetorian prefect 8, 12, 34, 40, 44, 49, 54, 85, 95, 102, 103, 116, 196
prayer, Christian 61, 77, 93, 94, 135, 157; of imperial cult 91, 117, 153; Jewish 111;

pagan 10, 30, 98, 101, 103, 113, 116, 119, 154; pagano-Christian 35
Price Edict 9, 197
priest, Christian 19, 35, 55, 57, 70, 72, 74, 130, 138, 144, 146; of imperial cult 152; pagan 12, 19, 33, 51, 81, 83, 90, 100–1, 103, 112, 115, 120, 125, 136, 137, 138, 141, 149, 151, 152, 153, 157, 161, 177, 184–5. *See also* clergy, high priest
Priscus, philosopher 112, 114, 148
prison, prisoner 13, 18, 20, 32, 42, 68, 69, 78; of war 22, 45, 50, 79, 92, 117, 155
proconsul, of Achaea 115; of Constantinople 37, 87, 88
Prohaeresius, Christian sophist 89, 107, 149
Projecta and Secundus, casket of 158
propaganda, religious 21, 89ff., 110–11, 117–18, 125
province, subdivision of 8
provincial assembly 122
public life xiii, 11, 25, 89, 90, 91, 149–57, 193; paganism and 90, 149–57. *See also* festival, official monument
public post 9, 66, 71, 105
Pythagoras, Pythagoreanism 100, 174

Qirqbize 144
quaestor 49, 114
quinquennalia 22, 156

Radiate Crown 35, 176, cf. 45; in imperial iconography 168; as pagan symbol on inscriptions 122
Raising of Lazarus, the 174, 182, 183, 185, 187, 188
Ravenna 16, 79, 168
recruiting, for army 3, 9, 40, 95; for *curiae* 105; for Senate 87
religious life xiii, 129–32, 157, 192–3, *and in general* 129–93; coexistence and toleration 77, 115, 128, 131, 135–7; violence 108–9, 129–31, *and see* riot. *See also* church, cult, festival, saint, sanctuary, temple, worship, etc.
reliquary, relics, Christian 56, 58, 109; pagan 123. *See also* martyrium
resurrection 45, 58, 133, 134, 192; of Christ 62, 189
rhetoric, rhetorician 7, 77, 85, 87, 88, 89, 95, 104, 107, 114–15, 148, 194. *See also* oratory, panegyric, sophist
Rhine, river xi, 1, 17, 34, 45, 51, 52, 172; army of 39, 47, 50, 95; Rhineland 137–8, 158, 181; glass production in 173–6
Rhône, Christianity in cities of 157, cf. 180
Richborough (Rutupiae) 139
Rimini, Council of 67, 78, 79
riot 49, 109; re food 38, 49; re religion 73, 76, 77, 108–9, 130
rite, ritual, Christian 35, 137, 193, cf. 121, 134; of court, etc. 8, 162; encaenia of Constantinople 35–6, 85, cf. 157; of imperial cult 81, 94, 142–3, 152, 157; pagan xiii, 6, 11, 34, 83, 86, 94, 100, 101, 102, 104, 115, 120, 124, 130, 131, 135, 137, 138, 142, 151, 152–3, 154, 156,

Index

rite—*cont'd*
 157, 167, 175, 179. *See also* incense, libation, prayer, sacrifice
Roma, goddess 24, 34, 37, 91, 154
Romanization 127
Romano-Celtic temple 125, 137, 139, 159
Rome, city of *passim*; bishops 34, 55, 69, 71,
 75–9, 150; capital moved from 7, 32ff.;
 catacombs 49, 56, 57, 134, 177, 181–6;
 churches 55–9, 62, 132, 135–6, 138, 142;
 eleventh centenary 45–6, 92; festivals
 150–5; glass factories 176–7; sarcophagus
 workshops 186–9, 190–2; Senate, *s.v.*;
 temples 24, 51, 81, 83, 90, 123–4, 135–6,
 142, 192; visit of Constantius II 50–1,
 83, 101

Sacrifice 5, 6, 10, 11, 12, 13, 18, 19, 25–7,
 35–6, 81, 82, 83, 91, 94, 100, 101, 103,
 111, 114, 115, 120, 135, 141, 151, 152,
 153, 154, 162, 165, 168, 178; as guarantee
 of genuine paganism in art 162, 165, 168,
 cf. 25–6, 178; of Isaac 174, 178, 182, 185,
 187, 188–9. *See also* incense, libation
saint 60, 36, 56, 145–9, 156, 177, 184, 185,
 192, 193; John 135; John the Baptist
 55, 156; Mary 186; Paul 49, 56,
 59, 135, 177, 183, 188, 185, 189;
 Peter 49, 56, 57–9, 142, 177, 183,
 185, 187, 188, 189, 190, *and see* St.
 Peter's, Rome; Petronilla 184, 186;
 Apostles, *s.v.*; Evangelists 50, 159, 168;
 of late Empire, *s.v. individual names*;
 burial *ad sanctos* 57; pagan 145, 147–9,
 192. *See also* catacombs, church, Sant . . .
St.-Bertrand-de-Comminges 142
St. Peter's, Rome 57–9, 62, 136, 138, 180,
 186, 187, 188–9
Sallust, praetorian prefect 102–3, 116
Salonae 14, 132
Salutius, *see* Secundus
salvation 2, 23, 50, 92, 171, 182, 185; god-
 dess of 2, 90, 115, 168. *See also* saviour
(Sebaste) Samaria 131
S. Callisto, catacomb of 185
S. Clemente 132, 136
S. Giovanni in Laterano, *see* Lateran
S. Lorenzo 57
S. Sebastiano, catacomb and basilica of 56
Sancta Sophia, church of 33, 36, 37
sanctuary, of church 60, 140; pagan 19, 22,
 35, 36, 62, 63, 80, 107, 111, 120, 123,
 124, 125–8, 132, 136, 137–8, 139, 140,
 141, 143, 148, cf. 51. *See also* temple
S. Agnese, catacomb and basilica 49, 57
S. Apollinare Nuovo 79
S. Cecilia in Trastevere 132
S. Costanza 49–50, 52, 57
S. Croce in Gerusalemme 56
S. Prisca 132, 135–6, 178
S. Pudenziana 62, 63
SS. Giovanni e Paolo 135
SS. Pietro e Marcellino, catacomb (and
 basilica) of 57, 185, 186
Sapor, *see* Shapur

Saracens 48, 58
sarcophagus 6, 23, 26, 57, 59, 148, 157,
 170, 173, 174, 176, 179, 181, 183, 186–92;
 Christian 50, 180, 186–90, 191; of
 Constantina 50; of Dioscuri 189–90;
 Dumbarton Oaks Season 191–2; of
 Junius Bassus 59, 188–9, 190; pagan 180,
 187, 190–2; of Two Brothers 188, 189
Sarmatians xi, 34, 38
Saturn, (Roman) 151, 153; Baal-Saturn 90,
 102, 165, 181; Saturnalia festival 115,
 150, 152–3; *Saturnalia* of Macrobius 115
saviour, Christian 2, 23, 63, 175, 193;
 pagan 2, 90, 110, 182, 193
Saxons 4; Saxon Shore 4, 139
schism 73, 79; Donatist 11, 67–70, 80, 112;
 Melitian 71, 72, 74, 75
sculpture 5–6, 121, 123, 130, 157, 180, 187,
 188, 189, 190, 191; of Arch of Constantine 25–8. *See also* sarcophagus, statue
Scythopolis, trials of 84, 114
Seasons, the four 155, 159, 165, 167–8, 186,
 189, 190–2; Dumbarton Oaks Sarcophagus 191–2; symbolism of 159, 186
Second Flavians (House of Constantine)
 143, 152
sect, Christian 10, 68, 112; pagan 181;
 used of the Christians 28, 110, 111
secularization, of imperial cult 81, 151–2,
 157; of pagan festivals 157
Secundus Salutius, praetorian prefect 54,
 94, 116
see (episcopal) 68, 70 73, 76, 77, 78, 147,
 167; in policy of Constantius II 75, 76,
 77, 78. *See also* bishop, diocese
Seleucia (in Asia Minor), Council of 78–9
Senate, senator, senatorial aristocracy 8, 38,
 44, 95; Christian 59, 95, 180; of Constantinople 37, 86, 87, 98, 105; pagan 81,
 83, 95–6, 115, 138, 142, 149, 153, 161, cf.
 191–2, 197, *and see* Praetextatus; of
 Rome xii, 24, 25, 27, 28, 34, 37, 43, 47, 51,
 59, 81, 83, 95, 115, 138, 149, 151, 154,
 158, 161, 180; Senate-house 6, 34, 51, 83,
 91
Septimius Severus, the Emperor 11, 25, 35
Serapis 109, 115, 130, 153, 154
Serdica, Council of 76–7
serf xi, 38, 41
service, *see* church, liturgy
Severus, tetrarch 14, 15, 16, 17, 28, 30
Shapur (Sapor) II, king of Persia 38, 45,
 51–2, 53
ship 22, 32, 47, 58, 100, 167, 177, 186, cf.
 45, 165, 166; *Navigium Isidis* 153; shippers 41–2. *See also* Jonah scenes, navy
shrine, Christian 56–9, 120; pagan 120, 125,
 137, 143, 151, 159, *and see* temple
Sicily 55, 162–3, 179
silverware xiii, 124–5, 140–1, 157, 158,
 170–3, 177, cf. 55
Singara 45, 52
Sirmium 34, 118
Siscia 91, 118
slave 30, 41, 66, 103, 153, 154
Sol Invictus 7, 26, 27, 35, 90, 91, 102;

Index

patron of Constantine 26, 90, cf. 22.
See also Sun-God (Unconquered)

soldier(s) 4, 41–2, 51, 101, 162, 188, 189; individual 14, 17, 52, 54, 94–5, 126, 146; religion of 50, 93–5, 109, 126; soldier-emperor 3, 18, 35. *See also* army, officer

Sopater, philosopher 35, 85, 88

sophist 49, 61, 84, 89, 95, 98, 103, 113, 114, 195, 196; political role of 114–15; as saint 148–9. *See also* orator

Sousse (Hadrumetum) 166

South Cadbury 126

Spain 5, 8, 17, 28, 33, 40, 43, 46, 71, 76, 81, 127, 132, 178

Split (Spalato) 14, 27

statue 6, 125–6, 197; Christian 55; of Constantine 24, 35, 61, 168; (pagan) at Constantinople 36–7; of emperor 10, 29, 30, 37, 51, 81, 122, 197; of gods 10, 34, 35, 37, 61, 80, 82, 83, 86, 98, 121, 123, 130, 137, 148, 151, 168, 172, 191

Stoicism 100, 111, 149, 168

Strasbourg (Argentorate), battle of 50, 52

Sun-God (Unconquered) 7, 26, 27, 43, 45, 90, 115, 152, 155, 168, 176; birthday of 43, 155; Christ as 58, 90, 186; Constantine as 35, 168; Julian as 35, 99, 102, 110, 168; as patron of Constantine 26, 27, 65, 90, cf. 22; solar cult, theology 115, 124; Sun and circus symbolism 155, 176. *See also* Sol Invictus

Sunday, Christian 93, 149, 159; Mothering 156; Passion 157

superstition xii, xiii, 11, 12, 14, 23, 81, 84, 151, 165; in Africa 164–6; of Constantius II 66, 82, 84; used of paganism 81, 152

Susanna and the Elders 174, 182, 185–6

Sylvester, bishop of Rome 34, 55, 71

symbol, symbolism 23–4, 25, 26–7, 49–50, 90, 118, 122, 124, 133–4, 158, 159, 160, 161, 163, 165, 171, 174, 175, 186, 190; of chi-rho and Cross 24, 91–2, *and s.v.*; of circus, *s.v.*; pagan cult-symbols 181; of salvation 182, 185, 186, *and s.v.*; of Seasons, *s.v.*

symbolism of fish 134, 175; Mystic Fisherman 58, 175, 186; sacred fish 123, 175

syncretism 102, 115, 138, 183

synod 31, 61, 79, 105. *See also* council

Syria *passim*; churches of 61, 143–4; Syrian gods, temple of 123–4, 142; Syrian goddess (Atargatis) 123, 175

talisman, talismanic 23, 24, 34, 141, 166, 175, 179. *See also* charm

Tarsus 30, 54, 59, 119, 122

taurobolium 138

taxation 2, 8–9, 41, 52, 65–6, 67, 74, 104, 105, 106, 145–6; Constantine's new taxes 38, 105; Diocletian's reform of 9

teacher, Christ as Teacher 148, 183, 186, cf. 36, 148. *See also* education, Libanius, sophist

Tebessa (Theveste) 167

Teleda (Deir Tell 'Ade) 145

temple xiii, 7, 11, 14, 37, 61, 74, 86, 91, 94, 95, 97–128 *passim*, 131–2, 135–7, 140, 147, 148, 154, 161, 172, 174, 175, 179, 198; attacks on, by Christians 83, 94, 109, 123–4, 129–30, 136, 145; building of 24, 94, 103, 104, 123–4, 125–8, 137–40, 141–3, 144, 159–60, 192; closure of 80, 82, 83, 99; confiscation of property of 38, 40, 80, 99, *and see* temple lands; at Constantinople 34–5, 36, 155; converted into churches 124, 130, 141, 143; destruction of 81, 83, 94, 123–4, 129, 130, 136, 137, 138, 139, 145; of imperial cult 152, cf. 142–3; Jewish in Jerusalem 111–12; restoration of 5, 19, 100, 104, 124, 139, 141, 143; of Rome 24, 51, 83, 90, 123, 153. *See also* sanctuary, shrine

temple lands 38, 80, 99, 132, 145

Tetrarchy, the 26, 27, 31, 40, 60, 90, 91, 94, 100, 118, 143, 153, 162, 186, 194; art of 5–6; creation of 3–4; First 1–14, 31, 139, 151; Second 14–17, 43; Third 17–30, 43

theatre 85, 89, 100, 103, 119, 120, 152, 154, cf. 164; of the mysteries 138

Thebes 51

Themistius, orator and philosopher 47, 85–9, 113, 160, 195

Theoderic, Ostrogoth king of Italy 79

Theodora, stepdaughter of Maximian 4, 42

Theodorus, bishop of Aquileia 133–4

Theodosius I, the Emperor xiii, 96, 109, 129, 136, 137, 153, 157, 195

theology, Christian xiii, 70, 71–2, 73, 74, 102; pagan 7, 98, 102–3; solar 115

Thessalonica 5, 6, 32, 109, 118, 172

theurgy, (Chaldaean) 83–4, 85, 86, 98, 99, 149

Thrace 29, 31, 32, 38, 40, 43, 76, 79, 106, 122, 161, 163, 185

Thuburbo Maius 167

Tigris, river 5, 52, 54

Tipasa 112, 132

tomb 41, 143, 144, 157, 164, 179–92; burial *ad sanctos* 57; of Christ, of Adam 62; of Constantine 36; of Julii 57–8; mixed Christian-pagan 158, 180–1; of saints 57, 132, 136

town council, *see* curia

trade 34, 37, 38, 46, 67, 93, 101, 105, 130, 134, 144, 162, 163, 167, 177, 186, 189, 191. *See also* market, ship

Trajan, the Emperor 10–11, 25, 111, 154

treasury, the imperial 5, 9, 17, 38, 62, 64, 80, 101, 120, 133, 172, cf. 111

Trebius Justus, hypogeum of 183–4, 185

tribunal 49, 53, 66

tricennalia 74

Trier 5, 34, 47, 60–1, 75, 78, 91, 132, 133, 174

Tyre 13, 21; Council of 63

Ulfilas, bishop of the Goths 79

Underworld, the 110, 163, 181, 182, 184, 190. *See also* after-life

uniform, of army 2, 3, 6, 9; of civil service 2, 9
university 5, 88, 104
Ursacius, bishop of Singidunum 76–8
Ursicinus, *magister equitum* 48–9
usurper 1, 2, 7, 8, 17, 21, 22, 29, 38, 40, 43, 69, 83, 92, 153, 194; proclamation of Constantine 15–16; proclamation of Julian 117; of 350 A.D. 24, 45, 46–7, 48, 77, 92, 141, 160, 172

Valens, bishop of Mursa 76–8
Valens, the Emperor 79, 84, 103, 115, 128
Valentinian I, the Emperor 79, 87, 94, 115, 128, 153
Valeria, daughter of Diocletian 4, 30
Valerian, the Emperor 12
Vandals xi, 1, 38
Vatican hill 57–8
Venus 24, 151, 155, 158, 161, 172–3, 174, 176, 190; Triumph of (Marine) 165–6, 167
Verona 22, 27
Verulamium 14
Vespasian, the Emperor 152
Vetranio, usurper 46–7, 87, 92, 160
Via Latina Catacombs 131, 181–3, 184, 185, 192
Vibia, hypogeum of 183, 184–5, 192
vicar, *see* deputy-prefect
vicennalia 5–6, 13, 14, 33–4, 48, 72
Victory, the goddess 24, 25, 27, 45, 50, 90, 91, 92, 117, 118, 164, 191; altar of in Senate-house 83, 91; Eucharistic 134
victory symbolism, of chi-rho 22–4, 93, cf. 92; of circus 166
Vienne 52, 138, 156, 175, 176, 180
Viennensis 5, 16
Vigna Massimo, catacomb of 185
villa 6, 97, 139, 140–2, 144, 158–62, 167, 169, 174, 176; Constantinian, Antioch 167–9, 170, 172; of Piazza Armerina 162–3
vision xii, 22, 30, 120; dream-vision of Constantine xii, 22–3, 25, 27, 92

vota 91, 117, 153–4; *Vota Publica* coins 153
votive offerings 121, 125–6, 137, 140, 159; to dead 141, 183–4, cf. 159; votive games 117

War 3, 20, 21, 25, 26, 37, 41, 42, 45, 71, 77, 194; Chlorus reconquers Britain 4; Constantine v. Licinius 32, 33, 93, 94; Constantine v. Maxentius 21–3; Constantius II v. Magnentius 45, 77; Galerius' Persian 5; Julian's Persian 53–4, 94, 111, 195; Licinius v. Maximin 29–30, 31; other civil 6, 7, 42, 44, 47, 53; Persian of Constantine and Constantius II 39, 45, 46, 51–2, 195. *See also* invasion, military campaign, usurper
Water Newton silver 140–1
Watling Street 139
wealth, rich xi–xii, 41, 42, 59, 64, 65, 66, 75, 100, 119, 120, 132, 133, 147, 157, 162, 164, 169, 170, 173, 179, 180, 181, 185, 197; of Church 66, 133, 134
Wint Hill Hunting Bowl 174
Wisdom, of Brahmins 147; Christian 36, 145, 148; Church of Holy Wisdom (S. Sophia) 33, 36; pagan 36, 113, 155. *See also* philosophy
Woodchester, mosaic of 160–1
workshop, *see* factory
worship, Christian 12, 19, 28, 32, 56, 61, 62, 64, 65, 67, 94, 112, 130, 131, 132, 133, 135, 136, 150; in imperial cult 2, 152; of Jews 110; liberty of xii, 28–9, 70, 80, 108, 192; pagan xii, 10, 29, 80, 82, 94, 103, 104, 108, 109, 123, 126, 127, 128, 129, 131, 132, 135, 138, 141, 192

York 5, 6, 15, 141

Zenobia, queen of Palmyra 1
Zoroastrianism 38
Zosimus, historian 30, 31, 33, 34, 35, 39, 194–5, 196

DATE DUE
